Malevolent Neutrality:

The United States, Great Britain, and the Origins of the Spanish Civil War

DOUGLAS LITTLE

Cornell University Press

ITHACA AND LONDON

First published 1985 by Cornell University Press.
Published in the United Kingdom by
Cornell University Press Ltd., London.

International Standard Book Number 0-8014-1769-4
Library of Congress Catalog Card Number 84-19930
Printed in the United States of America
*Librarians: Library of Congress cataloging information
appears on the last page of the book.*

*The paper in this book is acid-free and meets the guidelines for
permanence and durability of the Committee on Production Guidelines
for Book Longevity of the Council on Library Resources.*

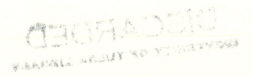

For Pat

Contents

The doctrine of non-intervention, to be a legitimate principle of morality, must be accepted by all governments. The despot must consent to be bound by it as well as the free States. Unless they do, the profession of it by free countries comes to this miserable issue, that the wrong side may help the wrong, but the right must not help the right.

JOHN STUART MILL,
"A Few Words on Non-Intervention,"
Fraser's Magazine, December 1859

If the Fascists win in Spain, with German and Italian help, the balance may be tipped against the anti-Fascist nations. Neither the policy of "splendid isolation" nor hundred per cent non-resistance will avail us in Britain if we abandon our friends on the Continent of Europe.

And yet the Tories blindly cheer the reports of rebel victories and our "National" Government adopts an attitude of malevolent neutrality towards the constitutionally elected Government of Spain.

"Those whom the gods wish to destroy, they first make mad."

LORD STRABOLGI,
"What Spain's War Means to Britain,"
Daily Herald, 10 August 1936

Preface

It has now been half a century since the civil war in Spain made headlines around the world, and the wounds have at last begun to heal. Exiled Loyalist figures such as Manuel Azaña nursed their broken hearts and died unnoticed in Mexico City or Paris, while victorious Nationalist generals basked in self-righteous glory before expiring quietly in Madrid, like Francisco Franco himself. Since Franco's death in 1975 constitutional monarchy and parliamentary democracy have once again blossomed south of the Pyrenees, and a new generation of political leaders has demonstrated that representative government can work in Spain. To be sure, there are those who still wave the bloody shirt and worship at the shrine of Largo Caballero or Primo de Rivera, but democratic institutions seem to be sinking deep roots in Spanish soil. Who would have dared prophesy a decade ago that Spain today would be governed by a Socialist regime that gained and has maintained power peaceably?

Yet if the wounds have healed, the scars are still visible, and the archives remain closed. Although many Spanish diplomatic records were destroyed or lost when the Loyalists hastily moved their official capital from Madrid to Valencia during the civil war, some have survived. Nevertheless, these materials are presently unavailable to scholars. Apparently the Spanish government still worries that they might contain sensitive information, information that could reopen painful wounds or reignite bitter recriminations dating from a bloody era that many Spaniards cannot forget and will not forgive. Fortunately, however, almost all the relevant British and American archival records are open for research. Indeed, they provide the documentary foundation for this book, permitting a fuller reconstruction of U.S. and U.K. relations with Spain in the mid-1930s than heretofore available.

The Spanish civil war has long fascinated observers on both sides of the Atlantic because, in retrospect, it seemed to be one of the last opportunities to sidetrack the aggressive designs of Nazi Germany and Fascist Italy. Many have concluded that once Britain and the United States chose to appease rather than to oppose Hitler and Mussolini in Spain, democracy was doomed, first in Madrid but ultimately in most of the other capitals of Europe as well. German and Italian leaders drew the same conclusions, and they did not concern themselves whether British and American officials adopted policies of nonintervention in the Spanish civil war out of prudence or out of pusillanimity. Ironically, this majority view holds, it was precisely because neither Washington nor London was willing in 1936 to risk wider war with Berlin or Rome to preserve democracy at Madrid that a much broader and more costly European conflagration became inevitable. Viewed through the prism of appeasement, the Spanish civil war has thus become one of the earliest and most notorious examples of the British and American diplomatic myopia that helped bring about the Second World War.

It is always dangerous, however, to read history backward, especially in an atmosphere as politically charged as that of the late 1930s. From the vantage point of 1939 it was certainly easy to view British and American neutrality in the Spanish civil war as one of the first steps down the road to armageddon, but that interpretation was at best incomplete. For if the conflict in Spain signaled in some sense the opening round of the Second World War, it also marked the final stage of a turbulent five years in American and British relations with the Spanish Republic. In April 1931 a bloodless revolution in Madrid had brought an abrupt end to the dismal reign of Alfonso XIII and reestablished parliamentary democracy in Spain after a half-century hiatus. The new regime was not well received in London or Washington, largely because skeptical British and American policy makers feared that it would amount to little more than a "Kerensky" interlude prior to a classic "Bolshevik" takeover. Republican Spain's chronic political instability, confiscatory attacks on foreign investments, and autarchic commercial policies did nothing to dispel such fears, and by July 1936 its relations with Great Britain and the United States were near the breaking point. On the eve of General Franco's uprising, then, a powerful antirepublican consensus had emerged on both sides of the Atlantic which soon predisposed U.S. and U.K. officials to adopt policies of nonintervention in the Spanish civil war.

Nevertheless, most studies of British and American diplomacy during the conflict in Spain have ignored this stormy legacy of the early 1930s. The first scholarly accounts of the origins of Britain's nonintervention policy, for example, bypassed the period from 1931 to 1936 and focused instead on balance-of-power considerations and the fear of a wider war. The Foreign Office, they held, was concerned primarily with preventing an Italo-German alliance and with buying time to rearm, not with influencing the outcome of the bitter struggle in Spain.[1] Those historians examining the American response to the Spanish civil war have likewise deemed the era before 1936 relatively insignificant. They have usually attributed U.S. neutrality to the tension between isolationist pressure in Congress and the State Department's quest for collective security. Thus a desire to cooperate with Britain and France without incurring the wrath of isolationists on Capitol Hill, not an animus against the Spanish Republic, brought the U.S. government to proclaim a stance of strict nonintervention in August 1936.[2]

Even those scholars who emphasize how ideological or economic factors shaped British and American policies after the civil war erupted have neglected the early 1930s. Several studies have detailed the antirepublican sentiments of American Catholics, British Conservatives, and U.S. and U.K. corporations during the civil war; but they fail to point out that policy makers on both sides of the Atlantic had expressed similar views long before the military uprising in July 1936.[3] To be sure, the two most recent accounts of British and American diplomacy during the crisis in Spain do ac-

[1] Patricia van der Esch, *Prelude to War: The International Repercussions of the Spanish Civil War, 1936–1939* (The Hague, 1951); William Laird Kleine-Ahlbrandt, *The Policy of Simmering: A Study of British Policy during the Spanish Civil War, 1936–1939* (Ambilly-Annemasse, 1961).

[2] F. Jay Taylor, *The United States and the Spanish Civil War* (New York, 1956); Richard P. Traina, *American Diplomacy and the Spanish Civil War* (Bloomington, Ind., 1968).

[3] Allen Guttmann, *The Wound in the Heart: America and the Spanish Civil War* (New York, 1962); K. W. Watkins, *Britain Divided: The Effect of the Spanish Civil War on British Political Opinion* (New York, 1963); and Dante Puzzo, *Spain and the Great Powers, 1936–1941* (New York, 1962).

knowledge that London and Washington encountered serious troubles with Madrid before 1936, yet both nevertheless fail to appreciate fully the impact that these difficulties had on later decisions.[4] In short, scholars in Great Britain and the United States have, to varying degrees, overlooked an important aspect of the diplomatic background to the Spanish civil war. This book seeks to fill that gap.

I am deeply indebted to many organizations and individuals without whose assistance this book would never have been completed. The Cornell University Graduate School, the International Studies Association, and the Clark University History Department supplied financial support for my research both in the United States and in Great Britain. William and Lynne Sheasgreen provided home cooking, good company, and a base of operations in London; Theresa Reynolds, Rene Baril, and Roxanne Rawson patiently typed and retyped the manuscript; and librarians and archivists too numerous to mention helped me track down hard-to-find books and documents. I am also grateful to Lawrence Malley and the entire staff of Cornell University Press for their swift and sure handling of prepublication matters. In particular, Roger Haydon's diligent and intelligent copy editing clarified many citations, streamlined my prose, and, on occasion, sharpened my argument.

Over the years, I have benefited from the insights and advice of friends, colleagues, and others who took the time to comment on my work. Tom E. Davis, Robert Divine, Gail Filion-Ullman, Lloyd Gardner, Gabriel Jackson, Steven Kaplan, Melvyn Leffler, and Theodore Von Laue read the manuscript at various points along the way and made useful suggestions, not all of which I followed. Ronald Formisano, William Ferguson, and George Billias encouraged my work and boosted my morale in ways they may not realize. My comrade Francis Couvares, formerly at Clark University and now at Amherst College, lent a sympathetic ear, superb editorial skills, and an unfailing sense of humor, all of which have improved this book enormously. My greatest scholarly debts, however, are to Walter LaFeber, who for more than a decade has been a teacher, critic, and friend whose wisdom and civility are models to

[4]James W. Cortada, *Two Nations over Time: Spain and the United States, 1776–1977* (Westport, Conn., 1978); Jill Edwards, *The British Government and the Spanish Civil War, 1936–1939* (London, 1979).

which all historians might aspire. He has read and reread this manuscript more times than I care to admit, and those who know him will realize that had I taken all his advice, this book would quite probably be error-free.

The book is dedicated to Pat, who knows very well that without her there simply would be no book. Her special contributions have been, and will always be, acknowledged in special ways.

Douglas J. Little

Worcester, Massachusetts

Acronyms

AEE	*Anuario estadístico de España*
BPLTC	Barcelona Power Light and Traction Company (the "Canadiense")
CAMPSA	Compañía Arrendataria del Monopolio de Petróleos
CEDA	Confederación Española de Derechas Autónomas
CID	Committee for Imperial Defence
CNT	Confederación Nacional del Trabajo
CTNE	Compañía Telefónica Nacional de España
DBFP	Documents on British Foreign Policy
DDF	*Documents diplomatiques français*
FAI	Federación Anarquista Ibérica
FRUS	*Papers Relating to the Foreign Relations of the United States*
IBC	International Banking Corporation
IBRD	International Bank for Reconstruction and Development
ITT	International Telephone and Telegraph Company
NA RG	National Archives, Record Group (with appropriate number)
ONI	Office of Naval Intelligence
PRO	Public Record Office
RTZ	Rio Tinto Zinc Company
SAUS	*Statistical Abstract of the United States*
UGT	Unión General de Trabajadores

Malevolent Neutrality

1

The Contours of British and American Diplomacy, 1919–1939

The rebels struck at dusk on a sweltering Friday in mid-July, seizing garrisons first in Morocco and then in mainland Spain. General Francisco Franco and a handful of other high-ranking right-wing military leaders hoped to deal a death blow to the republican regime in Madrid, which they held responsible for a half-decade of deepening political and economic turmoil south of the Pyrenees. The conspirators, however, miscalculated badly, anticipating neither the republican loyalties of many of their fellow officers nor the fierce determination of the left-wing popular militias. As a result, what had been intended as a swift and skillful coup d'état promised by August 1936 to become a long and bloody civil war. When the shooting stopped nearly three years later, Franco had emerged victorious, thanks in large measure to weapons and troops supplied by Germany and Italy.

Yet the United States and Great Britain also bore considerable responsibility for the outcome. Under the guise of nonintervention they had maintained arms embargoes against the Spanish Republic long after German and Italian military aid for rebel Spain had become common knowledge on both sides of the Atlantic. "Today," Julio Alvarez del Vayo, republican Spain's last foreign minister, wrote bitterly in 1940, "no one should be able to deny that the collapse of the Spanish Republic was due to Non-Intervention." Hitler's recent actions in Eastern Europe, he added sadly, "have confirmed our contention that appeasement, which reached the limits of folly in Spain, would lead inevitably to war."[1] Most con-

[1] Julio Alvarez del Vayo, *Freedom's Battle* (New York, 1940), p. 70.

temporary observers agreed and most historians have attributed short-sighted British and American policies during the Spanish civil war to domestic constraints imposed by public opinion or to broader international concerns such as a desire for collective security. Isolationism in the United States and pacifism in Great Britain seemed to make nonintervention the only sensible course, since it appeared to lessen the danger of a wider European conflagration. Viewed from London or Washington, the Spanish Republic had been cast as the unfortunate victim in a drama of great-power politics scripted by a madman in Berlin and a scoundrel in Rome.

British and American nonintervention in the Spanish civil war, however, represented not merely the first flicker of the fading light before the darkest days of the twentieth century but also the incandescent culmination of U.S. and U.K. diplomacy from 1919 to 1936. Following the Great War, the Foreign Office and the State Department struggled to create a stable international order out of the political and economic chaos unleashed by four years of carnage in Europe. Faced with rebuilding a world ruined by war, the White House and Whitehall shared three common concerns, which shaped American and British policies in similar ways. First, Great Britain and the United States, thoroughly alarmed by the wave of revolutionary upheavals in the wake of the Bolshevik takeover in Russia, strove steadfastly to contain left-wing nationalism. Second, both nations were firmly convinced that reconstruction could best be accomplished through foreign investment, and as a result, each was preoccupied with promoting and protecting its financial stake abroad. Finally, both London and Washington were deeply troubled by the postwar proliferation of discriminatory trade policies, and each in its own way sought to foster domestic prosperity through vigorous commercial expansion overseas. On the eve of the Spanish civil war these considerations constituted the ideological and economic underpinnings for the foreign relations of both Great Britain and the United States.

I

The specter of bolshevism haunted British and American policy makers during the two decades after the Great War. Lenin's seizure of power in Petrograd sent shock waves around the world and challenged concepts of democratic government and free enterprise sacred in London and Washington. Neither the United States nor Great Britain accepted the radical regime in Moscow, and after the Bolsheviks disbanded the constituent assembly and concluded a separate peace with Germany early in 1918, both nations dispatched first supplies and eventually troops to aid anti-Soviet forces in the Russian civil war. The Kremlin responded a year later by creating the Communist International (Comintern), a global revolutionary organization that sparked abortive left-wing uprisings in Germany, Austria, and Hungary during the spring of 1919. Although the Comintern threat to Central Europe had subsided by mid-summer, it touched off "Red Scares" on both sides of the Atlantic and prompted British and American leaders to contain the bolshevik virus by isolating Soviet Russia diplomatically.[2]

Not surprisingly, perplexed and frightened officials in Washington attributed most of the revolutionary upheavals that rocked the less developed regions of the world throughout the next fifteen years to Soviet subversion. The United States was particularly distressed by radical developments in Latin America, which threatened its interests and weakened its influence south of the Rio Grande. Moscow's alleged meddling in the Western Hemisphere surfaced first in Mexico, where as early as 1919 the State Department had labeled Venustiano Carranza's reformist government "Bolshevistic." Six years later, according to Undersecretary of State Robert Olds, the United States was on the verge of military intervention against the nationalist regime of Plutarcho Calles because of "great danger of a communist seizure of power" by "highly radical, perhaps communistic elements in the Mexican Government." By early 1927 Secretary of State Frank B. Kellogg claimed that "Bolshevist leaders" intent on using "Latin America and Mexico . . . as a base for activity against the United States" were responsible for the recent revolution in Nicaragua, which had necessitated the despatch of 5,000 marines to Managua. Overall

---

[2] For the reactions of British and American policy makers to the Bolshevik revolution and its aftermath, see N. Gordon Levin, Jr., *Woodrow Wilson and World Politics: America's Response to War and Revolution* (New York, 1968); Arno J. Mayer, *Politics and Diplomacy of Peacemaking: Containment and Counterrevolution at Versailles, 1918–1919* (New York, 1969); Richard Ullman, *Anglo-Soviet Relations, 1917–1921*, 3 vols. (Princeton, N.J., 1961–1973); and William Appleman Williams, *American Russian Relations, 1781–1947* (New York, 1952).

"Bolshevist Aims," Kellogg charged, included both "the destruction of what they term American Imperialism" and the "successful development of the international revolutionary movement in the New World."[3]

Kellogg's nightmare seemed about to be realized in the early 1930s as the Great Depression destroyed the world markets for such important Latin American exports as coffee, sugar, and bananas and touched off a fresh round of political instability. When plunging copper prices led to a left-wing military coup in Peru in 1931, Washington feared "a general disintegration of the country accompanied by communistic tendencies." After electoral fraud spawned unrest in Costa Rica a year later, U.S. minister Charles Eberhardt blamed Mexican and Nicaraguan subversives, who allegedly hoped to find "a fertile field for the doctrines and practices of communism" at San José.[4] From El Salvador, where left-wing radicals and landless Indian peasants revolted against a brutal military dictatorship in January 1932, American officials urged the State Department to do all it could to "prevent the establishment of a communistic state here accompanied by much bloodshed." Worried by "the serious situation in El Salvador resulting from the Communistic outbreaks," Washington stationed three warships in the Gulf of Fonseca and acquiesced in the slaughter of thousands of "communists" by the right-wing Salvadoran government during the six weeks that followed.[5] When political corruption and economic crisis brought down a pro-American regime in Cuba in 1933, U.S. policy makers such as Russian expert Robert Kelley and Ambassador Jefferson Caffery detected signs of "Soviet subversion" and welcomed Fulgencio Batista's January 1934 coup against the new and "frankly communistic" government at Havana.[6]

[3] Robert Freeman Smith, *The United States and Revolutionary Nationalism in Mexico, 1916–1932* (Chicago, 1972), pp. 168–71, 176–80, 232–41; Olds quoted in Hugh Wilson, *Diplomat between Wars* (New York, 1941), pp. 179–81; Bryce Wood, *The Making of the Good Neighbor Policy* (New York, 1961), pp. 17–18; Frank B. Kellogg, "Bolshevist Aims and Policies in Mexico and Latin America," *New York Times*, 13 January 1927, p. 2.

[4] Francis White (Division of Latin American Affairs) to Ambassador Fred Morris Dearing (Lima), 10 April 1931, United States, Department of State, *Papers Relating to the Foreign Relations of the United States, 1931*, 3 vols. (Washington, D.C., 1946), 2:918 (hereafter cited as *FRUS* for the appropriate year); Eberhardt to Stimson, tel. 17 February 1932, *FRUS, 1932*, 5:517–18.

[5] Chargé d'Affaires William McCafferty to Stimson, tel. 20 January 1932 and tel. 23 January 1932, and Stimson to McCafferty, tel. 23 January 1932, *FRUS, 1932*, 5:613–15.

[6] Robert Bowers, "Hull, Russian Subversion in Cuba, and the Recognition of the U.S.S.R.," *Journal of American History* 53 (December 1966), 542–54; David Green, *The*

Just as the State Department regarded recurrent political instability throughout Latin America as evidence of bolshevik interference in an informal U.S. sphere of influence, so too the Foreign Office interpreted revolutionary upheavals in the Near East and South Asia after the Great War as proof that Moscow was meddling in the affairs of the British Empire. As early as 1921 Lord Curzon, Britain's foreign secretary, charged that Soviet Russia was "plotting against British rule in India" by encouraging "the creation of a powerful united Moslem movement which would deal the final blow against . . . the colonial system upon which the power of Western European capital rests." Over the next two years Whitehall undertook a study of "Bolshevism as a Menace to the British Empire" and fretted about Comintern inroads in Iran, Turkey, and Egypt.[7] Convinced that Soviet agents were endangering both internal and imperial security, in October 1924 the Foreign Office released the celebrated "Zinoviev Letter," which purported to be a secret Kremlin directive to British Communists, and in the process tipped the general elections later that year to Stanley Baldwin and the Conservatives.[8]

The Tory government kept a watchful eye on the Comintern throughout the late 1920s. "Soviet agents are active against us," Foreign Secretary Austen Chamberlain told a gathering of Commonwealth officials in 1926, "because the character and stability of the British Empire make it the chief obstacle to the spread of revo-

---

Containment of Latin America: The Myths and Realities of the Good Neighbor Policy (Chicago, 1971), pp. 13–18; Luis E. Aguilar, *Cuba 1933: Prologue to Revolution* (Ithaca, N.Y., 1972), pp. 219–28. For ITT's concerns about the new government in Cuba, see the memorandum by Jay Pierrepont Moffat, 11 January 1934, 837.75/51, United States, Department of State, Record Group 59, State Department Decimal Files 1910–1939, National Archives, Washington, D.C., (hereafter cited as NA RG59 with appropriate file numbers).

[7] Curzon to the Soviet government, 7 September 1921, Cmnd. 2895, "A Selection of Papers Dealing with the Relations between His Majesty's Government and the Soviet Government, 1921–1927," Great Britain, Parliament, *Parliamentary Papers* (Commons), 1927, 27 vols. (London, 1927), vol. 26 (hereafter cited as *Parliamentary Papers* (Commons), for the appropriate year); Stephen White, *Britain and the Bolshevik Revolution: A Study in the Politics of Diplomacy, 1920–1924* (New York, 1979), pp. 102–3, 125–40.

[8] Zinoviev to the British Communist party, 15 September 1924, and Austen Chamberlain to M. Rosengolz, 26 May 1927, Cmnd. 2895, "A Selection of Papers Dealing with Relations between His Majesty's Government and the Soviet Government, 1921–1927," *Parliamentary Papers* (Commons), 1927, vol. 26; F. S. Northedge, *The Troubled Giant: Britain among the Great Powers, 1916–1939* (New York, 1966), pp. 308–11, 316.

lutionary communism." The Kremlin, he added, was "now at work on the borders of China, in Afghanistan, and in Persia where it is the object of the Soviet Government to establish a system of subordinate and affiliated Soviet republics."[9] Two years later Whitehall charged that "both military espionage and subversive activities throughout the British Empire were directed and carried out from the premises" of Arcos, the Russian trade agency in London raided by Scotland Yard in 1927. "The dangers to be feared," the Foreign Office claimed, "are those of Soviet intrigues in Afghanistan, the fomentation of hostile activity among the frontier tribes of India, and subversive propaganda in India itself."[10] Such fears were borne out over the following five years as M. N. Roy, an Indian nationalist linked to the Comintern, launched a series of anticolonial strikes that prompted British officials in Delhi to outlaw the Communist party there in 1934. Terming the Soviet Union a "purely negative and destructive" force in world politics, Permanent Undersecretary of State Robert Vansittart complained in the early 1930s that "wherever troubled waters exist, Russia is the compleat angler."[11]

The Great Depression unleashed an economic and political tempest not only in Latin America and South Asia but also in Europe itself, where in the decade after 1929 many U.S. and U.K. officials believed the Kremlin was angling for its biggest catch. As the Weimar Republic disintegrated in 1931, one State Department observer worried that "Germany may go Bolshevik once the radical wave gets under way, and Russia would not be slow to take steps to aid the situation."[12] A British policy maker likewise recalled that once Germany swung far to the right in 1933, many feared that "if the Nazis were overthrown, . . . the U.S.S.R. would be able to fish in troubled waters, and the end result might very well be a semi-

---

[9] "Statement Made by Sir Austen Chamberlain to the Imperial Conference on 20 October 1926," Great Britain, Foreign Office, *Documents on British Foreign Policy, 1919–1939*, ser. Ia, 7 vols. (London, 1966–1977), 2:945–46 (hereafter cited as *DBFP* for the appropriate series).

[10] Foreign Office Memorandum, "The Foreign Policy of His Majesty's Government," 5 April 1928, *DBFP*, ser. Ia, 4:657–58; Northedge, *Troubled Giant*, p. 316.

[11] John Patrick Haithcox, *Communism and Nationalism in India: M. N. Roy and Comintern Policy, 1920–1939* (Princeton, N.J., 1971), pp. 209–10; Robert Vansittart, "An Aspect of International Relations in 1930," 1 May 1930, *DBFP*, ser. Ia, 7:847–48; Vansittart, "Crying in the Wilderness: Jottings from the 1930s," in his *Even Now* (New York, n.d.), pp. 58–59.

[12] Paul Culbertson (Division of Western European Affairs) to Secretary of State Henry Stimson, 10 June 1931, Henry L. Stimson Papers, microfilm ed., reel 81, Sterling Library, Yale University, New Haven, Connecticut.

Communist Germany in alliance with a Communist Russia, which would represent, ultimately, a force capable of extending its influence over the whole of Western Europe."[13] The Kremlin seemed to be moving in just this direction by 1935, when the Seventh Comintern Congress convened at Moscow and endorsed a new tactical line, a "united front" of all antifascist parties, to combat the resurgent European right. Few observers on either side of the Atlantic, however, believed that this "Trojan Horse" policy had altered the Comintern's overall objective, which remained as always to produce a global revolution.[14]

As the new style of Soviet subversion became clearer, high-ranking British and American officials were able to pinpoint the Kremlin's targets. Secretary of State Cordell Hull, for example, claimed that the presence of leading U.S. Communists at the Seventh Comintern Congress indicated that the Soviets had reneged on their 1933 promise not to interfere in American domestic politics. They had reverted instead to a policy "directed toward overthrowing the political and social order in the United States."[15] Foreign Secretary Anthony Eden likewise held the Comintern responsible for recent domestic difficulties. He told Soviet foreign minister Maxim Litvinov at Geneva in January 1936 that "it was time that a full stop was put to Soviet aid for communistic propaganda in Great Britain."[16] Greece was also high on the Comintern's list according to U.S. ambassador Lincoln MacVeagh, who advised Hull from Athens in May that "the Communist Party acquired this spring a new importance in the Greek political line-up," thanks largely to its united-front alliance with more moderate elements.[17] When Léon Blum's Popular Front coalition, composed of Socialists and Communists, won the French elections early the next month,

---

[13] Lord Gladwyn (Sir Gladwyn Jebb), *The Memoirs of Lord Gladwyn* (New York, 1972), p. 55.

[14] Kermit E. McKenzie, *The Comintern and World Revolution, 1928–1943: The Shaping of Doctrine* (New York, 1964), pp. 140–65; William Bullitt to Cordell Hull, 19 July 1935, *FRUS: The Soviet Union, 1933–1939*, pp. 225–26; Viscount Chilston (Moscow) to the Foreign Office, 29 November 1935, and minute by J. L. Dodds, 19 December 1935, N6304/135/38, FO371 (General Political Correspondence of the Foreign Office, 1914–1945), vol. 19460, Public Record Office, Kew, Surrey, England (hereafter cited as PRO FO371 with the appropriate file number).

[15] Cordell Hull, *Memoirs*, 2 vols. (New York, 1948), 1:305.

[16] Eden to the Foreign Office, tel. 21 January 1936, N394/75/38, PRO FO371, vol. 20344.

[17] MacVeagh to Hull, 29 May 1936, in John Iatrides, ed., *Ambassador MacVeagh Reports: Greece, 1933–1947* (Princeton, N.J., 1980), p. 87.

the British ambassador to France, Sir George Clerk, predicted the worst. "It is extraordinarily reminiscent of the early days of the Russian Revolution," he warned Whitehall on 11 June 1936, "with Blum as an unconscious Kerensky and an unknown Lenin or Trotsky in the background."[18]

When political conditions in Europe and elsewhere deteriorated still further in the late 1930s, some British and American officials even suggested that the Kremlin secretly hoped to foment world revolution through world war. William Bullitt, the U.S. ambassador in Moscow, had been among the first to argue that Russia might actually seek to foster such a global conflagration. "The Bolsheviks do not expect communist revolutions in other parts of Europe," he warned Washington in April 1936, "except as a result of a general European war."[19] Two years later Sir Alexander Cadogan, Vansittart's successor at Whitehall as permanent undersecretary of state, was even blunter in rejecting a Kremlin proposal for an Anglo-Soviet pact against Nazi Germany. "The Russian object is to precipitate confusion and war in Europe," he remarked testily in March 1938. "They will hope for the world revolution as a result (and a very likely one, too)."[20]

Even as Stalin trimmed the Comintern's sails at the end of the decade and tacked briskly for an antifascist coalition with the Western democracies, few officials on either side of the Atlantic could forgive or forget his earlier efforts to export communism. Signs of Soviet subversion from Havana to Bombay, from Athens to Paris, had left both the Foreign Office and the State Department extremely suspicious of left-wing political movements everywhere. And in the process antibolshevism, the desire to curb Russian-style revolutions wherever they erupted, had become an article of faith among many influential policy makers in London and Washington.

II

British and American diplomacy after the Great War was shaped not only by ideological fears of global revolution but also by economic concerns, especially the expansion of foreign investment

---

[18]Clerk to Vansittart, 11 June 1936, C4355/1/17, PRO FO371, vol. 19857.
[19]Bullitt to Hull, 20 April 1936, 861.01/2120, NA RG59.
[20]Minute by Cadogan, 17 March 1938, and Halifax to Soviet ambassador Ivan Maisky, 24 March 1938, C1935/95/62, PRO FO371, vol. 21626.

and international trade. The 1920s witnessed the flowering of the modern multinational corporation. The United States, having emerged from Versailles for the first time as a creditor nation, saw its stake in direct investment abroad double from $3.7 billion in 1919 to $7.5 billion in 1929. Most U.S. ventures were concentrated in the Western Hemisphere, where General Motors, United Fruit, Kennecott, and other firms built manufacturing plants in Canada, operated enormous plantations in the Caribbean basin, and tapped the vast mineral wealth of South America. Bolder American multinationals, ITT and Firestone among them, established operations in Europe and Africa, either to supply consumer markets or to obtain raw materials. By the late 1930s U.S. petroleum giants such as Standard Oil and Texaco were firmly entrenched throughout the Middle East while others, most prominently Socony Mobil, had penetrated China and the East Indies. Total American direct foreign investment in 1939 had leveled off at slightly over $7 billion, and Wall Street controlled mines and factories in almost every corner of the globe.[21]

Accurate measurement of the growth of British multinationals following the Great War is much more difficult, largely because U.K. statistics fail to distinguish clearly between direct and portfolio investments. Best estimates nevertheless suggest that British firms, like their American counterparts, probably doubled their holdings abroad in the 1920s, from roughly $2 billion to nearly $4 billion. Perhaps as much as one-half of this stake was located within the Commonwealth, especially in mining and manufacturing operations in Canada, South Africa, and Australia, and in the United States, but some of the largest U.K. multinationals undertook important direct investments elsewhere. Unilever, for example, opened soap factories in Argentina, Italy, and the Dutch East Indies between 1919 and 1939; Imperial Chemical Industries likewise established subsidiaries in France, Germany, and Brazil. Taking their cue from competitors on the other side of the Atlantic, Royal Dutch Shell and Anglo-Persian Oil also expanded their operations in the Middle East. By the late 1930s the holdings of British multinationals were valued at approximately $7 billion, with most of the recent increase due to a shift away from portfolio to direct

[21] This summary of U.S. multinational expansion draws on Cleona Lewis, *America's Stake in International Investments* (Washington, D.C., 1938), and Mira Wilkins, *The Maturing of Multinational Enterprise: American Business Abroad from 1914 to 1970* (Cambridge, Mass., 1974).

investment triggered by massive defaults on both foreign private and public securities earlier in the decade.[22]

The rapid expansion of British and American corporations abroad after 1919 made the Foreign Office and the State Department extremely sensitive to the threat of nationalization. Having just witnessed the Soviets expropriate a multimillion-dollar foreign stake in Russia without compensation, Great Britain and the United States worked hard to prevent a recurrence elsewhere. During the 1920s both intervened diplomatically in Mexico after nationalists there threatened U.S. and U.K. oil and mining firms with confiscation.[23] When the Liberian government attempted to revoke Firestone's rubber concession in 1927, Washington hinted it might sever diplomatic relations with Monrovia.[24] Two years later, in the midst of a radical campaign to drive foreign businessmen out of the Middle Kingdom, London took the lead in bringing the Chinese nationalists to their senses.[25] After the Iranian government unveiled plans in late 1932 to nationalize the holdings of Anglo-Persian Oil, British threats of military intervention persuaded Teheran to reverse itself early in the new year.[26] The possibility that left-wing nationalists might expropriate the enormous U.S. investments in Cuba helped ensure that Batista's right-wing coup in early 1934 would be greeted warmly by the State Department.[27]

[22]This summary of U.K. multinational expansion draws on John M. Stopford, "The Origins of British-Based Multinational Enterprises," *Business History Review* 48 (Winter 1974), 303–35; Mira Wilkins, "Modern European Economic History and the Multinationals," *Journal of European Economic History* 6 (Winter 1977), 575–95; Alfred D. Chandler, "The Growth of the Transnational Industrial Firm in the United States and the United Kingdom: A Comparative Analysis," *Economic History Review*, 2d ser., 33 (August 1980), 396–410; S. J. Nicholas, "British Multinational Investment before 1939," *Journal of European Economic History* 11 (Winter 1982), 605–30; and Geoffrey Jones, "The Expansion of British Multinational Manufacturing, 1890–1939," in International Conference on Business History, *Proceedings of the Fuji Conference, no. 9: Overseas Business Activities* (Tokyo, 1984), pp. 125–53. The estimates of U.K. direct investment abroad are from Jones, "British Multinational Manufacturing," pp. 125–26, and have been converted from sterling to dollars at the 1929 rate of exchange ($4.85 = £1.00). For contemporary views of British investment abroad, see Mira Wilkins, ed., *British Overseas Investments, 1907–1948* (New York, 1977).

[23]Smith, *Revolutionary Nationalism in Mexico*, passim; Friedrich Katz, *The Secret War in Mexico: Europe, the United States, and the Mexican Revolution* (Chicago, 1981), pp. 527–40.

[24]I. K. Sundiata, *Black Scandal: America and the Liberian Labor Crisis, 1929–1936* (Philadelphia, 1980), pp. 33–79.

[25]Northedge, *Troubled Giant*, pp. 294–302.

[26]Peter J. Beck, "The Anglo-Persian Oil Dispute, 1932–33," *Journal of Contemporary History* 9 (October 1974), 123–51.

[27]Green, *Containment of Latin America*, pp. 13–18; Aguilar, *Cuba 1933*, pp. 219–28.

The most serious challenge to U.S. and U.K. multinationals between the two world wars came in March 1938. Mexico moved suddenly to resolve its long-standing dispute with British and American oil companies by expropriating them with only minimal compensation. Outraged by the nationalization of assets valued at nearly half-a-billion dollars, both Whitehall and the White House urged Mexican president Lázaro Cárdenas to rescind his confiscatory degree. When Cárdenas stood firm, British and American officials demanded prompt and adequate indemnification, encouraged Royal Dutch Shell and Standard Oil to organize a boycott of Mexican petroleum, and hinted at possible military intervention. The dispute would drag on for over three years until the United States and Great Britain, fearful that Mexico might sell its oil to Nazi Germany, agreed to a compensation formula through which U.S. and U.K. petroleum firms eventually received slightly under $100 million, or roughly one-fifth of the amount originally claimed.[28] In light of this crisis in Mexico City and earlier troubles from Monrovia to Teheran, it was by the late 1930s obvious that to protect the burgeoning British and American multinational stake abroad, both London and Washington would have to practice an increasingly vigilant and forceful brand of diplomacy.

The economic concerns of U.S. and U.K. policy makers after 1919 included not only the promotion and protection of foreign investment but the expansion of international trade as well. During the late nineteenth and early twentieth centuries a consensus had emerged among American business and political leaders that prosperity at home and increased sales abroad went hand in hand. As a result, the 1920s saw the State and Commerce departments cooperating successfully with private organizations such as the National Association of Manufacturers to stimulate exports, which by 1929 stood at $5.2 billion, slightly more than twice the prewar figure. The American share of total world trade rose as well over those same fifteen years, from 12 to 16 percent, mainly because the United States, unlike its major competitors, had emerged from the Great War economically unscathed. The portion of U.S. exports absorbed by Europe, however, shrank steadily from a high of 66 percent in 1919 to a mere 45 percent a decade later, thanks in large

[28] Karl Schmitt, *Mexico and the United States, 1821–1973: Conflict and Coexistence* (New York, 1974), pp. 176–88; Lorenzo Meyer, *Mexico and the United States in the Oil Controversy, 1917–1942* (Austin, Tex., 1977), pp. 173–93, 220–27; George Grayson, *The Politics of Mexican Oil* (Pittsburgh, 1980), pp. 13–18.

part to the imposition of protectionist policies from Paris to Prague. Thus although the United States maintained a healthy $1-billion annual trade surplus to help fuel the postwar boom, Herbert Hoover and other policy makers were by the late 1920s fearful that the spread of discriminatory commercial policies would disrupt the international economy.[29]

The commercial nightmare haunting Washington during the 1920s had already become stark reality in London. Great Britain, long dependent upon overseas sales for domestic prosperity, was mired in a decade-long slump. Despite the best efforts of the Foreign Office, the Board of Trade, and the Federation of British Industries, the U.K. share of total world exports shrank from 14 to 11 percent between 1913 and 1929. To be sure, British sales abroad did rise by 40 percent to $3.5 billion during that period, but imports rose even faster, producing an annual trade deficit of over $2 billion on the eve of the Great Depression. More and more, London blamed higher foreign tariffs and other trade barriers for unemployment that approached rates of 15 percent in such traditional British export industries as coal, steel, and textiles. As a result, Whitehall increasingly sought salvation in the markets of the Commonwealth, which by the late 1920s were absorbing nearly half of all U.K. exports. Autarchic commerical policies around the globe were forcing Britain to reconsider its long-term commitment to free trade.[30]

As both British and American officials had feared, the beggar-thy-neighbor trade practices of the 1920s did not produce universal prosperity but rather helped transform the Great Crash into a global commercial cataclysm. International commerce spiraled downward at an accelerating rate during the early 1930s as govern-

---

[29] This summary of U.S. trade policies during the 1920s draws on Joseph Brandes, *Herbert Hoover and Economic Diplomacy* (Pittsburgh, 1962); Carl Parrini, *Heir to Empire: United States Diplomacy, 1916–1923* (Pittsburgh, 1969); and Melvyn P. Leffler, *The Elusive Quest: America's Pursuit of European Stability and French Security, 1919–1933* (Chapel Hill, N.C., 1979). The statistics are from United States, Department of Commerce, Bureau of Foreign and Domestic Commerce, *Statistical Abstract of the United States, 1930* (Washington, D.C., 1930), pp. 481–85 (hereafter cited as *SAUS* for the appropriate year).

[30] This summary of U.K. trade policies during the 1920s draws on Great Britain, Board of Trade, *Final Report of the Committee on Industry and Trade*, Cmnd. 3282 (London, 1929), and Derek Aldcroft, *The Inter-War Economy: Britain, 1919–1939* (London, 1970). The statistics are from Great Britain, Board of Trade, *Statistical Abstract for the United Kingdom for Each of the Fifteen Years 1913 and 1920 to 1933*, Cmnd. 4801 (London, 1935), pp. 328, 338–45.

ments around the world scrambled to protect their own economies. By 1932 total world trade stood at barely one-third of the 1929 level, and many nations were resorting to bilateral bargaining and barter to revive their sagging exports. With unemployment epidemic and international trade in a shambles, commercial warfare on a global scale loomed ever larger.[31]

Convinced that the deepening economic crisis at home had been exacerbated by a 64-percent drop in U.S. sales abroad after 1929, American policy makers linked domestic recovery to the revival of foreign trade. Although President Hoover and his secretary of state, Henry L. Stimson, conceded that certain U.S. industries required modest protection, both men agreed that the quickest and simplest way to ensure economic recovery at home was to reconstruct a more liberal multilateral trading system. Their efforts to rekindle international commerce, however, were thwarted by Congress, which insisted on hiking the tariff to stratospheric levels in 1930. Resentful trading partners retaliated by imposing surcharges, quotas, and other discriminatory levies on American products.[32] After a brief flirtation with economic nationalism in 1933, the new administration of Franklin D. Roosevelt likewise operated on the assumption that "liberal commercial policy and reduction of trade barriers" would ensure a return to prosperity. Cordell Hull, the ardent apostle of commercial expansion who succeeded Stimson at the State Department, shepherded legislation through Congress authorizing mutual tariff reductions and creating the Export-Import Bank to foster U.S. sales abroad. By the late 1930s Hull and Roosevelt had concluded reciprocal trade agreements with over twenty nations, who promised equitable treatment for American exports, and threatened to sever relations with a handful of others, among them Nazi Germany, who persisted in their discriminatory ways.[33]

Whitehall's reaction to the 46-percent decline in U.K. exports after 1929 was considerably more complicated. Britain at first clung

[31] League of Nations, Economic Intelligence Service, *World Economic Survey, 1931–1932* (Geneva, 1934), pp. 144–60; Charles P. Kindleberger, *The World in Depression* (Berkeley, Calif., 1973), pp. 131–35, 172.

[32] Stimson to Lyman P. Hammond, 16 June 1931, Stimson Papers, microfilm ed., reel 81 (General Correspondence); Herbert C. Hoover, *The Memoirs of Herbert Hoover,* vol. 2: *The Cabinet and the Presidency* (New York, 1952), p. 79.

[33] Hull, *Memoirs,* 1:352–77; Lloyd C. Gardner, *The Economic Aspects of New Deal Diplomacy* (Boston, 1971), pp. 24–46.

stubbornly to its traditional policy of free trade and urged others to follow suit. As the depression deepened, however, protectionist pressures mounted both within the Conservative party and among the Dominions. By the time a conference of Commonwealth nations convened at Ottawa, Canada, in July 1932 to discuss economic recovery, Tory leader Stanley Baldwin had reluctantly accepted a system of imperial preference designed to expand British manufactured exports to and agricultural imports from the Dominions.[34] But U.K. officials were nevertheless well aware that the preferential arrangements growing out of the Ottawa meeting might jeopardize the lion's share of British trade outside the empire. As a consequence Britain worked hard during the mid-1930s to accommodate long-term trading partners such as Argentina and to cultivate new ones throughout the world.[35] As the decade drew to a close, London's commercial policy was still calculated to expand exports, through the paradoxical combination of bilateral preference inside and multilateral equality outside the Commonwealth.

During the 1920s and 1930s, then, policy makers on both sides of the Atlantic struggled to restore economic prosperity and political stability to a world devastated by war, revolution, and depression. Determined to prevent the growth of bolshevism in Central America, South Asia, and Western Europe, London and Washington were quick to interpret almost any turmoil from El Salvador to Afghanistan as evidence of Soviet subversion. Intent on shielding U.K. and U.S. investments from left-wing nationalist attacks, British and American officials interceded on behalf of Anglo-Persian Oil, Firestone, and other multinationals whose foreign holdings were in jeopardy. Convinced that recovery at home hinged on expanding markets abroad, the White House by the mid-1930s was struggling to reduce trade barriers; meanwhile Whitehall employed a double standard, protection inside and free trade outside the empire. Spain was destined to cross swords with Great Britain and the United States on all three counts.

---

[34] Richard Kottman, *Reciprocity and the North Atlantic Triangle, 1932–1938* (Ithaca, N.Y., 1968), pp. 19–35; Ronald S. Russell, *Imperial Preference: Its Development and Effects* (London, 1949), pp. 27–28.
[35] See, for example, Alfred E. Kahn, *Great Britain in the World Economy* (New York, 1946), pp. 236–56.

Acrimony rather than amity had long been the watchword in Madrid's relations with London and Washington, due in large measure to bitter imperial rivalry and long-standing cultural differences. The British had struck the first blow against the Spanish Empire in 1704 when they occupied Gibraltar, the Americans struck the last 194 years later when they seized the Philippines, and the Spaniards forgave neither. Royal bloodlines linked Spain's Alfonso XIII with Britain's George V, to be sure, and intellectual kinship linked some reformers south of the Pyrenees to liberals across the Atlantic. When the Great War erupted, however, neutral Spain leaned not toward Great Britain or the United States but rather toward Germany and Austria-Hungary. As a result, most Britons and Americans probably regarded Spain, with its rickety monarchy, its obscurantist clergy, and its primitive bullfights, as a twentieth-century holdover from the dark ages.

The 1920s witnessed modest Spanish rapprochements with Great Britain and the United States, thanks mainly to the emergence of a reformist military government at Madrid headed by General Miguel Primo de Rivera. Hoping to avoid further national humiliation at home and abroad, Primo saw himself as a Spanish Mussolini who would rejuvenate his country by fusing political autocracy with economic modernization. Washington and London were at first encouraged by the new regime's repression of the revolutionary left and by its relatively liberal approach to foreign trade and investment. By the end of the decade, however, Primo's star had begun to sink rapidly, and he was forced to step down in early 1930, a victim of his own venality and the global economic downturn. The ultimate casualty, as British and American officials knew only too well, was likely to be the monarchy itself. And indeed, assailed by a growing chorus of republican critics, Alfonso XIII reluctantly followed Primo into exile fifteen months later, in April 1931.

The birth of the Spanish Republic aroused mixed emotions among U.S. and U.K. policy makers. Although both the Foreign Office and the State Department were in theory committed to democratic principles, neither was entirely persuaded from a practical standpoint that Spain was fully prepared for representative government. The ensuing five years of political turmoil at Madrid did nothing to dispel such doubts, but they did do much to strengthen British and American suspicions that the republican regime would inevitably be superseded by a bolshevik tyranny with close ties to the Kremlin. Already troubled by the prospect of Soviet subversion in Spain, Whitehall and the White House were outraged when the Spanish Republic launched a nationalist economic program that threatened U.K. and U.S. investors and exporters. Any remaining British and American hopes that Spain's republican leaders might eventually provide the country with the orderly and moderate government it so sorely needed were dashed at the polls in February 1936 by the victory of a Popular Front coalition backed by Communists. On the eve of the Spanish civil war these long-standing ideological and economic misgivings about the deteriorating situation at Madrid had crystallized into consensus on both sides of the Atlantic: the republic had outlived its usefulness, and only some kind of authoritarian rule could avert total chaos in Spain.

British and American diplomacy in the wake of General Franco's uprising reflected this grim assessment. Although international law had customarily been interpreted as entitling a legitimate sovereign government to purchase from other nations the war matériel necessary to put down an internal rebellion, neither Britain nor the United States was eager to assist a left-wing Popular Front regime in its struggle against right-wing military insurgents. Nor did they wish to exacerbate tensions with Germany and Italy, whose clandestine support for Franco's rebels was tilting the military balance against the republican government at Madrid. By early August 1936 both Whitehall and the White House gravitated toward a policy of nonintervention in the Spanish civil war. They did so because, under the guise of impartial neutrality, such a course provided a convenient rationale for denying the Popular Front regime the weapons to which it might otherwise have had access.

Needless to say, policy makers on both sides of the Atlantic hotly contested this interpretation both then and later, indignantly dismissing allegations that their decisions had been calculated to influence the outcome of the conflict in Spain. A careful examination of British and American attitudes toward the Spanish Republic, however, reveals that the troubles estranging London and Washington from Madrid during the early 1930s persisted through the outbreak of the civil war. The growing strength of the extreme left, the widespread nationalist campaign against multinational corporations, and the proliferation of inequitable commercial policies, all ran counter to U.S. and U.K. diplomacy in the two decades following the Great War. Recurrent political and economic disputes poisoned British and American relations with Spain after 1931 and predisposed both the State Department and the Foreign Office to adopt strategies during the Spanish civil war that one contemporary critic so accurately labeled "malevolent neutrality."[36]

[36]The term "malevolent neutrality" was coined by Lord Strabolgi, a Labour peer, in an article critical of British policy in Spain that appeared in the *Daily Herald*, 10 August 1936; see the epigraph to this book. For the Foreign Office reaction, see Halifax to Strabolgi, 11 August 1936, W8416/62/41, PRO FO371, vol. 20530.

2

The Road to Revolution,
1919–1930

The broad currents that helped determine the general course of diplomacy on both sides of the Atlantic after the Great War also shaped American and British relations with Spain. During the 1920s Spain was shaken by left-wing upheavals, foreign capital poured into its mines and industries, and Spanish officials struggled to correct a chronic trade deficit. Given the preoccupation at the Foreign Office and the State Department with the containment of revolutionary nationalism, the promotion of investment abroad, and the expansion of export markets, it was only natural for Washington and London to monitor closely the sharp swings of the political pendulum at Madrid. Indeed, Spain soon stumbled down the road to revolution, and by 1930 the United States and Great Britain each feared that the increasingly chaotic state of Spanish politics would adversely affect its own interests in the Iberian Peninsula.

I

Although Spain had remained neutral during the Great War, it did not escape the dislocations generated by the conflict in Europe. Once the wartime industrial boom had crested, the Spanish economy slid into a serious recession. Unemployment and inflation spiraled upward, prompting a militant response from Spain's rapidly expanding labor movement. During 1920 alone workers staged over a thousand major strikes, while the anarchist Confederación Nacional del Trabajo (CNT) unleashed a campaign of terror against the employers that culminated in the assassination of Prime Minister Eduardo Dato in May 1921. Two months later Spain's tottering North African empire was dealt a stunning blow at Annual, where Moorish guerrillas led by Abd-el-Krim routed General Manuel Silvestre's much larger army and killed over 8,000 Spanish troops. By late 1922 many Spaniards held King Alfonso XIII and his moribund constitutional monarchy responsible for their nation's troubles and were clamoring for a change of regime.[1]

The crisis worsened over the next nine months, but at just the moment when the opposition seemed strong enough to topple the crown, General Miguel Primo de Rivera staged a coup d'état. Primo de Rivera, a fifty-three-year-old Andalusian who had distinguished himself in Spain's colonial wars, was an unlikely candidate for military dictator. Fond of horses, whores, and hard liquor, he was a self-styled liberal sympathetic to the urban workers and the rural poor. Although his outspoken criticism of the Moroccan campaign did not endear him to his fellow officers, the administrative expertise that Primo exhibited as captain general first at Cadiz and later at Barcelona earned him their grudging respect. A patriot who longed to restore his country to its former greatness, Primo had become convinced by the summer of 1923 that the resurgent separatist movement in Catalonia threatened to complete Spain's political disintegration. Attributing the current chaotic situation to the incompetence of the professional politicians, he issued a *pronunciamiento* from Barcelona on 12 September calling for the creation of a military directorate. Alfonso XIII, regarding this idea as the perfect solution to his own troubles, invited Primo to Madrid, where on 15 September a government composed of eight generals and one admiral was established by royal decree.[2]

The new dictator, whose coup was greeted by widespread popu-

---

[1] Raymond Carr, *Spain, 1808–1939* (London, 1966), p. 509; Gerald Meaker, *The Revolutionary Left in Spain, 1914–1923* (Stanford, Calif., 1974), pp. 338–45; Stanley Payne, *Politics and the Military in Modern Spain* (Stanford, Calif., 1967), pp. 166–77; Payne, *The Spanish Revolution* (New York, 1970), pp. 39–45; and Antonio Ramos Oliveira, *Politics, Economics and Men of Modern Spain, 1808–1946* (London, 1946), pp. 243–49.

[2] Gerald Brenan, *The Spanish Labyrinth* (New York, 1943), pp. 73–76; Dillwyn F. Ratcliff, *Prelude to Franco: Political Aspects of the Dictatorship of General Miguel Primo de Rivera* (New York, 1957), pp. 9–17; Salvador de Madariaga, *Spain: A Modern History* (New York, 1958), pp. 334–45; and Payne, *Politics and the Military*, pp. 187–207.

lar approval, undertook at once to bring Spain's nagging political crisis to an end. An admirer of Mussolini, Primo dissolved the Cortes on 3 October and suspended the Catalan provincial assembly in early 1924. He succeeded in quelling the street violence that had plagued postwar Spain by exploiting the bitter split between the anarchist CNT and its socialist rival, the Unión General de Trabajadores (UGT); while Primo subjected the CNT to a relentless campaign of repression, he invited the UGT to join his government. Most importantly, however, the military directorate brought the Moroccan war to a successful conclusion in 1926 by arranging a coordinated Franco-Spanish offensive against Abd-el-Krim. In three short years, then, Primo de Rivera had reestablished order south of the Pyrenees, and both the State Department and the Foreign Office hoped that his regime would become a permanent fixture in Spanish politics.[3]

Most American observers in Madrid welcomed the military coup because it promised political stability. Only ten days after Primo seized power, Alexander P. Moore, the U.S. ambassador to Spain, reported that the general was swiftly consolidating his power and "repressing the activities of labor agitators and communists." Three months later Moore confirmed that "Primo de Rivera and the present Government are the most popular government which Spain has had in years," largely because the military regime had stamped out the epidemic of "murders, strikes, and disorders" that had plagued Spaniards since the Great War.[4] Hallett Johnson, Moore's chief aide, echoed the ambassador's praise. Counting Primo among his "personal friends," Johnson later recalled the dictator as "a jovial man [who] cut off no heads but worked hard for the country, building much needed roads."[5]

British officials were even more enthusiastic about Primo's *pronunciamiento*. Alfonso XIII, who had married the English princess

---

[3] Carr, *Spain, 1808–1939*, pp. 567–72; Paul Preston, *The Coming of the Spanish Civil War* (New York, 1978), pp. 6–11; Shlomo Ben-Ami, "The Dictatorship of Primo de Rivera: A Political Reassessment," *Journal of Contemporary History* 12 (January 1977), 65–72; Shannon E. Fleming and Ann K. Fleming, "Primo de Rivera and Spain's Moroccan Problem, 1923–1927," ibid. 12 (January 1977), 85–99; Payne, *Politics and the Military*, pp. 208–23.

[4] Moore to Hughes, 22 September 1923, 852.00/950, and 3 December 1923, 852.00/1034, NA RG59. For further evidence of Primo's popularity, see Moore to Hughes, 29 September 1923, 852.00/951, and 6 October 1923, 852.00/963, NA RG59.

[5] Hallett Johnson, *Diplomatic Memoirs, Serious and Frivolous* (New York, 1963), p. 83.

Victoria Eugenia in 1906, was quite popular in Great Britain, where he could claim a close personal relationship with his consort's cousin King George V. Sir Esme Howard, the British ambassador to Spain, was convinced by 1923 that authoritarian rule was all that stood between the Bourbon Monarchy and "the Dictatorship of the Proletariat and the Soviet system."[6] He advised Whitehall on 21 September that most Spaniards were also "heartily tired" of corrupt parliamentary mismanagement and had welcomed the military seizure of power as the only alternative to "a revolution from below." G. H. Villiers, the head of Whitehall's Western Department, shared Howard's hope that Primo de Rivera would restore stability. "On the whole," Villiers remarked later in September, "I think one is justified in believing that the bloodless revolution will effect some purification of and improvement in the highly diseased Spanish body politic."[7] By early 1924 it seemed that Whitehall's optimism was wellfounded. "Complete tranquility, such as Spain has not known for many years," one British official at Madrid declared in March, "has reigned throughout the country since the Military Directorate commenced to govern."[8]

Primo's dictatorship found favor among British and American businessmen as well. Britain's economic stake in Spain probably approached $200 million by 1923, reflecting diverse holdings in natural resources, manufacturing industries, and public utilities.[9]

[6] Sir Charles Petrie, *King Alfonso XIII and His Age* (London, 1963), pp. 85–92, 190–93; Sir Esme Howard, *Theatre of Life,* vol. 2: *Life Seen from the Stalls, 1903–1936* (Boston, 1936), p. 425.

[7] Howard to Curzon, 21 September 1923, and minute by Villiers, 28 September 1923, W7602/623/41, PRO FO371, vol. 9490. See also Howard to Curzon, 20 December 1923, W9964/623/41, ibid.

[8] Great Britain, Department of Overseas Trade, *Report on the Industries and Commerce of Spain, 1924,* by Captain Ulick deB. Charles (London, 1924), p. 63.

[9] My estimate of total British direct investment in Spain is based on information from the following sources and has been converted into dollars at 1924 exchange rates ($4.85 to £1, 7 pesetas to $1): Charles E. Harvey, "Politics and Pyrites during the Spanish Civil War," *Economic History Review,* 2d ser., 31 (February 1978), 94, note 3, cites a 1929 market value for the Rio Tinto Company's common and preferred shares of £22.9 million ($111 million). M. W. Flinn, "British Steel and Spanish Ore," ibid., 2d ser., 8 (August 1955), 86, reports British holdings in Spanish iron mines in 1913 of £5.1 million ($24.7 million). Jaime Vicens Vives, *An Economic History of Spain* (Princeton, N.J., 1969), p. 724, estimates the assets of the Tharsis Sulphur Company in 1866 at 78.5 million pesetas ($11.2 million). Lord Bearsted, "Memorandum on the Present Situation in Spain," 9 February 1928, W1159/1/41, PRO FO371, vol. 13433, valued Royal Dutch Shell's Spanish facilities at roughly 38 million pesetas ($5.4 million). A Foreign Office minute, 18 June 1934, W5676/330/41, PRO FO371, vol. 18601, indicates that British investors were willing to sell their interest in the San-

British firms in Barcelona, whose operations had repeatedly been disrupted by anarchist organizers, breathed a collective sigh of relief when Primo outlawed the dreaded CNT soon after seizing power. The London-based Rio Tinto Company, which operated the world's largest open-pit copper mine at Huelva, likewise benefited greatly from military decrees prohibiting strikes and curtailing union activities.[10] Moreover, Primo encouraged other Britons to undertake fresh investment in Spain. In 1924, for example, he granted a multimillion-dollar concession to the newly created Anglo-Spanish Construction Company for the modernization of the railroad grid in Santander.[11] Sir Auckland Geddes, Rio Tinto's chairman, spent a month in Primo's Spain late in 1925 and came away with sentiments doubtless shared by many other British investors. "I returned to London," Geddes reported in April 1926, "satisfied that broadly the position at the mines, the foundation of our business, was sound."[12]

U.S. direct investments in Spain in 1923 were far smaller than Britain's, totaling approximately $30 million, mostly in petroleum refining and retail sales.[13] Nevertheless, American investors, like their British counterparts, regarded Primo's military coup as a hopeful sign. Indeed, the stable business conditions brought about

---

tander-Mediterranean Railway for £2 million ($9.7 million). Finally, Ramos Oliveira, *Modern Spain,* pp. 258–59, cites British investments in cork, electrical, and other manufacturing firms (including the Barcelona Power Light and Traction Company) of roughly 290 million pesetas ($41.4 million). The total of $203.4 million for 1923 probably underestimates the real value of British direct investments because many of the figures cited are for nineteenth-century concessions obtained at bargain-basement prices.

[10]Charles, *Report on the Industries and Commerce of Spain, 1924,* p. 65; David Avery, *Not on Queen Victoria's Birthday: The Story of the Rio Tinto Mines* (London, 1974), pp. 307–24.

[11]Memorandum by Sir Evelyn Wallers, 4 May 1931, W5108/5108/41; C. Howard Smith to Sir George Grahame, 26 October 1931, W11942/5108/41, PRO FO371, vols. 15780 and 15781.

[12]Geddes quoted in the *Times,* 8 April 1926, p. 21, col. d.

[13]I arrived at my estimate of total American direct investment in Spain by the following procedure: a memorandum by State Department Spanish desk officer Ellis Briggs (18 December 1930, 811.503152/6, NA RG59) placed U.S. holdings at $72 million, $47 million of which was in ITT's telephone subsidiary established in 1924. Subtracting $47 million from the $72 million total and then adding the $4.4 million that Standard Oil received in 1929 for its Spanish facilities (see Henrietta Larson et al., *History of Standard Oil Company (New Jersey): New Horizons, 1927–1950* [New York, 1971], p. 339), one comes up with $29.4 million as a rough approximation for American direct investment in 1923.

by the new authoritarian regime were very attractive on Wall Street, and in March 1924 Ambassador Moore, himself a successful businessman, predicted that the Spanish dictatorship would provide excellent opportunities for the expansion of American investment in Spain.[14]

The accuracy of his prediction was demonstrated later that same year by the achievements of the International Telephone and Telegraph Company (ITT). In late 1923 Primo de Rivera had announced plans to renovate Spain's ramshackle telephone system through the infusion of foreign technology. A lively competition ensued among ITT and its leading Swedish and German rivals for the lucrative right to modernize the Spanish phone network. With the arrival of ITT chairman Sosthenes Behn at Madrid in the spring of 1924 to handle his firm's negotiations, the balance tipped in favor of the Americans. Behn, a self-styled colonel who built ITT into a global communications empire during the 1920s, secured the energetic support of Ambassador Moore, wooed several Spanish officials with promises of high-paying jobs, and won an exclusive concession from Primo de Rivera on 29 August 1924 to provide Spain with modern, nationwide telephone service by 1929. ITT promptly established a Spanish subsidiary, the Compañía Telefónica Nacional de España (CTNE), capitalized initially at $45 million. Over the next five years telephone usage in Spain tripled, the CTNE's assets doubled to over $90 million, and ITT won praise from Primo and from Alfonso XIII himself.[15]

The warm welcome that Primo's authoritarian regime received from policy makers and investors coincided with a mild thaw in Spain's relatively frosty commercial relations with Great Britain and the United States. The Spanish government had decreed stiff duty hikes in July 1921 in an effort to combat the effects of the postwar recession, thereby earning itself the distinction of having imposed the world's highest tariff. British exports to Spain, particularly coal and machine tools, fell sharply. Faced with the prospect of even higher Spanish customs charges the next year, British officials were, according to Ambassador Howard, "forced against

---

[14] *New York Times*, 9 March 1924, sec. 1, pt. 2, p. 5:4.
[15] For a fuller discussion of the ITT concession, see Douglas J. Little, "Twenty Years of Turmoil: ITT, the State Department, and Spain, 1924–1944," *Business History Review* 53 (Winter 1979), 451–53.

our will" to renegotiate an 1894 trade agreement with Spain.[16] By October 1922 London and Madrid were able to conclude a new commercial treaty, which provided for most-favored-nation treatment and reciprocal concessions on wine and coal exports. Primo, who favored the expansion of markets overseas, agreed to broaden the Anglo-Spanish accord in April 1927 to include the dependent territories administered by the two nations. As a result, British sales to Spain increased by 75 percent during the mid-1920s, while Spain's exports to Great Britain nearly doubled.[17]

Spanish-American commercial relations had also been quite chilly immediately after the Great War. The inauguration of Prohibition in 1920 and the passage of the Fordney-McCumber Tariff two years later increased Spain's trade deficit with North America radically. Madrid retaliated in early 1923 by renouncing a 1906 commercial treaty that had granted the United States most-favored-nation status. Less than a month after his military coup in September, however, Primo agreed to a modus vivendi that restored equitable treatment to American exports on a conditional basis.[18] Unable to conclude a formal treaty, the two countries renewed this temporary accord four years later. Although the controversy surrounding American restrictions on the importation of Spanish agricultural products remained unresolved, Washington and Madrid were as late as 1928 on friendlier trading terms than they had been for at least a decade. American sales to Spain were up by nearly one-third over the 1920 total, and Spanish exports to the United States tripled over the same period.[19]

---

[16] International Bank for Reconstruction and Development (IBRD), *The Economic Development of Spain* (Baltimore, 1963), p. 142; *Board of Trade Journal,* 28 July 1921, p. 121, and 6 October 1921, p. 339; *Supplement to the Board of Trade Journal: Spain, New Draft Customs Tariff,* 28 July 1921, pp. iii, xxix–xxxi; Howard, *Life Seen from the Stalls,* pp. 465–66.

[17] Cmnd. 2188, "Treaty of Commerce and Navigation between the United Kingdom and Spain," 31 October 1922, *Parliamentary Papers* (Commons), *1924,* vol. 26; Cmnd. 2855, "Convention between His Britannic Majesty and His Majesty the King of Spain," 5 April 1927, *Parliamentary Papers* (Commons), *1927,* vol. 26; Spain, Ministerio de Trabajo y Previsión, Servicio General de Estadística, *Anuario estadístico de España, 1928* (Madrid, 1930), p. 187 (hereafter cited as *AEE* for appropriate year); *AEE, 1931,* p. 198.

[18] Joseph M. Jones, Jr., *Tariff Retaliation: Repercussions of the Hawley-Smoot Bill* (Philadelphia, 1934), pp. 34–36; Primo de Rivera to Moore, 6 October 1923, and Moore to Primo de Rivera, 22 October 1923, *FRUS, 1923,* 2: 873–74.

[19] Primo de Rivera to Ogden Hammond, 7 November 1927, *FRUS, 1927,* 3: 732–33; *AEE, 1928,* p. 187; *AEE, 1931,* p. 198.

During his first years in office Primo de Rivera enjoyed considerable popularity on both sides of the Atlantic. He had restored law and order, welcomed foreign investors with open arms, and reduced barriers to international trade, all of which pleased British and American diplomats enormously. Britain's ambassador applauded Primo's achievements and later recalled that by 1924 politics in Spain was "non-existent, and this I think came as a relief to the Spanish public quite as much as to us."[20] Alexander Moore likewise praised the dictator as "a wonderful patriot," who was "always thinking of what is best for Spain."[21] Indeed, both the United States and Great Britain seemed to regard Primo de Rivera as the answer to their nagging political and economic problems with Spain.

II

Much to the dismay of Whitehall and the White House, however, Primo de Rivera's political fortunes took a turn for the worse in the late 1920s. New problems threatened to reverse the trend since 1923 toward more cordial British and American relations with Spain. By 1925 Primo's popularity had begun to wane among liberal intellectuals and left-wing politicians, who denounced his regime as corrupt and repressive. The aging dictator nevertheless retained the support of both an officer corps gratified by his efforts to modernize Spain's antiquated armed forces and conservatives pleased by his attempt to revitalize Spanish political life through the creation of a nationalist party, the Unión Patriótica. Alfonso XIII likewise reaffirmed his royal commitment to the military regime as a bulwark of order.[22]

But as the decade drew to a close, even Primo's most ardent supporters were coming to doubt whether he could provide Spain with long-term political stability. As early as November 1926 the Marquis Arrilice de Ibarra, a wealthy right-wing industrialist, had remarked that a regime that was "permanent and not dependent

---

[20] Howard, *Life Seen from the Stalls*, pp. 475–76.
[21] Moore quoted in *New York Times*, 9 March 1924, sec. 1, pt. 2, p. 5:4.
[22] Payne, *Politics and the Military*, pp. 240–42; Petrie, *Alfonso XIII and His Age*, pp. 194–97; Ratcliff, *Prelude to Franco*, pp. 58–63.

on one man" was more likely to ensure "good government and stable business conditions" at Madrid.[23] Primo did attempt to legitimize his rule by establishing a national assembly in 1927, but this body was quickly discredited by charges of rank nepotism and financial scandal. By 1928 the Spanish treasury was straining under the burden of Primo's vast outlays for public works, while falling prices for agricultural exports pressed Spain's trade deficit steadily upward. Even the army grew restless; late that year a group of disillusioned military officers began to plan a coup.[24]

Throughout 1929 Primo's critics grew more vocal, while his adherents became more skeptical. In January José Sánchez Guerra, an exiled conservative politician, landed at Valencia and led the artillery corps there in an abortive revolt against the dictatorship. In following weeks disgruntled officers staged mutinies at scattered military outposts. Spring brought a fresh wave of unrest to Spain's universities, where students and their professors condemned Primo's arbitrary actions. Bankers worried that the previous year's poor harvest and the prospect of an even larger trade deficit might prompt the dictator to devalue the peseta. Industrialists in Catalonia, who had never felt comfortable about government intervention in the economy, feared that Spain might be on the verge of state socialism. As the year drew to a close, even Alfonso XIII confessed that the time had come for a change.[25]

Weakened by a long bout with diabetes, Primo decided privately in early 1930 that he would step down on the seventh anniversary of his 12 September *pronunciamiento*. The ailing dictator planned to use his remaining time in office to restore a semblance of political order and arrange a dignified return to private life, but he underestimated the depth of the opposition to his regime. When Alfonso XIII hinted in mid-January that the nine-month grace period was too long, Primo ignored the king's advice and instead appealed directly to the provincial military governors for a vote of

[23]The marquis expressed these views during a conversation with Ambassador Ogden Hammond. See Hammond to Castle, 15 June 1927, 811.503152/4, NA RG59.
[24]Ben-Ami, "Dictatorship of Primo de Rivera," pp. 66–70; Payne, *Politics and the Military*, pp. 243–46; IBRD, *Economic Development of Spain*, pp. 136–37; Madariaga, *Spain*, pp. 355–66.
[25]Shlomo Ben-Ami, *The Origins of the Second Republic in Spain* (London, 1978), pp. 36–44; Carr, *Spain, 1808–1939*, pp. 581–91; Ramos Oliveira, *Modern Spain*, pp. 192–202; Raymond Desmond, "The Aftermath of the Spanish Dictatorship," *Foreign Affairs* 9 (January 1931), 298–301.

confidence. Outraged by this violation of the royal prerogative, Alfonso XIII demanded that the dictator resign at once. When the military leaders advised Primo that they could not in good conscience support a government that had lost the king's favor, the dictator tendered his resignation on 28 January. Leaving Madrid in disgrace, Primo de Rivera went into voluntary exile at Paris, where he died two months later, a broken man. Alfonso XIII now turned to the task of rehabilitating his constitutional monarchy, and the State Department and the Foreign Office pondered Spain's political future.[26]

The sudden collapse of Primo's dictatorship was not altogether unexpected in Washington. As early as the autumn of 1924 the State Department, detecting "considerable Liberal opposition to the Directorate," had worried that "a radical change of Government would materially affect our relations with Spain."[27] Assistant Secretary of State Francis B. White wondered whether Spain was "finished" after he visited Madrid two years later. "Primo has reorganized the administration in a most remarkable and praiseworthy manner, but I am unable to bring myself to feel that he is building on a rock foundation," White advised the State Department. "Should anything happen to him his edifice would crumble, probably with far-reaching results."[28] By June 1927 Ogden Hammond, Moore's successor as U.S. ambassador to Spain, warned Washington that the popularity of the military regime was waning rapidly among Spanish businessmen.[29]

British policy makers were quick to express similar doubts about the long-term stability of Primo's dictatorship. In December 1924 Ambassador Horace Rumbold, Sir Esme Howard's replacement at Madrid, discovered "a certain amount of uneasiness in business and other circles here" regarding the future of the authoritarian government. Early the next year Lord Stamfordham, private secretary to King George V, confirmed that some British experts now believed that "a political catastrophe was sooner or later inevitable"

[26] E. Allison Peers, *The Spanish Tragedy, 1930–1936* (New York, 1936), pp. 6–12; Petrie, *Alfonso XIII and His Age*, pp. 208–10; Payne, *Politics and the Military*, pp. 250–55.
[27] Memorandum by Henry Carter, 6 November 1924, 852.00/1310, NA RG59.
[28] White to Castle, 1 January 1927, William R. Castle Papers, Box 8 (Spain 1923–1932), Herbert Hoover Presidential Library, West Branch, Iowa.
[29] Hammond to Castle, 15 June 1927, 811.503152/4, NA RG59.

in Spain. Having observed Primo at close range for eighteen months, Rumbold in August 1926 termed him "a cunning rather than a clever man . . . [who] becomes more autocratic the longer his regime lasts."[30] Sir Austen Chamberlain, the British foreign secretary, expressed many of the same reservations upon meeting the Spanish dictator for the first time a year later. Although Primo was "much more attractive than I had expected" and promised "the closest and most friendly relations" with Great Britain, Chamberlain nevertheless found the Spaniard "very amateurish" and "a little childish" when it came to matters of state.[31]

If both the State Department and the Foreign Office were well aware by the late 1920s that the dictatorship was steadily losing its appeal, neither American nor British policy makers were prepared for Primo's desperate effort to salvage his sagging prestige by unleashing a nationalist campaign against multinational oil companies operating in Spain. To be sure, Primo had earlier welcomed the influx of investors from abroad. By 1927, however, with the economy in disarray and the public disillusioned, he saw an assault on foreign petroleum firms as a convenient means of both providing a new source of badly needed revenue and flattering the Spanish sense of national pride. Accordingly, the military regime announced with considerable fanfare that effective 1 January 1928 the newly created Compañía Arrendataria del Monopolio de Petróleos (CAMPSA) would assume complete control of Spain's oil industry. Since Spanish petroleum refining and distribution were dominated by Royal Dutch Shell and Standard Oil of New Jersey, each of which claimed a $5-million stake in Spain, the formation of a government oil monopoly placed Madrid on a collision course with London and Washington.[32]

[30] Rumbold and Stamfordham are quoted in Martin Gilbert, *Sir Horace Rumbold: Portrait of a Diplomat, 1869–1941* (London, 1973), pp. 303–4, 312.
[31] Chamberlain to Rumbold, 14 October 1927, W9551/9551/41, PRO Fo371, vol. 12720; Sir Charles Petrie, *The Life and Letters of the Right Hon. Sir Austen Chamberlain*, 2 vols. (Toronto, 1940), 2: 317–18.
[32] George Gibb and Evelyn Knowlton, *History of the Standard Oil Company (New Jersey): The Resurgent Years, 1911–1927* (New York, 1956), pp. 516–17; Hammond to Kellogg, 16 November 1927, *FRUS, 1927*, 3: 687–93; Lord Bearsted, "Memorandum on the Present Situation in Spain," 9 February 1928, W1159/1/41, PRO Fo371, vol. 13433. For a concise summary of the entire episode, see Adrian Shubert, "Oil Companies and Governments: International Reaction to the Nationalization of the Petroleum Industry in Spain, 1927–1930," *Journal of Contemporary History* 15 (October 1980), 701–20.

The trouble started in mid-October 1927, when Primo authorized the seizure of all foreign petroleum properties but indefinitely postponed the question of indemnification. Neither the State Department nor the Foreign Office favored the creation of state-controlled monopolies abroad, yet both were willing to acquiesce to the Spanish proposal provided that Madrid and the two firms could agree on appropriate compensation.[33] No agreement was forthcoming, however, and by year's end British and American officials were worrying that Primo's action would set a dangerous precedent and jeopardize other foreign investments in Spain. "Today it is the turn of the Shell," Villiers fretted at the Foreign Office on 22 November. "Tomorrow it may well be the turn of those two huge [British] concerns, the Rio Tinto and . . . the Canadiense."[34] Primo's "arbitrary acts," Acting Secretary of State Robert Olds grumbled at Washington a month later, were convincing many Americans "that in Spain the law does not now protect property or property rights."[35]

The situation deteriorated in early 1928, when CAMPSA began to confiscate the holdings of Shell, Standard, and two smaller French enterprises. The Spaniards repeatedly promised that the oil companies would receive "fair and generous compensation," but Madrid continued to postpone the date for payment. The big petroleum corporations now began to doubt, with good reason, whether they would ever receive adequate indemnification from the Spanish government. Their worst fears were confirmed on 26 January, when Primo announced that the Compagnie Deutsch de la Meurthe, a small French refinery at Santander, was to receive only $130,000 for its assets in Spain, less than one-third of its $450,000 book value.[36]

The State Department regarded the compensation formula as hopelessly inadequate and believed that close cooperation with

[33] Castle to Hammond, tel. 13 August 1927, and Hammond to Kellogg, tel. 21 October 1927, *FRUS, 1927*, 3: 667–68, 673; Rumbold to Chamberlain, 18 November 1927, and minute by Villiers, 22 November 1927, W10770/5913/41, PRO Fo371, vol. 12719.

[34] Minute by Villiers, 22 November 1927, W10770/5913/41, PRO FO371, vol. 12719. "Canadiense" refers to the Barcelona Power Light and Traction Company, a firm legally incorporated in Canada but controlled by British capital.

[35] Olds to Percy Blair, tel. 20 December 1927, *FRUS, 1927*, 3: 711–12.

[36] Blair to Kellogg, 4 January 1928, tel. 10 January 1928, 11 January 1928, tel. 19 January 1928, and tel. 26 January 1928, *FRUS, 1928*, 3: 832–41.

Whitehall and the Quai d'Orsay would be the most effective way to protect foreign oil interests in Spain. But although the French were eager to act in concert with American officials, the British were reluctant. In early February Assistant Secretary of State William R. Castle warned Sir Esme Howard, now Britain's ambassador to the United States, that the confiscatory Spanish scheme was "likely to affect British and American interests in the same way" unless the two countries joined forces to block it.[37] On the other side of the Atlantic worried Shell representatives predicted that other British investors would suffer "much more serious losses" if Primo's plan were successful. They urged the Foreign Office to join the Quai d'Orsay and the State Department in presenting "a united front" against the petroleum monopoly.[38]

Despite such pressure, Whitehall hesitated to cooperate with the French and the Americans. In the first place, the Foreign Office was reluctant to intervene on behalf of an Anglo-Dutch corporation whose subsidiary was legally incorporated in Spain, especially since it had declined on the same grounds to assist Shell in a dispute the previous year over subsoil petroleum rights in Rumania. Furthermore, Whitehall had recently learned that Shell might be satisfied with less than book value for its holdings in Spain, provided that Primo paid the reduced compensation promptly. Finally, the Foreign Office hoped to avoid provoking a more serious Anglo-Spanish confrontation. Since Spain stood a-thwart Britain's imperial lifeline through the Mediterranean, Whitehall was loath to take any action what might provoke a nationalistic outcry at Madrid. Not surprisingly, then, Great Britain rejected the American proposal to act in concert on 23 February. Five months later Shell agreed to accept $3.4 million for its Spanish facilities, approximately two-thirds of what the firm had requested a year earlier.[39]

[37]Kellogg to Blair, tel. 27 January 1928; Blair to Kellogg, tel. 28 January 1928; Kellogg to Blair, 1 February 1928; Alanson Houghton to Kellogg, 8 February 1928, *FRUS, 1928*, 3: 841–46; Howard to Chamberlain, 9 February 1928, W1504/1/41, PRO FO371, vol. 13433.

[38]Lord Bearsted to Sir William Tyrrell, 9 February 1928, and minute by Tyrrell, 9 February 1928, W1159/1/41, PRO FO371, vol. 13433.

[39]Minutes by Villiers, 22 November 1927, W10770/5913/41, and 7 December 1927, W11289/5913/41; Villiers to Howard, tel. 30 January 1928, W750/1/41, PRO FO371, vols. 12719 and 13433; Hammond to Kellogg, tel. 24 August 1928, *FRUS, 1928*, 3: 873; Castle to Hammond, 13 July 1928, and Hammond to Castle, 3 August 1928, Castle Papers, Box 8 (Spain 1923–1932); Shubert, "Oil Companies and Governments," pp. 705–12.

Although the State Department was "distinctly disappointed by the failure of the British Government and the Shell group to stand with the French and American Governments and the oil companies," U.S. officials continued to work closely with their French counterparts to secure "increased compensation" for the remaining foreign firms. After six more months of wrangling, capped by threats to expel thousands of Spanish migrant workers from France and to exclude Spanish produce from grocery bins in France and the United States, collaboration between Paris and Washington bore fruit. Wearied by "long and concerted French and American pressure," Primo agreed in early May 1929 to sweeten his offer to the oil giants. Following some last-minute haggling, Standard Oil accepted $4.4 million in compensation on 15 June; the French companies received slightly more than $3.3 million for their combined holdings.[40]

If the State Department and the Foreign Office each handled the Spanish petroleum controversy differently, both recognized that the creation of CAMPSA augured ill for other American and British investments. Fearful lest Primo's eventual capitulation to foreign oil interests unleash an even more dangerous nationalist backlash, London and Washington cautioned businessmen to be extremely careful in Spain. When Colonel Constant Cordier of the Electric Bond and Share Company inquired about Spanish investment opportunities in June 1928, the State Department gave him a less than sanguine political forecast, emphasized the current difficulties being experienced by American oil firms, and suggested that he contact a good Madrid lawyer before securing any concession from Primo de Rivera.[41] Later that same year Rio Tinto received a scare, when the Spanish government filed suit alleging the British firm had evaded almost $5 million in export taxes during the early 1920s. A hasty note from Austen Chamberlain and a healthy bribe from Auckland Geddes brought swift assurances from Primo that the litigation did not presage a wholesale assault on the copper concession, but by now the message was clear to businessmen and

[40]Castle to Hammond, tel. 30 August 1928, and Hammond to Kellogg, tel. 5 September 1928, and tel. 6 December 1928, *FRUS, 1928,* 3: 874–75, 877–78; Castle to Sheldon Whitehouse, 14 February 1929; Hammond to Henry L. Stimson, 12 April 1929, and 9 May 1929; J. Reuben Clark to Hammond, 15 June 1929; Hammond to Stimson, 21 June 1929, *FRUS, 1929,* 3: 773–75, 777–80, 781–86; Shubert, "Oil Companies and Governments," pp. 712–18.
[41]Memorandum by J. Theodore Marriner, 6 June 1928, 811.503152/5, NA RG59.

to diplomats. As the decade drew to a close, one could no longer take the security of foreign investments in Spain for granted.[42]

Nor did Spain's modest commercial rapprochements with Great Britain and the United States survive the turmoil of the late 1920s. Primo de Rivera's increasingly protectionist policies and global economic dislocation combined to rekindle earlier trade disputes with London and Washington. British exports to Spain suffered heavily after 1927, thanks largely to Madrid's hefty customs increases on textiles and tighter restrictions on the use of foreign coal. Consequently, though Britain remained the biggest market for Spain's exports, it slipped from second to third place behind the United States and France as a source of Spanish imports.[43] Spanish-American commercial relations likewise worsened rapidly in 1928, after Washington hiked tariffs sharply on various fruits and vegetables. Tension mounted the following spring, when the Department of Agriculture embargoed Almerian grapes and oranges as a precautionary measure after the Mediterranean fruit fly, an insect pest endemic throughout much of southern Europe, devastated the Florida citrus crop. Angry Spanish officials threatened to renounce the 1923 modus vivendi and retaliate against U.S. exports. With Spain's worldwide trade deficit in 1929 still hovering near $70 million and exerting constant downward pressure on the peseta, Primo's regime felt it had much to gain and little to lose by resorting to old-fashioned commercial warfare.[44]

By late 1929, then, British and American relations with Spain had deteriorated markedly. The reemergence of political instability, the insecurity of foreign investments, and the resurrection of longstanding commercial grievances ensured that Primo de Rivera would have few mourners in London or Washington. One British diplomat, for example, recalled that Primo's increasingly erratic behavior had filled his former supporters with contempt, especially once the old man fell into the practice of "forecasting the end

[42] *Times,* 7 November 1928, p. 15; Carr, *Spain, 1808–1939,* p. 579; Avery, *Not on Queen Victoria's Birthday,* pp. 324–26, 339–40.

[43] Great Britain, Department of Overseas Trade, *Report on Economic Conditions in Spain, 1928,* by Alexander Adams (London, 1928), pp. 32–33; and *Economic Conditions in Spain, 1930,* by Adams (London, 1930), pp. 28–30.

[44] Jones, *Tariff Retaliation,* pp. 38–41; memorandum by Henry Stimson, 25 April 1929, Stimson Papers, microfilm ed., reel 163 (Memoranda of Conversations: Poland to Yugoslavia); Primo de Rivera to Hammond, 26 April 1929; Stimson to Hammond, 3 May 1929; Castle to Hammond, 3 May 1929, *FRUS, 1929,* 3: 790–95.

of his regime—a fatal habit in dictators."[45] Mounting political and economic troubles prevented the settlement of even minor issues, prompting the American Embassy in Madrid to complain that "unless the shoe pinches somewhere, the Spanish Government will allow the question to slumber."[46] Britain's permanent undersecretary of state Robert Vansittart probably expressed the sentiments of most policy makers on both sides of the Atlantic when he remarked simply that "Primo de Rivera's dictatorship was exhausted."[47] Yet neither the Foreign Office nor the State Department expected the dictator's departure to alter the political landscape at Madrid drastically; on the contrary, they anticipated that Alfonso XIII would lead Spain gradually back to constitutional monarchy.

III

Such British and American optimism soon proved to be mere wishful thinking, however, for Primo's demise failed to improve the political climate at Madrid. Ignoring the leading civilian politicians, Alfonso XIII again turned to the army for his new prime minister, General Damaso Berenguer. Eight years younger than his predecessor, Berenguer had distinguished himself during the 1920s as both an able military tactician and a vocal critic of Primo's excesses. The king, who hoped that this appointment would strengthen the bond between the army and the monarchy, instructed Berenguer on 28 January to prepare for a return to constitutional parliamentarism later in 1930.[48]

Although the general quickly lifted the censorship and eased some of the political restrictions imposed during the previous decade, he was unable to quell the tumultuous wave of unrest that swept Spain that spring. Students agitated for an immediate return to civilian rule, while workers launched a series of strikes to protest

---

[45] Maurice Peterson, *Both Sides of the Curtain* (London, 1950), pp. 153–55.

[46] Whitehouse to Stimson, 25 November 1929, *FRUS, 1929*, 3: 771–73.

[47] Lord Vansittart, *The Mist Procession: The Memoirs of Lord Vansittart* (London, 1958), pp. 415–16. British ambassador Sir George Grahame was much more graphic, cabling Whitehall that Primo de Rivera had finally "committed political suicide." Grahame to Arthur Henderson, 30 January 1930, W1087/35/41, PRO FO371, vol. 15040.

[48] Carr, *Spain, 1808–1939*, pp. 591–93; Payne, *Politics and the Military*, pp. 256–58; Petrie, *Alfonso XIII and His Age*, pp. 156–59.

low wages and high unemployment. Liberal and left-wing politicians weary of military rule alleged that Alfonso XIII himself had conspired with Primo to stage the 1923 coup. Radical members of the armed forces, among them Lieutenant Ramón Franco, an aviator who in 1930 was more widely known than his soon-to-be-famous older brother, called for the creation of a republic. Berenguer, faced with demands that a constituent cortes be convened to examine the charges against the king, repeatedly postponed the parliamentary elections originally scheduled for June 1930.[49]

Disgusted by the military regime's failure to restore more representative government, Alfonso XIII's critics gathered secretly at the Basque resort town of San Sebastián in August 1930. A broad coalition of liberal reformers, moderate Socialists, and Catalan separatists began to take shape, united by a common desire to replace the monarchy with a republic. After reaching an understanding known as the Pact of San Sebastián, the republican factions agreed to create a revolutionary committee that would coordinate plans for an uprising against the royal government. Upon securing the support of discontented army and navy officers, the conspirators set 15 December 1930 as the date for the revolution.[50]

But some republican officers stationed at Jaca, a small town in the foothills of the Pyrenees, grew impatient with this timetable. On 12 December, three days ahead of schedule, the Jaca garrison rose against the monarchy and proclaimed a republic. Other republican plotters were caught off guard by this unexpected turn of events, enabling the Berenguer regime to defeat the tiny band of military rebels in under forty-eight hours. The two officers who led the revolt were captured and executed; the members of the revolutionary committee, including Niceto Alcalá-Zamora, the future president of the Spanish Republic, were arrested in Madrid. British and American observers watching the political situation in Spain deteriorate throughout 1930, wondered if the monarchy could weather the gathering storm.[51]

---

[49] Ben-Ami, *Origins of the Second Republic*, pp. 22–25; Petrie, *Alfonso XIII and His Age*, pp. 212–14; Carr, *Spain, 1808–1939*, pp. 595–96.

[50] Ricardo de la Cierva, ed., *Los documentos de la primavera trágica* (Madrid, 1967), pp. 19–20; Petrie, *Alfonso XIII and His Age*, pp. 215–17; Ben-Ami, *Origins of the Second Republic*, pp. 76–84.

[51] Payne, *Politics and the Military*, pp. 260–62; Peers, *Spanish Tragedy*, pp. 14–17; Ben-Ami, *Origins of the Second Republic*, pp. 84–103.

The new American ambassador to Spain, Irwin B. Laughlin, was sympathetic to Alfonso XIII's efforts to reinvigorate the constitutional monarchy. A fifty-seven-year-old career diplomat who had served in posts from London to Tokyo, the ambassador was the scion of a wealthy Pittsburgh family that controlled the Jones and Laughlin Steel Corporation. After his arrival at Madrid in 1929 Laughlin, an outspoken conservative Republican with a Roman Catholic wife, had quickly established close ties with the king and the circle of aristocrats who advised him.[52] When Primo stepped down in early 1930, Laughlin confessed that Berenguer and his cohorts were "not men of outstanding reputation," but he predicted that the new government would remain in office only during the "transition period" between military and civilian rule. Indeed, the American ambassador was convinced that Alfonso XIII himself was the chief catalyst in this gradual restoration of parliamentary government, because the king realized that continued dictatorship would ultimately undermine his throne. By March, Laughlin was pleased to report, the Berenguer regime was keeping "excellent order . . . with a thoroughness and apparent ease that has perhaps surprised its adherents almost as much as it has disappointed its adversaries." Under the stewardship of the youthful king, he concluded, Spain seemed to be emerging from its long political crisis.[53]

Nevertheless, Laughlin watched uneasily during the spring of 1930 as support for the monarchy shrank and the ranks of those who favored a republic swelled. In April he noted signs of a loose republican alliance composed of disillusioned conservatives, anticlerical liberals, regional separatists, and left-wing radicals; but two months later he was assuring Washington that the army, the church, and the peasantry still constituted "the pillars upon which the monarchy rests." Not surprisingly, Laughlin tended to dismiss proponents of a republic as political charlatans determined to rekindle their dying careers at the expense of Alfonso and his new government.[54] As a result, the republican meeting at San Sebastián

---

[52]Grahame to Henderson, 24 January 1931, W1535/1535/41, PRO FO371, vol. 15779; "The Ambassadors of the United States of America," *Fortune*, July 1931, pp. 47, 96, 105.

[53]Laughlin to Stimson, tel. 31 January 1930, 852.00/1779; 3 March 1930, 852.00/1783; and 10 March 1930, 852.00/1782, NA RG59.

[54]Laughlin to Stimson, 26 April 1930, 852.00/1784, and 7 June 1930, 852.00/1786, NA RG59.

in the late summer of 1930 passed largely unnoticed by the State Department. The only detailed report about the secret gathering to reach Washington concluded that any republican success was still a long way off.[55]

This depiction of monarchist strength and republican weakness was in itself a serious misreading of the situation in Spain, but the error was compounded by the tendency of most American observers to minimize the influence of moderate elements and exaggerate the importance of Communists among Alfonso's opponents. As early as January 1925 the State Department's listening post at Riga, Latvia, had reported that the Comintern was preparing for "social revolution" south of the Pyrenees, "based on the overthrow of the existing dictatorship of Primo de Rivera, abolition of the monarchist system, and proclamation of the dictatorship of the proletariat and the Soviet system."[56] Five years later Irwin Laughlin argued that Alfonso XIII had less to fear from fragmented advocates of a republic than from the well-organized Spanish Socialist party, which believed that "such a Republic . . . should be similar to the present Soviet Government in Russia, albeit more moderate."[57] By October 1930 the State Department had received even more disturbing news from Valencia. The American consul there warned that "Communistic sentiment [was] strong" among the popular masses, who intended to "enter upon a program of violence and rapine" before which even "the horrors of the French Revolution would pale."[58] When revolutionary strikes erupted in November, the American Embassy in Madrid was quick to relay rumors of communist infiltration and "the influence of Moscow" to Washington.[59]

The abortive Jaca uprising, which Spanish officials labeled "markedly communistic," seemed to confirm the worst fears of American observers. In response to an urgent State Department request for an update on the current Spanish crisis, Chargé d'Af-

---

[55] Fletcher to G-2, 26 August 1930, 2657 S.123/15, Record Group 165, Records of the War Department, General Staff, Military Intelligence Division 1917–1941, National Archives, Washington, D.C. (hereafter cited as NA RG165).

[56] Felix Coleman to Hughes, 22 January 1925, 852.00 B/12, NA RG59.

[57] Laughlin to Stimson, 26 April 1930, 852.00/1784, NA RG59.

[58] Clement Edwards to Laughlin, 20 September 1930, enclosed in Sheldon L. Crosby to Stimson, 26 September 1930, 852.00/1787, NA RG59.

[59] Crosby to Stimson, 24 November 1930, 852.00 P.R./163, and tel. 25 November 1930, 852.00/1791, NA RG59.

faires Sheldon L. Crosby cabled a frightening account that attributed the recent insurrection to "very decided left and Communo-Bolshevist influences in this country doubtlessly directly inspired from Moscow." Crosby termed a purely republican revolution "extremely doubtful" in the near future. He instead advised Washington on 22 December that most Spaniards saw the real danger arising from a "Communist-Republican alliance" designed to topple the monarchy, after which "the Communists . . . following the example set by Russia in 1917, would make short work of their co-helpers and before long Spain would be ruled by a Soviet directed from Moscow."[60] Although the Spanish ambassador in Washington tried to assure the State Department later that same day that the recent uprising "was not a matter of great importance," American officials remained convinced that "communist agents" were hard at work in Spain. Indeed, on New Year's Eve the War Department received a summary of the Jaca revolt from Military Attaché R. H. Fletcher, which concurred in the bleak forecast offered by U.S. diplomats. "Those elements favoring a republic, having failed to gain their ends by political means, feel themselves to be strong enough to try force," Fletcher warned. "The army is not wholly loyal. . . . Communism is growing stronger."[61]

British observers at Madrid, on the other hand, tended to discount charges of communist subversion in the Iberian Peninsula. Sir George Grahame, the new British ambassador to Spain, had like Laughlin been hopeful that Alfonso XIII would succeed in restoring representative government. The fifty-six-year-old bachelor had been one of Curzon's favorites and was an old friend of Sir Robert Vansittart. A veteran of three decades in the British diplomatic service, Grahame had been stationed at Paris, Berlin, and Rome prior to his arrival at Madrid in 1928. In contrast to his American counterpart, however, the British ambassador considered himself to be a liberal and consequently never cultivated close personal ties with the royal couple or the aristocracy. Grahame's analysis of the political crisis in Spain down through the Jaca rebellion reflected this broader outlook. In the course of

[60]Crosby to Stimson, 16 December 1930, 852.00/1799, tel. 16 December 1930, 852.00/1796, and 22 December 1930, 852.00/1803, NA RG59.
[61]Memorandum by Castle, 22 December 1930, 852.00/1801, and Crosby to Stimson, 22 December 1930, 852.00 P.R./167, NA RG59; Fletcher to G-2, 23 December 1930, 2657 S.126/12, NA RG165.

1930 he provided the Foreign Office with an assessment of the situation at Madrid more accurate than the one the State Department had received from Laughlin and his aides.[62]

Grahame shared Laughlin's conviction that the Berenguer government would be transitional, but unlike his American colleague, he saw Alfonso's throne as increasingly vulnerable to attacks from democratic reformers. Thus although Grahame advised Whitehall in February 1930 that the new military regime had "made a good start" toward restoring constitutional monarchy, he emphasized that republicanism was becoming firmly rooted among the king's critics. Consequently, by early May the Foreign Office had begun to express "some considerable anxiety" over the deteriorating situation, anxiety stemming mainly from Spain's "geographical position" and "the close connection between the British and Spanish royal families." A month later Grahame replied that "wisdom, foresight, and firmness" on Alfonso's part might save his throne, but these qualities were currently in short supply. Since the monarchy was "not securely founded on the universal loyalty and devotion of the people," he concluded, the outcome "depended upon the behaviour of the troops."[63]

Once the Jaca revolt demonstrated that the troops were neither more loyal nor more devoted than the people, Grahame, in contrast to Laughlin, was careful to point out the overwhelmingly republican character of the uprising. He attributed wild charges that the aborted insurrection was "a by-product of Moscow bolshevism" to a "natural desire on the part of the [Spanish] Government to gloss over the republican aspect of the recent movement." Privately, Grahame assured Whitehall on 21 December, General Berenguer himself had admitted "that there really was no communism in this country." The Jaca revolt, Grahame stressed, resembled not so much the Bolshevik revolution but "revolutionary movements in other European countries during the 19th century, where the kind of liberties for which progressive Spaniards are still

[62] Claude G. Bowers, *My Mission to Spain* (New York, 1954), pp. 66–67; Peterson, *Both Sides of the Curtain*, pp. 159–62; Petrie, *Alfonso XIII and His Age*, p. 24; *Who Was Who, 1929–1940* (London, 1941), pp. 541–42.

[63] Grahame to Henderson, 4 February 1930, W1531/35/41; 20 March 1930, and minute by Howard Smith, 26 March 1930, W3026/35/41; Sir George Mounsey to Grahame, 13 May 1930, W4571/35/41; Grahame to Henderson, 7 June 1930, W6155/35/41, PRO FO371, vols. 15040 and 15041.

struggling have long ago ceased to be live political issues." If the Foreign Office remained distressed by the mounting opposition to Alfonso's arbitrary rule, there was relief in London that "communism finds Spain a most unfertile soil."[64]

If Whitehall and the State Department differed over the nature of the threat to the Berenguer regime, businessmen on both sides of the Atlantic were in agreement by late 1930 that the extended political crisis in Spain was endangering foreign investment. Rumors of bribery surrounding the 1924 telephone concession, held in abeyance by Primo's censorship, burst into a major national scandal in April 1930, when the Socialist leader Indalecio Prieto, speaking at Madrid's prestigious Ateneo Club, challenged the legitimacy of the CTNE monopoly and attacked ITT officials as "a group of North American capitalists" who saw Spain as "a picturesque colony where one courted the indigenes." Prieto, a moderate leftist known to favor the creation of a republic, went on to allege that Alfonso XIII had accepted a $600,000 bribe from Colonel Behn. The charge prompted a government libel suit but also ensured that ITT's activities in Spain would be subjected to intense scrutiny in the event of a republican triumph.[65] Rio Tinto experienced even worse problems the following December, when copper workers participating in the Jaca revolt briefly seized the mines at Huelva. Although the British firm regained control of its facilities and fired the culprits with the blessing of the royal government, the antimonarchist sentiments of the miners had begun to take on antiforeign overtones.[66]

British and American exporters also encountered fresh problems during 1930, for the Berenguer regime was as determined as its predecessor to eliminate the chronic Spanish trade deficit through protectionist policies. By May Whitehall worried that Spain's continuing political instability and high tariffs would reduce "her importance as a market for British goods." A month later the Department of Overseas Trade confirmed that Spanish customs officials were creating new obstacles for Britain's exports but predicted that

[64] Grahame to Henderson, 21 December 1930, and minute by Arthur Wiggin, 5 January 1931, W13896/35/41; Grahame to Henderson, 26 December 1930, W13897/35/41, PRO FO371, vol. 15042.

[65] *New York Times*, 30 April 1930, sec. 1, p. 10:4, and 1 May 1930, sec. 1, p. 7:2; Little, "Twenty Years of Turmoil," pp. 453–54.

[66] Avery, *Not on Queen Victoria's Birthday*, pp. 326–27.

better salesmanship and less ignorance of local regulations would eventually boost British sales to Spain.[67] These troubles were minor, however, compared to those experienced by American exporters. As late as March 1930 a Commerce Department official could proclaim that Americans "have reason to be proud of the fact that we rank as Number 1 among the nations supplying merchandise to Spain," but the passage of the Smoot-Hawley Tariff quickly silenced such boasts. When in June Congress imposed higher duties on cork and olive oil, items not even produced in North America but of crucial importance to Spain, the Berenguer regime retaliated swiftly. It directed a series of rate hikes specifically at the United States. On 22 July Spain doubled its import duties on tires, automobiles, and other products supplied primarily by American firms. Since such increases did not violate the existing Spanish-American commercial modus vivendi, Washington could only watch helplessly as U.S. exports to Spain fell sharply in subsequent months.[68]

As the year drew to a close, British and American relations with Spain had come almost full circle since 1923. Primo de Rivera's coup had calmed fears of left-wing revolution on both sides of the Atlantic, but his demise and the ineffectiveness of his successor raised fresh doubts. If the State Department erroneously interpreted the Jaca revolt as communist while the Foreign Office more accurately viewed it as republican, both could agree in its aftermath that political conditions in Spain were more uncertain than ever. The Spanish dictatorship had created a business climate favorable to British and American investors in the mid-1920s; but as support for the military regime ebbed, first Royal Dutch Shell and Standard Oil of New Jersey and later Rio Tinto and ITT became targets for ardent nationalists bent on reducing foreign control of Spain's economy. Although Washington and London might differ over the best way to protect these firms, they shared a growing fear

[67]Mounsey to Grahame, 13 May 1930, W4571/35/41, PRO FO371, vol. 15040; Adams, *Economic Conditions in Spain, 1930*, pp. 26–27, 33–37.
[68]Julius Klein, "American Influence and Interest in Spain," a radio talk given 23 March 1930, no. 13 in the CBS series "A Week of the World's Business" (Washington, D.C., 1930); Jones, *Tariff Retaliation*, pp. 49–55, 68–83, 104–13, 155–62; *AEE, 1934*, p. 296; Julian Greenup to the Bureau of Foreign and Domestic Commerce, 15 November 1930, 852.00 P.R./164, NA RG59. By November 1930 American automobile exports to Spain had fallen 40 percent from the period prior to the recent tariff hikes.

that chaos in Spain would jeopardize the entire quarter-billion-dollar British and American stake in the Iberian Peninsula. Finally, while Primo's commercial policies had reduced frictions with the United States and Great Britain after 1923, the persistent shortfall between what Spain exported and what it imported eventually prompted a new round of protectionism at Madrid. American exporters were, to be sure, hit much harder than their British counterparts, yet neither Whitehall nor the White House doubted that the widening global economic crisis would lead to even more restrictive Spanish trade practices.

By late 1930 three major aspects of British and American policy toward Spain had come into sharp focus. As opposition to military rule spread, the question of left-wing subversion in Spain became a matter that neither the State Department nor the Foreign Office could safely ignore. As nationalist attacks on foreign investment mounted, policy makers on both sides of the Atlantic questioned whether British and American firms operating in Spain were secure. As the Great Depression deepened, London and Washington wondered what new commercial restrictions Madrid would employ against their trade. The new year would bring a republican revolution to Spain, an event that not only exacerbated all three of these problems but also generated new tensions with Great Britain and the United States.

3

The Republic and the
Revolutionary Left, 1931–1933

Although British and American policy makers were well aware in early 1931 that time was running out on Alfonso's rather nonchalant attempt to salvage his throne, the bloodless birth of Spain's Second Republic that April came with a dramatic suddenness that caught the Foreign Office and the State Department unprepared. Neither Washington nor London was eager to recognize the republican government; indeed, both feared that the new regime would complete the political disintegration of Spain and usher in a period of revolutionary chaos. American officials, however, almost at once misinterpreted the collapse of the monarchy as proof of bolshevik subversion; in contrast, their British counterparts more accurately attributed the crisis to indigenous Spanish problems. These different perspectives notwithstanding, the tumultuous events of the next two years would leave observers from both countries in agreement by early 1933 that republican Spain had come perilously close to succumbing to the revolutionary left.

I

In the first weeks of 1931 Alfonso XIII and General Berenguer still believed that they could engineer a peaceful return to constitutional monarchy. Berenguer accordingly scheduled Spain's first free election in almost a decade for mid-March. Few doubted that with martial law and censorship in force throughout the country, the monarchists would triumph. But the opposition, claiming that balloting could hardly be either fair or free with the press muzzled and republican leaders behind bars, threatened to boycott the polls unless the general stepped down. Anxious to avoid another round of violent disturbances, the king reluctantly dismissed Berenguer on 14 February and replaced him with Admiral Juan Aznar, an officer of unquestioned integrity but limited political experience. Although Aznar quickly postponed parliamentary elections until June, he promised to hold the balloting for municipal councillors as scheduled in early April and, in a gesture of good faith, pardoned conspirators jailed for plotting the Jaca revolt. With the approach of spring the royal government was convinced that it had successfully defused the republican powderkeg.[1]

American and British observers were quite concerned over the continuing political crisis at Madrid, but by early 1931 they shared Alfonso and Aznar's faith that Spaniards would embrace constitutional monarchism rather than republicanism at the polls. Ambassador Irwin Laughlin continued, as he had throughout the preceding year, to minimize republican strength and magnify the communist danger south of the Pyrenees. He interpreted the replacement of Berenguer with Aznar not as a sign of royal weakness but rather as proof of Alfonso's political acumen. In late February he advised Washington that "the possibility of a successful republican revolution seems as distant as ever." The real threat, Laughlin insisted, lay in "the communist nature of the seditious movement last December."[2] When the State Department expressed renewed concern over possible Soviet subversion, the ambassador forwarded fresh reports of continued bolshevik activity in Spain. With the republican movement still in disarray and the Communists under constant military surveillance, however, Laughlin could assure the State Department by late March that "the situation looks brighter and the Monarchy seems more firmly established than at any time since the fall of the Dictatorship at the end of January 1930."[3]

[1] Peers, *Spanish Tragedy*, pp. 18–19; Petrie, *Alfonso XIII and His Age*, pp. 219–20; Payne, *Politics and the Military*, pp. 263–64; Ben-Ami, *Origins of the Second Republic*, pp. 206–13.

[2] Laughlin to Castle, 6 February 1931, Castle Papers, Box 8 (Spain 1923–1932); Laughlin to Stimson, 28 February 1931, 852.00/1811, NA RG59.

[3] Castle to Laughlin, tel. 26 February 1931, 861.504 Labor and Socialist International/75, NA RG59; Laughlin to Castle, 5 March 1931, Castle Papers, Box 8 (Spain 1923–1932); Laughlin to Stimson, 20 March 1931, 852.00/1813, NA RG59.

British officials likewise expected Alfonso XIII to weather the political tempest, but in contrast to their American counterparts they attributed the current crisis more to the ineptness of the royal government than to communist subversion. Ambassador George Grahame repeatedly dismissed reports of Soviet intrigue in Spain and warned instead in January that it was Berenguer's stubborn refusal to restore constitutional rule which was swelling the ranks of the increasingly powerful and overwhelmingly republican opposition. Whitehall's Spanish expert, Arthur Wiggin, agreed, quipping that "Communism is but a jackal to the Republican tiger . . . in Spain."[4] Alfonso's skillful shuffling of his cabinet early the next month did much of persuade London, as it had Washington, that he remained firmly in control at Madrid. Although Grahame admitted that a republican victory in the upcoming elections would render the king's position "untenable," he thought it more likely that the royalists would prevail. The Foreign Office shared his belief that the monarchists would "carry the day" in Spain. "Solid opinion regards the return of the old gangs with disgust, [and] the spectre of republicanism will rally many elements to the monarchy," Wiggin concluded on 16 February; "to most of them, republicanism & disorder are synonymous." As Alfonso's day of reckoning drew near, then, London was like Washington expecting the royal government to emerge from the polls victorious.[5]

Whitehall and the State Department could hardly have been more mistaken. Despite Admiral Aznar's confident predictions that government candidates would sweep the municipal elections on 12 April by a ten-to-one margin, a republican coalition of liberal reformers, moderate Socialists, and regional separatists staged a shocking upset at the polls. To be sure, the monarchists did return over 22,000 councillors as against slightly fewer than 6,000 for the opposition, but a closer look at the results revealed that the public had in fact repudiated the king. While the royalists had won the vast majority of seats in the smaller towns and rural areas, the republicans had swept the major cities, the only districts in Spain

---

[4]Grahame to Henderson, 26 December 1930, W13896/35/41, and 8 January 1931, W430/46/41; minute by Wiggin, 28 January 1931, W1002/46/41, PRO FO371, vols. 15042 and 15770.
[5]Grahame to Henderson, tel. 15 February 1931, and minute by Wiggin, 16 February 1931, W1737/46/41, PRO FO371, vol. 15770.

where the secret ballot rather than the cacique determined the outcome.[6]

The implications of this electoral debacle became obvious when enthusiastic republican crowds swarmed into the streets in urban centers and clashed with the Civil Guard, the national police force. The king swiftly appealed to the army for support but was stunned to learn that many high-ranking officers no longer backed him. Growing more desperate, he sought next to patch together a coalition of leading monarchists and conservative republicans, but this attempt also met with failure. Faced with a situation that might easily have deteriorated into civil war, Alfonso XIII heeded the advice of his cabinet and relinquished his authority to a provisional republican government on 13 April. The king left the country the next day without abdicating, clearly hopeful that his voluntary exile would be brief. In this remarkably bloodless and orderly manner, then, the monarchy was overturned and a republic established in its stead.[7]

The abrupt collapse of the monarchy caught both American and British officials off guard. Irwin Laughlin, who had continued to predict a royalist triumph even as the election returns were coming in, termed the outcome "astonishing," held Alfonso's "incompetent, selfish and ignorant" political advisers responsible, and cautioned Washington that there were "elements of the gravest nature in the resulting conditions." Once again he resorted to hyperbolic rhetoric and prophesied that communism, not republicanism, would ultimately fill the political vacuum. "Communistic falsities have captivated the seventeenth-century-minded Spanish people," Laughlin warned the State Department on 16 April. "All at once they see a promised land which does not exist. Ultimately they will be easily captured by the widespread Bolshevistic influences." Given such a bleak outlook, he did not believe immediate recognition of the republican regime was advisable.[8]

[6] Rhea Marsh Smith, *The Day of the Liberals in Spain* (Philadelphia, 1938), pp. 77–84; Henry Buckley, *Life and Death of the Spanish Republic* (London, 1940), pp. 34–39; Petrie, *Alfonso XIII and His Age*, pp. 220–21; Ben-Ami, *Origins of the Second Republic*, pp. 218–38.

[7] Ben-Ami, *Origins of the Second Republic*, pp. 238–52; Gabriel Jackson, *The Spanish Republic and the Civil War, 1931–1939* (Princeton, N.J., 1965), pp. 25–29; Payne, *Politics and the Military*, pp. 264–65; Peers, *Spanish Tragedy*, pp. 23–32.

[8] Laughlin to Stimson, tel. 13 April 1931, 852.00/1814; Stimson to Laughlin, tel. 14 April 1931, 852.00/1815a; Laughlin to Stimson, tel. 14 April 1931, 852.00/1815, tel. 15 April 1931, 852.00/1817, and tel. 16 April 1931, 852.00/1818, NA RG59.

Whitehall was equally surprised. As late as 14 April Sir George Grahame had been dismissing reports that Alfonso XIII would step down "as for the most part devoid of foundation," but unlike his American counterpart, he assured his superiors once the rumors proved true that "the revolution was accomplished without any tragic or bloody incidents." Moreover, Grahame chose not to raise the specter of bolshevism at all.[9] Although London possessed a picture more accurate than Washington's of recent developments at Madrid, British policy makers were nevertheless distressed by the collapse of the monarchy and complained that Grahame could have told them "a great deal more and a great deal earlier." Former foreign secretary Austen Chamberlain, who felt that "Spain was making real progress" under Alfonso and Aznar, "entirely mistrust[ed] the competence of the new governors—not to speak of their honesty" and hoped that the republic would "not be long-lived." Permanent Undersecretary of State Robert Vansittart likewise "was sorry" to see Alfonso XIII fall victim to "republicanism without democracy" and wished that the king had not entrusted his fate to "men of straw" like Berenguer and Aznar. In light of such continuing British sympathy for Spain's royal family and the growing uncertainty caused by Alfonso's refusal to abdicate formally, the Foreign Office, like the State Department, felt it "unwise" to act precipitously in recognizing the republican regime.[10]

Indeed, skeptical American and British observers believed that Spain's provisional government was as incongruous and unpredictable as the coalition that it represented. Prime Minister Niceto Alcalá-Zamora and Minister of the Interior Miguel Maura, both right-wing republicans, opposed radical social change and favored the formation of a conservative clerical regime. Foreign Minister Alejandro Lerroux, the septuagenarian leader of the centrist Radical party, advocated harsh anticlerical legislation but was ambivalent about reforms in other areas. Minister of War Manuel Azaña, a left-wing republican playwright-turned-politician, championed

[9] Grahame to Henderson, tel. 13 April 1931, and minute by Wiggin, 14 April 1931, W4084/46/41; Grahame to Henderson, tel. 14 April 1931, W4144/46/41, tel. 14 April 1931, W4145/46/41, tel. 15 April 1931, W4147/46/41, and 15 April 1931, W4153/46/41, PRO FO371, vol. 15770.

[10] Chamberlain quoted in Petrie, *Alfonso XIII and His Age*, p. 227; Vansittart, *Mist Procession*, pp. 415–16; Henderson to the governor general of Gibraltar, tel. 15 April 1931, W4465/46/41; Grahame to Henderson, tel. 15 April 1931, and minute by Howard Smith, 16 April 1931, W4202/46/41, PRO FO371, vol. 15771.

thoroughgoing alterations in land tenure and industrial relations but balked at complete nationalization. Labor Minister Francisco Largo Caballero and Finance Minister Indalecio Prieto, both Socialists, advocated the ultimate collectivization of agriculture and industry but were willing to work within the framework of a republic. Minister of the Economy Nicolau d'Olwer, a leading Catalan separatist, downplayed broader reforms and placed highest priority on regional autonomy. Finally, the Spanish Communist party, which claimed but 800 members in 1931, and the anarchist CNT, which counted nearly 800,000, both stood outside the republican fold; neither held a portfolio in the provisional government.[11]

The diversity and volatility of the provisional government reinforced the instinctive American and British reluctance to recognize the Spanish Republic. Secretary of State Henry L. Stimson, a Yale-educated Wall Street lawyer who had served as a diplomatic troubleshooter in revolutionary Nicaragua during the 1920s, preferred to postpone recognition pending the resolution of four questions: What was the legal status of the monarchy? How stable was the provisional government? Would the new regime respect existing Spanish international obligations? And what were the attitudes of such major European powers as Great Britain and France?[12] Stimson's cautious approach was welcomed by Irwin Laughlin, whose opinion of the Spanish Republic sank steadily lower. Seeking to assess the vitality of the provisional government, he called on Prime Minister Alcalá-Zamora on 17 April and expressed grave concern about the revolutionary left. Despite the Spaniard's assurances that "radical communistic" activities would not be tolerated, Laughlin questioned whether the republican regime could provide "protection against subversive elements . . . which existed in Spain as they did in every other country" and warned that "it would not do to go to sleep over dangerous possibilities." His fear of bolshevik intrigue undiminished, the ambassador urged Washington to adopt an attitude of watchful waiting.[13]

[11] Brenan, *Spanish Labyrinth*, pp. 221–22, 233, 238–40; Madariaga, *Spain*, pp. 382–91; Ben-Ami, *Origins of the Second Republic*, pp. 253–55; David T. Cattell, *Communism and the Spanish Civil War* (Berkeley, 1955), pp. 20, 217 note 4.

[12] Stimson to Laughlin, tel. 16 April 1931, 852.01/17, NA RG59. For Stimson's background, see Richard Current, *Secretary Stimson: A Study in Statecraft* (Hamden, Conn., 1970), pp. 18–42, and Henry Stimson and McGeorge Bundy, *On Active Service in Peace and War* (New York, 1948), pp. 155–89.

[13] Memorandum by Laughlin, 17 April 1931, Madrid (1931), File 800, vol. X, Record Group 84, Records of Foreign Service Posts, Part I, Records of Diplomatic Posts

Developments in the days that followed heightened American fears of Soviet subversion. U.S. diplomats in Berlin and Paris prophesied "a complete slide to the left" at Madrid and worried that "Spain may be swept by a communist wave." Laughlin reportedly called republican leaders "a collection of jailbirds" and expressed the hope that the Embassy walls would "keep out the probable attacks of the Bolshevist crowds." Believing that the new regime was not yet in complete control of the revolutionary left and having "no desire to be participants in a recognition race," the State Department decided on 19 April to defer normalizing relations with republican Spain.[14]

The Foreign Office was equally reluctant to establish formal ties with the Spanish Republic, but for different reasons. Although Ambassador Grahame, unlike Laughlin, predicted that the new regime would "consolidate itself" soon and urged speedy recognition, lingering British sympathy for Spain's royal family encouraged Whitehall to go slow.[15] Since the unexpected republican victory had been limited to the cities, the Foreign Office thought it "premature" to conclude that "the whole country is in favour of the new Govt." Moreover, "in view of the fact that King Alfonso ha[d] not abdicated," British officials felt it "wiser not to be in too great a hurry to rush in" with recognition. Indeed, Charles Howard Smith, the head of Whitehall's Western Department, pointed out that when King Manuel II of Portugal had been deposed under similar circumstances in 1910, Great Britain had declined to recognize his republican successors until a constitution was drawn up and ratified, eighteen months later.[16] Sir Robert Vansittart and

---

1788–1945, National Archives, Washington, D.C. (hereafter cited as NA RG84); Laughlin to Stimson, tel. 17 April 1931, 852.01/19, NA RG59.

[14] Ambassador Walter Edge (Paris) to Stimson, tel. 17 April 1931, 852.00/1823; Ambassador Frederick Sackett (Berlin) to Stimson, tel. 21 April 1931, 852.01/47; Stimson to Laughlin, tel. 19 April 1931, 852.01/30, NA RG59. For Laughlin's alleged comments, see Sir George Grahame to Henderson, 22 April 1931, W4733/46/41, PRO FO371, vol. 15772.

[15] Grahame to Henderson, tel. 16 April 1931, W4251/46/41, PRO FO371, vol. 15771. As recently as February 1931 Queen Ena, Alfonso's British-born consort, had received a resounding public welcome during a visit to London. See Chargé d'Affaires Ray Atherton (London) to Stimson, 24 February 1931, 852.00/1812, NA RG59.

[16] Minute by Howard Smith, 16 April 1931, W4251/46/41, PRO FO371, vol. 15771. For a discussion of the British reaction to the 1910 republican revolution in Portugal, see J. D. Vincent-Smith, "The Portuguese Republic and Britain, 1910–1914," *Journal of Contemporary History* 10 (October 1975), 707–27.

Foreign Secretary Arthur Henderson, an aging Labourite who deferred to the more conservative Whitehall bureaucracy on most issues, agreed on 16 April that the Portuguese precedent should be followed because it would postpone recognition for an indefinite period during which the absent king might reclaim his throne.[17]

Nagging British doubts about the weakness of the provisional government also made Whitehall hesitant to recognize republican Spain. In contrast to the State Department, however, the Foreign Office saw regional separatism rather than bolshevism as the real threat to Spanish political stability. Confident that the republican regime would be able "to prevent the Communist element from gaining the upper hand," British officials were less certain that it could control militant Catalan "nationalists," who had long agitated for regional autonomy. The promulgation of "the Republic of Catalonia" on 15 April as "an integral state of the Iberian Federation" confirmed these doubts. It simultaneously raised fresh fears that Basque and Galician separatists would follow suit, balkanizing Spain and creating a dangerous political vacuum south of the Pyrenees.[18] "Definite recognition" of republican Spain would now "clearly have to go slow," Vansittart concluded the next day, because of the "very much complicated" situation arising from the "self-constitution of the separate Catalan Republic whose relations with the rest of Spain must first be made clear." Even after Madrid and Barcelona reached an agreement on 18 April that reintegrated an autonomous Catalonia into a single Spanish republic, Whitehall continued to worry that "other separatist movements in other parts of Spain" would ultimately make even bolder demands. A serious crisis was almost inevitable, Spanish expert Arthur Wiggin prophesied, because "Spain cannot—by wholesale largesse—afford to encourage regionalism everywhere."[19]

[17]Minute by Vansittart, 16 April 1931, W4251/46/41, PRO FO371, vol. 15771. Vansittart noted in the margin "returned by the Foreign Secretary 16/4/31" and initialed the proposal without further comment. On Henderson's role as a figurehead, see Vansittart, *Mist Procession*, pp. 397–98, and Gladwyn, *Memoirs of Lord Gladwyn*, p. 39.

[18]Chargé d'Affaires Benjamin Thaw (London) to Stimson, 16 April 1931, 852.00/1827, NA RG59; Consul General Norman King (Barcelona) to Henderson, tel. 15 April 1931, minute by Howard Smith, 16 April 1931, and minute by Sir George Mounsey, 16 April 1931, W4216/46/41, PRO FO371, vol. 15771.

[19]Minute by Vansittart, 16 April 1931, and minute by Mounsey, 18 April 1931, W4251/46/41; Grahame to Henderson, tel. 18 April 1931, and minute by Wiggin, 20 April 1931, W4364/46/41, PRO FO371, vol. 15771.

British desire to delay formal recognition of the Spanish Republic indefinitely, however, ran counter to French preference to act swiftly. When France inquired on 17 April whether Britain wished jointly to normalize relations with Spain in the near future, Whitehall attempted to stall the Quai d'Orsay. The complex relationship between Great Britian and its Dominions, Charles Howard Smith suggested, "gives us a way out." Since Whitehall was responsible for the foreign policy of the entire British Commonwealth, "we can say that we cannot answer until we have consulted the Domns."[20] But before this scheme could be implemented, France unilaterally recognized republican Spain in a blatant effort to win commercial concessions from the new government. Unhappy over what it regarded as ill-considered French support for an "unconstitutional" regime, Whitehall realized that if Britain wished to preserve even the semblance of cordial relations with Spain, it must follow suit and recognize the republic. With Alfonso XIII safely on his way to Rome and with no further evidence of regional separatism outside Catalonia, the Foreign Office reluctantly authorized Sir George Grahame to extend formal recognition to the Spanish Republic on 21 April.[21]

Britain's normalization of its relations with republican Spain prompted similar action by the United States, which did not wish "to be conspicuous by withholding" recognition. Laughlin, who had learned of the British decision on 20 April, cabled the State Department that businessmen and diplomats at Madrid now agreed that "a further shift to the extreme left can best be halted and effectively so by immediate recognition." He asked Washington to authorize him to act accordingly.[22] The following morning Hernand Behn, president of ITT, telephoned the State Department. Foreign Minister Lerroux, a personal friend, had just assured him that "there is absolutely no communism in Spain" and that the new

---

[20] Grahame to Henderson, tel. 17 April 1931, W4314/46/41; minute by Howard Smith, 18 April 1931, W4251/46/41; Foreign Office to the Dominions, draft circular B no. 48, 18 April 1931, W4366/46/41, PRO FO371, vol. 15771.

[21] Ambassador Ronald Campbell (Paris) to Henderson, tel. 18 April 1931, minute by Howard Smith, 18 April 1931, and Howard Smith to Campbell, tel. 18 April 1931, W4347/46/41; Campbell to Henderson, tel. 18 April 1931, and minute by Howard Smith, 20 April 1931, W4366/46/41; Henderson to Grahame, tel. 21 April 1931, W4368/46/41, PRO FO371, vol. 15771.

[22] Stimson to Laughlin, tel. 19 April 1931, 852.01/30; Laughlin to Stimson, tel. 20 April 1931, 852.01/33, NA RG59.

regime "would be able to maintain order and would respect its international obligations." Behn urged swift American recognition so that "we would get the benefit of the beau geste, and not wait to trail in behind the British or others at a later time." Britain's decision to recognize the provisional government later that same day reinforced Laughlin's and Behn's arguments, and on 22 April the United States grudgingly reestablished formal diplomatic relations with Spain.[23]

The reluctance with which Great Britain and the United States recognized the new regime reflected lingering doubts about the future of the Spanish Republic. Never eager to write off Alfonso XIII, the Foreign Office soon had second thoughts about establishing ties with his successors. "We were hustled all through," one British official complained in early May 1931, first by France, which had "rushed in and recognized without consulting us," and then by Ambassador Grahame, who had urged "all the time that we should not be behind hand in doing what the French had done."[24] The State Department, which had followed Whitehall's lead, likewise believed recognition had been accorded precipitously. Even as he instructed Laughlin to relay the American decision to the provisional government, Secretary of State Stimson stressed that "the status of the new regime" was really still "awaiting settlement" and that U.S. officials must avoid as much as possible "the appearance of prejudging events."[25]

Yet if Washington and London both reserved judgment on the Spanish Republic, each did so for different reasons. Treated during the spring of 1931 to a steady diet of reports that overestimated support for the monarchy, underestimated the strength of republicanism, and exaggerated the danger of communism, the State Department suspected Soviet intrigue at Madrid and wanted to withhold recognition until the provisional government had proved able to maintain order and promised to respect its international obligations. Whitehall, on the other hand, possessed a more accurate picture of the situation in Spain and realized that the monarchy had fallen prey to republican reformers rather than the revolu-

---

[23]Behn quoted in Francis B. White, "Recognition of the New Spanish Regime," 21 April 1931, 852.01/40; Stimson to Laughlin, 21 April 1931, 852.01/33; Laughlin to Stimson, 22 April 1931, 852.01/36, NA RG59.
[24]Draft letter by Howard Smith, 8 May 1931, W5330/46/41, PRO FO371, vol. 15772.
[25]Stimson to Laughlin, tel. 21 April 1931, 852.01/33, NA RG59.

tionary left. Less concerned with the bolshevik bogey than with the uncertainty surrounding Alfonso's departure and the specter of regional separatism, the Foreign Office hoped to postpone its decision until a constituent assembly could clarify the status of the monarchy and resolve the explosive issue of Catalan autonomy. Nevertheless, French recognition of the republican regime forced first Great Britain and then the United States to follow suit, in order to avoid damaging relations with Spain. Violent developments in the Iberian Peninsula in the months that followed gave policy makers in both countries grounds to regret their hasty actions.

II

While the State Department and the Foreign Office agonized over recognition, Spain's republican leaders grappled with an array of domestic problems that threatened the stability of the new regime. Frightened monarchists spirited their families and their funds out of the country, draining badly needed capital from the fragile Spanish economy. At the other end of the political spectrum, militant anarchists were rumored to be plotting to overthrow the "bourgeois" republic. Furthermore, the republican movement itself was deteriorating into a loose alliance of radicals and reformers, who could agree on little more than their opposition to Alfonso XIII. In the fortnight following the bloodless revolution the provisional government did muster enough unity to restrict capital exports, impose modest land reforms, and extend the suffrage to all Spaniards over twenty-three years of age; but by early May even the cabinet had begun to show signs of splintering into warring factions.[26]

Any hope for a rapid resurgence of republican fraternalism was soon shattered by an outburst of anticlerical violence. The provisional government sequestered all clerical property on 2 May in an effort to prevent the church from removing its funds from Spain. Cardinal Pedro Segura, the archbishop of Toledo, responded pub-

---

[26]Leandro Benavides, *Política económica en la II república española* (Madrid, 1972), pp. 73–75; Edward Malefakis, *Agrarian Reform and Peasant Revolution in Spain: Origins of the Civil War* (New Haven, Conn., 1970), pp. 165–72; Ben-Ami, *Origins of the Second Republic*, pp. 264–68.

licly with a thinly veiled attack on the republic, an action that monarchists interpreted as an endorsement for their own antirepublican activities. Convinced that a religious and royalist conspiracy was afoot against the new regime, angry republican mobs sacked and burned half a dozen churches in Madrid on 10 May. Disturbances quickly spread to the provinces, apparently at the behest of well-organized anarchists who sought to discredit the provisional government. The republican regime was extremely slow to react to this anticlerical rioting. Prime Minister Alcalá-Zamora and Interior Minister Maura, both staunch Catholics, did seek cabinet approval on 10 May to use the army, but the anticlerical majority rejected the proposal, and the rioters continued their rampage. Finally on 12 May the government reversed itself, Alcalá-Zamora imposed martial law, and troops were ordered to put an end to the violence. Although there was little loss of life and serious damage to fewer than sixty churches and convents, the three days of rioting widened the rifts within the provisional government and shocked many middle-class republicans. Moreover, the tardiness of the republican regime's response rekindled old doubts in Washington and London about political stability at Madrid.[27]

In the three weeks between its reluctant recognition of the Spanish Republic and the suppression of the rioting, the State Department received a steady stream of grim news seemingly confirming its worst fears of bolshevik intrigue in Spain. The American Embassy in Paris alleged that "Spanish communists" had threatened the life of Queen Ena before she fled to France, while the U.S. listening post in Riga reported that "the Soviet press is displaying a lively expectation that events in Spain will serve the communist cause." When the republican government announced plans to establish diplomatic relations with the Soviet Union in early May, Irwin Laughlin warned Washington that Spain might be entering "a Kerensky interlude."[28] To make his point even clearer, he cautioned Secretary of State Stimson privately on 5 May that there would be "serious disorder" in the near future unless the provi-

---

[27]José M. Sanchez, *Reform and Reaction: The Politico-Religious Background of the Spanish Civil War* (Chapel Hill, N.C., 1962), pp. 85–99; Jackson, *Spanish Republic*, pp. 31–33; Ben-Ami, *Origins of the Second Republic*, pp. 255–60.
[28]"Strictly Confidential Report W. D. 897," by Warrington Dawson, enclosed in Edge to Stimson, 23 April 1931, 852.00/1835; Felix Coleman (Riga) to Stimson, 24 April 1931, 852.00/B18; Laughlin to Stimson, 4 May 1931, 852.00 P.R./186, NA RG59.

sional government prevented "a Bolshevistic turn" among the urban poor. Terming current, comparatively quiet conditions at Madrid "almost ominous," Laughlin foresaw "real troubles" coming when the new regime had to "face the growing disappointment of the people incited by extremist elements both within and without the country." When his prophecy was fulfilled a scant five days later by the anticlerical outburst, Laughlin blamed "irresponsible agents provocateurs" and requested permission to shelter religious refugees within the American Embassy. Stimson quickly authorized him to grant asylum to Spaniards endangered by mob violence and thanked him for keeping the State Department "in direct touch with the situation" in Spain.[29]

Anticlerical violence strengthened the conviction among American officials that the Spanish Republic would soon fall to Soviet subversion. Laughlin termed the recent riots "the beginning of a calculated movement to undermine the morale of the people and lead them to submit to a sort of bolschevistic [*sic*] tyranny of the extreme left." Years later he would recall with distaste "the corroding influence of the anti-religious anarchism and the teeth of communism that showed themselves from the very beginning and took hold of the infant democracy to devour it in its cradle."[30] Military Attaché R. H. Fletcher likewise believed that the church burnings had been inspired by the "many agents of communism . . . sent into Spain from abroad" since April; he complained that "no longer is Spain relatively free of the curse that threatens the peace of the world." Pierre Boal, soon to be promoted to chief of the State Department's Division of Western European Affairs, also suspected that "Communism" was undermining the Spanish Republic and requested additional information from Madrid in early June. Chargé d'Affaires Sheldon Crosby confirmed six weeks later that there was "a good deal of truth" in Boal's analysis. "I have felt all along that the Communist element in Spain, although small numerically, is at the same time powerful and determined," Crosby concluded, "and there is no doubt but that Russian Bolshevic

[29]Laughlin to Stimson, 5 May 1931, 852.00/1843; tel. 12 May 1931, 852.00/1839; and tel. 13 May 1931; and Stimson to Laughlin, tel. 13 May 1931, 852.00/1840, NA RG59.
[30]Laughlin to Stimson, 19 May 1931, Box 19 (General Correspondence—Stimson); undated draft speech (1938?) by Laughlin, Box 16 (Public Statements File 1929–1939), Irwin B. Laughlin Papers, Hoover Presidential Library.

Agents have kept their Spanish confreres well supplied with funds."[31]

Whitehall was equally disturbed by deteriorating political conditions in Spain during late April, but most British observers emphasized the anarchist rather than the communist danger. In a long despatch that arrived at the Foreign Office on 21 April, Sir George Grahame stressed that there was "really no communism in Spain," dismissed charges that Alcalá-Zamora was "a Spanish Kerensky," and suggested instead that the biggest threat to the new regime came from "extremist elements in and outside Syndicalist organizations."[32] Later that same day two reports arrived from Consul General Norman King at Barcelona, who challenged Grahame's views and alleged that "a communistic organisation in touch with Moscow" was at work in Spain. The contradictory analyses touched off a dispute at Whitehall. Persuaded by King that "the communist tail is wagging the republican dog," Sir George Mounsey, a career diplomat who specialized in Western European affairs, wondered whether recent developments at Madrid had been "engineered from Moscow." Parliamentary Undersecretary of State Hugh Dalton, an influential adviser to the Labour government, believed on the other hand that Spain was "one of the last countries in the world likely to go Communist" and rejected Mounsey's "silly" fears of Soviet subversion. "There is a certain sort of credulous person who sees Moscow everywhere, and regards all 'popular' and 'reformist' movements as 'communist,'" Dalton added acidly, "but we should be sceptical of such simplifications."[33] Information from the British Embassy in Moscow confirmed that the Kremlin had expressed little interest in Spain, and by early May even Consul General King admitted that there was only a minimal bolshevik threat in Catalonia. "This all seems to support the view," the Foreign Office concluded on 8 May, "that communism as such finds no general support with Spaniards."[34]

---

[31]Fletcher to G-2, 19 May 1931, 2657 S.126/19, NA RG165; Boal to Crosby, 10 June 1931, and Crosby to Boal, 28 July 1931, Madrid (1931), File 800, vol. X, NA RG84.
[32]Grahame to Henderson, 16 April 1931, W4453/46/41, PRO FO371, vol. 15771.
[33]King to Henderson, 17 April 1931, W4491/46/41; and 15 April 1931, minute by Mounsey, 25 April 1931, and minute by Dalton, 29 April 1931, W4463/46/41, PRO FO371, vol. 15771.
[34]Sir Edmund Ovey (Moscow) to Henderson, 21 April 1931, W4789/46/41;

The anticlerical outburst erupted two days later, however, and made British officials more sensitive to the danger of communist subversion. As details arrived of rioting in Madrid and its spread to the provinces, charges of bolshevik intrigue seemed less far-fetched. The rioters had "placed themselves hopelessly in the wrong," Spanish expert Arthur Wiggin remarked on 13 May, "and the obvious hand of communism in their activities should have increased the dislike which the average Spaniard must feel for all their methods and principles."[35] As further accounts of the violence filtered into London, the Foreign Office began to take comparisons between Alcalá-Zamora and Kerensky more seriously. Indeed, by late May Sir Robert Vansittart concluded that the republican regime "will have to show a good deal more courage and efficiency than hitherto if they are to get the better of communism in Spain." Even Grahame confessed that "propaganda of a modern communistic kind . . . emanating from Moscow" had begun to appear in Madrid, an admission that confirmed Whitehall's suspicion "that Communism is not likely in Spain, but that Moscow is working hard."[36] If with the approach of summer the Foreign Office, unlike the State Department, still regarded Spanish bolshevism as a disturbing threat rather than a dangerous reality, British and American officials shared a growing concern that Spain might soon slide very rapidly to the left.

The Kremlin was, in fact, working hard south of the Pyrenees, but with little success. Just days before Alfonso XIII's flight the Comintern had detected "elements of a revolutionary crisis" in Spain and predicted that the monarchy would soon be toppled by a radical alliance of the "proletariat," the "peasants," and the "petty bourgeoisie." When José Bullejos, the secretary general of the fledgling Spanish Communist party, journeyed to Moscow in May 1931, Comintern officials instructed him to "prolong the crisis by

---

Grahame to Henderson, 30 April 1931, W5281/46/41; King to Henderson, 5 May 1931, and minute by Wiggin, 8 May 1931, W5305/46/41, PRO FO371, vol. 15772.

[35]Minute by Wiggin, 11 May 1931, W5414/46/41; Grahame to Henderson, tel. 12 May 1931, and minute by Wiggin, 13 May 1931, W5515/46/41, PRO FO371, vols. 15772 and 15773.

[36]Maurice Peterson (Madrid) to Henderson, 13 May 1931, W5797/46/41; King to Henderson, 16 May 1931, W5827/46/41; Sir Ronald Graham (Rome) to Henderson, 22 May 1931, and minute by Vansittart, 28 May 1931, W6087/46/41; Grahame to Henderson, 25 May 1931, and minute by Howard Smith, 4 June 1931, W6520/46/41, PRO FO371, vol. 15773.

all possible means, to try and prevent the firm establishment of the republican regime, . . . and, where possible, create soviets." Trapped between the more popular anarchists on the left and the better-organized Socialists on the right, however, Spain's Communists proved that summer to be a party without a constituency. And once it became clear that the Stalinist Comintern was more interested in wiping out Trotskyites than in promoting the proletarian cause, Bullejos and his comrades began to ignore Soviet directives.[37]

Unaware of this growing friction between Communists in Moscow and Madrid, both London and Washington understandably regarded the upcoming selection of a constituent cortes, scheduled for 28 June, as an ideological litmus test, one that could reveal much about Spain's uncertain political future. With the monarchists intimidated by recent violence, the anarchists reluctant to participate in bourgeois politics, and the Communists unable even to field a slate of candidates, the election campaign quickly became a hard-fought contest among the various republican factions. Although the Socialists emerged from the balloting with 117 seats, the largest deputation returned by any single party, a loose coalition of "Left Republicans" headed by Manuel Azaña won 134 seats and would play the leading role in shaping the Spanish Republic. Lerroux's Radical party finished a respectable third with 93 seats, while Alcalá-Zamora's clerical republicans returned but 62 deputies. Only a handful of agrarian reactionaries and one solitary monarchist were elected, giving the Spanish right only minimal representation. Finally, not a single Communist would sit in the new assembly.[38]

The difficulties confronting the Constituent Cortes surfaced even before its initial session could be convened. On 4 July the anarchist CNT commenced a nationwide general strike to protest, among other things, the failure of republican leaders to implement radical labor and agrarian reforms. The work stoppages began in Madrid,

---

[37] "Theses of the Comintern's Eleventh ECCI Plenum, April 1931," in Jane De Gras, ed., *The Communist International, 1919–1943: Documents*, 3 vols. (New York, 1957–1965), 3:160; E. H. Carr, *Twilight of the Comintern, 1930–1935* (New York, 1982), pp. 293–300; Comintern instructions to Bullejos quoted in Hugh Thomas, *The Spanish Civil War*, 3d ed. (New York, 1977), pp. 120–21.

[38] Jackson, *Spanish Republic*, pp. 40–42; Payne, *Spanish Revolution*, pp. 88–89; Ben-Ami, *Origins of the Second Republic*, pp. 276–91.

Barcelona, and Valencia and spread rapidly to the anarchist strong-hold of Seville, where a revolutionary uprising was crushed by heavily armed police at a cost of twenty dead and three hundred wounded. Although the provisional government had restored order by the end of the month, the CNT's action once again dramatized the fragile nature of political stability in republican Spain.[39]

A recurrent fear of communism colored the American view of the Spanish elections and their violent aftermath. Evidence of bolshevik subversion in Spain, including a copy of Leon Trotsky's "La revolución española" advocating a proletarian uprising, continued to flow into the State Department in early June. Convinced that the upcoming elections constituted "a political phenomenon of world importance," Washington instructed all American observers in Spain to monitor the campaign even more closely.[40] Just two days before the balloting the State Department received a despatch from Chargé d'Affaires Sheldon Crosby confirming its worst fears. Although during the campaign republican leaders had "repeatedly discounted the importance of Communist influence," Crosby warned, there was mounting evidence of "Bolshevik agents and funds for propaganda purposes in Spain." Only "if the bogey of Communism" were defeated at the polls by the "conservative elements of the Republican ranks," he concluded, could "Spain's political and financial situation . . . be considered assured."[41]

If the communist failure to win a single seat in the Constituent Cortes was welcome news in Washington, the strong showings by the Left Republicans and the Socialists were hardly reassuring. Ambassador Laughlin held out some hope that clerical republicans such as Alcalá-Zamora would moderate the radical left, but the revolutionary strikes during July rekindled all his old fears of Soviet subversion. While admitting that the anarchists were primarily responsible for the labor violence, Laughlin was convinced that "communist elements" were deeply involved as well and pointed to the arrest of "large numbers" of "Communist agitators" as proof. Military Attaché Fletcher was "equally certain

[39] Peers, *Spanish Tragedy*, p. 62; Jackson, *Spanish Republic*, pp. 43–44; Laughlin to Stimson, 29 June 1931, 852.00 P.R./195, NA RG59; Grahame to Henderson, 7 July 1931, W8046/46/41, PRO FO371, vol. 15774; *New York Times*, 12 July 1931, sec. 1, p. 6:4.
[40] Leon Trotsky, "La revolución española," enclosed in Crosby to Stimson, 12 June 1931, 852.00/1855; circular telegram to all consular officers in Spain, 6 June 1931, 852.00 P.R./192, NA RG59.
[41] Crosby to Stimson, 15 June 1931, 852.00/1858, NA RG59.

that communist agents" were "at least partly responsible for the disorders and agitations." Relieved by the restoration of order at month's end, most American officials nevertheless regarded recent developments as further evidence of bolshevik intrigue.[42]

British officials, on the other hand, remained convinced during the summer of 1931 that "Extremism" and "Communism" were "by no means synonymous terms" in Spain. Ambassador Grahame, in contrast to American observers, reported that the provisional government was firmly in control on the eve of the elections; he prophesied a moderate republican victory. When "elements of moderation" indeed emerged "definitely in the ascendant," Whitehall termed the outcome "distinctively satisfactory." Grahame confirmed in early July that "no communist candidates were elected" and predicted the majority in the Constituent Cortes would "be of an advanced democratic but not revolutionary character."[43]

The bloody strikes that erupted shortly thereafter dampened Whitehall's optimism, of course, but British officials saw in them few signs of bolshevik subversion. Arthur Wiggin, for example, "did not think the atmosphere at all good" south of the Pyrenees, but he quite accurately blamed the disorders on the syndicalists rather than on the Kremlin. Grahame likewise emphasized that the labor unrest was "promoted as usual by the Confederación Nacional del Trabajo," not by Moscow. Yet if the Foreign Office was more aware than the State Department that the real threat to the Spanish Republic was not international communism but Iberian anarchism, British policy makers nevertheless questioned whether the republican regime could prevail over even home-grown revolutionaries. "I think the real trouble is before us," Charles Howard Smith observed in the wake of the July disturbances. "It is prophesied for the autumn."[44]

---

[42]Laughlin to Stimson, tel. 29 June 1931, 852.00/1859, and 1 July 1931, 852.00/1861; Consul General Claude I. Dawson (Barcelona) to Stimson, tel. 23 July 1931, 852.00/1862; Laughlin to Stimson, tel. 24 July 1931, 852.00 B/27, NA RG59; Fletcher to G-2, 14 July 1931, 2657 S.123/19, and 28 July 1931, 2657 S.126/35, NA RG165.

[43]Minute by Wiggin, 9 June 1931, W7631/46/41; Grahame to Henderson, 12 June 1931, W7135/46/41; 20 June 1931, W7515/46/41; and tel. 29 June 1931, and minute by Wiggin, 2 July 1931, W7660/46/41; Grahame to Henderson, tel. 1 July 1931, W7750/46/41, PRO FO371, vols. 15773 and 15774.

[44]Minutes by Wiggin, 7 July 1931, W7886/46/41, and 30 July 1931, W8735/46/41; Grahame to Henderson, tel. 5 September 1931, W10124/46/41; minute by Howard Smith, 30 July 1931, W8734/46/41, PRO FO371, vols. 15774 and 15775.

This bleak political forecast was borne out by a series of bitter conflicts within the Constituent Cortes, conflicts that threatened to tear the Spanish Republic asunder. While republican leaders agreed that Spain should be governed by a popularly elected unicameral legislature and that military influence in politics ought to be reduced, they saw eye to eye on little else. Socialists tangled with conservatives about the extension of state authority over the economy, necessitating a compromise. The result provided constitutional guarantees for private enterprise but also reserved the government's right to nationalize property with adequate compensation. Catalan separatists and Spanish nationalists disputed the merits of provincial autonomy, leading to another compromise. It granted regional self-government to Catalonia but left jurisdiction over foreign and military affairs in the hands of the central authorities.[45]

Amicable solutions, however, were impossible to achieve on two other issues—agrarian reform and religious disestablishment. A bitter dispute over how best to alter Spanish land-tenure patterns intensified republican factionalism in September. Prime Minister Alcalá-Zamora introduced a plan calling for both the expropriation of all estates held by absentee landlords (with generous compensation in long-term government bonds) and the resettlement of thousands of landless peasants on small farms. The Socialists, however, wanting more radical measures, aligned themselves with the Left Republicans to pass an agrarian reform clause that drastically reduced compensation and confiscated all large holdings, even those farmed by owner-operators.[46]

The debate over the status of the Catholic church in October stretched the republican coalition to the breaking point. When the Socialists and the Left Republicans again joined forces to insert an anticlerical clause in the constitution outlawing the Jesuits, eliminating government stipends for the clergy, and legalizing secular marriage and divorce, Alcalá-Zamora and Maura, the two practicing Catholics within the provisional government, resigned in disgust. Manuel Azaña, the new prime minister, shepherded the constitution through ratification in early December; he then

[45]Malefakis, *Agrarian Reform and Peasant Revolution*, pp. 182–83; Jackson, *Spanish Republic*, pp. 45–46, 73–74; Ben-Ami, *Origins of the Second Republic*, pp. 300–308.
[46]Preston, *Coming of the Spanish Civil War*, pp. 54–60; Malefakis, *Agrarian Reform and Peasant Revolution*, pp. 178–85, 188–93.

formed a Left Republican–Socialist government that excluded Lerroux's Radicals, who like many other middle-class Spaniards were disturbed by the recent assaults on private property. Although the Azaña regime attempted to reassure conservative critics by engineering the election of Alcalá-Zamora as president of the republic on 10 December 1931, it was clear to observers on both sides of the Atlantic that Spain's broad-based republican coalition had been shattered by the country's recent slide to the left.[47]

American officials monitored the wrangling in the Constituent Cortes with mounting apprehension. Ambassador Laughlin was impressed by the moderation of Alejandro Lerroux, whom he called Spain's "outstanding politician of the day," and held out some hope in early August that the "more conservative" forces within the republican movement would bring reform "through the orderly processes of law" rather than through "radical actions." Within a month, however, it was obvious that the Left Republicans and the Socialists held the initiative at Madrid, and Washington was by no means confident that these two groups could prevent revolutionary subversion. Indeed, on 5 September the State Department learned that Soviet leaders were now calling Spain "the weak link of European capitalism" and were urging the small Spanish Communist party to "deepen" the revolution into a classic "Bolshevik" upheaval. As if to demonstrate the power of the Kremlin's exhortations, Laughlin reported the following week that "communistic" disorders had erupted in Madrid and other cities.[48]

By the autumn of 1931 most Americans were convinced that the acrimony generated by the constitutional debate would prevent the "heterogeneous" provisional government from curbing "labor disorders" and "Communist disturbances" in Spain. "Quick action and a strong hand" were required, the U.S. military attaché warned in late September, because "Communist agents are unquestionably at work." Yet Spanish officials told Laughlin shortly thereafter to expect neither quickness nor strength, admitting that it was becoming increasingly difficult "to prevent the spread of

[47]Sanchez, *Reform and Reaction*, pp. 125–29; Peers, *Spanish Tragedy*, pp. 71–75; Preston, *Coming of the Spanish Civil War*, pp. 34–37.

[48]Laughlin to Stimson, 12 August 1931, 852.00/1867; Consul Thomas McEnelly (Barcelona) to Stimson, 21 August 1931, 852.00 B/32; Coleman to Stimson, 21 August 1931, 852.00 B/33; Laughlin to Stimson, 14 September 1931, 852.00 B/34, NA RG59.

Communism."[49] As winter drew near, the outlook grew as bleak as the `season. With Spanish conservatives unable to block the "shamefully bolshevist" assault on the landed estates of the wealthy and with Socialist minister of labor Largo Caballero promising "a new revolutionary movement" should the Cortes reconsider it confiscatory agrarian reform, Laughlin warned the State Department to expect more serious trouble. It came suddenly in early December, when the republican regime, under pressure from its left-wing supporters, unsuccessfully attempted to expropriate ITT's Spanish subsidiary without compensation, an effort that the State Department likened to what "the Soviet Government had done . . . when it succeeded to the Kerensky Government" in Russia. At year's end, then, the Azaña administration's recent actions seemed to have confirmed the worst American fears of communist subversion in Spain.[50]

The Foreign Office was also deeply troubled by the radical aspects of the new constitution and recurrent left-wing disorders. A report in late August that Spain's lawgivers intended "gradually to socialize private property" persuaded Whitehall that the country had "moved very far and very fast to the Left." Renewed labor unrest early in September convinced at least one British policy maker that Spain was "following the usual line" of revolutionary development. "The extreme left are becoming increasingly aggressive," Charles Howard Smith noted. "This time they failed, but they may prove next time better."[51]

The collapse later that month of Britain's Labour government, which saw a Liberal, the Marquess of Reading, replace Arthur Henderson as caretaker foreign secretary, did not alter Whitehall's belief that the Spanish Republic was "getting into deeper water." In

---

[49] Laughlin to Stimson, 16 September 1931, 852.00/1872, and 30 September 1931, 852.00/1874, NA RG59; Fletcher to G-2, 19 September 1931, 2657 S.126/39, NA RG165.

[50] Laughlin to Stimson, 11 November 1931, 852.00/1880; Chargé d'Affaires J. Webb Benton (Madrid) to Stimson, 22 November 1931, 852.00/1887, NA RG59. On the ITT expropriation, see memorandum by Undersecretary William R. Castle, 14 December 1931, 852.75 NTC/7, ibid.; Little, "Twenty Years of Turmoil," pp. 454–57; and chap. 4 below.

[51] Chargé d'Affaires Geoffrey Knox to Henderson, 14 August 1931, and minute by Louis Robertson Fullarton, 21 August 1931, W9534/6519/41; Grahame to Henderson, 25 August 1931, and minute by A. W. A. Leeper, 7 September 1931, W9933/46/41; Grahame to the Marquess of Reading, 7 September 1931, and minute by Howard Smith, 11 September 1931, W10355/46/41, PRO FO371, vols. 15775 and 15782.

contrast to American policy makers, however, British officials still regarded communism as only a minimal threat. Arthur Wiggin, for example, lamented in mid-October that Spain "could not be in a more uncertain plight," but he believed that the country's "spirit of independence" made it "very hard for communism to take any root."[52] Even after Rio Tinto and other British firms were harassed by Spanish authorities that autumn, few British observers took rumors of Soviet subversion seriously. Indeed, the views of Sir George Grahame in particular, reflected greater political acuity than those of his American counterparts. "It was expected in many quarters, when the revolution triumphed, that Spain would go down a slippery slope into bolshevism," Grahame wrote just before Christmas 1931. "Fortunately for all concerned, and not least for Great Britain, whose interests in this country are so important, these gloomy prophecies have not been fulfilled."[53]

Appalled by the anticlerical riots, shocked by recurrent labor violence, and dismayed by the radical aspects of the new constitution, policy makers on both sides of the Atlantic were questioning by late 1931 whether the Azaña regime would prevail over the revolutionary left. As it had all along, the State Department held "communism" responsible for Spain's woes and believed that "the struggle between labor and capital [was] being watched with satisfaction from Russia." But U.S. officials were beginning to appreciate that Spanish radicalism was often home-grown "without . . . being yet under any control by Moscow." A letter from Secretary of State Stimson to Herbert Hoover dated 17 December reflected this growing awareness of the complexity of left-wing politics in Spain. "Russian communism has not hitherto been nearly so important in Spain as an increasingly radical national socialism," Stimson told the president, "which, as its radicalism increases, naturally tends closer and closer to approximate the Russian variety."[54]

For their part, British observers continued to stress that "the

---

[52] Minute by Leeper, 9 October 1931, W11648/46/41; Grahame to Reading, 12 October 1931, W11929/46/41; and tel. 15 October 1931, and minute by Wiggin, 15 October 1931, W11915/46/41, PRO FO371, vol. 15775.

[53] Minute by Wiggin, 13 October 1931, W11771/46/41; Grahame to Foreign Secretary John Simon, 23 December 1931, W14821/46/41, PRO FO371, vols. 15775 and 15777.

[54] Stimson to Hoover, 17 December 1931, 852.75 National Telephone Company/7, NA RG59.

Spanish revolution has differed essentially from the Russian one."
The Foreign Office correctly saw problems indigenous to Spain—
anarchism, regional separatism, left-wing socialism—as more
dangerous during 1931 than international communism. More sanguine than Washington, London believed that Azaña and Alcalá-
Zamora, an odd couple to be sure, could lead the republic out of
the political wilderness. Indeed, by New Year's Day Whitehall was
convinced that "so long as the Government remain resolute and
the army continues loyal" in Spain, "extremist agitation" would
not "meet with any great success."[55] Unfortunately, however, both
governmental resolve and military loyalty were to become open
questions during 1932.

III

During the next year and a half British and American officials
watched nervously as the Azaña regime initiated a series of controversial reforms designed to usher Spain into the front ranks among
twentieth-century democracies. The Catholic church was stripped
of its pedagogical monopoly by legislation providing for compul-
sory secular education and the construction of nearly 10,000 new
schools. The swollen Spanish officer corps, which under the
monarchy could boast one general for every 150 men, was slimmed
down as half accepted the offer of early retirement at full pay.
Industrialists saw their authority reduced by the establishment of
"mixed juries" composed of workers and employers, which were
empowered to arbitrate labor grievances. The most explosive issue
confronting the Azaña government, however, was agrarian reform, long awaited by the republican left and much dreaded by the
republican right.[56]

Hoping to avoid alienating either group, Spanish officials employed radical rhetoric while working toward less extreme changes
in the land-tenure system. Nevertheless, violence erupted in January 1932 at the Estremaduran village of Castilblanco, where a mob

[55] Grahame to Simon, 23 December 1931, and minute by Wiggin, 1 January 1932,
W14821/46/41, PRO FO371, vol. 15777.
[56] Sanchez, *Reform and Reaction*, pp. 135–37; Jackson, *Spanish Republic*, pp. 62–64;
Payne, *Politics and the Military*, pp. 266–76; Preston, *Coming of the Spanish Civil War*,
pp. 669–72.

of tenant farmers angered by the slow pace of agrarian reform brutally murdered four Civil Guards. The victims' comrades retaliated by ruthlessly crushing several other rural disturbances later that month, killing fourteen peasants in the process. The Castilblanco affair widened the fissures within the republican movement and polarized the nation. On the one hand, the rural poor were now convinced that the Azaña regime was not serious about land reform and fell increasingly under the sway of the anarchist CNT. As a result, Spain was plagued throughout 1932 by agricultural strikes. They persisted even after the passage of an agrarian statute in September calling for the resettlement of thousands of landless peasants on small plots carved out of the holdings of the well-to-do. Members of the rural middle class, on the other hand, were frightened by the spread of violence to the countryside, and once it was obvious that the new agrarian reform law would imperil not only the estates of the nobility but their own medium-sized farms as well, they deserted the republic in droves and joined the ranks of its clerical and monarchist opponents.[57] Could republican Spain with Azaña at the helm navigate the narrows between Scylla on the left and Charybdis on the right, British and American policy makers were asking themselves by the summer of 1932?

Although the labor troubles that plagued the Azaña regime in its first nine months were almost always initiated by the CNT, American observers still made few distinctions between Spanish anarchism and Soviet subversion. The U.S. consul at Seville, for example, won accolades from the State Department in January 1932 for a "clear, comprehensive and timely" despatch that attributed the Castilblanco massacre not merely to the CNT but also to a "communistic party . . . of earnest young men recently returned from Moscow."[58] Irwin Laughlin was likewise convinced that anarchists and bolsheviks would eventually overthrow the Spanish Republic and establish "a communist-syndicalist government" unless Azaña took strong measures against "anti-republican activities in favor of a communistic regime."[59]

With the approach of spring Washington received even more

[57] Brenan, *Spanish Labyrinth*, pp. 256–59; Jackson, *Spanish Republic*, pp. 69–70; Malefakis, *Agrarian Reform and Peasant Revolution*, pp. 205–19, 310–14.

[58] Richard Ford to Stimson, 19 January 1932, and Assistant Secretary of State Wilbur J. Carr to Ford, 16 February 1932, 852.00/1890, NA RG59. Carr termed Ford's report *"Excellent."*

[59] Laughlin to Stimson, 25 January 1932, 852.00/1888, NA RG59.

disturbing information. Laughlin reported a fresh wave of "Communistic disorders" in February and passed along a recent Comintern publication praising the Spanish Communist party for expanding its membership from 800 to nearly 10,000 in less than one year. The military attaché at Madrid confirmed the twelvefold increase in Communist strength and added that the Kremlin was reported to have funneled $500,000 into Spain to finance extremist activities. This news thoroughly alarmed Soviet specialists at the State Department's Division of Eastern European Affairs, among them Loy W. Henderson, who urged that Laughlin be instructed to keep Washington "fully informed regarding the manner in which the Communist International and other Moscow controlled organizations are endeavoring to bring about the transformation of the Spanish revolution into a communist revolution."[60]

By April 1932 the American perception of bolshevik danger south of the Pyrenees had become so indiscriminate as to encompass nearly the entire Spanish left. Irwin Laughlin admitted that "strictly speaking" there was "no great communist party proper in Spain," but he believed nonetheless that "a powerful Communist organization [was] operating in the Peninsula." Even after Laughlin departed on a two-month leave to attend to family matters in Pittsburgh, Chargé d'Affaires Sheldon Crosby continued to warn that Spain was very susceptible to "contagious political diseases" from abroad. Blurring the very real differences among the various left-wing groups, he reminded Washington on 2 May that "Communism has made tremendous strides since the advent of the Republic" and cautioned that "large numbers of foreign agents liberally supplied with funds" had recently entered Spain "with a view to forcing Communistic principles upon the country."[61]

Although the Comintern clearly did hope to transform Spain's "bourgeois-democratic revolution" along bolshevik lines, Laughlin, Crosby, and other Americans badly overestimated Moscow's effectiveness in Madrid. The self-proclaimed twelvefold increase in Communist party membership, for example, seems inflated; it probably reflects an effort by Bullejos to boost morale among the

---

[60] Laughlin to Stimson, 15 February 1932, and undated memorandum "WE from EE" initialed L. W. Henderson, 852.00 B/41, NA RG59; Fletcher to G-2, 17 February 1932, Madrid (1932), File 800, vol. X, NA RG84.
[61] Laughlin to Stimson, 2 April 1932, 852.00 B/44; Crosby to Stimson, 18 April 1932, 852.00 B/46; 2 May 1932, 852.00/1895; and 9 May 1932, 852.00 B/47, NA RG59.

Spanish faithful and win points at the Kremlin. And if in early 1932 Soviet officials did exhort their comrades in Spain to launch "revolutionary mass struggles of the proletariat," Stalin's minions also rebuked the Spaniards for "not fighting with sufficient determination counter-revolutionary Trotskyism." Moreover, precisely because the Comintern at this juncture regarded socialism, not fascism, as its chief nemesis, Moscow directed Spanish Communists to squander what little political clout they possessed in attacks on such popular left-wing leaders as Largo Caballero rather than on the military and clerical right. By April even Secretary General Bullejos was beginning to challenge the Kremlin's line, and with the approach of summer the bolshevik steamroller in Spain ground slowly to a halt, stalled by sectarian warfare and bureaucratic intrigue.[62]

British officials, while not privy to these internecine squabblings, sensed the disarray and consequently discounted the persistent rumors of Soviet subversion at Madrid which so troubled their American counterparts. Sir George Grahame, for example, rightly attributed the peasant uprisings sweeping the countryside in January to anarchism, not communism, and repeatedly assured Whitehall that "the situation is well under control." As a result the Foreign Office, unlike the State Department, believed that Azaña had "improved his position considerably by his prompt action and the consequent collapse of those movements." Even when the anarchists disrupted the operations of several British firms in late March, Grahame was still convinced that a moderate republican government would "remain in power for some time to come." Relieved that Azaña seemed "to be getting little by little more firmly into the saddle," Whitehall viewed him increasingly as "a strong man and no Kerensky."[63] Indeed London, in contrast to Washington, dismissed "the possibility of a Union of Iberian Soviet Republics" because "the Spanish extremist is an anarchist rather than a communist." Persuaded by late spring that "no concerted

[62] "Comintern's West European Bureau to the Spanish Communist Party, January 1932," in De Gras, *Communist International, 1919–1943*, 3:180–87; Thomas, *Spanish Civil War*, pp. 121–22; Carr, *Twilight of the Comintern*, pp. 300–307.
[63] Grahame to Simon, 23 January 1932, and minute by Wiggin, 29 January 1932, W994/12/41; Grahame to Simon, 16 March 1932, and minute by Wiggin, 29 March 1932, W3462/12/41; Grahame to Simon, 30 March 1932, and minute by Howard Smith, 8 April 1932, W3882/12/41, PRO FO371, vol. 16505.

and widespread revolutionary movement is probable" in Spain, Whitehall regarded Azaña as the republican leader most likely to maintain political stability.[64] His mettle, however, would soon be tested, and not by the anarchists but by the army.

Although many Spanish officers were disturbed by the chronic unrest and disorder that had plagued Spain since the collapse of the monarchy, most remained loyal to the republic until the impact of Azaña's army reforms was felt. Arousing particular resentment among the military was a January 1932 decision to strip several younger generals, including Francisco Franco, of promotions awarded them by Primo de Rivera. Then on 5 February Azaña relieved General José Sanjurjo as commander of the Civil Guard after left-wing critics held Sanjurjo responsible for the repression following Castilblanco. Throughout the spring of 1932 Sanjurjo was in contact with both monarchist conspirators and right-wing republicans disenchanted by Spain's recent drift to the left. By July a handful of officers at several key garrisons had agreed to lead the rebellion that would topple the Azaña regime. Conflict between royalist and republican plotters over whether to restore the monarchy, however, sapped the strength of the conspiracy from the very start. Moreover, the Spanish government had become privy to the details of the revolt through wiretaps and was well prepared when Sanjurjo issued his futile call to arms on 10 August. The uprising, successful only in Seville, was crushed in under forty-eight hours and its leaders jailed. Surprised by the ease with which Azaña suppressed the attempted coup, policy makers on both sides of the Atlantic feared that the right-wing fiasco would strengthen the hand of the revolutionary left.[65]

The State Department's understanding of the deepening political crisis was enhanced by John C. Wiley, a career foreign service officer who had served at several posts in Eastern Europe before being stationed at Madrid in June 1932 to assist Irwin Laughlin. A protégé of Soviet expert Robert Kelley and a skilled analyst of left-wing and right-wing ideologies, Wiley provided Washington with

[64] Minute by Wiggin, 21 April 1932, W4447/12/41; Grahame to Simon, 25 May 1932, and minute by Wiggin, 2 June 1932, W6200/12/41; Leeper to Grahame, 7 June 1932, W 6603/12/41; Grahame to Simon, 8 June 1932, W6810/12/41; Grahame to Leeper, 9 June 1932, W6899/12/41, PRO FO371, vol. 16505.
[65] Payne, *Politics and the Military*, pp. 277–91; Jackson, *Spanish Republic*, pp. 75–77; Richard A. H. Robinson, *The Origins of Franco's Spain: The Right, the Republic, and Revolution, 1931–1936* (Newton Abbott, England, 1970), pp. 96–104.

its first accurate picture of Spanish politics since the advent of the republic.[66] He first demonstrated his superior political acumen in the aftermath of the Sanjurjo revolt. While Laughlin puzzled over the implications, Wiley specifically predicted that the Azaña regime would employ exaggerated charges of aristocratic complicity in the uprising to rally the masses behind a confiscatory land reform program, a prophecy fulfilled less than a month later by the passage of an agrarian statute authorizing the seizure of large estates without compensation. He likewise foresaw a systematic Left Republican campaign to muzzle the right-wing press and confirmed later that autumn that the Ministry of the Interior had indeed imposed strict censorship. Distressed by such "extraordinary measures," Wiley warned Washington in early November that "Azaña is certainly a dictator" whose tenure was predicated upon "the ruthless use of the iron hand."[67]

British officials shared American fears that the ill-conceived military conspiracy would spark a bitter left-wing backlash. Several weeks after the right-wing fiasco Sir George Grahame reported that Spanish radicals were "demanding that the real revolution should now be carried through and declaring that if Señor Azaña is unwilling to lead this movement, he should cede his place to someone who is." By mid-September Whitehall viewed the Sanjurjo revolt as "a most lamentable mistake" through which conservative Spaniards had "brought disaster on themselves and strengthened the Republic in a tendency to the Left."[68] The Foreign Office, however, dismissed charges that republican Spain was becoming a dictatorship. In early December, for example, Spanish expert Arthur Wiggin called Azaña "a very strong man, with the keenest of political noses," whose recent swing to the left was "more apparent than real" and whose "solid republicanism" proscribed all shades

[66] United States, Department of State, *State Department Register 1934* (Washington, D.C., 1934), p. 275; Stimson to Wiley, tel. 26 May 1932, John C. Wiley Papers, Box 1 (Spain), Franklin D. Roosevelt Presidential Library, Hyde Park, New York. Wiley carried on an extensive correspondence with Kelley while stationed at Berlin and Warsaw. See Wiley Papers, Box 1 (DivEE).

[67] Laughlin to Stimson, tel. 10 August 1932, 852.00/1900, and 12 August 1932, 852.00/1903, NA RG59; Wiley to Laughlin, 22 August 1932, Madrid (1932), File 875, vol. XVII, NA RG84; Wiley to Ellis Briggs, 7 November 1932, Wiley Papers, Box 1 (Spain).

[68] Grahame to Simon, 30 August 1932, W9944/12/41, minute by Leeper, 21 September 1932, and minute by Howard Smith, 22 September 1932, W10388/12/41, PRO FO371, vol. 16506.

of extremism. "It is hard, in all the circumstances," Wiggin concluded in words doubtless endorsed by other British policy makers, "to see what better man one could wish for Spain at this critical juncture."[69] Even Azaña, however, was unable to forestall a left-wing uprising early the next year, a failure that discredited his government at home and dismayed policy makers abroad.

Throughout 1932 the anarchists, eager for rapid revolutionary change, had been critical of the slow pace of republican reform. Having made major inroads among landless peasants and urban workers, the CNT proclaimed in January 1933 an "anarchist revolution" designed to topple the republic. Although gun battles erupted in several cities, the government swiftly restored order, with little bloodshed. The revolt was even less successful in the countryside, but at the Andalusian village of Casas Viejas an incident occurred that would seal the fate of the Azaña regime. On 11 January republican gendarmes cornered a dozen heavily armed anarchist peasants in a hovel in the center of town. When the anarchists refused to surrender, the police set fire to the building and gunned down the occupants as they fled the flames.[70]

The massacre at Casas Viejas shocked Azaña's supporters and opponents alike. The Socialists, not altogether displeased at the retribution visited upon their anarchist rivals, maintained a troubled silence in the Cortes. Lerroux's Radical party, however, labeled Azaña a "murderer" and claimed that realistic agrarian reform administered by a stronger government could have averted the tragedy. The Left Republican regime hoped to obtain a popular mandate for its tough stance, but the public repudiated its candidates in the April municipal elections by nearly a two-to-one margin. Although Azaña managed to remain in office for five more months, it was obvious in Washington and London by the spring of 1933 that republican unity had evaporated and that Spain's two-year period of radical experimentation had come to an end.[71]

The Casas Viejas massacre and its aftermath confirmed U.S. doubts about the Azaña regime, but it also encouraged a fuller

[69]Minute by Howard Smith, 22 October 1932, W11542/12/41; Grahame to Simon, 24 November 1932, and minute by Wiggin, 2 December 1932, W13213/12/41, PRO FO371, vol. 16506.
[70]Jackson, *Spanish Republic*, pp. 101–2; Peers, *Spanish Tragedy*, pp. 128–33; Brenan, *Spanish Labyrinth*, pp. 247–49.
[71]Malefakis, *Agrarian Reform and Peasant Revolution*, pp. 258–63; Robinson, *Origins of Franco's Spain*, pp. 121–23; Preston, *Coming of the Spanish Civil War*, pp. 81–83.

American appreciation of the diversity of the revolutionary left in Spain. John Wiley remained an especially perceptive student of Spanish politics, emphasizing on the eve of the January uprising that profound differences between bolshevism and anarchism made it impossible for the Comintern to flourish in the peninsula. "The Communist danger is small," he assured Washington on 21 December 1932, because the "unity and discipline . . . essential for a successful Communist movement are entirely lacking." Despite charges by some American officials that the subsequent insurrection was "communistic," Wiley correctly held the Federación Anarquista Ibérica (FAI), a terrorist offshoot of the CNT, responsible and reported no evidence of any "inspiration, guidance or support from Moscow." Even Irwin Laughlin admitted in late January that the anarchists, not the Comintern, had spearheaded the uprising, and by February 1933 the State Department at last had a relatively accurate picture of the left-wing menace to republican Spain. The real threat, Wiley reiterated, was the home-grown CNT and its one million supporters rather than the Communist party, whose membership of 12,500 he termed "not particularly impressive."[72]

If Washington had finally become aware that the revolutionary left in Spain was largely indigenous, the revelation was less than comforting. Azaña's ability to provide effective leadership remained questionable, and few Americans believed his coalition would fare well at the polls in April. But having watched the growing popularity of such right-wing leaders as Alejandro Lerroux and José María Gil Robles during the previous year, many U.S. observers eagerly expected the emergence of a more conservative regime, one capable of bringing order and stability. Indeed, although Wiley complained in February that it was "only a marvel that under the present motley government conditions have not been worse than they were," he thought it "safe to forecast that the present Rightward tendency in Spain" meant that by summer "a more conservative cabinet will be in the saddle" and that "left radicalism . . . will no longer enjoy the free reign it now has." Weeks before the April municipal elections, then, it was common

---

[72]Wiley to Briggs, 21 December 1932, Wiley Papers, Box 1 (Spain); Dawson to Stimson, 13 January 1933, 852.00/1926; Laughlin to Stimson, 27 January 1933, 852.00/1927, NA RG59; Wiley to Kelley, 12 January 1933, and 21 February 1933, Wiley Papers, Box 1 (Spain).

and not unwelcome knowledge among American officials that Azaña's days in office were numbered.[73]

Although London and Washington now both saw anarchism rather than communism as the real menace to the Spanish Republic, the Foreign Office, in contrast to the State Department, did not necessarily regard Azaña's demise as a welcome development. Grahame praised the "stability and strength" of the Left Republican leader in the wake of the anarchist uprising; Arthur Wiggin agreed "it was lucky that a strong man of comparatively moderate views was available to take the helm." Even after the opposition at Madrid grew more vocal in March, British policy makers hoped that Azaña "would survive the storm," largely because they, unlike their American counterparts, regarded Lerroux, his likely successor, as "no good." The results of the municipal elections a month later, however, confirmed that Azaña's influence was ebbing and convinced Whitehall that he would have to step down in the near future.[74]

Two years after the collapse of the monarchy American and British relations with the Spanish Republic remained circumspect. Neither the State Department nor the Foreign Office had been eager to recognize the new regime, nor were they pleased by the controversial reforms and the periodic assaults on private property in the months that followed. The sporadic right-wing and left-wing upheavals that rocked Spain in 1932 and 1933 merely reinforced nagging doubts on both sides of the Atlantic about the reliability of the republican government. Washington and London were, in short, profoundly skeptical of recent revolutionary changes at Madrid, largely because the Russian experience of 1917 was still fresh in their minds.

British policy makers, however, did adopt a more indulgent at-

[73] Laughlin to Stimson, 23 February 1932, 852.00/1892; Wiley to Stimson, 13 July 1932, 852.00/1897, NA RG59; Fletcher to G-2, 8 March 1933, 2657 S.126/63, NA RG165; Wiley to Kelley, 15 February 1933, Wiley Papers, Box 1 (Spain). For predictions of Azaña's impending defeat, see for example Laughlin to Stimson, 1 March 1933, 852.00/1929, NA RG59.

[74] Grahame to Simon, 10 January 1933, and minute by Leeper, 16 January 1933, W472/116/41; Grahame to Simon, 17 January 1933, and minute by Wiggin, 26 January 1933, W810/116/41; Grahame to Simon, 28 February 1933, and minute by Howard Smith, 10 March 1933, W2571/116/41; minute by Howard Smith, 24 March 1933, W3167/116/41; minute by Mounsey, 25 April 1933, W4248/116/41, PRO FO371, vol. 17426.

titude toward the young republic. They did so partly as a result of Whitehall's awareness early on that there was only a minimal communist danger in Spain, a view sharply at odds with the portrait produced at the State Department by suspicious U.S. observers at Madrid. The dispassionate and penetrating despatches of Sir George Grahame and the exaggerated and at times erroneous reports of Irwin Laughlin epitomize the contrast between British and American perspectives. Yet even after John Wiley finally provided Washington with a more accurate account of anarchist strength and communist weakness, London remained more tolerant of the Azaña regime for several other reasons. First, because British officials were much more accustomed than American policy makers to the compromises necessitated by coalition government under a parliamentary system, Whitehall had greater respect for Azaña's astute if occasionally erratic leadership. While the Foreign Office came to view him as "a strong man," he never transcended his "Kerensky" image at the State Department. Second, having already been outmaneuvered by the Quai d'Orsay over recognition in April 1931, Whitehall was "careful not to show coolness" toward the republican regime in order to avoid "pushing them into the eager arms of France." American officials, by contrast, apparently never considered this complication.[75]

The most important reasons why the State Department continued to take a dimmer view of the Spanish Republic than did the Foreign Office, however, were linked to the increasingly radical economic program of the Azaña regime. Republican officials were as eager as their monarchist predecessors to reduce Spain's persistent trade deficit. As a result they imposed autarchic commercial policies, which affected American exporters much more adversely than their British counterparts. In addition Azaña was pressured by left-wing nationalists both inside and outside his cabinet to undertake a concerted campaign against multinational corporations operating in Spain. Although British companies encountered their share of difficulties, Left Republican and Socialist leaders

[75]Grahame to Vansittart, 29 March 1932, Vansittart to Grahame, 5 April 1932, and minute by Howard Smith, 11 April 1932, W3959/3959/41; Grahame to Howard Smith, 3 October 1932, W11659/432/41, PRO FO371, vols. 16508 and 16511. I found no evidence in the State Department files that American officials feared a Franco-Spanish political rapprochement.

quickly singled out ITT as a symbol of foreign exploitation and called for the expropriation of the American firm without compensation. In so doing they precipitated a full-scale diplomatic crisis whose implications would frighten investors on both sides of the Atlantic.

4

Manhandling the Multinationals, 1931–1933

British and American policy makers were not alone in worrying over the increasingly uncertain situation at Madrid; businessmen were also deeply troubled by deteriorating political conditions in republican Spain, and with good reason. Britain's stake in the Spanish economy still stood at roughly $200 million in 1931, concentrated largely in mines and railroads, while U.S. holdings had topped $100 million, thanks mostly to the rapid growth of the American-owned telephone system.[1] Although few British or American businessmen at first expected the collapse of the monarchy to endanger their interests in Spain, left-wing republican nationalists soon launched a campaign to end humiliating foreign control over Spanish natural resources and public utilities. Prime Minister Azaña and his colleagues eventually sanctioned this crusade against multinational corporations because it provided them with the potent issue of Spanish sovereignty around which to unite their fragmented and unwieldy coalition of radicals and reformers. As a result, between 1931 and 1933 such convenient symbols of foreign domination as Rio Tinto and ITT became targets of Spanish nationalists demanding tighter regulation or even outright

---

[1]In December 1930 the State Department estimated U.S. investment in Spain at $72 million, two-thirds of which was accounted for by ITT's holdings (see chap. 2, note 13, above). The $47-million figure for ITT's Spanish assets seems low, however, since Secretary of State Stimson valued them at "over $70 million" in December 1931 (Stimson to Hoover, 17 December 1931, 852.75 National Telephone Company/7, NA RG59), and *Poor's Public Utilities 1932* listed them at approximately $100 million. Given these higher figures, an estimate of total American investment in Spain in 1931 of slightly in excess of $100 million does not seem unreasonable.

expropriation. Not surprisingly, republican Spain's manhandling of these and other multinationals complicated its relations with Great Britain and strained those with the United States almost to the breaking point.

I

From the very inception of the republic, in April 1931, Spain's new leaders and the international financial community regarded each other with mutual suspicion. Indeed, this reciprocal mistrust had surfaced during the final days of Alfonso XIII's rule, when a syndicate of American and European bankers organized by J. P. Morgan and Company extended a $60-million revolving credit to the Bank of Spain in a desperate effort to reverse the sinking economic fortunes of the monarchy.[2] Two of the king's leading republican critics, Niceto Alcalá-Zamora and Indalecio Prieto, greeted the announcement of the Morgan credit in late March with charges that the royal government had sold out to the international bankers. Nevertheless, the king's financial advisers maintained that the $60-million deal was both "expedient and necessary," and the arrangement went into effect on 1 April 1931.[3]

The fall of the monarchy two weeks later, however, altered the status of the Morgan credit drastically. Upon joining the provisional government, both Alcalá-Zamora and Prieto reversed themselves, admitted that the republic needed the infusion of foreign funds to stabilize the sagging peseta, and promised on 17 April to honor the recent agreement. The new regime nonetheless incurred the instant wrath of the international banking community that same day by imposing unorthodox measures, including rigid exchange controls, to stem the massive flight of capital from Spain in the wake of Alfonso's departure. J. P. Morgan officials reacted swiftly, notifying the State Department on the afternoon of 17 April that the revolving credit was "no longer in operation" because all

---

[2] Russell C. Leffingwell to Assistant Secretary of State Wilbur Carr, 27 March 1931, and Carr to Economic Adviser Frederick Livesey, 28 March 1931, 852.51/202, NA RG59.

[3] Laughlin to Stimson, 30 March 1931, 852.51/207, and 6 April 1931, 852.00 P.R./ 182; memorandum by Ellis Briggs, 15 April 1931, 852.00/1825, NA RG59; Benavides, *Política económica*, pp. 71–72.

drawings had to be backed by "notes guaranteed by the *Kingdom* of Spain," a condition that the Spanish Republic could not fulfill.[4] Surprised and angered by this unilateral cancellation, Minister of Finance Prieto proudly renounced the $60-million deal four days later. He claimed that the Spanish treasury now possessed ample reserves that made continued foreign assistance unnecessary. Privately J. P. Morgan's Parker Gilbert expressed relief at Prieto's action and informed the State Department on 25 April that his firm had really canceled the agreement because "the whole situation had changed" and "the Party now in power in Spain had denounced this credit as illegal and improper in their campaign prior to the setting up of the Provisional Government." The international financial community had delivered what amounted to a vote of no confidence in the republican regime.[5]

Other businesses operating in Spain were initially more sanguine about the reliability of the republican government. Rio Tinto chairman Sir Auckland Geddes admitted on 16 April that recent developments at Madrid made it "impossible for the moment to foresee what is going to happen," but he assured the annual shareholders' meeting that "political changes in Spain are no new experience to us." Reminding his listeners that the firm had "worked under Republican, Dictatorial, and Monarchical Spanish Governments," Geddes concluded that there was "no reason to suppose that in [the] future our treatment will be essentially different from what it has always been."[6] Buoyed by personal assurances from Spanish foreign minister Alejandro Lerroux that "all foreign property and investments in Spain would be respected, supported, and protected," ITT president Hernand Behn likewise advised the State Department on 21 April that the new regime was "perfectly stable" and recommended speedy American recognition.[7]

As political instability continued, however, fresh questions arose about the security of foreign investments. Troubled by persistent

---

[4] *New York Times,* 18 April 1931, sec. 1, p. 8:1; Jackson, *Spanish Republic,* pp. 38–39; memorandum by Carr, 17 April 1931, 852.51/204; Laughlin to Stimson, 18 April 1931, 852.51/206, NA RG59.

[5] Crosby to Stimson, 21 April 1931, 852.51/207; Gilbert to Carr, 24 April 1931, 852.51/208; memorandum by Carr, 25 April 1931, 852.51/209, NA RG59.

[6] Geddes, annual Rio Tinto chairman's address, 16 April 1931, RTZ Corporate Archives, London, England.

[7] Quoted in "Recognition of the New Spanish Regime," memorandum by Francis B. White, 21 April 1931, 852.01/40, NA RG59.

reports of communist intrigue in Spain, the State Department cautioned potential U.S. investors in early May that conditions remained "somewhat unstable" and instructed Ambassador Irwin Laughlin to determine "the probable attitude of the new administration [at Madrid] toward American interests and investments."[8] When republican officials made no move to prevent armed workers from occupying the Rio Tinto copper mines and several other British holdings later that same month and then announced plans to sequester the personal property of King Alfonso and his British-born consort, Queen Ena, Whitehall expressed similar concerns. Indeed, Foreign Secretary Arthur Henderson privately warned his Spanish counterpart Lerroux at a League of Nations meeting at Geneva on 14 May that any further confiscatory measures would probably destroy the relatively favorable attitude toward republican Spain that currently existed in Britain.[9]

Despite Lerroux's assurances that Spanish policies toward foreign investments "would not raise apprehensions abroad," businessmen grew steadily more skeptical about the new regime at Madrid. Rio Tinto, for example, moved swiftly to reduce its vulnerability. "There is a possibility of Spain passing through a Communistic phase, probably preceded and succeeded by a Socialistic phase," Sir Auckland Geddes warned the firm's board of directors on 21 May, in which case "the Company will be faced with some form of demand to surrender the Mines." Convinced that Rio Tinto ran "considerable risk of seeing [its] property interfered with, as regards to its management and ownership," the board agreed "that the Company should not embark upon any further capital expenditure in Spain except in case of absolute necessity" and "that there should be a cessation of actual writing down of property and plant, in order that the Balance Sheet figures be kept high, in case such are used as the basis of valuation." To offset potential losses resulting from "expropriation" or "nationalization" in Spain, Rio Tinto

---

[8]Hollie Lepley to the State Department, 1 May 1931, and Pierre de la Boal to Lepley, 7 May 1931, 811.503152/8; Castle to Laughlin, 8 May 1931, 811.503152/8a, NA RG59.

[9]On the dangers to private property see in particular the materials relating to the claims of British subjects in Files W5837/5837/41 and W6826/6826/41, PRO FO371, vols. 15781 and 15782. On the British response see Grahame to Henderson, tel. 15 May 1931, W5691/46/41, and 15 May 1931, W5931/46/41; and Henderson to Vansittart, 14 May 1931, W5798/46/41, PRO FO371, vol. 15773.

simultaneously expanded its operations in the Rhodesian copper belt, safely inside Britain's African empire.[10]

Rio Tinto's Spanish nightmare became all too real for ITT during the summer of 1931. The trouble began with a lengthy strike by left-wing nationalists against the American firm's $70-million Spanish subsidiary, the Compañía Telefónica Nacional de España (CTNE). As late as 29 June the firm's officials remained "entirely optimistic" about the situation at Madrid, but five days later anarchist phone workers walked off the job to protest low wages, automation, and foreign control. Although the Spanish government crushed the strike with considerable bloodshed at month's end, the left-wing call for nationalization of the CTNE struck a responsive chord in the Constituent Cortes, where on 12 August a parliamentary commission cited numerous irregularities during Primo's dictatorship and recommended the nullification of ITT's 1924 concession. The republican regime postponed such action indefinitely in September, but only after ITT chairman Sosthenes Behn had warned several Spanish cabinet members that abrogation of the CTNE contract would create serious friction with the United States.[11]

No sooner had the Spanish government tabled the nullification proposal than the Constituent Cortes drafted legislation in early October that augured ill for all foreign investments in Spain. Article 42 of the republican constitution permitted an absolute majority of the Cortes to expropriate any public utility without compensation. British firms were quick to call attention to the dangerous implications of this clause. As early as 13 October Whitehall learned that Rio Tinto was "very worried" about the possible expropriation of its copper mines at Huelva; during the next month executives of the Barcelona Power Light and Traction Company (BPLTC) and the Great Southern Railway of Spain expressed similar fears and requested formal representations to protect their holdings. Moreover, King George V himself pressured the Foreign Office to take a strong stand in support of property rights after the republican regime threatened in mid-October to sell Queen Ena's

---

[10]Henderson to Vansittart, 14 May 1931, W5798/46/41, PRO FO371, vol. 15773; Geddes quoted in Charles E. Harvey, *The Rio Tinto Company: An Economic History of a Leading International Mining Concern, 1873–1954* (Penzance, England, 1981), pp. 259–61.

[11]Little, "Twenty Years of Turmoil," pp. 454–55.

personal effects at public auction.[12] Nevertheless, Whitehall held that as long as British investors were treated no differently than their Spanish counterparts and received adequate compensation for any losses, there were no grounds for protest.[13]

As winter approached, however, the Foreign Office grew less confident about the intentions of the new Azaña government. "Conditions in Spain are almost as bad as they could be," Spanish expert Arthur Wiggin noted grimly in early November, "there can be little of British capital invested in that country which is not in grave peril." Under mounting pressure from the Department of Overseas Trade, the Board of Trade, and Buckingham Palace to make strong representations on behalf of British interests, Whitehall requested an update on the expropriation threat from Ambassador George Grahame at Madrid.[14] Grahame, who doubted that the confiscatory clause would ever be enforced strictly, advised London on 23 November that neither Rio Tinto nor the Great Southern Railway now believed a formal protest was necessary. By month's end both bureaucrats and businessmen were agreed that the rising nationalist campaign against foreign investments could best be stemmed through pressure applied by local Spanish commercial organizations rather than by the British Embassy.[15]

ITT, like its British counterparts, had adopted a relatively low-key approach to Article 42 through the autumn of 1931. In early December, however, the communications giant once again became

[12]Minute by Wiggin, 13 October 1931, W11771/46/41; E. R. Peacock (BPLTC) to Vansittart, 30 October 1931, W12565/58/41; "A Memorial from the Great Southern Railway of Spain," 2 November 1931, W12542/12221/41; Sir Clive Wigram (personal secretary to King George V) to Vansittart, 28 October 1931, W12593/46/41, PRO FO371, vols. 15775, 15777, and 15783.

[13]Minute by Wiggin, 28 October 1931, W12308/46/41, PRO FO371, vol. 15776. Regarding the appeals of British railway firms in Spain, Wiggin observed on 6 November that "all the railways in Spain, Spanish and foreign alike, are in the same plight in regard to these [confiscatory] measures; and as the original concession granted to these particular companies contained a provision subjecting their terms to such general dispositions of Spanish law as might at any time be promulgated, it is hard to see what we can do." W12542/12221/41, PRO FO371, vol. 15783.

[14]Minute by Wiggin, 12 November 1931, W12820/5108/41; memorandum from the Department of Overseas Trade, 4 December 1931, W13817/46/41; H. Fountain (Board of Trade) to Vansittart, 11 December 1931, W14126/12221/41; and Charles Howard Smith (Western Department) to Grahame, 7 November 1931, W12565/58/41, PRO FO371, vols. 15777, 15781, and 15783.

[15]Grahame to Simon, 23 November 1931, W13685/58/41; Grahame to Howard Smith, 26 November 1931, W13691/12497/41; and Grahame to Simon, 4 December 1931, W14254/12221/41, PRO FO371, vols. 15777 and 15783.

the target of ardent Spanish nationalists in the Cortes. Legislative investigators ruled that ITT had acquired its 1924 contract through collusion with Primo de Rivera, had established a discriminatory pay scale for its Spanish employees, and had annually repatriated from Spain millions of pesetas in excess profits. As a result they recommended that the Azaña regime annul the original CTNE concession and nationalize the firm's holdings. The cabinet agreed that ITT's conduct had been an affront to the nation and introduced a bill on 10 December nullifying the telephone concession and postponing indemnification for at least six months. ITT's Sosthenes Behn dispatched a sharply worded telegram to the Spanish government the next day warning that such action was "bound to have a very important influence on the confidence of American and other foreign investors in Spain." Then on the twelfth he appealed directly to the State Department for assistance.[16]

Having watched ITT's situation deteriorate for nearly six months, Washington responded vigorously. Terming the expropriation of the CTNE "manifestly unfair," Secretary of State Henry Stimson instructed the U.S. Embassy in Madrid to cooperate fully with the firm's officials and to warn the Spanish authorities that the confiscatory proposal might convince the American public "that all investments in Spain were exceedingly unsafe." Chargé d'Affaires Sheldon Crosby dutifully cautioned President Alcalá-Zamora on 14 December "without beating around the bush" that should Spain revoke the ITT concession, it "could no longer count on American financial aid and must reckon with hostility instead." The Spaniard, who later termed this "the final manifestation of the greedy and inconsiderate diplomacy of the dollar," indignantly replied that the dispute was really a question of "Spanish sovereignty" and refused to discuss the matter further.[17]

[16] Manuel Azaña, "Memorias política y de guerra," 10 December 1931, in *Obras completas*, ed. Juan Marichal, 4 vols. (Mexico City, 1966–1968), 4:266–67; "Translation of Appendix Number 89 to the Journal of the Session of the Constitutent Cortes of the Spanish Republic, December 10, 1931," 852.75 National Telephone Company/21 (hereafter this file will be cited as 852.75 NTC); Behn to Alcalá-Zamora, tel. 11 December 1931, and memorandum by Castle, 12 December 1931, 852.75 NTC/3, NA RG59.

[17] Stimson to Crosby, tel. 12 December 1931, 852.75 NTC/3; Crosby to Stimson, tel. 14 December 1931, 852.75 NTC/6; Niceto Alcalá-Zamora, *Memorias* (Barcelona, 1977), p. 327.

That same morning in Washington Undersecretary of State William R. Castle tangled with Luis de Irujo, the Spanish chargé d'affaires. Castle called the CTNE expropriation bill "one of the most high-handed performances" he had ever seen and made it clear that the State Department "could not stand passively at one side while American interests were being played with in this way." When Irujo retorted that the controversy was entirely a Spanish domestic affair, the undersecretary likened the confiscatory proposal to Bolshevik actions in 1917, promised that the United States would demand prompt and just compensation for ITT, and warned that failure to comply "would certainly be a staggering blow to Spanish credit in this country."[18] Convinced by the Azaña regime's continuing intransigence that the Cortes would quite probably pass the CTNE expropriation bill and confiscate "by far the most important American interest" in Spain, Secretary of State Stimson outlined the dangerous implications of the crisis in a 17 December letter to President Herbert Hoover and prophsied "a further swing to the left" at Madrid.[19]

At the last moment, however, Prime Minister Azaña drew back from full-scale diplomatic confrontation with the United States. Unnerved by American fulminations against a proposal that he himself now termed "a monstrosity" created by radical nationalists, Azaña privately assured ITT officials shortly before Christmas that the confiscatory plan would be "held in abeyance." He announced publicly on 12 January 1932 that the bill had been withdrawn from the Cortes for further study.[20] Policy makers on both sides of the Atlantic breathed a collective sigh of relief. Whitehall, which had monitored the State Department's struggle against the nationalization plan carefully, believed that a satisfactory outcome would provide "a precedent for us in the case of British companies" facing similar difficulties.[21] Despite the absence of any real

[18] Memorandum by Castle, 14 December 1931, 852.75 NTC/7, NA RG59.

[19] Stimson to Hoover, 17 December 1931, 852.75 NTC/7, NA RG59. There is no record in either the Hoover Presidential Library or the National Archives that Hoover ever responded to this letter.

[20] Azaña quoted in Behn to Castle, 18 December 1931, 852.75 NTC/11, NA RG59; Azaña, "Memorias," 12 January 1932, in *Obras completas*, 4:305–6; Frank Page (ITT) to Castle, 15 January 1932, 852.75 NTC/13, NA RG59.

[21] Grahame to Simon, 11 December 1931; minute by Wiggin, 16 December 1931; minute by Howard Smith, 17 December 1931; and minute by Mounsey, 18 December 1931, W14261/14261/41, PRO FO371.

assurance that the expropriation bill would not be suddenly resurrected, American officials, like their British counterparts, were quite heartened by Azaña's willingness to shield a foreign firm from attacks by Spanish nationalists.

II

Although staunch U.S. opposition to Spain's assault on ITT dampened the nationalist campaign against foreign investment for the time being, British and American corporations, like their Spanish competitors, repeatedly ran afoul of republican regulatory and labor laws in the course of 1932. Rio Tinto, which had unaccountably escaped attack since the previous May, was the first foreign firm to encounter difficulty in the new year. Recent advances in mining technology had boosted productivity rapidly at precisely the time that worldwide depression had reduced demand for copper, creating a situation where by early 1932 fully half of Rio Tinto's 6,000 employees were "redundant." But republican labor reforms, especially the establishment of mixed juries that gave workers a greater voice in setting wages and handling grievances, made it virtually impossible for the company to reduce its operating costs. Indeed, when Rio Tinto announced massive layoffs that spring, the Azaña regime forbade such action and even ordered the firm to rehire miners returning from conscript duty in the army. Shortly thereafter the mayor of Huelva, incensed by rigidly segregated housing and public accommodations in the copper fields, forced management to open the British enclave at Bella Vista to Spaniards. Terming conditions in Spain during 1932 "still difficult," Rio Tinto not surprisingly complained in its annual report that recent labor legislation had had "far reaching effects upon foreign companies operating in Spain."[22]

Other British investors encountered similar problems in 1932. The Tharsis Sulphur Company, which held a huge mining concession not far from the Rio Tinto copper fields, was plagued by strikes and sabotage orchestrated by workers protesting wage cuts

---

[22]Geoffrey Knox (Madrid) to Howard Smith, 5 February 1932, W1693/12/41, PRO FO371; Avery, *Not on Queen Victoria's Birthday*, pp. 349–51; *1933 Rio Tinto Annual Report*.

and layoffs.[23] The Zafra and Huelva Railway, a small London-based firm that linked the British mining companies to the coast, saw its operations repeatedly disrupted by work stoppages, its installations bombed by unidentified militants, and its taxes raised arbitrarily by the Madrid authorities.[24] The Anglo-Spanish Construction Company, which eight years earlier had been awarded a lucrative concession under questionable circumstances to lay several hundred miles of railway track, complained that the Azaña regime had reneged on a $5-million payment.[25] Later that same summer the Great Southern Railway faced possible expropriation when, due to substantial operating losses, its directors in London suspended service in defiance of republican regulations.[26] Even the estates of the Duke of Wellington came under fire in September 1932, when Spain's newly created Institute for Agrarian Reform placed them on its list of expropriable properties.[27]

Whitehall, however, resisted pressures to assist these troubled British investors through formal diplomatic protests. Still convinced that Britain "cannot . . . claim better than national treatment," the Foreign Office preferred a policy of watchful waiting while the affected firms muddled through "on the verge of bankruptcy." British officials might deliver "quiet hints" to the Azaña regime that its "scandalous" treatment of such companies as Rio Tinto "must inevitably discourage foreign capital," but they steadfastly rejected any commercial or financial reprisals against Spain. Whitehall's patience regarding these "delicate matters" eventually paid off. Although most British firms doing business in Spain complained about sporadic disruptions and government harassment throughout 1932, none saw its concession revoked or its operations nationalized.[28]

[23] S. G. Checkland, *The Mines of Tharsis: Roman, French and British Enterprise in Spain* (London, 1967), pp. 215–16.

[24] Minute by Wiggin, 7 March 1932, W2643/2643/41, PRO FO371, vol. 16510.

[25] See the extensive correspondence on this complex case in File W432/432/41, PRO FO371, vols. 16507 and 16508.

[26] F. Higgs (Great Southern Railway) to Vansittart, 26 April 1932, W4814/2643/41, and 10 August 1932, W9074/2643/41, PRO FO371, vol. 16510.

[27] See File W10694/10694/41, PRO FO371, vol. 16514, for Wellington's appeals to the Foreign Office in this matter. The Duke of Wellington had received large landholdings in Spain after 1815 from a Cortes grateful for his help in driving out the Napoleonic invaders.

[28] Knox to Howard Smith, 5 February 1932, W1693/12/41; minute by Wiggin, 7 March 1932, W2643/2643/41; and Howard Smith to Vansittart, 11 October 1932, W11060/432/41, PRO FO371, vols. 16506, 16507, 16510.

U.S. investors were also harried by Spanish bureaucrats and labor leaders. Having narrowly avoided cancellation of its original contract the previous December, ITT was plagued by minor problems during the new year. In February 1932 the Cortes passed legislation that regulated the CTNE more closely and for the first time opened its books to public scrutiny. Two months later the Azaña regime hinted that it might unilaterally force the renegotiation of the 1924 concession in the near future. Within weeks republican officials inaugurated a series of annoying lawsuits against the American firm, suits arising from its suspension of service during the telephone strike a year earlier. That summer the Cortes struck a potentially fatal blow to the CTNE monopoly by authorizing the government to create its own independent telecommunications system. Finally, following the abortive military coup in August 1932, left-wing trade unionists charged that ITT officials had willingly placed calls from General José Sanjurjo to his fellow conspirators around the country. In this increasingly violatile atmosphere American officials worried that such allegations would become "powerful weapons" against the CTNE.[29]

The first U.S. firm to encounter serious trouble in 1932 was not ITT, however, but rather the International Banking Corporation (IBC), the Spanish subsidiary of National City Bank. Late that autumn the Azaña regime unexpectedly commenced litigation designed to hike IBC's taxes to confiscatory levels by calculating them not on the firm's Spanish assets but rather on its "worldwide capital." Ambassador Laughlin termed this proposal "clearly excessive," as did bank officials, who swiftly requested State Department assistance. W. W. Lancaster, a National City executive, discussed the IBC imbroglio in early December with Undersecretary of State Castle, who complained that the unstable and potentially "revolutionary" state of affairs south of the Pyrenees complicated matters enormously. Lancaster agreed, pointing out that on a recent trip to Moscow he himself had detected "unusual" Soviet interest regarding "the development of Communist influence in

---

[29]Lewis Proctor (CTNE) to Behn, tel. 24 February 1932; Behn to Page, tel. 24 February 1932; Stimson to Laughlin, tel. 25 February 1932, 852.75 NTC/15; Laughlin to Stimson, 4 April 1932, 852.51/227; Wiley to Stimson, 28 June 1932, 852.75 NTC/21; Laughlin to Stimson, 22 August 1932, 852.75 NTC/30, NA RG59. For a complete discussion of ITT's troubles, see Douglas Little, "Malevolent Neutrality: The United States, Great Britain, and the Revolution in Spain, 1931–1936" (Ph.D. diss., Cornell University, 1978), pp. 199–256.

Spain." Castle urged National City to exhaust all legal redress under Spanish law before requesting official U.S. representations, but he promised that the State Department (unlike the Foreign Office) would lodge a formal protest, if necessary, to protect national interests.[30] This emphatic pledge was prompted less by IBC's own difficulties than by the eruption of a major Spanish-American diplomatic crisis, before which such relatively minor tax problems paled. As 1932 drew to a close, republican nationalists at Madrid resurrected their earlier plan to expropriate ITT's valuable Spanish subsidiary, and this time American businessmen and bureaucrats alike feared the Spaniards would succeed.

III

Given the repeated skirmished between ITT executives and Spanish officials throughout the spring and summer of 1932, U.S. policy makers were well aware by autumn that the CTNE was "already in a vulnerable position." The State Department was nonetheless shocked when terrorist bombs rocked ITT's Spanish facilities in late October and was further dismayed when the Madrid press unleashed fresh attacks on the telephone concession, replete with charges of bribery and corruption, in the weeks that followed.[31] Worse was to come. Citing pressure from its own members as well as outside critics, the Cortes announced on 18 November that the 1931 CTNE expropriation bill would be "resuscitated" and granted the firm only two weeks to prepare its defense. When both Prime Minister Azaña and President Alcalá-Zamora refused to block the confiscatory proposal, ITT appealed once again to the State Department for help.[32]

Alarmed not just by the real threat to the CTNE but also by the

[30] Lancaster to Castle, 1 November 1932, and Stimson to Laughlin, tel. 18 November 1932, 852.5123/60; Laughlin to Stimson, tel. 22 November 1932, 852.5123/62; and tel. 26 November 1932, and memorandum by Briggs, 3 December 1932, 852.5123/63, NA RG59.

[31] Laughlin to Stimson, tel. 15 October 1932, *FRUS, 1932*, 2:557; Laughlin to Stimson, 31 October 1932, 852.75 NTC/32 and 2 November 1932, 852.75 NTC/34, NA RG59.

[32] Laughlin to Stimson, 8 November 1932, 852.75 NTC/45, NA RG59; Military Attaché R. H. Fletcher to G-2, 16 November 1932, S.126/54, NA RG165; Laughlin to Stimson, tel. 18 November 1932, *FRUS, 1932*, 2:563; Page to Castle, 30 November 1932, 852.75 NTC/90, NA RG59.

more symbolic precedent for all U.S. investment abroad, American officials moved swiftly to thwart the expropriation plan. On 22 November Secretary of State Stimson instructed Ambassador Laughlin to lodge a confidential protest reminding the republican regime of its earlier guarantees to foreign investors and warning of possible U.S. retaliation should those guarantees be repudiated. Laughlin delivered the message the following day and later spoke with Azaña himself regarding the fate of this "American investment of first importance." But he returned to the Embassy convinced that with the prime minister governed by "domestic political expediency" and the Cortes "ruled by mob psychology," ITT would probably have to fend for itself against left-wing nationalists.[33] Counselor John C. Wiley paid an equally fruitless visit to the Spanish Foreign Ministry on 25 November. Explaining that Washington viewed the present crisis with "much gravity," Wiley emphasized that aside from "the very large intrinsic value of the American investment involved," Spain's assault on ITT "would as a precedent endanger the American investments in other foreign countries which exceed $14,000,000,000 in value." The United States "could not admit such a precedent," he added, because "its dangerous character had not been surpassed outside of Soviet Russia." Disheartened by the lame responses of Spanish officials, Wiley could only warn that "there would certainly be consequences" if the CTNE were expropriated.[34]

In light of these inconclusive developments State Department officials conferred with ITT vice president Frank Page in Washington about how best to protect the firm's interests. Everyone present agreed that Prime Minister Azaña faced a Hobson's choice in the CTNE controversy: outright opposition to the expropriation bill would alienate many of his left-wing followers, continued support for the measure would alienate the United States. The most effective way to ensure an outcome favorable to ITT in these "precarious" circumstances, Page believed, was to threaten to make Laughlin's confidential protest public unless the Spanish government blocked the confiscatory proposal.[35] Persuaded that such

---

[33] Stimson to Laughlin, tel. 22 November 1932, 852.75 NTC/43; Laughlin to Stimson, tel. 23 November 1932, 852.75 NTC/44; and tel. 25 November 1932, 852.75 NTC/47, NA RG59.

[34] Memorandum by Wiley, 25 November 1932, 852.75 NTC/47, NA RG59.

[35] Memoranda by Briggs, 25 November 1932, 852.75 NTC/51, and 26 November 1932, 852.75 NTC/56, NA RG59.

heavy-handed pressure would produce the desired results, the secretary of state instructed Laughlin to issue the warning on 28 November. The Spanish Foreign Ministry, which had earlier dismissed American complaints out of hand as "unjustified," was taken aback by the blunt threat of unfavorable publicity and offered fresh assurances that the ITT dispute would be settled amicably. Concerted action by corporate executives and U.S. policy makers appeared to have forced the Azaña regime to back down.[36]

If by late November State Department officials believed that recent American pressure had produced "a more malleable spirit in Madrid," developments early the next month caused them to change their minds. To be sure, the Spaniards did offer a compromise of sorts on 1 December. The Azaña regime promised to withdraw the expropriation bill from the Cortes immediately, but in return ITT must accept a public denunciation of its operations and submit to a binding "joint examination" of the telephone concession by a team of CTNE executives and Spanish officials. The U.S. Embassy, however, objected that joint examination might all too easily lead to "unilateral action in repudiation of contractual rights" and reminded Madrid authorities that "American interest throughout the world were so enormous that the various principles which governed economic international relationships had to be defended by the [U.S.] Government at all costs."[37] Since both ITT executives and American policy makers in Washington agreed that accepting the Spanish proposal would weaken the U.S. position, the State Department decided to "stand firmly" behind its earlier protest. When Ambassador Laughlin relayed this message to Foreign Minister Luis de Zulueta the next day, the Spaniard angrily retorted that all aspects of the CTNE concession deemed "in derogation of Spanish sovereignty" would still be subject to cancellation. "The chances for an acceptable reply to our note of November 23," Laughlin warned Washington afterward, "are not bright."[38]

[36] Stimson to Laughlin, tel. 28 November 1932, 852.75 NTC/56; memoranda by Wiley, 28 and 29 November 1932, 852.75 NTC/124; Laughlin to Stimson, tel. 29 November 1932, 852.75 NTC/61, NA RG59.
[37] Jay Pierrepont Moffat, Diplomatic Journals, 30 November 1932, Jay Pierrepont Moffat Papers, Houghton Library, Harvard University, Cambridge, Massachusetts; memorandum by Wiley, 1 December 1932, 852.75 NTC/124, NA RG59.
[38] Memorandum by Briggs, 1 December 1932, 852.75 NTC/67; Laughlin to Stimson, tel. 3 December 1932, 852.75 NTC/73, NA RG59; Moffat, Diplomatic Journals, 1 December 1932, Moffat Papers.

This gloomy forecast was confirmed in short order. The Spanish cabinet considered the CTNE expropriation bill during an "extraordinary session" on the morning of 3 December, and a few hours later the long-awaited reply to Laughlin's note arrived at the Embassy. In a two-page statement the Azaña regime summarily dismissed the American protest, contended instead that the CTNE controversy was fundamentally Spanish in character, and reiterated its support for revision of the telephone concession. With the situation now very much "up in the air," American officials and businessmen moved into high gear.[39] At the behest of ITT executives, who believed that the threat of a "semi-diplomatic rupture" between the United States and Spain would force the Azaña regime to modify its *"intransigeant* attitude," the State Department instructed Laughlin to let it be known privately that Washington might sever relations with Madrid should the confiscatory proposal become law. Outraged by Spain's "utterly unsatisfactory" handling of the CTNE affair, most U.S. officials agreed that "the moment has pretty nearly come when it may be necessary to have an actual showdown."[40]

That showdown came on 5 December, when Juan Cárdenas, the Spanish ambassador to the United States, called at the State Department to discuss the ITT crisis with Secretary of State Stimson and Undersecretary Castle. Although Cárdenas promised that his government intended to handle matters "in a most friendly way," he insisted that the CTNE controversy remained "a purely domestic question between the Spanish Government and a Spanish corporation," a question that could best be resolved through "joint examination" of the telephone concession by the interested parties. Stimson retorted that he regarded the dispute as "a very serious International question between our government and Spain." Emphasizing that the principle of joint examination was acceptable only so long as it implied "mutual agreement" between American businessmen and Spanish officials, he demanded that Prime Minister Azaña intervene personally to prevent the Cortes from moving unilaterally against ITT. When Cárdenas replied that "he

[39] Zulueta to Laughlin, 3 December 1932, Box 18 (Spain–Madrid), Laughlin Papers; Laughlin to Stimson, tel. 3 December 1932, 852.75 NTC/73, NA RG59.
[40] Laughlin to Stimson, tel. 3 December 1932, and Stimson to Laughlin, tel. 3 December 1932, 852.75 NTC/71, NA RG59; Moffat, Diplomatic Journals, 3/4 December 1932, Moffat Papers.

did not think that the Spanish Government had any power to interfere with the action of the Cortes," Stimson snapped back that "it did not make any difference to us whether our head was cut off by an axe in the hands of the Cortes or an axe in the hands of the Spanish Government, . . . it was equally an injury and a violation of our rights in either case." With this the conversation broke up, Cárdenas departed "much troubled," and the two Americans made good on the earlier U.S. threat to go public with the dispute.[41]

Stimson and Castle held a special press conference on the CTNE affair later that same day. Noting that "a rather serious situation" had developed in Spain, Stimson turned matters over to the under-secretary, who recounted the entire episode with particular emphasis on the legality of the original concession and the unparalleled improvement in Spain's telephone service achieved by ITT. Although both men were determined to protect ITT's $90-million stake south of the Pyrenees, they were even more concerned with avoiding a dangerous precedent. "The principle of the validity of a contract made with a foreign state during a prior regime was at stake," Castle told the journalists, "and its implications extended to nearly every country of the globe." Stimson agreed that "the sanctity of agreements underlies the whole problem" and emphasized that "the question was of very serious import because of . . . the size and the good reputation of the Telephone Company." After explaining that the State Department could only accept a settlement based on "mutual agreement" between the American firm and the Spanish government, the two men released the texts of the notes recently exchanged by the United States and Spain. When asked what action was contemplated should the expropriation bill become law, Stimson and Castle warned that it might be necessary to sever relations with the Azaña regime.[42]

Spain was shocked by this open threat of diplomatic rupture. A storm of protest swept through the Cortes and the Madrid press, while Minister of Justice Álvaro de Albornoz labeled American strong-arm tactics "brutal, impolite, and humiliating." Prime

---

[41]Stimson to Laughlin, 5 December 1932, 852.75 NTC/84; memorandum by Stimson, 5 December 1932, 852.75 NTC/86, NA RG59; Stimson, Diary, 5 December 1932, microfilm ed., reel 5 (vol. XXIV). Stimson noted: "We are having a little crisis now with Spain, and this morning has been rather spent over it."

[42]"Memorandum of the Special Press Conference: Spain, December 5, 1932," by M. J. McDermott, 852.75 NTC/119, NA RG59; Moffat, Diplomatic Journals, 5 December 1932, Moffat Papers.

Minister Azaña realized, however, that he had little choice but to act swiftly to prevent a formal breach between the two nations. "This is a question of economic and political power," he lamented in his diary on 5 December. "If I had a billion pesetas or fifteen battleships at El Ferrol, it would be resolved in another manner."[43] The next morning Azaña accordingly delivered a passionate speech to the Cortes opposing the expropriation bill and calling instead for revision of the CTNE contract only on the basis of "mutual consent." His proposal was sustained by a lopsided 181-to-11 vote, with most proponents of expropriation refusing to vote at all. "First round won on points," a jubilant John Wiley cabled Washington that afternoon. "Congratulations," came the reply on 7 December, "Magnates ecstatic!"[44]

Indeed, official Spanish confirmation that the telephone concession would not be revised without ITT's approval came as a great relief to bureaucrat and businessman alike. Sosthenes Behn was quick to thank State Department officials personally both for defending the interests of his own firm and for reaffirming the sanctity of all investments abroad.[45] *Bradstreets*, the influential business weekly, confirmed on 17 December that Wall Street had been watching the U.S. defense of the CTNE "with keen interest" because "any weakness in facing the Spanish problem . . . would tend to encourage similar affronts by Latin American countries" against the "great corporations holding electric, cable and telephone concessions" in the Western Hemisphere.[46] Frank Page doubtless spoke for many other investors, then, when at month's end he praised Washington's handling of the recent crisis in Spain as not merely beneficial to ITT but as "most far-reaching and important to American interests in Latin America" as well.[47]

The State Department's successful defense of ITT's Spanish holdings did not pass unnoticed at Whitehall. Although publicly

---

[43] Albornoz and Azaña both quoted in Joaquín Arrarás, *Historia de la segunda república española*, 4 vols. (Madrid, 1956–1967), 2:51, my translation.

[44] Laughlin to Stimson, 7 December 1932, 852.75 NTC/129, and 12 December 1932, 852.00/1923, NA RG59; Arrarás, *Historia de la segunda república*, 2:51–52; Wiley to Briggs, tel. 6 December 1932, and Briggs to Wiley, tel. 7 December 1932, File 875 (Madrid 1932), vol. XVII, NA RG84.

[45] Memorandum by Briggs, 6 December 1932, 852.75 NTC/95, NA RG59.

[46] *Bradstreets*, 17 December 1932, p. 1669. See also stories in the *New York Times*, 7 December 1932, sec. 1, p. 6:3, and the *Washington Post*, 6 December 1932, sec. 1, p. 5:1.

[47] Page to Stimson, 28 December 1932, 852.75 NTC/140, NA RG59.

British officials maintained that multinational subsidiaries incorporated in Spain could claim no better than national treatment, privately they welcomed "tenacious" U.S. resistance to the expropriation bill. Expressing "great and direct interest" in the ITT controversy because of its obvious implications for British investments, the Foreign Office encouraged Ambassador Grahame to cooperate closely with his American colleague at Madrid. Whitehall, not surprisingly, saw "certain advantages" to be gained from the U.S. diplomatic victory over the Azaña regime. First, "the American lead on this shd. be very useful" because it provided "an excuse for tackling" the Spaniards on behalf of British firms facing similar problems. Moreover, Whitehall, like the State Department, believed that the outcome of the ITT affair constituted a cautionary tale for other nationalist regimes and would help prevent "further defaulting" on commitments to foreign investors far beyond the borders of Spain.[48] In short, the precedent established in December 1932 provided the Foreign Office with the best of both worlds: Britain could enjoy the benefits of diplomatic intervention by proxy without incurring the costs of more strained relations with Spain.

By early 1933, then, British and American investments in Spain seemed more secure than at any time since the advent of the republic in April 1931. To be sure, Irwin Laughlin did warn Washington shortly after Christmas that "the people who are after the phone company's scalp haven't given up the fight which they will try to win in the end," but few observers on either side of the Atlantic believed that the Azaña regime would risk another full-scale diplomatic confrontation by repudiating its commitments to ITT or other foreign firms.[49] The Spanish government simply could not afford new problems abroad at precisely the time when mounting domestic troubles foreshadowed its eventual collapse. The

---

[48]Grahame to Simon, 7 December 1932, minute by Wiggin, 15 December 1932, minute by Howard Smith, 16 December 1932, and minute by Mounsey, 17 December 1932, W13696/1836/41; Howard Smith to Grahame, tels. 14 December 1932, and 19 December 1932, W13825/1836/41, PRO FO371, vol. 16509. British officials had good reason to be concerned about nationalist assaults on foreign investments around the world, for at precisely this time the Iranian government suddenly announced the cancellation of the Anglo-Persian Oil Company's petroleum monopoly. See Beck, "Anglo-Persian Oil Dispute," passim, and Donald N. Wilbur, *Riza Shah Pahlavi, 1878–1944: The Resurrection and Reconstruction of Iran* (Hicksville, N.Y., 1975), pp. 141–52. The concession was restored in the spring of 1933.

[49]Laughlin to Moffat, 3 January 193[3], Box 13 (General Correspondence–Moffat), Laughlin Papers.

fates of the multinational corporations and the Azaña regime in the spring of 1933 were inversely related; British and American investors waxed optimistic while left-wing nationalism at Madrid waned.

Indeed, the fortunes of such foreign firms as ITT and Rio Tinto had been closely linked to the ebb and flow of Spanish domestic politics throughout the preceding two years. The republican revolution, sparking as it had a responsive chord among Spanish nationalists determined to restore their country to its former greatness, raised serious doubts in international financial circles and prompted an Anglo-American banking syndicate to cancel a $60-million revolving credit for Spain. When the republican government failed to shield foreigners from mob violence, labor disorders, and legislative assault during the latter half of 1931, policy makers on both sides of the Atlantic pressured the Azaña regime to protect economic interests as diverse as Queen Ena's personal effects and the telephone company. When Madrid's attention shifted from restoring national pride to reforming archaic systems of land tenure and industrial relations, British and American firms encountered trouble less because they were foreign than because they violated newly enacted republican regulations. Relatively minor disputes over layoffs or taxes in early 1932, however, laid the groundwork for vastly more serious problems later that year, when resurgent left-wing nationalists in the Cortes targeted ITT's Spanish subsidiary for expropriation without compensation. Since such a precedent could easily have jeopardized billions of dollars in British and American investments in Spain and elsewhere, there was palpable relief in London and Washington when forceful U.S. intervention blocked the confiscatory proposal in December 1932.

Although both British and American firms had encountered serious problems at the hands of the Azaña regime, Spain's clashes with the United States were nevertheless more acrimonious than those with Great Britain. Part of this difference stemmed from the contrasting approaches adopted on opposite sides of the Atlantic. While Whitehall regarded disputes between multinational subsidiaries and host governments as primarily internal matters and accordingly refrained from formal diplomatic representations, the State Department contended instead that such controversies were clearly international in scope and intervened forcefully. British investors also fared better in Spain than their American counterparts because such firms as Rio Tinto had reputations for usually operating within the bounds of Spanish law; ITT, on the other hand, was suspected of having gained its concession through bribery, collusion, and influence peddling. Finally, international commerce had an important impact on foreign firms operating in Spain. Throughout the early 1930s Spain maintained a substantial trade surplus with Great Britain but incurred an enormous trade deficit with the United States. If the Azaña regime was reluctant to jeopardize one of its best export markets by attacking British investments, it had little to lose commercially, and perhaps much to gain, by implicitly linking the fate of ITT's telephone concession to better American treatment for Spanish exports.

5

Commercial Cold War, 1931–1933

If the United Kingdom and the United States were deeply troubled by republican Spain's treatment of foreign investments from 1931 to 1933, they were equally disturbed by the Azaña regime's adoption of an autarchic trade program that threatened British and American exports. As the devastating tremors of the Great Crash spread outward in the early 1930s from their epicenter in North America, Spain's exports fell a remarkable 71 percent from their predepression levels, the steepest decline registered for any major trading nation.[1] Faced with awesome trade deficits and a dangerously weak peseta, the Spanish Republic resorted to preferential tariffs and import quotas to protect its ailing economy. Spain's formal treaty commitments and favorable balance of trade with Great Britain ensured relatively equitable treatment for British exports. The uncertain status of the 1927 Spanish-American modus vivendi and Spain's huge trade deficit with the United States, on the other hand, virtually guaranteed that U.S. exports would suffer serious discrimination. Consequently, while Anglo-Spanish economic relations had cooled slightly by 1933, the United States and Spain were engaged in what amounted to a commercial cold war.

I

Variations in both balance of trade and treaty commitments shaped Spain's commercial relations with Great Britain and the

[1] League of Nations, Economic Intelligence Service, *World Economic Survey, 1931–1932* (Geneva, 1934) p. 157; Benavides, *Política económica*, p. 71; AEE, 1930, p. 128.

United States in distinctive ways during 1931. Although total Spanish exports had plummeted by over two-thirds in 1930 alone, producing an overall trade deficit of nearly 200 million pesetas, sales to the United Kingdom had slumped by less than half, leaving Madrid a healthy trade surplus with London. Indeed, the British market for Spanish exports ranked throughout the early 1930s second only to the French. Moreover, since the Anglo-Spanish treaty of 1922 guaranteed reciprocal most-favored-nation treatment, both national self-interest and international law made the Azaña regime understandably anxious to avoid a commercial rupture with Britain.[2] Well aware of the importance of coal, iron, and textile sales south of the Pyrenees for the depressed British economy, Minister of Finance Indalecio Prieto offered public assurances in mid-April 1931 that the Spanish Republic would honor the commercial obligations of its predecessors. To be sure, the new regime in Spain did on occasion exhibit signs of discarding its existing multilateral trade program in favor of the bilateral bargaining strategy practiced by such trading partners as France and the Soviet Union; but few British exporters expected the collapse of the monarchy to damage their interests.[3]

Anglo-Spanish commercial relations, however, were complicated by the severe financial crisis that swept Europe in the summer of 1931. After a month-long run on sterling had depleted London's gold supply and split the Labour cabinet, Britain's reorganized National government was forced to devalue the pound by one-third in September. This action, which worked to raise the price of Spanish exports to Great Britain, was extremely unpopular at Madrid. Britain's chargé d'affaires there, Geoffrey Knox, reported on 1 October that Spain might respond to the devaluation with "a depreciated currency surtax" on all British products entering the country. Nevertheless, Arthur Wiggin, the Spanish expert at the Western Department of the Foreign Office, hoped a week later that despite the threat of exchange controls, "British goods in

<hr />

[2] *AEE, 1934,* pp. 295–96; League of Nations, *World Economic Survey, 1932–1933,* p. 218; Charles, *Report on the Industries and Commerce of Spain, 1924,* pp. 31, 36; Jones, *Tariff Retaliation,* p. 62.

[3] Great Britain, Department of Overseas Trade, *Economic Conditions in Spain, 1933,* by Alexander Adams (London, 1934) pp. 25–34; *Times,* 18 April 1931, p. 10, col. c; Jackson, *Spanish Republic,* p. 39; John T. Davies (British Ford) to Vansittart, 31 March 1931, W3671/3671/41, PRO FO371, vol. 15780.

general may . . . have, for the time being at any rate, a better sale in Spain."[4]

Rather than levying a surtax on British exports, the Spanish government responded to the devaluation of sterling indirectly, by concluding a preferential treaty with France. Madrid and Paris had opened commercial talks a year earlier, but an impending agreement—reducing Spanish duties on French manufactured products in exchange for lower tariffs on Spain's produce shipments to France—had fallen through in March 1931 because of Spain's political instability. Later that spring, however, republican Spain resumed the trade negotiations, and by early autumn the Spaniards were on the verge of granting major concessions on French exports in return for a substantial currency stabilization loan from the Bank of France. Although the two nations failed to reach an agreement on the proposed credit, they did hammer out a commercial pact in mid-October. The new treaty went into effect on 10 November 1931, slashing Spain's duties on French automobiles, motorcycles, tires, and films by 50 percent and slicing tariffs on Spanish wine exports to France by a similar margin.[5]

British policy makers had monitored the Franco-Spanish trade negotiations throughout the year, but few were perturbed by rumors of preferential treatment for French exports. Indeed, Whitehall believed that existing most-favored-nation treaties with both Spain and France guaranteed Britain equitable treatment. If British officials were quick to view the terms of the November trade pact as "surely discrimination against us," they were equally quick to predict that the Franco-Spanish commercial alliance would be short-lived. Burdensome administrative restrictions on Spanish agricultural exports and heavy-handed tactics by the Bank of France in negotiations for a 300-million-franc loan did in fact prompt Spain to retaliate in short order by extending the preferential concessions recently accorded the French to their British competitors. As a re-

---

[4] Knox to Reading, 1 October 1931, and minute by Wiggin, 9 October 1931, W11651/46/41, PRO FO371, vol. 15775. On the 1931 sterling crisis see Aldcroft, *Inter-War Economy*, pp. 269–78; Robert Skidelsky, *Politicians and the Slump: The Labour Government of 1929–1931* (London, 1967), pp. 334–83; and Kindleberger, *World in Depression*, pp. 157–67.

[5] Castle to Pyke Johnson, 10 July 1931, 652.113 Auto/29A, NA RG59; minute by Howard Smith, 31 March 1931, W3671/3671/41; Sir Ronald Campbell (Paris) to Reading, 10 November 1931, W12909/3671/41; and Grahame to Reading, 10 November 1931, W13099/3671/41, PRO FO371, vol. 15780.

sult British exports were permitted by early December "to enter Spain on the same terms as French goods."[6]

American exporters, for a variety of reasons, did not fare nearly as well as their British counterparts. Unlike Great Britain, the United States lacked a formal most-favored-nation guarantee and was therefore vulnerable to Spanish manipulation of the modus vivendi of 1927. Furthermore, Spain's huge trade deficit with the United States, which in 1930 had soared to 184 million pesetas and by itself more than accounted for Madrid's negative commercial balance with the world as a whole, made it inevitable that the Azaña regime would exploit that vulnerability. Charging that recent barriers against Almerian grapes and other produce had reduced the U.S. market for Spanish exports to but one-fourth the size of the British, republican Spain resorted to discriminatory tactics designed to curb American sales.[7]

The first sign of an offensive against U.S. trade in Spain came late in the spring of 1931. On 25 May Madrid announced an exclusive three-year contract with Moscow for the purchase of 750,000 tons of Soviet gasoline at a price 18 percent below that quoted by Cities Service Corporation, the American firm that had previously supplied the bulk of Spain's petroleum needs. The Spanish-Soviet agreement effectively shut the United States out of a lucrative gasoline market, and it augured ill for other American exporters in Spain as well.[8] Six weeks later Pyke Johnson, the president of the National Automobile Chamber of Commerce, warned Washington that the Spanish Republic was likely to grant preferential treatment to French automotive exports, a move clearly directed against the United States, the leading foreign supplier of motor cars to Spain. By autumn Johnson worried that should Madrid discriminate against American automobiles, other governments might follow suit, seriously eroding Detroit's already depressed sales abroad.[9]

[6]Grahame to Reading, 18 November 1931, and minute by A. W. A. Leeper, 3 December 1931, W13682/3671/41; minute by Wiggin, 10 December 1931, W13952/481/41; Grahame to Reading, 24 December 1931, W14822/3671/41, PRO FO371, vols. 15778 and 15780; Adams, *Economic Conditions in Spain, 1933*, p. 37.

[7]*AEE, 1934*, pp. 295–96; Jones, *Tariff Retaliation*, pp. 49–55, 68–83, 104–13, 155–62; Commercial Attaché Julian Greenup (Madrid) to the Bureau of Foreign and Domestic Commerce, 15 November 1930, 852.00 P.R./164, NA RG59.

[8]Laughlin to Stimson, 25 May 1931, 852.00 P.R./189, NA RG59; *New York Times*, 31 May 1931, sec. 1, p. 14:2; Jackson, *Spanish Republic*, p. 39.

[9]Crosby to Stimson, 22 June 1931, 651.5231/55; Johnson to Castle, 10 July 1931, 652.113 Auto/28, NA RG59; Jones, *Tariff Retaliation*, p. 55.

The State Department was not at first alarmed when Ambassador Irwin Laughlin confirmed on 24 October that Spain and France had indeed concluded a preferential commercial treaty, since the existing Spanish-American modus vivendi was believed to ensure the United States most-favored-nation status, albeit informally. Early the next month, however, Washington was stunned to learn that Madrid had rejected Laughlin's routine request to extend the lower duties recently granted to French exports to comparable American products. Despite charges of discrimination, the Spaniards maintained that because the 1927 modus vivendi applied only to the consolidated import duties existing at the time, the United States was not entitled to rate reductions resulting from the abolition of Spain's old two-column tariff structure and the creation of a third column receiving preferential treatment.[10] Even after Laughlin warned Spanish officials in mid-November that continued discrimination might force the White House to employ the "retaliatory powers" specified in Section 338 of the Smoot-Hawley Tariff, Foreign Minister Alejandro Lerroux replied that Madrid "must find some means to correct . . . the staggering balance of trade against Spain in the United States." If Washington "expected to receive the advantages accorded France they must offer something in return." American concessions on Spanish fruit exports, for example, might prompt better treatment for U.S. automobiles in Spain.[11]

Sentiment in the United States ran decidedly in favor of retaliation rather than accommodation. The Rubber Export Association, Ford Motors, the Studebaker Corporation, and other business interests bombarded the State Department with calls for the application of Section 338, which would permit President Herbert Hoover to raise duties on Spanish exports to the United States by 50 percent. Spanish desk officer Ellis Briggs agreed that "unless we are

---

[10]Laughlin to Stimson, tel. 24 October 1931, 651.5231/56, and tel. 10 November 1931, 651.5231/57; memorandum by Briggs, 12 November 1932, 611.5231/604, NA RG59; Jones, *Tariff Retaliation*, pp. 35–36. Jones observes that the Spanish position on the matter was essentially correct: "[T]he Spanish Government on November 12, 1927 issued a royal decree granting the United States most-favored-nation treatment for unlimited time, but revocable upon ninety days notice, and limiting most-favored-nation treatment to *consolidations in force at that date*, reserving all commitments as to further consolidations" (emphasis in the original).

[11]Laughlin to Stimson, tel. 11 November 1931, 611.5231/603, tel. 13 November 1931, 611.5231/606, and tel. 13 November 1931, 611.5231/601, NA RG59.

prepared to consider jettisoning unconditional most-favored-nation treatment and adopting in its stead a bargaining policy, we should be willing to employ in defense of the former the instrument already provided by Congress for just such a contingency."[12] President Hoover himself received a telegram in mid-December from the National Automobile Chamber of Commerce demanding such retaliation, and he passed this message along to Secretary of State Henry Stimson with the frosty comment that the protest "speaks for itself." Senator Arthur Vandenberg of Michigan, whose constituents were adversely affected by declining automobile sales abroad, also urged the Hoover administration to apply Section 338 if Spain persisted in its discriminatory policy. Robert L. O'Brien, the chairman of the Tariff Commission, likewise denounced the Franco-Spanish commercial treaty and advocated swift retaliation by the United States.[13]

High-ranking American policy makers were nevertheless reluctant to resort to Section 338. Hoping to protect what U.S. trade remained with Spain and also to avoid Spanish reprisals against ITT and other American firms operating south of the Pyrenees, Secretary of State Stimson favored a more moderate course. So did Secretary of Commerce Robert P. Lamont, who feared that a tariff war would have a devastating impact on both countries and believed that relatively minor concessions by both sides would produce a negotiated settlement. Bolstered by Lamont's support, Stimson recommended on December 18 that President Hoover temporarily table consideration of Section 338 in order to permit the State and Commerce Departments to undertake a "careful study" of this "important question of broad national policy." Hoover concurred, and as the year drew to a close Stimson and Lamont began the search for a compromise formula that could placate both angry American exporters and adamant Spanish

---

[12] Pyke Johnson to Stimson, 12 November 1931, 652.113 Auto/31; memorandum by Briggs, 13 November 1931, 652.113 Auto/32; A. G. Cameron (managing director of the Rubber Export Association) to Stimson, 18 November 1931, 611.5231/609; illegible (Studebaker Corporation) to Stimson, 18 November 1931, 652.113 Auto/42; memorandum by Briggs, 12 November 1931, 611.5231/604, NA RG59.

[13] Alvan Macauley (National Automobile Chamber of Commerce) to Hoover, tel. 12 December 1931, and Hoover to Stimson, 12 December 1931, Hoover Presidential Papers, Box 994 (Foreign Affairs—Spain), Herbert Hoover Presidential Library; Vandenberg to Stimson, 15 December 1931, 652.113 Auto/46; O'Brien to Stimson, 17 December 1931, 611.5231/618, NA RG59.

officials. Unable to win from Spain the tariff reductions Whitehall had obtained for British traders, the White House remained hopeful that the new year would bring a speedy restoration of most-favored-nation treatment for the United States.[14]

II

Far from improving, however, U.K. and U.S. commercial relations with Spain deteriorated steadily throughout 1932, owing to the ravages of deepening global depression and to the recovery programs adopted on opposite sides of the Atlantic. Having won an impressive victory in parliamentary elections held the previous November, Britain's National government inched ever closer to protectionism. To be sure, Prime Minister Ramsay McDonald, a Labourite long opposed to higher tariffs, and Foreign Secretary John Simon, a Liberal who had recently replaced Reading at Whitehall, still hoped that the historic British policy of free trade would eventually restore prosperity. But Conservatives such as Lord President of the Council Stanley Baldwin and Chancellor of the Exchequer Neville Chamberlain had for years maintained that only a bilateral system of imperial preference could cure Britain's commercial woes, and by early 1932 their arguments carried the day. As a result, the cabinet first endorsed the passage of an Import Duties Act in February, which levied a 10-percent surcharge on all manufactured products entering the United Kingdom except those originating within the Commonwealth, and then arranged an imperial conference to consider the consolidation of a sterling bloc based on mutual preferences.[15]

[14]Lamont to Stimson, 15 December 1931, 80911, Record Group 40, General Records of the Department of Commerce, Office of the Secretary, Box 504 (General Correspondence), National Archives, Washington, D.C. (hereafter cited as NA RG40 with appropriate box numbers); Stimson to Hoover, 17 December 1931, Hoover Presidential Papers, Box 994 (Foreign Affairs—Spain). I have been unable to locate any record of Hoover's response in the Hoover papers, the Stimson papers, or the State Department files, but the White House must have concurred with the State and Commerce Departments' position because Section 338 was never invoked.

[15]Speech by Chamberlain, 3 November 1930, Great Britain, Parliament, *Parliamentary Debates* (Commons), 5th ser., *1930–1931*, vol. 244, 508–9; Keith Middlemas and John Barnes, *Baldwin: A Biography* (London, 1970), pp. 219–22, 657–59; Russell, *Imperial Preference*, pp. 27–28; Royal Institute of International Affairs, *Survey of British Commonwealth Affairs*, vol. 2, pt. 1: *Problems of Economic Policy, 1918–1939*, by W. K. Hancock (London, 1940), pp. 214–15; Aldcroft, *Inter-War Economy*, pp. 285–86.

Representatives of Great Britain and the Dominions gathered at Ottawa, Canada, in July 1932 to discuss the feasibility of an imperial preference system. Stanley Baldwin, who headed the British delegation, stressed that "the United Kingdom is so highly industrialized that it is vital to the physical existence of her people to find adequate markets for her products." But since fully one-half of Britain's exports were absorbed by nations outside the Commonwealth, commerce within the empire should not be expanded at the expense of further restricting the overall volume of international trade. He proposed instead that imperial preference be based upon mutual tariff reductions by the Dominions rather than upon fresh duty hikes against foreign countries. Canadian prime minister Richard Bennett, however, objected to Baldwin's formula and succeeded in uniting the Dominions against it. Bennett argued that because most foodstuffs and raw materials entered Great Britain duty-free, the only way to expand the imperial share of this trade was in fact the imposition of high tariffs on such products originating outside the Commonwealth. Baldwin struggled to defeat Bennett's proposal, but rather than return to London empty-handed, he finally agreed to preferential duties favoring the Dominions on most primary commodities. As a result, while prior to 1932 over four-fifths of Britain's non-empire agricultural and mineral imports had been admitted duty-free, after the Ottawa Conference only one-fourth of such products escaped customs charges.[16]

Among the beneficiaries of the new imperial preference system were South African and Palestinian orange growers. Before the Ottawa gathering Spain had supplied over three-fifths of all oranges entering the United Kingdom. The favorable duties accorded Commonwealth members under the economic agreements of July 1932, however, threatened Spain's share of the British orange market. With Spanish citrus production up sharply and sales abroad restricted by tariffs and quotas, the London press reported that "trainloads of fruit" were "rotting at the frontier." Spanish fruit growers, angered by the recent announcement of British ad valorem duties on fresh produce, met at Valencia in late

---

[16]Cmnd. 4175, "Imperial Economic Conference at Ottawa, 1932," *Parliamentary Papers* (Commons), *1931–1932*, vol. 10; Kottman, *Reciprocity and the North Atlantic Triangle*, pp. 19–35; Middlemas and Barnes, *Baldwin*, pp. 676–84; Hancock, *Problems of Economic Policy, 1918–1939*, pp. 218–20.

July to draw up a protest. Although the impact of the imperial preference system was not as drastic as many Spaniards had feared, South African and Palestinian oranges did begin to replace Valencian produce in British grocery bins. While total Spanish orange exports in 1932 rose by nearly 4 percent, shipments to Great Britain actually fell by a similar percentage.[17]

Outraged by this blow against the Valencian orange trade, Spain threatened retaliation. As early as November 1931 Spanish officials had warned that unless all preferential duties accorded members of the Commonwealth in the future were also extended to Spain, Britain's exports would suffer.[18] Nine months later, in the wake of the Ottawa Conference, the Azaña regime made good on this threat and announced plans to slash Spanish purchases of British coal "by something like 300,000 tons per annum." Fearful that such punitive action might fatally weaken Britain's already ailing coal industry, both the Board of Trade and the Foreign Office worked to block "this new proposal to enforce a further serious reduction in the trade of this country to Spain." Although Ambassador George Grahame at Madrid did manage to persuade the Azaña regime in mid-October to rescind for the time being its restrictions on British coal shipments, he was not optimistic about Anglo-Spanish commercial relations. Newcastle's colliers might continue to call at Barcelona or Cadiz, but Grahame warned Whitehall that unless "more favorable treatment for Spanish fruit exports" was forthcoming in return, there would probably be more trouble in the following months.[19]

Britain's commercial disputes with Spain during 1932 paled in comparison to the mounting problems encountered by the United States. In contrast to the program of bilateral preferences pursued by their British counterparts, high-ranking American policy makers adhered to a multilateral nondiscriminatory trade policy as the international economic crisis deepened. Indeed, it remained an

---

[17] Russell, *Imperial Preference*, pp. 87–88; Jackson, *Spanish Republic*, pp. 88–90; *Times*, 27 July 1932, p. 11, col. f; *AEE, 1931*, p. 222; *AEE, 1932–1933*, p. 262.

[18] Alexander Adams (Madrid) to the Department of Overseas Trade, 27 November 1931, and minute by A. W. A. Leeper, 23 December 1931, W13548/46/41, PRO FO371, vol. 15777.

[19] A. E. Overton to Vansittart, 29 September 1932; minute by Mounsey, 1 October 1932; and Vansittart to Grahame, tel. 1 October 1932, W10774/58/41; Grahame to Simon, 14 October 1932, W11353/58/41, PRO FO371, vol. 16506; *Times*, 15 October 1932, p. 5, col. d.

article of faith within the Hoover administration that commercial expansion abroad was the best way to ensure rapid recovery at home.[20] Secretary of State Stimson, for example, emphasized at the time that "the development of the foreign trade of this country has now become essential to its prosperity."[21] The president himself agreed years later that "there was no quarter from which reconstruction and employment could come faster and more efficiently than in the restoration of our foreign trade."[22] Although neither Stimson nor Hoover had much sympathy for nations such as Spain, whose own discriminatory protectionist policies retarded rather than expanded U.S. exports, both men hoped that a conciliatory approach would improve Spanish-American commercial relations.

Preliminary trade talks between the two nations began in January 1932 at Madrid. Ambassador Laughlin, who expressed renewed displeasure at continued Spanish discrimination against U.S. automobiles, learned that Spain's new foreign minister, Luis de Zulueta, was equally concerned over alleged American discrimination against Almerian grapes. The Spaniards seemed "anxious to settle these outstanding questions," however, and by month's end Laughlin was predicting that serious commercial negotiations would begin "within the next few days."[23] Nevertheless a snag developed, when in February the State Department demanded that Spain restore most-favored-nation treatment to the United States prior to the start of negotiations in Washington, something that Azaña regime was unwilling to do until afterward. But upon receiving Spanish assurances that discrimination against American exports would cease once the talks were under way, State Department officials opened formal discussions with Juan Cárdenas, the Spanish ambassador, in early March.[24]

---

[20] Julius Klein, *Frontiers of Trade* (New York, 1929), passim, especially pp. ix–xi; Stimson and Bundy, *On Active Service*, pp. 298–99; Joan Hoff Wilson, *American Business and Foreign Policy, 1920–1933* (Lexington, Ky., 1971), pp. 87–92.

[21] Stimson to Lyman Hammond, 16 June 1931, Stimson Papers, microfilm ed., reel 81 (General Correspondence).

[22] Hoover, *Memoirs*, vol. 2: *The Cabinet and the Presidency*, p. 79.

[23] Laughlin to Stimson, tel. 22 December 1931, 611.5231/620, tel. 22 January 1932, 611.5231/627, tel. 23 January 1932, 611.5231/628, and tel. 28 January 1932, 611.5231/629, NA RG59.

[24] Stimson to Laughlin, tel. 30 January 1932, 611.5231/629; Laughlin to Stimson, tel. 7 February 1932, and Stimson to Laughlin, tel. 8 February 1932, 611.5231/633; memorandum by Boal, 8 March 1932, 611.5231/638, NA RG59.

Progress was made on some specific Spanish grievances. Convinced that Spain "would welcome even a *mediocre concession,*" State Department economic adviser Herbert Feis recommended on 11 March that the United States stop requiring expensive labels on imported cork stoppers and outlaw widespread pirating of the "Almerian" and "Valencian" brand names by California fruit growers. American negotiators demonstrated a willingness to yield on such minor issues two weeks later, when the Tariff Commission abolished "administrative requirements" on a few Spanish exports, and the Federal Trade Commission ordered a halt to the fraudulent use of Spanish trademarks.[25] Washington, however, was reluctant to consider Spain's major complaint, the U.S. Department of Agriculture's embargo on Almerian grapes rumored to be contaminated by the Mediterranean fruit fly, until reciprocal concessions were forthcoming from Madrid. Particularly galling to American officials was the Azaña regime's proposal to restore equitable treatment not to all U.S. exports, as it had pledged earlier, but only to a specific list of products to be drawn up by Washington. Terming the Spanish offer "a further whittling away of our commercial rights," the State Department rejected it on principle. "Complete most-favored-nation treatment," Undersecretary of State William Castle explained tersely on 31 March, "is the only kind that this Government grants or could recognize."[26]

Despite this apparent impasse, Ambassador Cárdenas and Undersecretary Castle did hammer out an informal trade agreement in April. Insisting that it was legally "impossible" for his government to extend unconditional commercial equality to any country, the Spaniard assured Castle on 4 April that most-favored-nation treatment could be arranged for "a list of everything we exported to Spain" and that all other items enumerated by the United States at a later date "would automatically be added." After Castle agreed that "some formula might be worked out along these

[25] Undated handwritten memorandum (probably 11 March 1932) by Feis, attached to Assistant Secretary of State James Rogers to the secretary of commerce, 11 March 1932, 611.5231/619; memoranda by Briggs, 25 March 1932, 611.5231/647, and 30 March 1932, 611.5231/706, NA RG59.
[26] Memorandum by Boal, 28 March 1932, 611.5231/658; Castle to Laughlin, tel. 29 March 1932, 611.5231/643; Laughlin to Stimson, tel. 30 March 1932; Castle to Laughlin, tel. 31 March 1932; and memorandum by Briggs, 31 March 1932, 611.5231/645, NA RG59.

lines," the Azaña regime formally offered two days later to extend "maximum benefits granted by Spain to other countries, on all those articles which may concern the United States" in exchange for renewed American efforts to alleviate "the onerous and adverse balance in the commercial interchange" between the two nations.[27] The State Department remained reluctant to accept a Spanish offer that clearly violated general American commercial principles, but it was clear by mid-April that rejection of the compromise formula would probably destroy what little U.S. trade remained with Spain. Aware that the Azaña regime had requested the list in order to placate Almerian fruit growers, who objected to any agreement until the American embargo on their grapes was lifted, and that Madrid's earlier concessions to France had already seriously eroded U.S. exports to Spain, Washington decided on 21 April to accept the Spanish proposal.[28]

Although Spain learned of this decision two days later, unexpected problems delayed implementation of the agreement. On 26 April Cárdenas warned the State Department that one-sided American press accounts of the commercial talks, which emphasized Spain's discriminatory actions but ignored those of the United States, "might jeopardize the successful conclusion of our negotiations." American officials promised to minimize such "premature publicity," but commercial relations between the two nations received a fresh blow at month's end when the Spanish request that the Department of Agriculture's embargo on Almerian grapes be lifted was rejected for "sanitary reasons."[29] The Azaña regime's reaction was swift and predictable. On 6 May Spain requested an "amplification" of the American export list prior to the restoration of most-favored-nation treatment, ostensibly to forestall third-country criticism of repeated Spanish concessions to the United States. The real reason for the delay, however, was Madrid's displeasure at the "unsatisfactory manner" in which "the

[27] Memorandum by Castle, 4 April 1932, 611.5231/660; Cárdenas to the secretary of state, 6 April 1932, 611.5231/656; Zulueta to Laughlin, 5 April 1932, 611.5231/688; Laughlin to Stimson, tel. 6 April 1932, 611.5231/652, NA RG59.

[28] Commercial Attaché Charles Livengood (Madrid) to the Bureau of Foreign and Domestic Commerce, 6 April 1932, 611.5231/673; W. B. Pitts (Department of Commerce) to Briggs, 15 April 1932, 611.5231/667; Castle to Crosby, tel. 21 April 1932, 611.5231/664, NA RG59.

[29] Crosby to Castle, tel. 23 April 1932, 611.5231/669; memorandum by Boal, 26 April 1932, 611.5231/724; Castle to Cárdenas, 29 April 1932, 611.5231/705A; Cárdenas to Stimson, 30 April 1932, 611.5231/710, NA RG59.

negotiations in Washington concerning Spanish grievances were progressing." American officials insisted that "considerable progress" had been made on Spain's trade complaints and that the Department of Agriculture was still "exploring every possibility" for lifting its embargo on Almerian grapes. Accordingly, unless the Azaña regime fulfilled its obligations under the April exchange of notes, the United States would have "no alternative" but to retaliate.[30]

The negotiations remained stalemated throughout the spring. On 21 May Ambassador Cárdenas reiterated Spain's position that restoration of most-favored-nation treatment for American exports hinged on the suspension of the embargo on Almerian grapes. California fruit growers, he hinted darkly, not the Mediterranean fruit fly, were behind a sanitary quarantine that had reduced Spanish grape sales to the United States from $1 million as recently as 1923 to zero in 1931. Outraged by what he regarded as Spanish intransigence, Undersecretary Castle retorted angrily that "rather than to let grapes into this country which were infested with the Mediterranean fruit fly, I should prefer not to have any trade with Spain."[31] Convinced that "our tariff relations with Spain . . . now appear to have reached an impasse" that might "seriously affect our most-favored-nation position throughout Europe," the State Department prepared a fresh study of the probable effects of a Spanish-American trade war in early June.[32]

Indeed, with the approach of summer the case for reprisals

[30]Zulueta to Crosby, 5 May 1932, 611.5231/719; Crosby to Castle, tel. 6 May 1932, 611.5231/674; Castle to Crosby, tel. 7 May 1932, 611.5231/712A, NA RG59.

[31]United States, Department of Commerce, Bureau of Foreign and Domestic Commerce, *Foreign Commerce and Navigation of the United States, 1923* (Washington, D.C., 1924), p. 41; *Foreign Commerce and Navigation of the United States, 1931*, p. 241; Crosby to Stimson, tel. 20 May 1932, 611.5231/720; memorandum by Castle, 21 May 1932, 611.5231/726, NA RG59. It is difficult to determine whether the sanitary quarantine was warranted. At a 2 June 1932 meeting with State and Agriculture Department officials, Ambassador Cárdenas pointed out that despite the presence of the Mediterranean fruit fly in Argentina, the United States still imported grapes from Buenos Aires. Edgar Sasscer of the Department of Agriculture tried to explain the distinction between the Almerian and the Argentinian grapes, but even Ellis Briggs was forced to admit that "I was unable clearly to follow Mr. Sasscer's reasoning even though I was considerably more familiar with the intricacies of the English language than were either of the Spaniards present." Memorandum by Briggs, 2 June 1932, 811.612 Grapes—Spain/175, NA RG59.

[32]Stimson to Wiley, tel. 26 May 1932, Wiley Papers, Box 1 (Spain); memorandum by Boal, 8 June 1932, 611.5231/751, NA RG59.

against Spanish exports was growing stronger. American automobile sales in Spain had plummeted from 7,415 in 1929 to 473 in early 1932, the American Chamber of Commerce in Spain reported a net loss of eighteen members since 1930, and numerous firms interested in the Spanish market continued to press the State Department for retaliation unless Madrid ceased discriminating against the United States.[33] Secretary of State Stimson perhaps best captured the gravity of the crisis when he noted on 28 June that Spanish-American commercial relations were "very acute now" because the Azaña regime had "set up a bargaining tariff" that was "killing off our trade, particularly in automobiles." Since the Department of Agriculture was unlikely to lift its embargo on Almerian grapes in the near future, he concluded that "a fight" between the two nations seemed inevitable.[34]

With the trade talks still at a standstill in mid-August, the State Department termed the informal commercial accord of the previous April "a dead letter" and prepared for retaliation against Spain. "The only thing left to us," Pierrepont Moffat, the chief of the Division of Western European Affairs, noted privately on 18 August, "is to make use of Section 338 of our Tariff Bill raising all duties 50 percent against countries that discriminate against us."[35] Castle and Stimson had already begun to discuss just such action with Roy Chapin, who had recently succeeded Lamont as secretary of commerce. Since Spain absorbed only a small fraction of overall American exports, State and Commerce Department officials concluded that the United States stood to lose next to nothing in a tariff war while Spain stood to lose a great deal. Both Stimson and Chapin accordingly agreed in early October that the time had come to invoke Section 338 and teach the Azaña regime a lesson about international trade.[36] With American exporters still subject to discrimination that their British competitors had escaped, the Hoover

[33] Jones, *Tariff Retaliation*, pp. 61–63; excerpt from *Export Trade & Finance*, 7 May 1932, filed at State Department, 11 May 1932, 611.5231/716; John B. Tower (U.S. Rubber Company) to Stimson, 6 May 1932, 611.5231/713; Pyke Johnson to Castle, 15 June 1932, 651.113 Auto/53, NA RG59.

[34] Stimson Diary, 28 June 1932, microfilm ed., reel 4, vol. XXIII.

[35] Moffat, Diplomatic Journals, 18 August 1932, Moffat Papers; memorandum by Briggs, 19 August 1932, 611.5231/740, NA RG59.

[36] Memorandum by Briggs, 27 September 1932, 611.5231/739; Rogers to Assistant Secretary of Commerce Julius Klein, 28 September 1932, and memorandum by Briggs, 30 September 1932, 611.5231/738; Castle to Laughlin, tel. 10 October 1932, 611.5231/742, NA RG59; Moffat, Diplomatic Journals, 10 October 1932, Moffat Papers.

administration by the autumn of 1932 was hovering on the verge of open commercial warfare with the Spanish Republic.

III

Winter brought frostier Spanish commercial relations not only with the United States but also with the United Kingdom, whose interests in Spain endured reprisals for imperial discrimination against Valencian oranges. Careful to avoid outright retaliation against such important British exports as coal and iron, Madrid chose instead to apply pressure indirectly, by imposing exchange controls in October 1932 that prevented such London-based firms as the Barcelona Power Light and Traction Company from repatriating their profits.[37] Although the Foreign Office warned that should Spanish officials become "intolerably harsh towards our interests" the Board of Trade might be forced to take "a strong line . . . against their orange crop," the Azaña regime tightened the exchange controls on 5 January 1933 and linked liberalization to more favorable treatment for Spain's fruit exports to the British Commonwealth.[38]

Three months later Anglo-Spanish trade disputes had become so rancorous that Whitehall, like the State Department, was contemplating a tariff war. "I think we shd. seriously consider the possibility of having a show-down with Spain on all the questions outstanding," Western Department head Charles Howard Smith remarked testily on 10 April, "provided that we can find some stick to beat her with." A gloomy analysis prepared shortly thereafter by C. N. Stirling, who had recently replaced Arthur Wiggin as Whitehall's Spanish expert, concluded that such a "stick" would be difficult to employ. Attributing Madrid's "attitude of intransigence" on exchange controls and other minor matters to "our refusal to accommodate Spain in the matter of the duty on oranges," Stirling was uncertain how to combat the "petty chauvinism" of

[37] Minute by M. Shearman (Western Department), 5 October 1932; Howard Smith to Grahame, 20 October 1932, W11019/38/41; Grahame to Howard Smith, 25 October 1932, W12017/38/41, PRO FO371, vol. 16506.
[38] Grahame to Howard Smith, 27 October 1932, and minute by Wiggin, 5 November 1932, W12064/38/41, PRO FO371, vol. 16506; Adams, *Economic Conditions in Spain, 1933,* p. 30.

the Azaña regime. "Our only effective weapon seems to be the tariff, and we have already shot our two best bolts from this bow," he confessed. "However, the fact remains that there is a large balance in favour of Spain in Anglo-Spanish trade for us to attack . . . which will give us some hold over them."[39] In short, by the spring of 1933 Stirling, like his opposite numbers on the other side of the Atlantic, was convinced that the Spanish Republic would prove more responsive to retaliation than to conciliation.

Washington had even greater cause than London to consider reprisals, since Spain practiced not more subtle forms of harassment but outright discrimination against American commercial interests. Yet the Hoover administration, as it had throughout 1932, hesitated to retaliate against Spanish exports. To be sure, the State and Commerce Departments had favored the application of Section 338 in early October, but they reversed themselves later that month on the recommendation of Ambassador Laughlin at Madrid. Although he admitted that American exporters now had little to lose from such action, Laughlin warned Washington on 15 October that "the animus raised by trade reprisals would not help American enterprises in Spain, in particular the telephone company which is already in a vulnerable position." The ITT situation was so delicate that even the American Chamber of Commerce in Spain believed U.S. retaliation against Spanish exports would be "extremely unfortunate and ill-advised." Finally, Laughlin pointed out that "repeated prognostications of Mr. Roosevelt's election" had convinced Spanish negotiators that "whatever we may do now, they might get better terms later."[40]

Fearing "a political boomerang" against ITT and other American interests in Spain, the Hoover administration postponed further consideration of retaliatory action indefinitely. Although Laughlin continued to press the Azaña regime to live up to its promise to restore most-favored-nation treatment, the State Department expected the Spaniards "to drag out the negotiations interminably in order to win as much ground as possible." Washington longed to

---

[39] Minute by Howard Smith, 10 April 1933, and minute by Stirling, 21 April 1933, W3809/3809/41, PRO FO371, vol. 17434. See File W115/115/41, PRO FO371, vol. 17425, for the details of the complex dispute arising out of the new Spanish exchange controls and British restrictions on the Valencian orange trade.

[40] Laughlin to Stimson, tel. 15 October 1932, 611.5231/743, NA RG59; Moffat, Diplomatic Journals, 17 October 1932, Moffat Papers.

retaliate with Section 338, but as Secretary of Commerce Chapin put it in mid-November, "the resultant tariff war arising from such a step would, of course, involve grave difficulties for many aspects of American trade and investment."[41] In any case, Hoover's resounding defeat at the polls earlier that month made retaliation against Spain a moot question for a lame-duck administration. Counselor John Wiley did make one final request in December for lower duties on American exports, but he told Laughlin that Spanish officials had only "smiled indulgently."[42] Commercial negotiations between Madrid and Washington, Spanish desk officer Ellis Briggs concluded acidly in a February 1933 summary of American trade disputes with Spain for outgoing Secretary of State Stimson, had broken down entirely. When the new Roosevelt administration took office later that spring, Spanish-American commercial relations remained, as they had been since the inception of the republic two years earlier, deadlocked.[43]

If by early 1933 major trade problems seemed to have placed both Great Britain and the United States on a collision course with Spain, Madrid nevertheless remained on slightly better terms with London than with Washington. In the first place, while Spain's formal treaty commitments precluded discrimination against British exports, no such constraints protected comparable American products. The 1922 Anglo-Spanish commercial treaty guaranteed both countries reciprocal most-favored-nation treatment, but the Spanish-American modus vivendi of 1927 was specifically limited to Madrid's existing two-column tariff. When the Azaña regime elected to grant additional preferences to French products in 1931, the lower duties were automatically extended to British goods but were denied to American exports. As a result, while American observers at Madrid watched Detroit's automobile sales there plummet over the next year, Britons in Spain could hail "the steady

---

[41] Moffat, Diplomatic Journals, 19 and 20 October 1932, Moffat Papers; Stimson to Laughlin, tel. 21 October 1932, 611.5231/743, NA RG59; Chapin to W. H. Lalley (president of Kelley-Springfield Tire Company), 22 November 1932, 82220/1, NA RG40.

[42] Laughlin to Stimson, tel. 3 November 1932, 611.5231/747, and 3 December 1932, 852.75 NTC/124, NA RG59; Moffat, Diplomatic Journals, 5 November 1932, Moffat Papers.

[43] Undated memorandum by Briggs (probably February 1933), Stimson Papers, microfilm ed., reel 166 (Spain—Division of Western European Affairs).

increase in the number of British motor cars which have reached this market."[44]

Furthermore, Madrid's peculiar balance-of-payments position in the early 1930s dictated different commercial policies toward London and Washington. In 1933, for example, Spain continued to maintain a trade surplus with Britain of almost 75 million pesetas—in sharp contrast to its 84-million-peseta deficit with the United States. Consequently, although Spaniards might charge that the preferential treatment Britain accorded Palestinian orange growers was as objectionable as the American embargo on Almerian grapes, they recognized that a tariff war with the United Kingdom would be much more costly to Spanish exports than one with the United States. Not surprisingly, then, the Azaña regime discriminated against U.S. interests blatantly while it harassed British commerce more discreetly.

Finally, London's switch to an exclusive system of imperial preference at a time when trade expansionist sentiment was growing in Washington virtually ensured that Madrid's discriminatory commercial policies would arouse fewer objections at Whitehall than at the State Department. Convinced that bilateral agreements provided the only solution to international economic stagnation, British policy makers succeeded in creating a preferential trading bloc at Ottawa in 1932. American officials, on the other hand, opposed such exclusive policies and supported a program of multilateral most-favored-nation treatment instead. Hoping to reduce their own huge trade deficits, Spanish leaders pursued an autarchic strategy that more closely approximated Britain's new attitude than the commercial orthodoxy prevailing in the United States.

The contrast between Spain's cool economic relations with the United Kingdom and its commercial cold war with the United States provides a fairly accurate gauge of the overall standing of the Spanish Republic among British and American policy makers during the first two years of its existence. If officials on both sides of the Atlantic had been shocked by and suspicious about Spain's persistent political instability since 1931, Whitehall, unlike the White House, did not permit exaggerated accounts of bolshevik subversion to bedevil its relations with the Azaña regime. As a

[44] Adams, *Economic Conditions in Spain, 1933*, pp. 35–36; Jones, *Tariff Retaliation*, pp. 61–62.

result, even after Sir George Grahame and Irwin Laughlin finally agreed in early 1933 that the real threat to the republic was not communism but rather anarchism, London remained more cordial toward Madrid than did Washington. Similarly, the Foreign Office and the State Department were each outraged by repeated Spanish assaults on multinational investments in 1931 and 1932, but in handling such problems British officials displayed patience and propriety, both of which their American counterparts lacked. Consequently, Rio Tinto's troubles only soured Spain's relations with Great Britain; the ITT controversy poisoned those with the United States.

Two years of republican rule in Spain, then, had generated serious political and economic problems with Great Britain and the United States. The Azaña regime's inability to control the extreme left, its harassment of foreign investors, and its autarchic commercial program had raised hackles in London and had nearly produced a diplomatic breach with Washington. By the spring of 1933, however, the political tide at Madrid was surging to the right, sweeping conservatives into power and soothing policy makers on both sides of the Atlantic. As a result, during the next eighteen months both British and American relations with the Spanish Republic would improve markedly.

6

The Republic and the Reformist Right, 1933–1935

Worried by the Azaña regime's inability to restrain the revolutionary left, outraged by mistreatment of multinational corporations, and frustrated by discriminatory commercial policies, both the Foreign Office and the State Department were heartened by the rightward swing of the Spanish political pendulum in 1933. When a coalition of moderate and conservative republicans emerged from the polls triumphant in November, hope spread on both sides of the Atlantic that the new regime would resolve the many internal and international problems created by its predecessors. During the next two years such right-wing reformers as Alejandro Lerroux reversed many of Azaña's more controversial policies, dealt harshly with left-wing dissidents, and seemed by 1935 about to provide Spain with the political stability it had lacked for the better part of a decade. Spanish relations with both the United States and Great Britain improved accordingly, but prospects for lasting rapprochement were dashed later that year when charges of corruption and repression discredited the reformist right and opened the door to another round of ideological polarization.

I

By the spring of 1933 the Left Republican regime that had governed Spain for nearly two years was on its last legs. Disenchanted with Azaña's reluctance to pursue more radical reforms, militant young Socialists bent on revolutionary change drifted leftward. Wary of rural disorder and industrial strife, moderate republicans moved in the opposite direction, drawn rightward by the promise of law and order. Despite the splintering of his coalition, Manuel Azaña labored steadfastly to consolidate recent republican reforms. At his behest, the Cortes passed a fresh anticlerical bill outlawing all religious teaching orders in May and imposed government regulation of rural rents to protect tenant farmers two months later. But such legislation was regarded as too mild by the left and too harsh by the right. Caught in a withering political crossfire, the Azaña regime suffered a humiliating defeat at the polls in early September, when its candidates won fewer than one-third of the seats on the new Tribunal of Constitutional Guarantees, Spain's supreme court. President Niceto Alcalá-Zamora, who interpreted these returns as a repudiation of the Left Republican coalition, secured Azaña's resignation on 8 September 1933 and asked Alejandro Lerroux, the aging leader of the center-right Radical party, to form a new government.[1] Vexed by the chronic instability that had plagued the Spanish Republic since its inception, both British and American policy makers regarded this change as a harbinger of better relations.

While the Azaña regime crumbled and collapsed at Madrid, the new Roosevelt administration was busy consolidating itself in Washington. Although Franklin Roosevelt devoted most of his first year in office to domestic matters, he made several changes at the State Department that affected American relations with Spain. Cordell Hull, trade expansionist and back-country lawyer from Tennessee, succeeded Stimson as secretary of state while William Phillips, a Harvard-trained professional diplomat, replaced Castle as undersecretary. The only holdovers from the previous administration with any expertise regarding Spain were chief of the Division of Western European Affairs Pierrepont Moffat and John Wiley, the former counselor at Madrid who had recently taken over the Spanish desk from Ellis Briggs.[2]

The most important personnel change, however, occurred not within the State Department but at the American Embassy in Madrid, where Claude Bowers replaced Irwin Laughlin. A popular

---

[1] Jackson, *Spanish Republic*, pp. 110–15; Malefakis, *Agrarian Reform*, pp. 268–78; Robinson, *Origins of Franco's Spain*, pp. 124–26; Sanchez, *Reform and Reaction*, pp. 150–57.

[2] Hull, *Memoirs*, 1:352–54; William Phillips, *Ventures in Diplomacy* (Boston, 1952), pp. 3–6, 154–56; *State Department Register, 1934*, p. 15.

historian, partisan journalist, and life-long Jeffersonian liberal whose temperament and outlook contrasted sharply with those of his predecessor, Bowers received his ambassadorship as a reward for his yeoman service during the 1932 presidential campaign. He looked forward to spreading the democratic gospel south of the Pyrenees.[3] Eager to improve Spanish-American relations, the freshman ambassador called on his old friend Franklin Roosevelt on 2 May. The president proved equally "anxious to have Spain on our side of the table with us" but was nevertheless "greatly disturbed over the trend in the world toward dictatorships." Consequently, he asked Bowers to undertake a personal study of the current status of democracy in Spain and to contact the White House directly "whenever you find anything you think I should know." Convinced that with Roosevelt's backing he could engineer a rapprochement between Washington and Madrid, Bowers departed for Spain two weeks later.[4]

American observers at Madrid, however, remained deeply suspicious of the Azaña regime. Chargé d'Affaires Joseph Flack warned in early May that the Spanish Republic was on the verge of an unspecified "dictatorship." His fear was shared by businessmen, among them Cornelius Vanderbilt, who from his luxury suite atop the Ritz predicted "a strong fight by Russian communists and German and Italian fascists for the control of Spain."[5] Augustin M. Ferrin, the consul at Malaga, offered an even grimmer assessment that spring: "What appears at this writing the most probable development," he cautioned John Wiley on 17 May, "is that the Socialists will continue their socialization of Spain until it provokes a spontaneous rising of all the non-Leninist classes."[6]

Upon his arrival at Madrid in late May Claude Bowers took issue with such gloomy forecasts and attempted to use his personal in-

---

[3] Claude G. Bowers, *My Life: The Memoirs of Claude Bowers* (New York, 1962), pp. 1–26, 249–63; Douglas Little, "Claude Bowers and His Mission to Spain: The Diplomacy of a Jeffersonian Democrat," in K. Paul Jones, ed., *U.S. Diplomats in Europe, 1919–1941* (Santa Barbara, Calif., 1981), pp. 130–32.

[4] Claude G. Bowers, Diary, 2 May 1933, Claude G. Bowers Papers, Lilly Library, Indiana University, Bloomington, Indiana; Bowers, *My Life*, p. 265.

[5] Flack to Hull, 10 May 1933, 852.00/1933; Vanderbilt to Secretary of Commerce Daniel Roper, 21 April 1933, enclosed in Roper to Hull, 5 May 1933, 852.00/1931, NA RG59. Vanderbilt, a self-styled "revolution expert," had stopped off in Madrid during his annual tour of Europe.

[6] Ferrin to Wiley, 17 May 1933, Wiley Papers, Box 7 (General Correspondence—"F").

fluence to dispel the mutual misunderstandings that had bedeviled Spanish-American relations since 1931. Distressed that "all Americans here are against democracy and republicanism" and outraged in particular that "our ambassadors here have been high flying monarchists for years and never more so than since the advent of the republic," the historian-turned-diplomat "did not endeavor to conceal a certain sympathy for left republicans and even socialists." Determined to erase the "stuffed shirt" image associated with his predecessor, Bowers stripped away the pomp and formality so dear to Laughlin and impressed both Spaniards and Americans alike as "a democrat, accessible and friendly, who sits at his typewriter, sucking an unlit cigar, and hammers out his own dispatches with two aching finger tips." Such charming geniality and democratic proclivities "made an unusual appeal to the Spanish," especially among kindred spirits like Prime Minister Azaña, whom Bowers termed "a genius in government." Indeed, Bowers could assure Roosevelt as early as 28 June that despite the dire predictions of some American observers, there was "not the slightest possibility of either a communistic or a fascist dictatorship" in Spain.[7]

As the political fortunes of the Left Republicans waned, Bowers likened their travail to that of the Jeffersonians in late eighteenth-century America and hoped that Azaña would prevail over Spain's Hamiltonians. "There are extreme parties and elements but nothing extreme has been done thus far from our American point of view," he wrote his old friend and fellow ambassador Josephus Daniels in early July. "They have confiscated the surplus land of the great land hogs, but that is essential."[8] Other Americans, however, did not share Bowers's faith in the Azaña regime. "Acts of violence," ITT's Frank Page warned Undersecretary Phillips on 12 July, "take place with unusual frequency" in the Spanish countryside. Military Attaché R. H. Fletcher confirmed a week later that

---

[7] Bowers, Diary, 31 May 1933, Bowers Papers; Bowers to Josephus Daniels, 3 July 1933, Josephus Daniels Papers, Box 67, Library of Congress, Washington, D.C.; Louis Fischer, Writings of Louis Fischer 1935–1939—Spanish Diary 1936, Box 36, Louis Fischer Papers, Seeley G. Mudd Manuscript Library, Princeton University, Princeton, New Jersey; Bowers to Roosevelt, 28 June 1933, in Edgar B. Nixon, ed., *Franklin D. Roosevelt and Foreign Affairs*, 3 vols. (Cambridge, Mass., 1969), 1:259–61 (hereafter cited as *FDR & Foreign Affairs*).
[8] Bowers to Daniels, 3 July 1933, Daniels Papers, Box 67.

the Left Republicans were losing their grip on the situation.[9] As late as 2 August Bowers could assure the White House that Azaña remained the "strong man of Spain," but at month's end Fletcher foresaw conditions "similar to gang warfare on a large scale" unless the republican regime took "energetic action soon."[10] Even Bowers admitted long afterward that by early September Azaña "had run the parliamentary machinery at high speed" for too long and that Lerroux, "a benevolent and easy boss," was likely to replace him soon. Relieved at last that "the drift was strongly to the right" at Madrid, the State Department viewed Lerroux's ascendancy later that month as "a sign of stability and strength."[11]

Although the Foreign Office, in contrast to the State Department, had shown much respect for Azaña's reformist program and able leadership down through early 1933, British officials were reluctantly agreeing before the year was out that only a more conservative regime could restore order to Spain. Whitehall's faith began to ebb in May when Sir George Grahame reported "premonitory signs" of a "general crisis," especially among Madrid's moderates, who expressed "great uncertainty and some discouragement" regarding the intentions of the left. Convinced nonetheless that the Azaña government still desired "a closer parallelism between British and Spanish policies in a general sense," Grahame warned Whitehall that any sign of "antagonism to the Republican regime" might drive Spain to align itself more closely with France. Although Permanent Undersecretary Robert Vansittart denied any "intention whatever of altering our present policy towards Spain, which is one of friendly encouragement of her efforts to put her own house in order," he did instruct Grahame on 2 June to apply "firm but patient pressure to secure fair treatment for our own interests where they are affected."[12]

By the summer of 1933, however, most British officials were convinced that the Left Republicans had stumbled into political

[9] Page to Phillips, 12 July 1933, 851.00/1227, NA RG59; Fletcher to G-2, 21 July 1933, 2657 S.126/70, NA RG165.
[10] Bowers to Roosevelt, 2 August 1933, *FDR & Foreign Affairs*, 1:342–43; Fletcher to G-2, 26 August 1933, 2657 S.123/22, NA RG165.
[11] Bowers, *My Mission to Spain*, pp. 34, 38; memorandum by Phillips, 28 September 1933, 852.00/1954, NA RG59.
[12] Grahame to Simon, tel. 3 May 1933, W4820/74/41; 6 May 1933, W5321/116/41; and 5 May 1933, and Vansittart to Grahame, 2 June 1933, W5425/116/41, PRO FO371, vols. 17424 and 17426.

quicksand. Chargé de'Affaires Courtenay Forbes reported in early July that Azaña's inability to placate either the extremists or the moderates ensured the disintegration of his coalition, a forecast that worried Whitehall, where it was believed that the prime minister "could not easily be replaced without bloodshed." As the summer drew to a close, even Grahame confessed that Azaña's days in office were numbered. When the axe finally fell in September, the Foreign Office interpreted the formation of Lerroux's center-right cabinet as "a hopeful sign" because the new regime seemed likely to follow "a quiet path."[13]

Such British and American hopes proved a bit premature, for Spain endured yet another season of turmoil as Lerroux and the reformist right struggled to thwart the left at the polls. Sensing an opportunity to deal Azaña's rickety anticlerical coalition a death blow, President Alcalá-Zamora dissolved the Cortes in early October and scheduled parliamentary elections for 19 November 1933. As expected, the left fragmented into reformist and revolutionary wings and failed to field a unified slate of candidates. The right, on the other hand, spearheaded by José María Gil Robles and his Confederación Española de Derechas Autónomas (CEDA), created a broad coalition of monarchists and clerical republicans. It ran on a single ticket appealing to Spain's frightened middle class. As a result, in perhaps the fairest Spanish elections in a century, Gil Robles and his allies won 201 seats in the new Cortes, Lerroux's Radical party returned 104 deputies, and the Socialists placed a distant third with 58. Azaña's own Left Republicans claimed only 5 seats. Despite his impressive victory, Gil Robles commanded neither a parliamentary majority nor the respect of Alcalá-Zamora, who questioned his commitment to the republic and turned instead to Lerroux to form a government. Confident that the CEDA still held the balance of power, Gil Robles acquiesced, Lerroux took office once again on 19 December, and policy makers on both sides of the Atlantic hoped Spain's long political crisis had come to an end.[14]

[13]Forbes to Simon, 7 July 1933, and minute by A. W. A. Leeper, 17 July 1933, W8280/116/41; Grahame to Simon, tel. 8 September 1933, W10251/116/41; minute by Philip Leigh-Smith, 12 September 1933, W10357/116/41; minute by C. N. Stirling, 20 September 1933, W10650/116/41, PRO FO371, vols. 17426 and 17427.
[14]Jackson, *Spanish Republic*, pp. 116–20, 520–21; Robinson, *Origins of Franco's Spain*, pp. 140–57; Arrarás, *Historia de la segunda república*, 2:208–217.

The outcome of the elections was neither unexpected nor unwelcome in Washington. In spite of his own sympathy for the Azaña regime, Claude Bowers advised the State Department on 28 November that the conservative triumph resulted from popular rejection of "the extreme social policies" initiated by a Cortes "hopelessly out of tune with the country." The Socialists, he explained, had "overshot the mark and incurred a bitter and desperate opposition which . . . finally rallied around Señor Gil Robles and the admirable organization which he devised." Furthermore, Bowers assured Roosevelt two weeks later, recent events meant "a more conservative republican policy" but "nothing like a restoration of the monarchy." The return of Lerroux, whom Bowers called a "very good friend" and "a typical American politician [*sic*]," seemed in particular to augur well for improved relations between Spain and the United States.[15]

The Lerroux regime demonstrated shortly thereafter that such optimism was well-founded, by moving to resolve a dispute that had kept Madrid and Washington at odds for more than six months. Following a fracas with local units of the Civil Guard at Palma de Mallorca the previous June, five drunken American artists had been jailed for forty-six days without bail and had then been remanded to a military court for trial. Citing "wide spread [*sic*] indignation . . . both in the press and in Congress" over the handling of the case, Secretary of State Hull had warned that American opinion was "being embittered all out of proportion to the gravity of the offense." Prime Minister Azaña, however, had repeatedly declined to intercede on behalf of the five defendants.[16] Lerroux, once he had taken over the government in September, agreed to expedite the proceedings. "I will do everything I can within the law," he promised Bowers "and outside it, if necessary." The election campaign delayed matters, but two months after Lerroux returned as prime minister in December he "kept his word" and pardoned the Americans, a gesture of good faith Azaña had

---

[15]Bowers to Hull, 28 November 1933, 852.00/1964, NA RG59; Bowers to Roosevelt, 13 December 1933, Franklin D. Roosevelt Papers, Official File 303, Franklin D. Roosevelt Presidential Library (hereafter cited as FDR Papers, OF, with appropriate file number).

[16]Bowers to Phillips, tel. 15 July 1933, and 1 August 1933; Hull to Bowers, tel. 7 September 1933, *FRUS, 1933*, 2:708–12.

been unwilling to make.[17] This subtle improvement in Spanish-American relations did not go unnoticed at the White House. "I am glad to see," Roosevelt wrote Bowers on 5 February 1934, "that Spain seems to be going along all right with the change of government."[18]

Weary of the constant tumult in Spain, British officials also anticipated a surge to the right in the autumn of 1933. Sir George Grahame, no friend of the Spanish conservatives, admitted early in the campaign that a center-right victory at the polls probably offered the best hope "of preventing the country from falling into chaos." By early November Whitehall expected the Left Republicans to be soundly defeated in a "three-cornered struggle" on election day. "All the indications are that Señor Azaña and the advanced radicals will be swept away," the Western Department's J. W. Nicholls observed on the eve of the balloting, "and the real interest of the elections will be to see how far the reaction against socialism will play into the hands of the clericals and conservatives."[19] Although surprised by "the unexpected extent of the success of the reactionaries," Ambassador Grahame was quick to point out that the the decisive issue had been law and order, not "the Republic versus the Monarchy." Interpreting the outcome as "a success for the Church rather than the Monarchy," Whitehall now believed the real question to be "Will Spain produce a Salazar?"[20]

The answer at first seemed to be "no." Fearful that renewed conflict between the Socialists and Gil Robles' CEDA would paralyze the reformist right, Grahame warned that "there are not quiet times ahead in this country." The healthy vote of confidence for Lerroux's cabinet in late December, however, was an encouraging sign. As the year drew to a close, Spanish expert C. N. Stirling

---

[17]Bowers to Hull, tel. 19 September 1933, 21 January 1934, tel. 23 January 1934, and tel. 3 February 1934, *FRUS, 1933*, 2:713–18; Bowers, *My Mission to Spain*, p. 38.

[18] Roosevelt to Bowers, 5 February 1934, in Elliott Roosevelt, ed., *F.D.R.: His Personal Letters, 1928–1945*, 2 vols. (New York, 1950), 1:389 (hereafter cited as *FDR, Personal Letters*).

[19]Grahame to Leeper, 10 October 1933, W11842/1318/41; Grahame to Simon, 9 November 1933, and minute by Nicholls, 16 November 1933, W12998/116/41, PRO FO371, vols. 17427 and 17430.

[20]Grahame to Simon, 21 November 1933, W13297/116/41, and 24 November 1933, and minute by Nicholls, 2 December 1933, W13657/116/41, PRO FO371, vol. 17427.

believed that this "swing to moderate conservatism in a country of violent political feeling" meant that "the outlook for a stable govt. in Spain is brighter."[21] As if to confirm Stirling's forecast, progress was made within a month on several outstanding British claims stemming from the 1931 anticlerical riots, prompting Whitehall to conclude that the "moderate" Lerroux regime was "more likely than previous Governments" to bring about better relations with Great Britain. If by early 1934 Lerroux was not yet a Spanish Salazar, the Foreign Office could take heart that neither was he a Spanish Kerensky.[22]

After nearly three years of left-wing disorder, then, the emergence of an impressive center-right coalition at Madrid came as something of a relief in both London and Washington. Even Claude Bowers and Sir George Grahame, who shared a common sympathy for Azaña and the Left Republicans, admitted reluctantly that Lerroux and the moderate right would reverse only the most radical republican reforms and would employ strictly constitutional means. The State Department was delighted that Spain had become "serene and lawful" during the spring of 1934, as was the Foreign Office, which remained confident that the Lerroux regime would "have a chance as long as the parties of the Right are content to play a waiting game and support a moderate policy."[23] Much to the dismay of policy makers on both sides of the Atlantic, however, neither the right nor the left exhibited much moderation in the months that followed.

II

While British and American observers watched anxiously, the new regime at Madrid wasted little time in reversing many Left

---

[21] Grahame to Simon, 12 December 1933, W14192/116/41, and tel. 22 December 1933, and minute by Stirling, 28 December 1933, W14654/116/41, PRO FO371, vol. 17427.

[22] Minute by Stirling, 2 January 1934, W14776/116/41; Leeper to Sir Evelyn Wallers (Santander and Mediterranean Railway), 2 January 1934, W14561/74/41; minute by Nicholls, 16 January 1934, W12849/250/41, PRO FO371, vols. 17424, 17427, and 17428.

[23] Bowers to R. Walton Moore, 12 February 1934, R. Walton Moore Papers, Box 3, Franklin D. Roosevelt Presidential Library; minute by Stirling, 5 February 1934, W1185/27/41, PRO FO371, vol. 18595.

Republican reforms. In short order Lerroux restored public stipends for parish priests, permitted rural wages to slip back to prerevolutionary levels, and promised to deal with popular disorders harshly. But when Gil Robles and the CEDA pressured the reformist right in April to pardon all the conspirators involved in the abortive Sanjurjo uprising two years earlier, President Alcalá-Zamora rebuked Lerroux for freeing known enemies of the republic. The prime minister angrily resigned on 25 April and was replaced by Ricardo Samper, a Valencian Radical with questionable parliamentary skills and little experience in national politics.[24]

Throughout the spring of 1934 British and American officials had shared the hope that Lerroux and the reformist right would prevail over the radicals at both ends of the ideological spectrum. Discounting rumors of "an inevitable struggle between the extremes of Left and Right," Sir George Grahame as late as March saw "nothing sufficiently definite to warrant real alarm."[25] Although wary of "reactionaries" like Gil Robles, who seemed bent on "knocking the Constitution into a cocked hat" and imposing autocratic rule, Claude Bowers likewise reported that conditions at Madrid were presently "much quieter" than under Azaña, largely because Lerroux had adopted a "strong line of action" against left-wing troublemakers.[26] "From what we hear in Washington," one State Department official remarked with obvious relief, "the general situation in Spain is much better than in most nations."[27] Convinced that the Lerroux regime was "neither dominated by the Right nor weak," Whitehall too was increasingly confident that a solution to Spain's nagging political troubles would "eventually be found by Parliamentary means" without resorting to a "strong Govt. of dictatorial character."[28]

Lerroux's resignation and Samper's ascendancy quickly demonstrated that such optimism was premature. Greeted by a fresh

[24] Brenan, *Spanish Labyrinth*, pp. 265–70; Jackson, *Spanish Republic*, pp. 122–24, 130–32; Preston, *Coming of the Spanish Civil War*, pp. 97–108.

[25] Minute by Stirling, 21 February 1934, W1781/27/41; Counselor George Mounsey (London) to Grahame, tel. 12 March 1934, W2466/27/41; Grahame to Simon, tel. 12 March 1934, W2467/27/41, PRO FO371, vol. 18595.

[26] Bowers to Hull, 28 March 1934, 852.00/1989, NA RG59; Bowers, Diary, 12 and 22 April 1934, Bowers Papers.

[27] R. Walton Moore to Bowers, 2 March 1934, Moore Papers.

[28] Minute by Stirling, 1 March 1934, W2101/27/41; "Spanish Politics, 1931–1934," by Stirling, 17 March 1934, W2654/27/41; Grahame to Simon, 21 March 1934, and minute by Leigh-Smith, 27 March 1934, W2912/27/41, PRO FO371, vol. 18595.

wave of left-wing disorders, the new prime minister responded by jailing hundreds of workers and peasants later that spring and summer. Spanish Socialists, who interpreted such repression as proof that the republic was now controlled by the reactionary rather than the reformist right, began to smuggle arms along the Biscayan coast in August and September. Meanwhile, conservative republicans like Gil Robles and royalists like José Calvo Sotelo stepped up their own criticism of the government for failing to punish the left-wing opposition even more severely. With Samper powerless to prevent a new round of ideological polarization, Spain seemed by the autumn of 1934 on the verge of political cataclysm.[29]

Whitehall and the White House were understandably dismayed by the erosion of the center-right coalition of republican moderates that had seemed so promising earlier in the year. For a time American observers believed that Samper had weathered Spain's most recent crisis "more successfully than we had feared," but his inability to prevent "terrorist crimes and excesses" left little doubt in Washington that his days were numbered.[30] Worried because "practically the whole proletariat" had expressed "violent hostility" toward Samper's new "middle class Government," Sir George Grahame likewise warned London that conditions in Spain were "neither normal nor satisfactory." As early as June the Foreign Office conceded that the Spanish situation was "potentially extremely dangerous"; four months later U.K. officials agreed that "the signs of impatience" with Samper's weak leadership were "getting ominous."[31] It was Claude Bowers, however, who expressed most bluntly the dark mixture of disgust and foreboding that colored British and American views of the increasingly rickety regime at Madrid. "Samper has both the features and the brain of a frog," the Hoosier Democrat told Roosevelt on 19 September. His cabinet "will fall, and it will have no mourners," Bowers

---

[29]Robinson, *Origins of Franco's Spain*, pp. 164–81; Jackson, *Spanish Republic*, pp. 122–24, 130–32; Preston, *Coming of the Spanish Civil War*, pp. 97–108.

[30]Moffat, Diplomatic Journals, 27 April 1934, Moffat Papers; Moffat to Bowers, 7 May 1934, Bowers Papers; Military Attaché Stephen Fuqua to G-2, 30 May 1934, 2657 S.126/94, NA RG165.

[31]Grahame to Simon, 27 April 1934, W4329/27/41, and 23 May 1934, W5170/27/41; minute by Nicholls, 13 June 1934, W5650/27/41; Grahame to Simon, 23 September 1934, and minute by Stirling, 1 October 1934, W8621/27/41, PRO FO371, vols. 18595 and 18596.

prophesied, but "just what will happen then is on the lap of the gods."[32]

Such misgivings soon proved well-founded. On 1 October Gil Robles made good on a long-standing threat to withdraw support from the Samper regime and then refused during the ensuing cabinet crisis to endorse Lerroux's latest government until President Alcalá-Zamora conceded the CEDA three ministerial posts. Having repeatedly warned that they would regard any CEDA role in the cabinet as a betrayal of the republic to its clerical enemies, the Socialists called for a nationwide general strike. To the north, in the Asturias, armed miners seized the provincial capital of Oviedo, while at Barcelona Luis Companys, a left-wing separatist, proclaimed the autonomous state of Catalonia. By 6 October 1934 Spain was in the throes of a major revolutionary upheaval.[33]

As he had during his previous tenure, Prime Minister Lerroux moved swiftly against the revolutionary left. In a matter of hours he imposed censorship, decreed martial law, and unleashed the army against the left-wing rebels. Although the uprising soon burned itself out in Madrid and Barcelona, where the left had remained disunited, the fighting raged for over a week in the Asturias, where the Socialists had forged an alliance with their long-time anarchist rivals. A crack battalion of Moorish troops finally crushed the Asturian revolution in mid-October after a campaign of rape and torture that left over one thousand dead. With the left-wing press gagged and thirty thousand dissidents awaiting trial, the Lerroux regime was firmly in control of the country at month's end.[34] The abortive revolution bolstered Lerroux's standing as a republican strong man and discredited the Spanish left on both sides of the Atlantic.

The revolutionary uprising came as no surprise to American observers, who had monitored the mounting tension at Madrid for months. Claude Bowers warned Washington in early October that any CEDA participation in the government was likely to spark an "immediate socialist revolutionary general strike," and once the

---

[32] Bowers to Roosevelt, 19 September 1934, *FDR & Foreign Affairs*, 2:218.
[33] Paul Preston, "Spain's October Revolution and the Rightist Grasp for Power," *Journal of Contemporary History* 10 (October 1975), 555–78; Peers, *Spanish Tragedy*, pp. 161–68; Robinson, *Origins of Franco's Spain*, pp. 188–92.
[34] Jackson, *Spanish Republic*, pp. 143–53; Brenan, *Spanish Labyrinth*, pp. 282–84; Payne, *Spanish Revolution*, pp. 150–52.

Catholics joined Lerroux's cabinet he concluded that "it looks like real trouble." With the revolutionary left "growing steadily stronger" and the country "rapidly drifting into . . . civil war," Bowers telephoned Hull on 6 October to emphasize that the outcome of the crisis depended largely on Lerroux, who was "holding firm and preparing to act with great vigor."[35] The next day it was clear at the State Department that "the forces of the loyal government" were growing "stronger with time." By nightfall on 8 October Bowers confirmed that the worst seemed to be over everywhere except the Asturias, and two days later ITT's Frank Page reported that conditions in Spain were "rapidly approaching normal."[36]

The implications of the abortive left-wing revolt were not immediately clear to American officials. Some, such as Chargé d'Affaires Alexander Magruder at Lisbon and Consul General Claude Dawson at Barcelona, believed that the swift repression visited upon the Spanish left would ensure political stability throughout the Iberian Peninsula.[37] Others, such as Pierrepont Moffat in Washington, worried that Gil Robles and the CEDA might overestimate their own power, demand "a new Government more to the Right with a strong military tinge," and in the process touch off further disorders. Most, however, agreed with Claude Bowers that the unsuccessful uprising would probably strengthen the republic, since Lerroux's forceful actions had chastened critics on the left and reassured skeptics on the right.[38]

Indeed, as Christmas drew near, Bowers, his Jeffersonian proclivities notwithstanding, was becoming more sympathetic toward Lerroux, Gil Robles, and the Spanish right. "My impression is that the republic has been greatly strengthened by the manner in which

[35] Bowers, Diary, 4 October 1934, Bowers Papers; Bowers to Hull, tel. 4 October 1934, 852.00/2025; "Memorandum of Telephone Conversation between the Secretary of State and Ambassador Bowers, October 6, 1934," by Moffat, 8 October 1934, 852.00/2039, NA RG59.

[36] Moffat, Diplomatic Journals, 6/7 October 1934, Moffat Papers; Bowers to Hull, tel. 8 October 1934, 852.00/2037; memorandum for Hull by Moffat, 8 October 1934, 852.00/2042; Page to Moffat, tel. 10 October 1934, 852.00/2047, NA RG59.

[37] Magruder to Hull, 13 October 1934, 852.00/2064; Dawson to Hull, 15 October 1934, 852.00/2065, NA RG59.

[38] Memorandum by Moffat, 17 October 1934, 852.00/2052; Bowers to Hull, tel. 19 October 1934, 852.00/2053, NA RG59; Bowers, Diary, 20 October 1934, Bowers Papers.

it put down the socialist revolution," he wrote fellow journalist Arthur Krock on 11 December, "and by the fact that [Gil] Robles has gone republican to such an extent that the monarchists here hate him." The extreme left, Bowers told his old friend Josephus Daniels that same day, was more responsible than the right for the October carnage. Noting that even Azaña regarded the left-wing uprising as "suicidal and stupid," Bowers stressed that the threat constituted by the presence of three CEDA ministers in the cabinet "was not great enough to justify a resort to arms." Nevertheless, Socialist leader Francisco Largo Caballero, who had "gone over so far to the extreme left that he is really a communist," had touched off a revolt that discredited not only his own party but Azaña's Left Republicans as well. Fortunately, however, no widespread military bloodbath ensued, thanks mainly to Lerroux, whose restraint convinced Bowers that moderation, not reaction, would be the watchword at Madrid.[39]

British officials, like their American counterparts, never doubted the outcome of the left-wing rebellion. Sir George Grahame assured Whitehall that the "subversive movement" which exploded on 5 October was doomed to failure and prophesied, as had Bowers, that Lerroux and Gil Robles "would be masters of Spain for some time to come." At the Western Department C. N. Stirling was heartened because "the comparative ease with which the various revolutionary movements . . . have been suppressed" demonstrated that "Spain contains a larger backbone of solid law-abiding citizens than the frequency of these outbreaks would lead one to suppose." By mid-October Grahame confirmed that with Lerroux firmly in control, conditions in Spain had "cleared up" and were "much more normal."[40]

In London as in Washington Lerroux's victory was greeted with mixed emotions. "The liberals of all shades have been crushed & discredited," Stirling wrote on 16 October, "& the triumph of the

---

[39]Bowers to Krock, 11 December 1934, Arthur Krock Papers, Box 18 (Correspondence—Bowers), Seeley G. Mudd Manuscript Library, Princeton University; Bowers to Daniels, 11 December 1934, Daniels Papers, Box 67.

[40]Grahame to Simon, tel. 6 October 1934, W8910/27/41, and tel. 7 October 1934, W8934/27/41; minute by Stirling, 8 October 1934, W8926/27/41; Grahame to Simon, tel. 8 October 1934, W8945/27/41, and tel. 11 October 1934, W9052/27/41, PRO FO371, vol. 18596.

Right may give Spain at last some model of orderly government."
Yet, he continued, the country was still in desperate need of reform, and with the "progressive forces" now "branded as potential
enemies of law & order," the outlook for "peaceful development in
the long run" seemed bleak. Assistant Undersecretary of State
Orme Sargent, on the other hand, was much less equivocal. "The
Spanish people in enjoyment of universal suffrage," he thundered,
had "returned a Chamber with a definite conservative tendency."
Rather than "submitting to the will of the people," however, the
revolutionary left "preferred to resort to arms to overthrow the
Government" and thereby demonstrated an utter disregard for
"democratic parliamentar[ism]." Notwithstanding such quibbles,
most British officials acknowledged that "the elements of the
Centre and the Moderate Right have all the cards in their hand"
and felt that "if they could only agree to play them properly they
ought to have a chance of giving Spain a period of orderly government."[41]

Throughout 1934, then, both the Foreign Office and the State
Department held out the hope that the reformist right would provide the stability and the order which the Spanish Republic had
lacked since its inception. To be sure, Lerroux's sudden resignation
in April, Samper's inept six-month interregnum, and Largo Caballero's ill-fated rebellion in October worried policy makers on both
sides of the Atlantic, but the resurgence of the right-wing moderates that autumn augured well for more cordial British and American relations with Spain during the new year. Despite his own
liberal sympathies, Bowers confirmed in November that the new
and more conservative republican officials at Madrid had been "exceedingly friendly to me." With Spain adrift in a sea of "post-
revolutionary confusion," Whitehall agreed that the present government was "struggling to keep to the path of moderation."[42] The
central question in London and Washington was whether the Lerroux regime was making for a safe port or slipping into deeper
water.

[41] Minute by Stirling, 16 October 1934, and minute by Sargent, 19 October 1934,
W9132/27/41; minute by Stirling, 2 November 1934, W9526/27/41, PRO FO371, vols.
18596 and 18597.
[42] Bowers to Roosevelt, 21 November 1934, *FDR & Foreign Affairs*, 2:279; minute by
I. P. Garran, 30 November 1934, W10313/27/41, PRO FO371, vol. 18597.

III

During the first half of 1935 Lerroux performed a delicate balancing act that placated his left- and right-wing critics at home and reassured skeptics abroad that he intended to steer a center course. He acquiesced, for example, in reactionary legislation evicting tenant farmers from their leaseholds and restoring religious properties to the Jesuits, yet he refused to carry out death sentences against twenty leftists involved in the recent armed uprising in the Asturias. After some bickering with the CEDA in May, Lerroux reorganized his cabinet, giving Gil Robles a portfolio for the first time as minister of war but appointing Joaquín Chapaprieta, a moderate republican lawyer, as minister of finance. By mid-summer this center-right coalition was calling for further modifications in the anticlerical statutes, stronger guarantees for private property, and the creation of a republican senate as a bulwark against unicameral radicalism. Moreover, the economy-minded Chapaprieta pressed for fiscal austerity and a balanced budget by abolishing hundreds of government sinecures, slashing civil service salaries, and hiking inheritance taxes. Despite much grumbling among discredited reformers and disgruntled bureaucrats, the Lerroux regime had by the autumn of 1935 shown Spaniards and foreigners alike that both political stability and economic solvency were possible under moderate republican rule.[43]

Impressed by Lerroux's political acumen and Chapaprieta's economic wizardry, American officials welcomed the return of law and order engineered by the reformist right. Claude Bowers cited the cessation of the "mad-dog persecutions growing out of the [Asturian] revolution" and the commutation of the death sentences meted out to its leaders as proof that Spain now possessed "a truly republican government." Indeed, he told Hull in April 1935, the present Lerroux regime was "one of the best from the point of view of technical ability that has been formed under the Republic."[44] Hallett Johnson, a Columbia-trained career diplomat and chief aide

[43] Jackson, *Spanish Republic*, pp. 166–73; Robinson, *Origins of Franco's Spain*, pp. 193–98, 205–6; Brenan, *Spanish Labyrinth*, pp. 289–92; Benavides, *Política económica*, pp. 124–29.

[44] Bowers to Hull, tel. 1 April 1935, 852.00/2093, tel. 3 April 1935, 852.00/2094, and 8 April 1935, 852.00 P.R./389, NA RG59.

to Bowers at Madrid, agreed in June that the current center-right cabinet was Spain's strongest in years and was likely to "continue in power for some time." Both Lerroux and Gil Robles, Johnson emphasized, "realize the need of a stable Government to liquidate the effects of the October revolution and to face the disorder and crime which are notable in Barcelona and . . . other parts of the country as well." Although Bowers had begun to question the republicanism of Gil Robles and the other CEDA ministers, he was forced to admit at the end of July that the Lerroux regime had achieved its paramount objective, the restoration of order.[45]

Washington was understandably heartened by the "more settled political conditions" at Madrid. Progress on mutual trade disputes and favorable American press coverage of the Lerroux regime suggested that relations between the United States and Spain were gradually improving. As late as 19 November 1935 a Treasury Department study would stress that despite persistent economic woes, the "political situation in Spain has greatly improved since the advent of the republic in 1931." Although the "possibility of conflict between the conservative groups now in power and the radical elements" was always present, the report concluded that Lerroux and his colleagues had "shown their strength by putting down the disturbances of October and November 1934" and had since indicated their intention to steer a moderate course between revolution on the left and reaction on the right.[46]

British observers were at first less optimistic than their American counterparts that moderation would prevail in Spain. In January 1935 Sir George Grahame reported a "disquieting state of affairs" at Madrid. He warned that the left and the right regarded each other "with sullen hatred" and likened the Lerroux regime to "a heavy stage coach being slowly dragged by tired horses over a dilapidated road with deep holes and ruts which have to be avoided as far as possible." Sir Maurice Peterson, the new head of the

---

[45]Johnson to Hull, 2 July 1935, 852.00/2104; Bowers to Hull, 31 July 1935, 852.00/2106, NA RG59. On Johnson's background see Johnson, *Diplomatic Memoirs*, pp. 9–15, 106–8.

[46]William Lingelbach, "Conservative Rule in Spain," *Current History* 42 (September 1935), 655–57; memorandum for the secretary of the treasury by "E. G. C.," 19 November 1935, General Records of the Department of the Treasury, General Correspondence of the Secretary, "Spain—Fin & Econ Data," Record Group 56, National Archives, Suitland, Maryland (hereafter cited as NA RG56).

Western Department, saw signs of "communist subversion" in Spain that winter and complained as late as 11 April that "the Republic has so far failed to produce a stable administration."[47] The emergence in May of a Radical-CEDA partnership committed to reversing earlier republican reforms by "Constitutional means," however, suggested to both Grahame and his superiors that the Lerroux regime was now "the best safeguard against a complete reaction" at Madrid. "What remains to be seen," Spanish expert C. N. Stirling emphasized on 17 May, "is whether the Radicals & the Catholics can cooperate effectively."[48]

While Lerroux struggled to tame both the left and the right at Madrid, Stanley Baldwin finally succeeded in reshuffling the British cabinet in London. The Conservative leader, who replaced the ailing Ramsay MacDonald as prime minister on 7 June, named fellow-Tory Sir Samuel Hoare to succeed the Liberal Simon as foreign secretary but made few other changes at Whitehall.[49] Britain's own drift to the right had little impact on its relations with Spain that summer, and Grahame was quick to assure Hoare that Madrid wished to remain on friendly terms with London. Although Spain was "still far from being in a normal condition," Grahame did believe by early July that the Lerroux regime would prevent further polarization by "increasing its influence with the middle class" and by placating the workers with measures resembling "Christian socialism." With the approach of autumn the Foreign Office, like the State Department, concluded that "it would clearly be for the good of the country if the Radicals and Catholics could continue to sink their differences in order to give Spain a period of non-contentious, practical government."[50]

This relatively stable interlude, which had blossomed in early 1935 after half a decade of stormy weather, nevertheless withered much sooner than anyone on either side of the Atlantic had ex-

[47]Grahame to Simon, 28 January 1935, W1074/18/41, and 31 January 1935, W1079/18/41; Peterson to Grahame, 4 February 1935, W1039/18/41; minute by Peterson, 11 April 1935, W3141/18/41, PRO FO371, vol. 19735.
[48]Grahame to Simon, 9 May 1935, and minute by Stirling, 17 May 1935, W4139/18/41; Grahame to Simon, 9 May 1935, minute by Stirling, 17 May 1935, W4140/18/41, PRO FO371, vol. 19736.
[49]Middlemas and Barnes, *Baldwin*, pp. 821–25; Norman Rose, *Vansittart: Study of a Diplomat* (London, 1978), pp. 163–65; Viscount Templewood (Sir Samuel Hoare), *Nine Troubled Years* (London, 1954), pp. 107–10.
[50]Grahame to Hoare, 19 June 1935, W5498/18/41, and 2 July 1935, W5991/18/41; minute by Stirling, 20 August 1935, W7224/18/41, PRO FO371, vol. 19736.

pected, a victim not of modern ideological conflict but of old-fashioned political scandal. In late September rumors linking Prime Minister Lerroux to the Catalan underworld forced him to resign his post and return to the Foreign Ministry in a new cabinet headed by Chapaprieta. When fresh evidence surfaced a month later confirming that Lerroux and several associates had accepted bribes in return for granting licenses to operate a roulette-like gambling device called the *straperlo* and had also received kickbacks on army supply contracts, the old man had no choice but to retire from the government in disgrace. The *straperlo* scandal completely destroyed the Radical party and seemed to guarantee that the CEDA would at last be allowed to form a cabinet. Yet when the tottering Chapaprieta regime finally collapsed in mid-December, President Alcalá-Zamora bypassed Gil Robles once again, asked Manuel Portela Valladares, a Galician conservative, to head a caretaker government, and scheduled new elections for early 1936.[51] Spanish politics had come almost full circle since November 1933, with the crucial difference that now the discredited Radicals could provide no buffer between a vengeful left and a fearful right.

American officials condemned Lerroux's corrupt practices but lamented the demise of his Radical party. Claude Bowers predicted as early as September 1935 that the collapse of the reformist right would strengthen the hand of the "shifty" and increasingly "anti-democratic" Gil Robles, a forecast shared by John H. Morgan, the career foreign service officer who had recently succeeded John Wiley at the State Department's Spanish desk.[52] By late November Bowers confirmed that Chapaprieta's moderate coalition was "crumbling rapidly" and two weeks later complained that "disunion exists everywhere." Gil Robles and his CEDA, now openly "hostile to democracy," threatened to "smash the revolution and forever exclude the Lefts from power." The "more extreme" Socialists, Bowers confessed, with their shrill cries that "the revolution must begin over again," were no better. The destruction of the center parties and the growing boldness of extremists at both ends of the ideological spectrum worried the historian-turned-diplomat,

---

[51] Arrarás, *Historia de la segunda república*, 3: 219–31, 264–70; Robinson, *Origins of Franco's Spain*, pp. 231–37; Peers, *Spanish Tragedy*, pp. 181–86.

[52] Bowers, Diary, 13 September 1935, Bowers Papers; Bowers to Hull, 30 October 1935, and attached memorandum for Hull by Morgan, 14 November 1935, 852.00/2116, NA RG59.

who concluded grimly that "the political future of the new republic presents a gloomy picture."[53] For more than two years Bowers had labored valiantly to improve relations between Washington and Madrid, only to see his efforts thwarted by Spain's seemingly incurable political instability.

British disappointment with the collapse of moderate rule at Madrid during the autumn of 1935 was equally great. Sir Henry Chilton, a fifty-eight-year-old career "diplomatist of the old school" with prior service in Chile and Argentina, had succeeded Sir George Grahame as ambassador to Spain upon the latter's retirement in August. If his penchant for "showing the Embassy flag socially" and his profound conservatism contrasted sharply with Grahame's liberal disdain for aristocratic privilege, Chilton nevertheless shared his predecessor's belief that for the time being Lerroux and the reformist right offered the only real hope for stable government at Madrid. The new ambassador, who had the misfortune to present his credentials in the midst of the *straperlo* crisis, took pains to assure Whitehall that Foreign Minister Lerroux had promised to maintain "the best possible relations with Great Britain," but the Spaniard's resignation shortly thereafter deepened the gloom in London.[54]

Few at the Foreign Office believed that the Chapaprieta regime could weather the ensuing tempest. Certain that the scandal would "weaken the Catholic-Radical coalition" and leave "no satisfactory alternative to new elections," Spanish expert C. N. Stirling foresaw a very bitter campaign, one that could easily lead to "the extremists on one side or the other refusing to bow to an adverse decision of the electorate & resorting to violent measures." Chilton agreed in mid-November that conditions at Madrid had become "somewhat ominous," and Philip Leigh-Smith, one of Stirling's colleagues at the Western Department, expected "plenty of trouble ahead."[55] Chapaprieta's fall three weeks later confirmed what Whitehall had

[53]Bowers to Hull, 13 November 1935, 852.00/2117, tel. 9 December 1935, 852.00/2119, and 10 December 1935, 852.00/2122, NA RG59; Bowers, Diary, 5 December 1935, Bowers Papers.

[54]Sir Geoffrey Thompson, *Front Line Diplomat* (London, 1959), pp. 75, 130–31; Bowers, *My Mission to Spain*, p. 291; *Times*, 22 November 1954, p. 8, col. d; Chilton to Hoare, 11 October 1935, W8975/18/41, and 11 October 1935, W9010/18/41, PRO FO371, vol. 19736.

[55]Chilton to Hoare, 30 October 1935, and minute by Stirling, 6 November 1935, W9535/18/41; Chilton to Hoare, 12 November 1935, and minute by Leigh-Smith, 19 November 1935, W9890/18/41, PRO FO371, vol. 19736.

suspected for some time: the balance of political power in Spain was shifting rapidly from the moderates to the extremists. "The Spaniards are, it appears, too bitter as partisans to make a success of parliamentary govt.," Stirling, echoing Bowers's lament, grumbled on 11 December, "Unless, however, equilibrium is found somewhere—of which presently there seems little prospect—the country is likely to despair of parliamentary govt. and an attempt will be made to set up a dictatorship."[56] By the end of the year, then, the Foreign Office, like the State Department, was well aware that with the collapse of the reformist right, Spain was once again on the verge of ideological polarization.

Confident as recently as the summer of 1935 that Spain's political center was powerful enough at last to control both the revolutionary left and the reactionary right, British and American officials were understandably disheartened the following winter by the increasing weakness of such Spanish moderates as Lerroux and Chapaprieta and the mounting strength of such extremists as Largo Caballero and Gil Robles. In the wake of the conservative triumph at the polls in November 1933 policy makers on both sides of the Atlantic had hoped that the most radical left-wing reforms could be reversed without unleashing a more thoroughgoing right-wing backlash. Lerroux's cautious but capable leadership, his swift repression of the Socialist upheaval in 1934, and his shrewd rejection of the CEDA's most extreme proposals in 1935 impressed even those observers, among them Bowers and Grahame, who had been quite sympathetic to Azaña and the Left Republicans. Then in late 1935, just when such moderation seemed to promise better Spanish relations with Great Britain and the United States, the *straperlo* scandal discredited Lerroux and the reformist right and ushered in another round of political chaos. By December Sir Henry Chilton acknowledged that the "middle course" was increasingly "unpopular" at Madrid, while Claude Bowers confessed a month later that if Spain escaped its current crisis "without much violence and possibly civil war it will be a marvel."[57]

This latest manifestation of republican Spain's congenital insta-

---

[56]Chilton to Hoare, tel. 10 December 1935, and minute by Stirling, 11 December 1935, W10521/18/41, PRO FO371, vol. 19736.
[57]Chilton to Hoare, 13 December 1935, W10667/18/41, PRO FO371, vol. 19736; Bowers, Diary, 7 January 1936, Bowers Papers.

bility proved especially frustrating in London and Washington for other reasons as well. Not only had Lerroux's moderate program reduced political friction with the Roosevelt and Baldwin administrations, it had also produced better economic relations. Lerroux, to be sure, was as eager as his predecessors to eliminate his country's recurrent balance-of-payments deficit, but unlike Azaña he believed that a trade truce could accomplish this more easily than a tariff war. As a result Spain had by the summer of 1935 at last concluded tentative commercial agreements with both the United States and Great Britain. In addition, the reformist right proved much more sympathetic than the Left Republicans and the Socialists had been to foreign investors. Consequently, such multinational giants as Rio Tinto and ITT encountered remarkably little trouble between 1933 and 1935, while other firms, among them Ford and General Motors, actually constructed new branch factories in Spain—all of which was welcome news both at Whitehall and at the White House.

7

Fair Field for Foreign Investment, 1933–1935

Spain's drift to the right between 1933 and 1935 was as welcome in corporate board rooms on both sides of the Atlantic as it was in diplomatic chanceries. Having endured repeated attacks at the hands of Azaña and his left-wing allies, most multinational executives anticipated a more hospitable business climate under Lerroux and the reformist right. British and American businessmen were not disappointed. In the wake of the November 1933 conservative landslide the Spanish government curbed the labor unrest and eased the economic regulations that had long made life so difficult for Rio Tinto, ITT, and other foreign firms. Moreover, Lerroux's nononsense approach to the 1934 Asturian revolution and his conciliatory attitude toward corporate concerns actually helped attract fresh multinational capital into Spain's automobile industry. By the summer of 1935, then, a fair field for foreign investment existed for the first and, as it turned out, the last time under the Spanish Republic. When the Lerroux regime collapsed later that autumn, the multinationals feared that Spain would revert to the dreadful business conditions of the early 1930s.

I

As Azaña's coalition crumbled during the spring and summer of 1933, British and American businessmen feared that he might try to recoup his waning political fortunes at their expense. Having narrowly averted expropriation the previous December, ITT's

Spanish subsidiary remained especially vulnerable to Spain's "radical, aggressive, prehensile, and head strong [sic]" left. Convinced that the CTNE was still very much "a political football," Colonel Sosthenes Behn worried that the incoming Roosevelt administration would be less sympathetic to ITT's troubles in Spain than Hoover and Stimson had been. Behn need not have fretted. In March John Wiley, an old friend, had moved from the embassy at Madrid to the State Department's Spanish desk, where he was able to brief key members of the new team about the CTNE controversy.[1] Wiley's defense of ITT's interests was so fervent that it left Claude Bowers with the impression that "apparently we have just one matter of importance pending—the monopoly given the Spanish auxiliary of the American [sic] Telephone and Telegraph Company which is being attacked by the radical enemies of the Spanish Government." Secretary of State Cordell Hull was likewise convinced that the recent expropriation crisis in Spain "went to the very heart of international confidence," as was Franklin Roosevelt himself. The president told Bowers in early May that "we expect of course that the terms of the [CTNE] contract will be observed."[2]

ITT's excellent connections with the Roosevelt administration were tested later that month when, as expected, the Azaña regime renewed its assault on the CTNE. On 14 May Socialist minister of public works Indalecio Prieto denounced the telephone concession as a "stupendous act of robbery" and rescinded the CTNE's contractual exemption from Spanish labor regulations. Faced with the prospect of what amounted to workers' control under the republican "mixed jury" system of arbitration, ITT officials urged Washington to reiterate its support for their Spanish subsidiary and to postpone all trade negotiations with Spain until Madrid ceased its efforts "to chisel away the [CTNE] contract bit by bit." Although both the State Department and the White House were "opposed to the idea of making tariff readjustments . . . a mere club to be used in the interest of the telephone company," Hull did instruct American diplomats at Madrid to protest these latest infringements on

---

[1]Memorandum by Briggs, 13 December 1932, 852.75 NTC/120; Behn quoted in memorandum by Briggs, 23 February 1933, 852.75 NTC/157; Moffat to Frank Page (ITT), 8 March 1933, 852.75 NTC/160; and Page to Moffat, 10 March 1933, 852.75 NTC/164, NA RG59. For a fuller discussion of ITT's problems in the spring of 1933, see Little, "Twenty Years of Turmoil," pp. 462–65.

[2]Bowers, Diary, 11 and 28 April and 2 May 1933, Bowers Papers.

ITT's contractual rights.[3] Not only did ITT's labor problems persist, however, but other American firms including the International Banking Corporation encountered similar difficulties later that summer. Frustrated by the intransigence of the Azaña regime, Hull angrily reversed himself in early September and announced that the United States would not start commercial talks with Spain until he was "assured that American investments in Spain will be adequately protected in all their legitimate rights."[4]

British investors fared no better than their American counterparts during Azaña's last months in office. In March 1933 Catalan officials hiked taxes arbitrarily on the Barcelona Power Light and Traction Company and did nothing to prevent "the parties of the extreme Left" from sabotaging the British firm's generators. The following month Madrid moved forward with its plans to confiscate the estates of the Duke of Wellington and in May threatened to cancel unilaterally the Anglo-Spanish Construction Company's railway concession. By mid-summer even Rio Tinto was experiencing "manifold difficulties" with its unruly work force at the copper mines in Huelva. Finally, in September antiforeign riots exploded in the Canary Islands against the London-based Bank of West Africa, creating "elements of danger" for British lives and property at Las Palmas.[5] By the autumn of 1933 it was obvious to businessmen on both sides of the Atlantic that the crippled Azaña regime was neither willing nor able to shield foreign firms from left-wing radicals.

The rise of Lerroux and the reformist right later that year, however, augured well for multinational interests in Spain. As early as the previous April Cornelius Vanderbilt had predicted, after conferring with CTNE personnel in Madrid, that once Lerroux became prime minister he would "be under the thumb of Capt. Logan Rock . . . of the telephone company" and would, unlike Azaña, be "favorably inclined to the US." Bowers confirmed five months later

[3] Flack to Hull, 16 May 1933, 852.75 NTC/174; 17 May 1933, 852.75 NTC/175; and tel. 19 May 1933, and Hull to Flack, 19 May 1933, 852.75 NTC/170, NA RG59; Flack to Wiley, 31 May 1933, Wiley Papers, Box 7 (Flack); Bowers, Diary, 28 April 1933, Bowers Papers.
[4] Bowers to Hull, 25 July 1933, 852.75 NTC/182, and 28 August 1933, 852.0442/2; Hull to Bowers, tel. 6 September 1933, 652.113 Auto/77, NA RG59.
[5] Consul General Norman King (Barcelona) to Simon, 24 March 1933, W3809/3809/41; Grahame to Simon, tel. 29 April 1933, W4718/114/41; Sir Evelyn Wallers to Mounsey, 18 May 1933, W5588/74/41; Leeper to Grahame, 30 September 1933, W10989/1318/41, PRO FO371, vols. 17424, 17425, 17430, and 17434; *Times*, 20 April 1934, p. 23, col. a.

that "the present drift to the Right" in the wake of Azaña's resignation guaranteed that "Spain will never yield to the extremists" demanding the confiscation of the CTNE without compensation.[6] Although ITT officials still feared that the Socialists would make the CTNE controversy an election issue, the conservative triumph in the November balloting killed the expropriation bill once and for all. Indeed, when the Socialists made a feeble last-ditch effort to revoke ITT's concession, Prime Minister Lerroux promised CTNE officials that he himself "would choke off debate if it should go as far as to discuss the legality or the terms of the [telephone] contract." With a more hospitable regime in power at Madrid, Sosthenes Behn concluded with considerable relief, "the situation in Spain looked a little brighter" in early 1934.[7]

British firms were equally relieved by the drift to the right at Madrid. Lerroux moved swiftly in early October to restore law and order in the troubled Canary Islands, mainly to prevent the disruption of Spain's lucrative tourist industry but also to reassure London that British holdings at Las Palmas were secure. Later that month the Lerroux regime intervened with Catalan officials to shield the BPLTC from recurrent strikes and sabotage. Determined "to protect the public services in Barcelona from extremist agitation and disorders," Madrid actually placed Spanish military and naval personnel in Catalonia at the disposal of the British utility giant to help quell labor unrest. "The company," Whitehall admitted in early November, "have good reason to be thankful to Senor Lerroux."[8] Even the Anglo-Spanish Construction Company, which had all but given up hope of collecting payments long overdue from Spain's Ministry of Public Works, saw its claims "vindicated" in mid-December when a Madrid appeals court staffed by Lerroux's appointees returned a "favourable decision" in the case and ordered compensation for the British firm.[9] By late 1933, then, the

---

[6] Vanderbilt to Roper, 21 April 1933, enclosed in Roper to Hull, 5 May 1933, 852.00/1931; Bowers to Hull, 27 September 1933, 652.113 Auto/79, NA RG59.

[7] Bowers to Hull, 10 November 1933, 852.75 NTC/187, NA RG59; Bowers, Diary, 21 December 1933, Bowers Papers; Bowers, *My Mission to Spain*, p. 60; Captain Logan Rock to Colonel Behn, tel. 23 December 1933, File 875 (Madrid–1933), vol. XVI, NA RG84; memorandum by Moffat, 11 January 1934, 837.75/51, NA RG59.

[8] Grahame to Leeper, 10 October 1933, W11842/1318/41; Grahame to Simon, 6 October 1933, W11497/3809/41, and 16 October 1933, and minute by Nicholls, 3 November 1933, W12411/3809/41, PRO FO371, vols. 17430 and 17434.

[9] Wallers to Mounsey, 18 December 1933, and minute by Leeper, 2 January 1934, W14561/74/41, PRO FO371, vol. 17424.

business climate in Spain looked rosier than it had at any time since the advent of the republic in 1931. After two years of fear and frustration at the hands of Azaña and his left-wing allies, multinationals anticipated that the more conservative Lerroux would once again provide a fair field for foreign investment in Spain.

II

Although the new year did bring more hospitable business conditions to Spain, neither British nor American firms managed to escape the barbs of Spanish nationalists entirely. ITT, the most visible of the multinationals operating in Spain, repeatedly ran afoul of technical and economic regulations during 1934. Despite its personal ties with Prime Minister Lerroux, for example, the CTNE saw its monopoly on radio traffic between Madrid and New York broken and its rate increases postponed by Spanish officials in January. Later that spring Madrid delayed the repatriation of $5 million in profits by ITT, Twentieth Century Fox, and other American firms in an effort to curb Spain's balance-of-payments deficit with the United States.[10] These relatively minor difficulties notwithstanding, the security of American holdings in Spain was never really at issue under Lerroux or his successor, Ricardo Samper. Indeed, after Samper blocked yet another Socialist effort to rekindle the dormant expropriation bill in May and then tabled a proposal by his own followers to require ITT to divest 51 percent of its holdings to Spanish nationals in June, CTNE officials felt their firm's position had been strengthened considerably.[11]

The sailing for British multinationals in Spain was not entirely smooth in early 1934 either, but their difficulties, in contrast to those of their American counterparts, stemmed less from bureaucratic regulation than from labor agitation. The big British mining firms at Huelva—Rio Tinto and Tharsis Sulphur—were plagued by sabotage and short-lived strikes throughout the winter, as were the estates of wealthy Britons, among them the Duke of Wellington.

---

[10] Moffat, Diplomatic Journals, 2 and 3/4 February 1934, Moffat Papers; Bowers to Roosevelt, 10 January 1934, *FDR & Foreign Affairs*, 1:586–87; Bowers to Hull, tel. 10 January 1934, 652.116/34, and 20 March 1934, 852.5151/76, NA RG59.

[11] Bowers to Hull, 9 May 1934, 852.75 NTC/194, and 12 June 1934, 852.75 NTC/198, NA RG59; Rock to Behn, tel. 6 June 1934, File 875 (Madrid–1934), vol. XV, NA RG84.

Conditions grew so grim at one point that a Rio Tinto official actually appealed to the governor general of Gibraltar, who promised to dispatch British troops if necessary to protect the mines. Lerroux and Samper, however, quickly made it clear that such extreme measures would not be required. First, in March 1934 Lerroux reversed Azaña's policy and permitted Rio Tinto and Tharsis to dismiss more than one thousand redundant miners. After these layoffs sparked a fresh round of violence that culminated in the attempted murder of several British managers, Samper stationed four hundred soldiers in the mining district to ensure law and order. Thanks largely to the presence of these troops, Rio Tinto's Sir Auckland Geddes reported, "between March and October no troubles occurred."[12] Despite sporadic problems with Spanish bureaucrats and miners, then, by the autumn of 1934 both British and American businessmen felt their holdings in Spain were more secure than they had been in years.

This burgeoning multinational faith in the reformist right at Madrid was sorely tested during the brief but bloody left-wing rebellion in October 1934. American firms encountered surprisingly few problems during the uprising, due mainly to the vigilance of the Lerroux regime. The Barcelona offices of IBC were vandalized and CTNE headquarters in Madrid was raked by machine gun fire, but Spanish troops prevented any more serious harm to Americans and their property. Indeed, in the wake of the abortive revolt ITT reported that damage to its facilities in Spain had been limited to one exchange and two hundred trunk lines.[13] The gratitude of American businessmen for the protection accorded them by the Lerroux regime took tangible form a month later, when ITT and IBC each donated 100,000 pesetas "to a national fund to reward the armed forces that suppressed the recent rebellion."[14]

The situation that confronted the British mining firms at Huelva that autumn, on the other hand, was much more threatening. Just before violence erupted throughout Spain in early October, Sir

[12] Avery, *Not on Queen Victoria's Birthday*, pp. 351–53; Checkland, *Mines of Tharsis*, pp. 217–19; Geddes, Annual Rio Tinto Chairman's Address, 24 April 1935, RTZ Corporate Archives.

[13] Bowers, Diary, 8 October 1934, Bowers Papers; Page to Moffat, tel. 10 October 1934, 852.00/2047; Behn to Page, tel. 9 October 1934, attached to memorandum by Moffat, 10 October 1934, 852.00/2048, NA RG59; Phillips, Journal, 17 October 1934, William Phillips Papers, Houghton Library, Harvard University.

[14] *New York Times*, 9 November 1934, sec. 1, p. 5:3.

George Grahame had warned Whitehall to expect "trouble at the Rio Tinto mines." No sooner had Grahame's message arrived than hundreds of left-wing miners, angered by recent layoffs and armed with dynamite and hunting rifles, clashed with the Spanish army garrison defending the copper fields. Despite "some shooting and bomb throwing" and "a good deal of noise," Rio Tinto officials reported later, the defenders "were able to maintain their position until reinforcements arrived," and as a result "no serious damage was done to the company's property."[15] Grahame confirmed on 11 October that the atmosphere at Huelva was "much more normal" and that British businessmen there were "satisfied with the state of things." Britain's consul at Seville noted a week later that mining operations had been resumed without further incident, and by month's end Whitehall agreed that "Rio Tinto seems to have come off lightly."[16]

Never a company to miss an opportunity to reduce costs, Rio Tinto used the violence at Huelva as a pretext for slicing its payroll. Arguing that recent advances in mining technology made still more of its work force redundant, the British firm appealed to the Madrid authorities in November for further reductions. As he had earlier in the year, Prime Minister Lerroux authorized Rio Tinto to fire nearly one thousand miners, some "for whom no useful work could be found" but most "for implication in the revolutionary movement." Lerroux's swift and forceful handling of the left-wing uprising made it clear that a wholesale assault on private enterprise, whether domestic or foreign, would no longer be tolerated in Spain. As a consequence, few British or American businessmen would have taken issue with Sir Auckland Geddes, who told a group of Rio Tinto shareholders in early 1935 that "we are profoundly grateful" to the Spanish government for its "prompt and energetic action" in protecting the copper fields at Huelva.[17] In-

---

[15] Grahame to Simon, tel. 5 October 1934, and minute by Stirling, 5 October 1934, W8856/27/41, PRO FO371, vol. 18596; Geddes, Annual Rio Tinto Chairman's Address, 24 April 1935, RTZ Corporate Archives.

[16] Grahame to Simon, tel. 11 October 1934, W9052/27/41; Coultas (Seville) to Grahame, 17 October 1934, enclosed in Grahame to Simon, 19 October 1934, and minute by Stirling, 25 October 1934, W9351/27/41, PRO FO371, vols. 18596 and 18597.

[17] Avery, *Not on Queen Victoria's Birthday*, pp. 353–54; Lerroux quoted in Geddes, Annual Rio Tinto Chairman's Address, 24 April 1935, RTZ Corporate Archives.

deed, the close ties that ITT and Rio Tinto had cultivated with the Lerroux regime since 1933 seemed at last to have paid off.

III

The political stability and social tranquillity generated by the Lerroux regime in the following months favorably impressed foreign businessmen. Free from left-wing disruptions for the first time in years, ITT watched earnings on its Spanish operations soar by nearly 50 percent during 1935. Despite the company's influence with Lerroux, however, ITT's accounts remained blocked at Madrid because of rigid exchange controls designed to correct the huge adverse balance in Spain's trade with the United States. Eager to repatriate almost $5 million in profits, CTNE officials apparently struck a deal with the Spanish government. If ITT could obtain a sizable credit in New York for Spain to stabilize the peseta, Madrid would release the frozen funds. Captain Logan N. Rock, the CTNE's managing director and also the Lerroux regime's de facto financial representative, arrived in the United States in January 1935 determined to secure a loan on Wall Street so that ITT and other American firms operating in Spain "could unblock their accounts right away." The bankers, however, were "unwilling to touch it" and told him that "it would have to be a Government loan." And so Rock took his case to Washington.[18]

ITT's scheme received mixed reviews from the Roosevelt administration. Both the Export-Import Bank and the Treasury Department favored a revolving credit that would enable Spain to liquidate its foreign-exchange arrears and expand its foreign trade. The State Department, on the other hand, found the idea of "bailing out" ITT or any American multinational "objectionable as a general proposition." Determined to prevent bureaucratic rivals or corporate executives from meddling in commercial policy, Cordell Hull tabled the loan proposal pending the conclusion of Spanish-American trade negotiations. Although Rock returned to Madrid empty-handed, Spanish finance minister Chapaprieta assured him

---

[18]Bowers to Hull, 20 March 1934, 852.5151/76; memorandum by Moffat, 21 January 1935, 852.51/271, NA RG59; CTNE, *Annual Report 1935*, pp. 12–13.

nonetheless that in return for his recent efforts the CTNE would be permitted to repatriate some of its frozen funds to New York. Ironically, ITT now seemed more influential with the Lerroux regime than with its own government in Washington.[19]

ITT's exchange problems did not deter other American multinationals from expanding their operations in Spain. The U.S. economic stake south of the Pyrenees, Roosevelt's special adviser on foreign trade George N. Peek pointed out in early 1935, was diverse enough to include firms producing "licorice, lead, sulfur, shoe machinery, medicine, and toiletries." The most important new investments, however, were in "electrical and automobile manufacturing plants."[20] Indeed, restrictions on Spanish motor car imports and the more favorable business climate under Lerroux combined to lure auto makers to Spain. The Ford Motor Company had opened a branch plant in Barcelona as early as 1925 in an effort to "hop over" Spain's extremely high tariff wall, but its output had remained relatively insignificant for nearly a decade. Then new import quotas and tax incentives prompted Ford to quadruple its output, to 1,700 units in 1934, and to expand production still further in 1935.[21] At the invitation of the Spanish government other American auto makers followed suit, and in July 1935 General Motors drew up plans to build a new branch factory at Barcelona capable of producing 20,000 vehicles per year. Bowers reported that General Motors had agreed to employ as much Spanish labor and materials as possible and to export 70 percent of its output in order to supply Spain with badly needed foreign exchange.[22] Such cooperation between Detroit and Madrid during 1935 demonstrated that, under

---

[19] Memorandum by Moffat, 21 January 1935, 852.51/271; George N. Peek to Assistant Secretary of State Francis B. Sayre, 12 April 1935, and handwritten memorandum by Sayre, 16 April 1935, 611.5231/956; memorandum by Arthur Upgren (Tariff Division), 21 May 1935, 611.5231/981, NA RG59; Henry J. Morgenthau, Jr., Diaries, Book 7, p. 142, 21 June 1935, Morgenthau Papers, Franklin D. Roosevelt Presidential Library; Chapaprieta's assurances are in Johnson to Hull, 21 May 1935, 852.5151/118, NA RG59.

[20] Peek, "United States–Spain Economic Relations," February 1935, FDR Papers, OF 422A.

[21] Mira Wilkins and Frank Ernest Hill, *American Business Abroad: Ford on Six Continents* (Detroit, 1964), pp. 140–45; James Mitchel Elston, "Multinational Corporations and American Foreign Policy in the Late 1930s" (Ph.D. diss., University of Michigan, 1976), pp. 165–69; O. Holm (Ford Motor Company) to Richard Stephenson, 11 June 1935, File 531 (Spain), NA RG151.

[22] Johnson to Hull, tel. 22 June 1935, 652.113 Auto/87, and 25 June 1935, 164.21/350; Bowers to Hull, 17 July 1935, 164.21/352, NA RG59.

the right circumstances, multinational corporations could benefit both home and host country.

While British multinationals did not expand their operations in Spain in 1935, they were as encouraged as the Americans by Lerroux's policies. The Anglo-Spanish Construction Company, for example, told Whitehall that the Madrid authorities had promised to settle all its claims before the year was out. BPLTC vice president Miller Lash likewise told a group of shareholders in June that "the outlook was reassuring" for the big utility firm. Stressing that "the labour situation had so far been satisfactory" at Barcelona, Lash predicted that "reasonably quiet political and social conditions" in Spain would boost the utility's earnings for 1935 sharply.[23] Although the Rio Tinto Company had gradually begun to make its new investments in the politically more secure copper fields of British Rhodesia, the giant mining concern still remained confident that its multimillion-dollar stake in Spain was secure. Indeed, Sir Auckland Geddes praised the Lerroux regime for authorizing still more reductions in the work force at Huelva and for providing modest unemployment relief for hundreds of jobless and potentially dangerous miners in the region. Furthermore, Geddes added, Spanish officials had recently agreed to lower taxes on copper exports in order to make Rio Tinto more competitive in the tight international metals market.[24] For most British and American multinationals operating in Spain, the more favorable business climate fostered by Lerroux and the reformist right seemed almost too good to be true.

Lerroux's resignation in October and the subsequent parliamentary crisis at Madrid were as disappointing for businessmen as for diplomats. Fearing that the collapse of the reformist right would worsen business conditions in Spain, some multinationals moved to reduce their vulnerability. Chrysler, which had submitted a proposal to build an assembly plant at Barcelona the previous July, never followed through on its plan to join Ford and General Motors in Spain. The British armaments firm of Vickers-Armstrong, which

---

[23] Grahame to Peterson, 27 February 1935, W2005/678/41, PRO FO371, vol. 19744; Lash quoted in the *Times*, 2 July 1935, p. 23, col. d.

[24] Geddes, Annual Rio Tinto Chairman's Address, 24 April 1935, RTZ Corporate Archives; Charles E. Harvey, "Business History and the Problem of Entrepreneurship: The Case of the Rio Tinto Company, 1873–1939," *Business History* 21 (January 1979), 16–17.

had operated a Spanish shipbuilding subsidiary called Constructora Naval at Bilbao for several years, pulled out of Spain in late 1935, citing nationalist pressures.[25] Although multinational giants like ITT and Rio Tinto had too much at stake to withdraw abruptly from the country, they made it clear that they were as discouraged as Chrysler and Vickers by the unexpected return of political instability at Madrid. After President Alcalá-Zamora dissolved the Cortes in December and scheduled new elections, Captain Logan Rock expressed concern over the safety of ITT's $100-million subsidiary, telling Claude Bowers that many Spanish businessmen were "getting their money out of Spain and into banks in New York."[26] Captain Ulick deB. Charles, Rio Tinto's representative at Madrid, agreed that conditions were "quite uncertain" and told British officials in January 1936 that his firm anticipated "outbreaks of violence during the elections."[27]

As the Spanish Republic braced itself for its third round of balloting in less than five years, few foreign investors expected the business climate in Spain to brighten in the near future. Rio Tinto and ITT, like the Foreign Office and the State Department, recalled all too well the stormy weather British and American interests had encountered at the hands of Azaña and the Left Republicans. The steady swing to the right between 1933 and 1935 had temporarily cleared the air at Madrid and generated optimism among businessmen on both sides of the Atlantic. ITT used its personal influence with Lerroux to ease the CTNE's political and financial problems, Rio Tinto persuaded Spanish officials to approve massive layoffs at its copper mines, and nearly all multinationals emerged from the abortive left-wing uprising in 1934 unscathed. More stable business conditions during 1935 brought higher profits for firms such as the BPLTC and tempted Ford, General Motors, and others to expand their operations in Spain. Then just when the storm clouds seemed to have vanished from Spanish skies, the Lerroux regime collapsed, and British and American multination-

<hr />

[25] On Chrysler see Johnson to Hull, 1 July 1935, 652.116 Auto/15, and 1 July 1935, 164.21/347, NA RG59. On Vickers-Armstrong see Puzzo, *Spain and the Great Powers,* p. 19, and Anthony Sampson, *The Arms Bazaar: From Lockheed to Lebanon* (New York, 1977), p. 73.

[26] Bowers, Diary, 23 December 1935, Bowers Papers; Bowers to Hull, 23 December 1935, 852.00/2127, NA RG59.

[27] Minute by Stirling, 8 January 1936, W225/62/41, PRO FO371, vol. 20519.

als readied themselves for another political and economic tempest. The rekindling of old fears among foreign investors and diplomats, however, was not the only consequence of the renewed turmoil at Madrid. The demise of Lerroux and the reformist right also disrupted British and American commercial negotiations with Spain, which by late 1935 had produced a pair of tentative trade agreements.

8

Trade Truce, 1933–1935

The better treatment that the Lerroux regime accorded British and American multinationals was paralleled by a more general improvement in Spain's commercial relations with Great Britain and the United States between 1933 and 1935. Well aware that the commercial cold war waged by his predecessors had trimmed Madrid's huge trade deficit only slightly and had done nothing at all to expand Spanish exports, Lerroux adopted a more conciliatory approach to London and Washington. As a result Britain's mounting commercial troubles with Spain in early 1933 gradually gave way to a rapprochement symbolized by the conclusion of a preliminary agreement for mutual trade stabilization in mid-1935. Washington's economic relations with Madrid, which had been much stormier than London's during the early 1930s, likewise improved markedly under Lerroux, culminating in an October 1935 Spanish-American draft reciprocal trade treaty. Lerroux's sudden resignation later that same month, however, raised the unpleasant possibility that the trade truce he had so carefully engineered with Great Britain and the United States might give way once again to tariff war.

I

Desperate to reverse the downward spiral of Spanish exports and, perhaps, rebuild its own dwindling political support, the Azaña regime resorted during the spring and summer of 1933 to increasingly autarchic commercial policies that disrupted both British and American trade with Spain. Although entitled by treaty to most-favored-nation status, Britain's commerce was harassed by

Madrid authorities angry over London's recent adoption of an imperial preference system that discriminated against Spanish fruit exports. The Azaña regime, for example, stiffened its exchange controls in February, forcing many British traders and investors to wait months before they could repatriate funds abroad. Easier access to hard currency, Ambassador George Grahame learned, hinged on more favorable treatment for Valencian oranges in Britain.[1] Spain raised the stakes in May by granting a 32-percent tariff rebate on French automobiles and then refusing to extend the lower duties to British motor cars. The rebates, Grahame explained, were intended to kill two birds with one stone by placating France, Spain's largest export market, while at the same time extracting concessions from Britain on Spanish fruit. Whitehall pressed its most-favored-nation claim throughout the summer and even hinted it might seek redress from the World Court at the Hague, but such pressure had little effect on the embattled Azaña regime.[2]

Once Lerroux became prime minister that autumn, however, British commercial relations with Spain began to improve. The new government quickly agreed to ease Azaña's troublesome exchange regulations, and by 1 December 1933 British exporters and investors were able to convert their pesetas into sterling freely.[3] The rebate issue proved considerably more difficult to resolve. The Lerroux regime still hoped to link lower duties for British motor cars to reciprocal reductions on Valencian oranges. The Foreign Office, on the other hand, was under pressure from auto makers not only in Britain but also in Canada to force Spain to honor its most-favored-nation commitments. Whitehall's tough talk of "Hague-courting Spain" finally persuaded Madrid in early November to offer rebates on British automobiles provided that London withdrew its support for the Canadian claim. Well aware that acceptance of the

---

[1] Adams, *Economic Conditions in Spain, 1933*, p. 20; British Chamber of Commerce in Spain to Foreign Secretary Simon, 24 January 1933, and Simon to Grahame, 26 February 1933, File W115/115/41, PRO FO371, vol. 17425.

[2] J. J. Wills (Board of Trade) to Vansittart, 5 July 1933, and Simon to Chargé d'Affaires Courtenay Forbes (Madrid), 7 July 1933, W8340/1319/41; Forbes to de los Rios, 13 July 1933, enclosed in Forbes to Simon, 13 July 1933, W8436/1319/41; memorandum by Alexander Adams, enclosed in Grahame to Simon, 20 July 1933, W8747/1319/41; Wills to Vansittart, 24 August 1933, W9777/1319/41, PRO FO371, vol. 17431.

[3] Grahame to Simon, tel. 1 December 1933, File W115/115/41, PRO FO371, vol. 17426.

Spanish proposal would compromise Canada's bargaining position yet mindful as well that rejection would decimate Britain's automobile exports, Foreign Secretary John Simon reluctantly approved the deal on 14 November but emphasized that the arrangement should not be construed as relinquishing any British or Canadian treaty rights. After last-minute legal haggling had delayed matters for another six weeks, the Lerroux regime finally granted the rebates to British motor cars on 1 January 1934.[4]

Although the swing to the right at Madrid was also welcome among exporters on the other side of the Atlantic, the improvement in Spanish-American commercial relations in the course of 1933 was more modest. Secretary of State Cordell Hull, who preached "lower tariffs and fewer trade barriers" with almost religious zeal, joined the Roosevelt administration with a team of disciples, among them Francis B. Sayre and Henry Grady, trained in international economics and committed to resolving the bilateral disputes that had bedeviled U.S. commerce with Spain and other nations in the early 1930s.[5] Grumbling that "Spain, of course, is a very high tariff country," Hull questioned as early as April 1933 whether the Azaña regime was really committed to freer trade; he refused to open commercial talks until Madrid ceased its two-year campaign against American exports. The preferential auto rebates that Spain accorded France in mid-May further eroded Detroit's already weakened position and confirmed Hull's suspicion that Azaña intended to reduce Spanish trade deficits at the expense of U.S. manufacturers. The State Department accordingly lodged a formal protest with Spain's ambassador to the United States, Juan Cárdenas, and reaffirmed in June that "we were not eager to go forward with the Spanish treaties at this time."[6]

[4] Canadian prime minister Richard Bennett to the Dominions Office, tel. 10 October 1933, and A. W. A. Leeper to the Dominions Office, 26 October 1933, W11636/1319/41; Grahame to Simon, 27 October 1933, W12417/1319/41; T. Quintin Hill (Board of Trade) to Vansittart, 20 October 1933, W11975/1319/41; Grahame to Simon, tel. 5 November 1933, W12596/1319/41; minute by Legal Adviser Hugh Malkin, 13 November 1933, W12802/1319/41; Simon to Grahame, 14 November 1933, W13058/1319/41; Dominions Office to Bennett, 18 November 1933, W13325/1319/41, PRO FO371, vol. 17431; Grahame to Simon, tel. 4 January 1934, W327/225/41, PRO FO371, vol. 18598.
[5] Speech by Hull, 19 May 1932, United States, Congress, Senate, *Congressional Record*, 72d Cong., 1st sess., 75, pt. 10, p. 10644; Hull, *Memoirs*, 1:352–53, 356, 366; *State Department Register, 1934*, pp. 151, 166, 177, 185, 247; Herbert Feis, *1933: Characters in Crisis* (Boston, 1966), p. 263.
[6] Memoranda by Hull, 6 and 20 April 1933, Papers of Cordell Hull, microfilm ed.,

Despite these fresh troubles, however, Ambassador Claude Bowers reported that the Spaniards were actually quite interested in American proposals for a reciprocal lowering of trade barriers. "I find the people here eager for commercial understandings with us," he wrote Roosevelt on 28 June, "and, with the atmosphere friendly, [I] think that something can be accomplished when the Administration is ready to move in that direction." Pleased by Bowers's "splendid relations" with Spanish officials, the president urged him on 11 July to "search for individual commodities which Spain could sell here with the understanding that the proceeds from such sales would be spent in the United States for a return cargo!"[7]

The State Department remained committed nonetheless to its hard-line approach toward Spain. Indeed, when Ambassador Cárdenas called on Undersecretary William Phillips in mid-July to discuss the American embargo on Almerian grapes, he got an icy reception. The Spaniard charged that the sanitary quarantine was not designed to prevent contamination by the Mediterranean fruit fly but rather to protect the California grape industry from Spanish competition. After all, Cárdenas pointed out, during the North American winter the United States imported grapes from Argentina despite the presence of the insect pest in that country, but during the summer harvest in California all Spanish grapes were embargoed. Could not the Department of Agriculture ascertain whether certain areas in Spain, as in Argentina, might be uncontaminated? Phillips dismissed Cárdenas's argument, rejected the inspection proposal, and reiterated instead Washington's unwillingness to consider any concessions until Madrid stopped discriminating against American exports.[8] Convinced that "the Spaniards are deeply interested in a treaty," Bowers urged the State Department to be more flexible. "I do not believe," he advised Hull on 19 July, "that we will gain anything by appearing indifferent to, or contemptuous of, this country commercially."

reel 32 ("Spain"), Library of Congress (hereafter cited as Hull Papers, microfilm ed.); Bowers to Phillips, tel. 10 June 1933, and Phillips to Bowers, tel. 12 June 1933, *FRUS, 1933*, 2:704; Bowers to Phillips, tel. 26 June 1933, 652.113 Auto/62; memorandum by Phillips, 27 June 1933, 611.5231/761, NA RG59.
[7] Bowers to Roosevelt, 28 June 1933, and Roosevelt to Bowers, 11 July 1933, FDR Papers, OF 303.
[8] Memorandum by Phillips, 14 July 1933, *FRUS, 1933*, 2:695–96.

The State Department however, remained adamant that, given Spain's "extensive discrimination against American commerce," there was "no hope that such negotiations could be undertaken at this time."[9]

Claude Bowers was deeply troubled by this turn of events. Certain that Hull's subordinates were subverting plans to ease global commercial tensions while the secretary was in London at the World Economic Conference, Bowers carried his case directly to the White House in early August. He sent Roosevelt a "Memorandum on what Spain wants to see in the U.S." listing six areas of concern to Spaniards, the most important of which was the embargo on Almerian grapes. Failure to redress these grievances, Bowers warned, would play into the hands of France, which was already angling to expand its markets in Spain at the expense of the United States.[10] Roosevelt passed the Spanish desiderata along to the State Department, but upon his return from London Hull made it clear that he would not permit Madrid's preferential tariff system to jeopardize his cherished liberal commercial policies. Angered by the Azaña regime's continued unwillingness to restore most-favored-nation treatment to American exports, Hull bluntly explained on 6 September 1933 that "it is not our present intention to undertake commercial treaty discussions with the Spanish Government . . . so long as that Government practices such extensive discriminations against our trade and . . . investments."[11]

There were subtle signs of better Spanish-American commercial relations, however, after Lerroux replaced Azaña in mid-September. Cordell Hull, who now attributed the ongoing trade troubles as much to "overwhelming" American sentiment favoring "extreme high tariffs" as to Spanish protectionism, adopted a more cordial tone with Ambassador Cárdenas and encouraged him to call "from month to month" for a "frank" assessment of the stalemated negotiations. Claude Bowers reported in October that the Lerroux regime seemed even more eager than its predecessor

[9] Bowers to Hull, 19 July 1933, 611.5231/776; Phillips to Bowers, tel. 21 July 1933, 611.5231/764, NA RG59.

[10] Bowers to Josephus Daniels, 26 July 1933, Daniels Papers; Bowers to Roosevelt, 2 August 1933, FDR Papers, PPF 730.

[11] Roosevelt to Hull, 21 August 1933, Roosevelt to Bowers, 22 August 1933, and Hull to Roosevelt, 26 September 1933, FDR Papers, PPF 730; Hull to Bowers, 6 September 1933, 652.113 Auto/77, NA RG59.

for closer commercial ties with the United States and added that a growing rift between Madrid and Paris might soon prompt the new government to rescind the preferential rebates accorded French autos earlier in the year. The time was ripe, he concluded, to make some kind of concession to Spain.[12]

The end of Prohibition later that autumn provided the State Department with an opportunity to do so. As early as October 1933 Pierrepont Moffat had noted that the projected repeal of the Volstead Act might provide "a very useful trading card with Spain." If the United States was "generous" to the Spaniards regarding their wines and spirits, "they might be disposed to remove some of the discriminatory trade practices with which they are hampering our commerce at present."[13] Following the passage of the Twenty-First Amendment in December, the Roosevelt administration accordingly announced a temporary annual wine quota of 400,000 gallons for Spain and promised to raise the figure should Madrid offer "a quid pro quo preferably benefiting American agricultural exports." The Spaniards were nevertheless disappointed by the size of their quota, which amounted to barely one-tenth that accorded France, and Bowers warned Washington in early January 1934 that American interests should expect "bad weather" in Spain unless the United States made "immediate concessions [on] basic Spanish products."[14]

Undaunted by this bleak forecast, the State Department maintained that Spain must make the next concession. Irked by Bowers's pro-Spanish outlook, Pierrepont Moffat argued that any American "free will gesture" to a nation such as Spain, which was "actively discriminating to our disfavor," would "dislocate our entire world policy." Yet Bowers, Moffat remarked privately, "seems to regard his role as primarily that of the Ambassador of rather than to Spain, and gives all the Spanish arguments without assur-

[12]Bowers to Hull, 27 September 1933, 652.113 Auto/79; memorandum by Hull, 28 September 1933, 611.5231/774; Bowers to Hull, 13 October 1933, 651.5231/94, and 6 November 1933, 651.5231/96, NA RG59.
[13]Moffat, Diplomatic Journals, 2 October 1933, Moffat Papers; Feis, *1933: Characters in Crisis*, pp. 332–33.
[14]Bowers to Phillips, tel. 21 December 1933, and Phillips to Bowers, tel. 21 December 1933, *FRUS, 1933*, 2:697–98; Bowers, Diary, 21 December 1933, Bowers Papers; Moffat, Diplomatic Journals, 21 December 1933, Moffat Papers; Bowers to Hull, tel. 10 January 1934, 652.116/34, NA RG59.

ing us that he presses our case in Spain with anything like the same vigor."[15] Hoping to "keep Bowers and the Department walking hand in hand," Undersecretary Phillips sent a soothing cable to Madrid on 13 January offering to increase Spain's wine quota in exchange for larger Spanish purchases of American tobacco. But, Phillips hastened to point out, additional concessions were out of the question until Madrid treated American exports more equitably. "We cannot," he concluded, "extend gratuitous favors to Spain and thus give other countries, whose markets are more important to us than Spain, and who do not discriminate against us, ground for complaint."[16]

Still convinced that Spain was "anxious to straighten out all our commercial tangles," Bowers appealed directly to the White House. Outraged by "the idiotic notion" at the State Department that American interests could "best be served by treating Spain with contempt," he warned Roosevelt that "unless we show a generous disposition in the negotiations now on in Washington I expect a flare-up." Better treatment for Spanish exports, Bowers emphasized, was imperative if punitive quotas for American products were to be avoided. Alarmed by this storm warning, Roosevelt pressed the State Department on 24 January to make concessions on Spain's wines.[17] Such White House pressure worked wonders, for in less than a month the United States agreed to triple its Spanish wine quota to 1.1 million gallons. In return Spain pledged to purchase an additional 4 million pounds of American tobacco. Ratified by a mutual exchange of notes in February 1934 and financed by a $675,000 Export-Import Bank credit later that year, the wine and tobacco deal marked the first major step toward better Spanish-American commercial relations since 1931.[18] By early 1934 the problems that had disrupted U.S. trade with Spain,

[15]Memorandum by Moffat, 11 January 1934, 611.526 Wines/10, NA RG59; Moffat, Diplomatic Journals, 11 and 12 January 1934, Moffat Papers.
[16]Moffat, Diplomatic Journals, 13 January 1934, Moffat Papers; Phillips to Bowers, tel. 13 January 1934, 652.116/34, NA RG59.
[17]Bowers to Roosevelt, 10 January 1934, and Roosevelt to Phillips, 24 January 1934, *FDR & Foreign Affairs*, 1:586-87, 609.
[18]Memorandum by Hull, 25 January 1934; Hull to Bowers, tel. 15 February 1934; Cárdenas to Hull, 16 February 1934; Hull to Cárdenas, 23 February 1934; Sayre to Bowers, 13 March 1934, *FRUS, 1934*, 2:687-91; Phillips to Roosevelt, 29 January 1934, *FDR & Foreign Affairs*, 1:616-17; agreement between the S. B. Smith Company and the Second Export-Import Bank, Credit File no. 11, Record Group 275, Records of the Export-Import Bank, National Archives, Washington, D.C.

like those which had plagued Britain's exports there, were at last beginning to abate.

II

Under the steady and able leadership of Alejandro Lerroux, Spanish commercial relations with both Britain and the United States continued to improve in 1934. Total British exports to Spain edged upward for the first time in over five years by a modest 2 percent, due mainly to increased automobile sales. The Lerroux regime did impose restrictions on a variety of imports in an effort to stabilize the sagging peseta, but Britain, which had recently surpassed France as the leading market for Spanish exports, was largely unaffected.[19] Madrid limited the importation of British diesel motors and leather goods in 1934, but Commercial Counselor Alexander Adams believed that "United Kingdom trade could hardly be prejudiced very greatly" by a system directed primarily against those nations with which Spain maintained a trade deficit. Rumors that the Lerroux regime might shift its coal purchases from Britain to Poland in September did prompt the Board of Trade to consider "threatening the Spanish Government with an increased duty on oranges," but "the adverse effect of such a threat . . . on U.K. trade relations" led the board to "rule it out." The alleged Spanish plan to substitute Silesia for Newcastle never materialized, and by year's end Adams saw "every prospect that the market for United Kingdom coal can be considerably extended, providing there are no reverses in the steady march towards stability in both political and economic spheres" at Madrid.[20]

Arthur Mullins, a commissioner for the British Overseas Trade Development Council who toured Spain in late 1934, confirmed that Anglo-Spanish commercial relations were improving rapidly. Impressed by the cordiality and high caliber of the Spanish officials he encountered, Mullins assured the Board of Trade on 4 December that the Lerroux regime was quite eager to expand its purchases

---

[19] *AEE*, 1934, p. 296; Adams, *Economic Conditions in Spain, 1935*, pp. 13–14.

[20] Adams, *Economic Conditions in Spain, 1935*, pp. 10–13; minutes of the Board of Trade meeting 27 September 1934, C. R. T. 7625/34, ser. 549, vol. 306, BT-11, Records of the Board of Trade, Commercial Relations and Treaties Department, Public Record Office (hereafter cited as PRO BT11).

from Britain in return for reciprocal concessions on Spain's orange exports. Upon his return from Madrid two weeks later Mullins reiterated that the Spaniards were well aware of the importance of the British market for their produce and were willing to offer Britons "considerable advantages in the Spanish market." But "in order to 'grease the wheels,'" the Board of Trade must "obtain from the Ministry of Agriculture something to whet the Spanish palate." Should Britain lower its duty on Valencian oranges for example, Mullins pointed out, it would "reap substantial reward." The best way to reach a speedy solution, he concluded, was to commence preliminary commercial negotiations with Spain at once.[21] The Board of Trade agreed on 19 December, and after Whitehall gave its approval the Lerroux regime was invited "to send a small official delegation to London early in the New Year." By February 1935 "the growth of confidence in the stability of the country" and the promise of an Anglo-Spanish commercial agreement led Alexander Adams at Madrid to predict that British trade with Spain would "steadily improve during the coming year."[22]

Spain's commercial relations with the United States, like those with Great Britain, grew gradually better throughout 1934. Well into February some State Department officials were still complaining that Spain, with its "discriminations against our trade," was "giving us more trouble than any other country" and that the United States should "show that it means business" by retaliating against Spanish exports.[23] Most American officials, however, including Assistant Secretary Sayre and Economic Adviser Herbert Feis, shared Tariff Commission staffer Joseph Jones's conviction that mutual concessions of the sort embodied in the wine and tobacco deal were more likely to resolve outstanding trade disputes than "pressure or punishment."[24] Bowers agreed with this latter judgment. He predicted "something of a crisis" in March unless

[21] Mullins to the Board of Trade, 4 December 1934; minutes of the Board of Trade meeting 19 December 1934; and minutes of the Board of Trade meeting 20 December 1934, C. R. T. 9740/34, ser. 549, PRO BT11, vol. 327.

[22] J. J. Wills (Board of Trade) to Vansittart, 4 January 1935; Mounsey to Grahame, 7 January 1935, W139/25/41; Grahame to Simon, 10 January 1935, W416/25/41, PRO FO371; Adams, *Economic Conditions in Spain, 1935*, p. 1.

[23] Moffat, Diplomatic Journals, 2 February 1934, Moffat Papers; "Spanish Trade," by Paul T. Culbertson, 10 February 1934, 611.5231/928, NA RG59.

[24] Feis to Sayre, 17 February 1934, 611.5231/929, NA RG59; Jones, *Tariff Retaliation*, pp. 66–67.

the United States opened serious trade talks with Spain soon. Despite his own "friendly interest in maintaining the best possible relations between the two countries," Secretary of State Hull explained on 28 March that the absence of reciprocal trade legislation made it impossible for Washington to start commercial negotiations with Madrid. Two weeks later the unhappy Lerroux regime tightened its financial restrictions on American exporters and investors.[25]

Faced with fresh evidence that Spanish officials were quite prepared to stifle U.S. trade, the Roosevelt administration moved to lift the embargo on Almerian grapes. Following extensive tests, the Department of Agriculture announced in mid-April that improved refrigeration techniques made it possible to rescind the American sanitary quarantine effective 1 May 1934. Washington's latest concession, Bowers reported with satisfaction in mid-May, had produced "a great improvement" in the commercial situation at Madrid and had dispelled at last the mistaken notion "that for some reason the United States was not friendly to Spain." Indeed, once the Almerian grape dispute was settled amicably, Spanish foreign minister Leandro Pita Romero assured Bowers that "the trade difficulties of our two countries [could] be settled speedily and to their mutual benefit." The removal of the embargo, what one American had labeled "a jewel of great price," had brought Washington and Madrid another step closer to resolving their longstanding economic grievances with each other.[26]

Congress finally passed the Reciprocal Trade Agreements Act on 4 June 1934. The president signed it into law eight days later, opening the door to formal commercial negotiations between the United States and Spain. In an effort to expedite matters, Madrid tapped Foreign Ministry trade expert Luis Calderón as its new ambassador in Washington. Calderón presented his credentials at the White House on 14 June, pledged to work for a swift resolution of Spanish-American commercial troubles, and received Roosevelt's per-

---

[25]Bowers to Hull, tel. 26 March 1934, and Hull to Bowers, tel. 28 March 1934, *FRUS, 1934*, 2:693–94; Bowers to Hull, 28 March 1934, 611.5231/799, and 11 April 1934, 852.5151/78, NA RG59.

[26]Hull to Bowers, tel. 20 April 1934, 811.612 Grapes—Spain/200a, NA RG59; Moffat, Diplomatic Journals, 20 April 1934, Moffat Papers; Moffat to Bowers, 7 May 1934, and Bowers, Diary, 14 May 1934, Bowers Papers; Bowers to Roosevelt, 16 May 1934, 611.5231/802, NA RG59.

sonal assurance that U.S. officials would "do all in their power to cooperate" with him. At the end of the month the Spaniard paid his first call on Cordell Hull, who confirmed the State Department's earnest desire for "a satisfactory adjustment" of outstanding grievances through "a mutual expansion of our trade."[27] Spain's unwillingness to rule out import quotas and restore most-favored-nation treatment to American exports delayed the start of trade talks in July and tempted U.S. officials "to decline to negotiate with the Spaniards [and] put into effect tariff retaliation" instead. Calderón, however, prevented a serious breach by promising that "Spain would grant an equitable share of the [import] contingents to American products" based on "a period of unrestricted trade." Once Madrid officially confirmed that "the total volume of North American exportation to Spain would continue to keep its present characteristics" throughout 1934, Washington announced that the long-awaited commercial negotiations would start formally on 17 September.[28]

After eighteen months of haggling, the news that Spanish-American trade talks were under way evoked an enthusiastic response at Madrid. "The atmosphere for negotiations with Spain is ideal and Spain actually is giving us more concessions than she has given any other country just now," Bowers jubilantly advised Roosevelt in mid-September. "The Government here is enormously pleased with our agreement to get together." At the end of the month he informed the State Department as well that recent American concessions on Spanish wines and fruits had left Madrid in an extremely conciliatory mood. The Spaniards still hoped that a commercial treaty would help reduce their huge deficit with the United States, but they now realized that this effect could be best achieved by multilateral trade expansion rather than by bilateral trade discrimination. Heartened by such encouraging reports, Washington decided on 26 September to press its negotiations with Madrid "with greater vigor than the others."[29]

[27] Hull, *Memoirs*, 1:357; Roosevelt quoted in "The Ambassador of Spain Presents His Letters of Credence, June 14, 1934," United States, Department of State, *Press Releases*, no. 246 (16 June 1934), pp. 410–11; Hull to Calderón, 25 June 1934, and Calderón to Hull, 27 June 1934, *FRUS, 1934*, 2:697–99.

[28] Moffat, Diplomatic Journals, 26 June and 2 and 6 July 1934, Moffat Papers; memorandum by Grady, 6 July 1934, 611.5231/806-1/2, NA RG59; memorandum by John D. Hickerson, 17 July 1934; memorandum by Moffat, 6 September 1934; and Calderón to Hull, 6 September 1934, *FRUS, 1934*, 2:701–2, 705–6.

[29] Bowers to Roosevelt, 19 September 1934, FDR Papers, PPF 730; Bowers to Hull,

Not all Americans, however, were as eager to press forward with trade talks. Businessmen and farmers threatened by potential Spanish competition peppered the State Department with vehement protests urging stiff protection for the domestic market. During the months of September and October alone Hull received dozens of telegrams from cherry and almond growers, iron and mercury producers, and California vintners opposing a commercial treaty with Spain.[30] Nevertheless, these complaints were offset by counterpressures from other sectors of the business community, such as the automobile and tire industries, which hoped that a Spanish-American trade agreement would boost their sagging exports.[31] As a result, by late 1934 most observers in Madrid and Washington expected the new year to bring a commercial rapprochement. "The entire atmosphere of Spanish-American relations has been changed since I came," Bowers noted with pride on 11 December, and the prospects for a trade agreement were good. "If it all works out in the end," he concluded, "it will justify my own theory that good diplomacy is just a spirit of justice and sympathy and that a spirit of good will goes farther than trickery, slyness or a big stick."[32] Indeed, Bowers's tireless efforts on behalf of a trade truce seemed about to pay off. He, like Britain's Arthur Mullins, believed that modest concessions accorded Spanish exports during 1934 were certain to earn big dividends in the future.

III

Spain's increasingly cordial commercial relations with Great Britain and the United States bore fruit during 1935 in a pair of trade agreements. At the invitation of the Board of Trade, Lerroux sent a negotiating team to London that spring to iron out mutual griev-

---

26 September 1934, 611.5231/837, NA RG59; Moffat, Diplomatic Journals, 26 September 1934, Moffat Papers.

[30] For opposition to a commercial treaty with Spain, see Henry Stubbs (almonds) to Hull, 28 September 1934, 611.5231/831; Irving Ballard (mercury) to Hull, 28 September 1934, 611.5231/834; Ralph Eltse (wines) to Hull, 8 October 1934, 611.5231/846; E. Pearce (iron barytes) to Hull, 19 October 1934, 611.5231/852; and Frank Swett (cherries) to Hull, 24 October 1934, 611.5231/857, NA RG59.

[31] For support for a commercial treaty with Spain, see W. D. Blood & Company (auto parts) to Grady, 10 October 1934, 611.5231/854, and Florsheim Shoe Company to Hull, n.d., 611.5231/892, NA RG59.

[32] Bowers to Daniels, 11 December 1934, Daniels Papers.

ances, and by early May the key issues were clear. The Spaniards wanted more favorable treatment for Valencian oranges, the Britons sought simplification of Madrid's complex system of import quotas and exchange controls. Since neither side was willing to make the first move, however, the two delegations engaged in bitter recriminations, and the trade talks deadlocked six weeks later amidst rumors of a tariff war. Indeed, after the Board of Trade threatened to hike duties on Spanish produce by as much as 40 percent, Lerroux warned that in retaliation he would withdraw the rebates extended to British automobile exports eighteen months earlier.[33]

Eager to avoid such commercial warfare if possible, the two delegations met again in early August to hammer out a truce. Although both sides thought it wise to adjourn the talks temporarily so that each could examine its bargaining position "afresh," they also hoped that "goodwill" would govern their relations in the interim. As a result Britain and Spain initialed "a standstill agreement" on 2 August designed to ensure that "each country would pursue a benevolent policy towards the other" until negotiations were resumed in the autumn. Under the terms of this arrangement London and Madrid pledged to "refrain from any action . . . which would in a substantial degree detrimentally affect the other's economic interests." While several thorny matters remained unresolved, this preliminary standstill agreement suggested that both sides were willing to compromise in order to improve commercial relations between their two nations.[34]

Fresh obstacles to an Anglo-Spanish accord emerged that autumn. The exchange situation facing British exporters in Spain went "from bad to worse" in September, when the Lerroux regime tripled the waiting period required to convert pesetas to sterling (from 30 to 90 days). As the delays grew longer, the Board of Trade complained that "there would be no use in continuing the negotiations regarding tariffs . . . and other means of increasing our exports to Spain as long as the Spaniards fail to make punctual provi-

---

[33]Minutes of the meeting between the British and Spanish commercial delegations, 27 June 1935, W6340/25/41; minute by Stirling, 22 July 1935, W6552/25/41, PRO FO371, vols. 19737 and 19738; *Times*, 3 August 1935, p. 9, col. a.

[34]John Colville (Board of Trade) to Garcia Conde, 2 August 1935; Garcia Conde to Colville, 3 August 1935; minute by Stirling, 13 August 1935, W7058/25/41, PRO FO371, vol. 19738.

sion of sterling exchange to pay for what we already send them."
British diplomats, however, believed "it would be an error to abandon the negotiations altogether," and the Foreign Office persuaded
the Board of Trade in mid-November to make one final effort to
conclude a commercial agreement with Spain.[35]

The trade talks adjourned the previous August in London were
accordingly resumed at Madrid on 22 November. British officials
found the Spaniards quite willing, even anxious, to resolve the
convertibility problem amicably provided that modest concessions
were forthcoming on Spanish exports. Spain's trade surplus with
Britain would provide an easy source of sterling to eliminate the
exchange backlog south of the Pyrenees. "The outlook is not altogether unhopeful for some kind of agreement with Spain," Spanish expert C. N. Stirling noted in early December, "if we do not
open our mouths too wide." Just before Christmas 1935 British and
Spanish negotiators came to terms. Spain agreed to establish a
special account at the Banco Exterior in Madrid, where it would
deposit sufficient sterling to liquidate current exchange arrears and
to ensure prompt payment for future British exports. In return
Britain promised privately to reconsider its duties on Spanish produce. The Foreign Office termed this arrangement "very satisfactory" while the Board of Trade was "very favorably impressed indeed," and the Anglo-Spanish payments agreement went into
effect early in the new year.[36]

Rapid progress in the ongoing reciprocal trade negotiations in
Washington led to a more comprehensive Spanish commercial accord with the United States during 1935. Spain's "petty bargaining
spirit" and its penchant for reducing its big deficit with the United
States through bilateral balancing ran counter to the American

[35] Memorandum by Commercial Secretary Arthur Pack (Madrid), 13 September
1935, enclosed in Chargé d'Affaires George Ogilvie-Forbes to Hoare, 20 September
1935, W8318/25/41; Ogilvie-Forbes to Hoare, 28 September 1935, W8567/25/41;
Mounsey to Chilton, 5 November 1935, W9243/25/41; Chilton to Mounsey, 15
November 1935, W9993/25/41; Ronald Fraser (Board of Trade) to Hoare, 18 November 1935, W9980/25/41, PRO FO371, vol. 19738.

[36] Memorandum by Pack, 22 November 1935, enclosed in Chilton to Hoare, 22
November 1935; minute by Stirling, 5 December 1935, W10174/25/41; memorandum
by Pack, 14 December 1935, enclosed in Chilton to Hoare, 14 December 1935; minute by Stirling, 17 December 1935, W10731/25/41, PRO FO371, vol. 19738; Cmnd.
5097, "Payments Agreement between the Government of the United Kingdom and
the Spanish Government," 6 January 1936, *Parliamentary Papers* (Commons), *1935–
1936*, vol. 28.

"view of opening up trade policy along broad lines" and nearly derailed the talks during the winter. The Spaniards answered U.S. requests for most-favored-nation treatment and an end to preferential import quotas and exchange controls with higher duties on American cigarettes, tighter restrictions on ITT's profit remittances, and outright default on the $675,000 Export-Import Bank tobacco credit.[37] When Madrid unveiled a proposal in February freezing American automobile exports at fewer than 500 per year, Washington termed the plan "unjust and unfair" and warned that such action would "in all probability end the commercial negotiations with the United States."[38]

A growing rift between Spain and France, however, worked in favor of the United States as the year wore on. For months Paris had been threatening to embargo Spanish fruits and wines in order "ruthlessly to bulldoze" Madrid into granting "special advantages" for French manufacturers. The Lerroux regime intended to adopt a hard line against such pressure, but Claude Bowers pointed out in late February that "Spain would be in [a] better position to resist French demands and threats had she some assurance that she could find markets to make up for the losses that might result." Hoping to profit from the Franco-Spanish falling out, Hull and Roosevelt agreed later that spring to reduce American duties on Spanish cork, olives, and other commodities in the near future.[39] Bowers applauded these U.S. concessions, which he believed were responsible in part for Lerroux's decision in early May to sever commercial relations with France. Indeed, he advised Hull that the Spaniards' "annoyance with the French and their desire to find new markets makes the moment psychologically a good one to bring our new negotiations to a successful conclusion." The secretary of state apparently agreed, for he cabled Bowers on 6 May that

---

[37] Morgan to Hickerson, 14 December 1934, 611.5231/904; John E. Walker (R. J. Reynolds Tobacco) to Hull, 5 February 1935, 852.5151/101; memorandum by Moffat, 21 January 1935, 852.5151/271; Bowers to Hull, tel. 15 February 1935, 652.116 Auto/1, NA RG59; Hull to Bowers, tel. 14 February 1935, File 851 (Madrid—1935), vol. XV, NA RG84.

[38] Bowers to Hull, tel. 15 February 1935; Hull to Bowers, tel. 19 February 1935; Bowers to Hull, tel. 21 February 1935, *FRUS, 1935,* 2: 697–99.

[39] Bowers, Diary, 21 February 1935, Bowers Papers; Bowers to Hull, tel. 21 February 1935, *FRUS, 1935,* 2:699; Bowers to Hull, 13 March 1935, 651.5231/129; memorandum by Morgan, 22 April 1935; Hull to Roosevelt, 26 April 1935; and Roosevelt to Hull, 30 April 1935, 611.5231/967, NA RG59.

American and Spanish negotiators were now "meeting daily in order to expedite matters as much as possible."[40]

Some major sticking points nevertheless delayed the conclusion of a commercial accord between Spain and the United States over the summer. Despite recent American concessions on a variety of Spanish products, the Lerroux regime steadfastly refused to raise its quota for U.S. automobile exports. The 472 units allotted the Americans for 1935, the Madrid authorities explained, matched precisely Detroit's sales in Spain the previous year. The State Department, however, was quick to point out that recent discrimination against American motor cars had slashed their share of the Spanish market from 50 to 4 percent. A more equitable base period such as the late 1920s, U.S. officials suggested, would give Detroit a quota in excess of 5,000 units. Unless the Spaniards proved more receptive to this line of reasoning, Cordell Hull warned, it would be impossible to conclude "more than a very limited [trade] agreement."[41]

Determined to soften the State Department's unyielding position on auto exports, Claude Bowers returned to Washington in June 1935 to lobby for a compromise. Although he complained later that "everyone [was] on my back every day from the President on down," Bowers insisted that an American quota of 5,000 motor cars "was asking too much considering the great adverse balance of trade in Spain." Terming a figure around 2,000 much more realistic, he warned that continued inflexibility would probably result "in depriving us of most of [our] exports to Spain which amounted last year to over $38,000,000."[42]

Two developments that summer strengthened Bowers's hand. First, in an effort to evade Spanish import barriers both Ford and General Motors had established new branch plants at Barcelona, moves that Hull believed had "considerable importance in view of our current negotiations with Spain." Expanded local output by

---

[40]Bowers to Hull, tel. 1 May 1935, 651.5231/136, NA RG59; Phillips, Journal, 2 May 1935, Phillips Papers; Bowers to Hull, tel. 2 May 1935; Hull to Bowers, 6 May 1935, *FRUS, 1935,* 2:703–4.

[41]Bowers to Hull, tel. 6 May 1935; memorandum by Grady, 17 May 1935; Hull to Bowers, tel. 17 May 1935, *FRUS, 1935,* 2:704–8.

[42]Bowers to Daniels, 27 November 1935, Daniels Papers; Bowers to Sayre, 27 June 1935, 611.5231/987, NA RG59; Bowers to Hull, 12 July 1935, Hull Papers, microfilm ed., reel 12; Hull to Bowers, 12 July 1935, Bowers Papers.

U.S. multinationals would offset any losses caused by discriminatory Spanish import quotas.[43] Second, after a full-fledged tariff war erupted between Spain and France in July, the Lerroux regime levied a 50-percent surcharge on all French exports. Should Washington bypass this opportunity to move closer to Madrid, Bowers prophesied, similar treatment would await U.S. products. The State Department must show "greater flexibility" on the auto quotas or risk "ruining American export trade with Spain" entirely. After "careful and detailed consideration" of these and other aspects of the matter, the Roosevelt administration in September reluctantly accepted a compromise that gave Detroit a quota of 2,500 units for 1935.[44]

No sooner had the auto controversy been settled than a financial flare-up threatened to disrupt the negotiations. Its 90-million-peseta trade deficit with the United States producing an ever-greater shortage of foreign exchange, Madrid announced in late August that it could not guarantee American exporters and investors that their pesetas would be converted into dollars unless Washington arranged a $200-million currency stabilization credit. Firms such as ITT and General Motors supported the Spanish proposal, for obvious reasons. So did the Treasury Department, which still hoped to expand American exports through bilateral credits.[45] Cordell Hull, however, was outraged that the Spaniards still seemed "disposed to place obstacles in the way of our trade rather than to remove them" and ruled as a result on 19 September that "the question of a commercial agreement with Spain should not be complicated in any way by the [proposed] loan." Only after the conclusion of a trade treaty guaranteeing Americans "fair and equitable" access to foreign exchange, he told Spanish negotiators, would the United States even consider "loans or advances in mod-

---

[43] Hull to Johnson, 28 June 1935, 164.21/346, NA RG59. For more details on Ford and General Motors in Spain see chap. 7, sec. III, above.

[44] Secretary of the Treasury Henry J. Morgenthau, Jr., to Hull, 2 July 1935, 651.5231/148; Bowers to Hull, 10 July 1935, 651.5231/155, tel. 12 July 1935, 651.5231/151, and 14 August 1935, 611.5231/1017, NA RG59; Hull to Bowers, 13 September 1935, and Bowers to Hull, 20 September 1935, *FRUS, 1935*, 2:720, 722.

[45] Bowers to Hull, tel. 14 August 1935; Hull to Bowers, tel. 3 September 1935; Bowers to Hull, tel. 7 September 1935, *FRUS, 1935*, 2:717–19; Bowers to Hull, tel. 16 September 1935, 852.5151/140, and tel. 8 October 1935, 852.51/308, NA RG59; On ITT and Treasury Department activities, see Little, "Malevolent Neutrality," pp. 492–99.

est amounts." Unwilling to jeopardize a commercial accord that promised to broaden Spanish access to the American market, Madrid dropped its demand for a stabilization credit in October and in so doing removed the final obstacle to a reciprocal trade agreement.[46]

With the loan issue at least temporarily out of the way, Secretary of State Hull and Ambassador Calderón were able at last to initial a preliminary draft of the Spanish-American commercial treaty on 23 October 1935. Under the terms of the proposed agreement Madrid could look forward to tariff reductions on agricultural products ranging from wines to onions while Washington received lower duties on cotton, wheat, and tobacco. Moreover, Spain guaranteed American merchants most-favored-nation treatment on foreign exchange and import quotas in return for "sympathetic consideration" by the United States for any complaints concerning administrative or sanitary restrictions on Spanish produce.[47] If in the short run Madrid stood to gain appreciably more than Washington from the treaty in terms of increased exports, the Roosevelt administration nevertheless emerged from the negotiations with its commercial principles largely intact and with long-run prospects for trade expansion in Spain markedly enhanced. As one American observer put it as the year drew to a close, a half-decade of "quiet tariff war" between Spain and the United States had apparently come to an end.[48]

By late 1935, then, Spanish commercial relations with both Great Britain and the United States were better than at any time since the inception of the republic four years earlier. Azaña's autarchic trade program had given way to the more flexible policies of Lerroux, who gradually phased out the preferential import duties and currency controls imposed prior to 1933. Britain's role as the most important overseas market for Spanish products made it relatively easy for Whitehall to secure equitable treatment for British export-

---

[46] Hull to Bowers, 19 September 1935, 852.51/299a, and tel. 9 October 1935, 611.5231/1037, NA RG59; memorandum by Grady, 16 October 1935, *FRUS, 1935,* 2:724.

[47] "Draft Trade Agreement between the United States and Spain," 23 October 1935, *FRUS, 1935,* 2:724–32.

[48] "Comment on the Proposed Trade Agreement with Spain," undated, unsigned memorandum [probably October 1935], Hull Papers, microfilm ed., reel 50; George Haas to Morgenthau, 19 November 1935, Morgenthau Papers.

ers through tariff and foreign exchange accords hammered out in 1935. Washington's quest for most-favored-nation treatment from Madrid, on the other hand, was complicated by Spain's substantial trade deficit with the United States, but the White House connections of Claude Bowers and the hard bargaining of Cordell Hull produced a series of mutual concessions that eventually culminated in the tentative Spanish-American commercial agreement initialed in October 1935.

The more favorable climate for British and American exporters was, however, only as secure as the Lerroux regime itself. Once the *straperlo* scandal touched off a new round of political instability at Madrid, policy makers in London and Washngton worried that their recent commercial accords with Spain might come unglued overnight. Whitehall, for example, wondered whether the caretaker regime of Portela Valladares would honor the Anglo-Spanish standstill agreement on tariffs concluded the previous summer with Lerroux.[49] The outlook across the Atlantic was even less sanguine. Indeed, some State Department officials believed that the political and financial uncertainties unleashed by the collapse of the Lerroux regime would delay Spanish ratification of the reciprocal trade treaty with the United States indefinitely.[50]

The British and American sense of frustration and foreboding in the wake of the *straperlo* scandal was, of course, not limited to commercial matters. The more conservative atmosphere at Madrid between 1933 and 1935 had also fostered better political relations with London and Washington, both of which applauded the restoration of law and order and the return of fiscal responsibility under Lerroux and Chapaprieta. The sudden parliamentary crisis during the autumn of 1935 came as a rude shock for many British and American officials, who had hoped to build a lasting rapprochement with Spain's reformist right. The more hospitable business climate generated by the Lerroux regime likewise enabled some multinationals, among them ITT and Rio Tinto, to resolve nagging problems and encouraged others, including Ford and General Motors, to expand their operations. To no one's great surprise foreign investors, like merchants and policy makers on both sides of the Atlantic, lamented Lerroux's demise in late 1935 and readied

---

[49] Chilton to Hoare, tel. 26 December 1935, W10938/25/41, PRO FO371, vol. 19739.
[50] Memorandum by Morgan, 30 December 1935, 852.75 NTC/203-1/2, NA RG59.

themselves for another season of stormy weather south of the Pyrenees.

For most British and American observers, the interlude of relatively moderate rule by the reformist right from 1933 to 1935 had been a welcome respite from the left-wing chaos and confusion of the previous two years. Under Lerroux and his allies the specter of bolshevik subversion faded, threats against multinational investment waned, and discrimination against foreign trade abated. These pleasant developments did not go unnoticed in London or Washington. Indeed, Spain's overall relations with both the United States and Great Britain were by the summer of 1935 more cordial than anyone could have imagined just two years earlier.

As a result the Lerroux era became something of a benchmark against which Whitehall and the White House could measure the frightful disorder of the early 1930s and the renewed turmoil that looked ever more certain for 1936. When the Roosevelt and Baldwin administrations compared Azaña, who had been unable to curb left-wing excesses and unwilling to compromise on commercial matters, with Lerroux, who had swiftly quelled the 1934 Socialist uprising and had shown considerable flexibility in trade negotiations, they found that there really was no contest. Nor was there any doubt in corporate board rooms about which regime, the Left Republican or the reformist right, had been more sympathetic to foreign investments.

For British and American businessmen and diplomats alike, the two-year period of relative tranquillity that Spain had known after 1933 seemed almost too good to be true. And so it was. With the collapse of the Lerroux regime in the autumn of 1935, frustrated and frightened policy makers in London and Washington grimly concluded that the Spanish Republic had unknowingly passed some dreadful point of no return and that the new year would bring more political violence and, perhaps, even civil war.

9

The Road to Civil War, 1936

Two years of relative political stability, favorable business conditions, and more equitable trade policies had fostered better British and American relations with Spain. The collapse of Lerroux and the reformist right, however, and the resurgence of the revolutionary left in early 1936 rekindled old fears on both sides of the Atlantic of bolshevik subversion, economic nationalism, and commercial autarchy. Both London and Washington were shocked when a left-wing Popular Front coalition based on concepts favored by the Kremlin emerged from the chaos at Madrid to win a narrow victory at the polls in February 1936. Rapid ideological polarization and widespread popular disturbances made effective government impossible during the months that followed, leaving little doubt at the Foreign Office or the State Department that the Spanish Republic had fallen prey to international communism. Moreover, as Spain swung sharply to the left Rio Tinto and ITT once again encountered serious troubles, and the British and American trade truce concluded with the Lerroux regime gradually unraveled. By July 1936 Great Britain and the United States could only watch with despair and disgust as the left-wing government at Madrid careened down the road to civil war.

I

Both British and American officials saw ominous parallels between the 1936 Spanish election campaign and recent developments at the Kremlin. The previous summer the Seventh Comintern Congress had convened in Moscow and, chastened by Nazi decimation of the German Communists, had urged its member parties to forge "united front" alliances with all antifascist organizations. Six months later Spanish Communists joined a Popular Front coalition of Socialists, Left Republicans, and Catalan separatists patterned loosely on the Comintern model. Led by former prime minister Azaña, this left-wing alliance endorsed a moderate program of religious, educational, and agrarian reforms and on 15 January 1936 promised amnesty for the thousands of political prisoners jailed after the Asturian revolution. Although neither the Socialists nor the Communists were willing to serve in any forthcoming "bourgeois" cabinet, both groups pledged full parliamentary support for a progressive republican regime.[1] Precisely because the Spanish left appeared more united and more confident that it had for years, policy makers on both sides of the Atlantic feared that a Popular Front triumph on 16 February would reignite the radical aspirations of workers and peasants and in so doing plunge Spain into a revolutionary firestorm.

Neither the State Department nor the Foreign Office placed much faith in the Comintern's united front or its Spanish analog. As early as 19 July 1935 Ambassador William Bullitt had warned Washington that despite the Russian call for an antifascist alliance, the Kremlin's ultimate goal remained "to produce a world revolution." Undersecretary of State William Phillips likewise saw the united front as a Soviet charade and complained in August that the Comintern was still "encouraging communistic efforts in other countries." Moreover, Secretary of State Cordell Hull interpreted the presence of the American Communist leader Earl Browder at the Moscow conclave as proof of renewed Soviet subversion in the United States; he bitterly protested the Kremlin's violation of its 1933 pledge to refrain from such activities.[2]

Although preoccupied with the deepening crisis in Abyssinia, London shared Washington's misgivings about recent Russian maneuvers. Viscount Chilston, the British ambassador to the Soviet Union, compared the Kremlin's united front strategy to "the Trojan horse" and, like Bullitt, cautioned in August that "world revolution

---

[1] Cattell, *Communism and the Spanish Civil War*, pp. 23–24; Jackson, *Spanish Republic and the Civil War*, pp. 184–86; Payne, *Spanish Revolution*, pp. 163–64.

[2] Bullitt to Cordell Hull, tel. 19 July 1935, tel. 26 July 1935, and tel. 21 August 1935, *FRUS: The Soviet Union, 1933–1939*, pp. 225–26, 228–29, 244–47; Phillips, Journal, vol. 7, n.d. [probably early August 1935], Phillips Papers; Hull, *Memoirs*, 1:305; Beatrice Farnsworth, *William C. Bullitt and the Soviet Union* (Bloomington, Ind., 1967), pp. 142–49.

remains as ever the ultimate end of Comintern policy." Whitehall agreed that the Comintern was "certainly not dead" but was merely "being driven underground" in order to "give more scope for communist activities." The Kremlin's new and "far cleverer line of attack," Chilston prophesied later that autumn, was "eventually more likely to bear fruit in democratic countries than the former line of preaching open revolution."[3]

The formation of a Popular Front coalition in Spain during the winter of 1935–1936 seemed to confirm such dire predictions of Soviet subversion. The emergence of a left-wing electoral bloc "thoroughly alarmed" Spanish conservatives, who warned Ambassador Claude Bowers shortly before Christmas that a Popular Front triumph would mean "the immediate disbandment of the Civil Guard and the socialization of the banks and the major industries." Although Bowers initially discounted rumors that "a victory for the Left would not only mean a proletarian revolution but one as bloody as that of Russia," by New Year's Eve he was confessing that such prophecies had been "substantiated to a considerable extent by the developments of the week," particularly the shrill calls of some Socialists for class war.[4] Sir Henry Chilton also questioned whether a left-wing victory at the polls would unleash "a revolution more bloody than the French and Russian revolutions," but he had to admit that "the unexpected happens more frequently and more suddenly in Spain than in any other country." Distressed by "the leftward swing" at Madrid, Permanent Undersecretary of State Robert Vansittart reckoned early in the new year that Spain was "in for a fresh wave of troublous times" and instructed Chilton "to consider the situation at the Rio Tinto mines."[5]

Indeed, British and American multinationals worried that the resurgence of the revolutionary left during 1936 would endanger their quarter-billion-dollar stake south of the Pyrenees. ITT execu-

---

[3]Chilston to Hoare, 30 July 1935, and minutes by B. A. B. Burrows, 6 August 1935, and J. L. Dodds, 7 August 1935, N3894/54/38; Chilston to Hoare, 13 August 1935, N4118/54/38, and 29 November 1935, and minutes by Dodds, 19 December 1935, and Laurence Collier, 20 December 1935, N6304/135/38, PRO FO371, vols. 19457 and 19460.

[4]Bowers, Diary, 23 December 1935, Bowers Papers; Bowers to Hull, 23 December 1935, 852.00/2127, and 31 December 1935, 852.00/2128, NA RG59; Bowers, *My Mission to Spain*, pp. 175–76.

[5]Chilton to Eden, 27 December 1935; minute by Vansittart, 2 January 1936; Vansittart to Chilton, tel. 3 January 1936, W11051/18/41, PRO FO371, vol. 19736.

tives in Madrid and Washington complained that the political and economic uncertainty surrounding the upcoming elections seriously handicapped their Spanish operations.[6] Rio Tinto officials likewise displayed "a definite hostility to the Left . . . based on a general disapproval of the Republic." Captain Ulick deB. Charles, the copper firm's representative at Madrid, called at Whitehall on 8 January and confirmed that the situation in Spain was "quite uncertain." Although "he did not seem to think the Communist danger very serious," Charles claimed that the caretaker regime of Manuel Portela Valladares was "biased to the Left" and predicted that a Popular Front triumph would spark "a coup d'etat by the Right sooner or later." Five years of turmoil, he grumbled, had finally persuaded Rio Tinto "to discount the possibility of any successful form of Republican government," and Spanish expert C. N. Stirling conceded that "events certainly do not justify any optimism" regarding parliamentary rule in Spain.[7]

British and American commercial relations with Spain in early 1936 also showed signs of strain. To be sure, the Anglo-Spanish payments agreement went into operation in January, making it much easier than in the past to convert pesetas into sterling. But Madrid's decision to grant Britons preferred access to scarce foreign exchange at the expense of their American competitors placed London and Washington on a collision course with each other. The State Department viewed this preferential arrangement as a blatant act of bad faith by both Spain and Britain and lodged protests against it, first with Spanish ambassador Luis Calderón and then with his British colleague, Sir Ronald Lindsay. Terming the payments plan "narrow" and "short-sighted," Cordell Hull warned Lindsay on 22 January that Britain's effort to siphon off Spain's foreign exchange would "drive trade straight into the bilateral channel" and would have "obstructive and handicapping effects" on American efforts to restore world commerce on a multilateral basis. When Lindsay explained that London and Madrid regarded the recent accord as "more or less natural" given their trading relationship, Hull angrily retorted that those nations "sit-

---

[6]Bowers, Diary, 23 December 1935, Bowers Papers; Colonel Sosthenes Behn to Assistant Secretary of State Francis B. Sayre, 31 December 1935, 852.5151/164, NA RG59.

[7]Stirling to Charles, 6 January 1936, W98/62/41; minute by Stirling, 9 January 1936, W225/62/41, PRO FO371, vol. 20519.

ting behind tariff walls and Empire preference" would in the long run do more to stymie than to stimulate global economic recovery.[8] As election day neared, all the old ideological, multinational, and commercial problems that had bedeviled British and American relations with Spain in the early 1930s had begun to resurface.

The outcome of the partisan struggle in Spain remained very much an open question, for Spaniard and foreigner alike, right down through the balloting on 16 February 1936. As the campaign moved into full swing, the left-wing Popular Front coalition, in early January seemingly unbeatable, began to show signs of political schizophrenia. Manuel Azaña and his moderate Left Republicans were promising progressive reforms at the same time that Francisco Largo Caballero and his Socialist militants were preaching proletarian revolution. Despite the erstwhile efforts of José María Gil Robles and CEDA to mount a broad "antimarxist crusade," the Spanish right was in even greater disarray. With royalists like José Calvo Sotelo favoring the restoration of the monarchy and with José Antonio Primo de Rivera and his Falange Española calling for a military coup, Gil Robles was unable to patch together a conservative National Front coalition until the first week in February. The political center had, of course, atrophied with the collapse of Lerroux and his Radical party, rendering the last-minute attempts of President Niceto Alcalá-Zamora to rally Spaniards to his middle-of-the-road republicanism futile. In such a volatile atmosphere the upcoming elections were simply too close to call.[9]

Both the United States and Great Britain monitored these developments closely. Convinced that "the accumulated passions" of the previous two years made for an explosive situation, Claude Bowers predicted "a campaign of extreme bitterness" during which "numerous political grievances . . . are certain to be well ventilated." The right and the left in Spain, he warned Hull on 15 January, were like "two gamblers with revolvers on the table, one of whom, seeing the other about to win will bring the revolver into

---

[8]Memorandum by Feis for Hull, 9 January 1936, 611.5231/1093; memorandum by Grady for Sayre, 10 January 1936, 611.5231/1094, NA RG59; memorandum by Hull, 22 January 1936, *FRUS, 1936*, 1:629–32.

[9]Jackson, *Spanish Republic and Civil War*, pp. 186–88; Preston, *Coming of the Spanish Civil War*, pp. 145–50; Robinson, *Origins of Franco's Spain*, pp. 239–45; Stanley Payne, *Falange: A History of Spanish Fascism* (Stanford, Calif., 1961), pp. 89–95; Payne, *Spanish Revolution*, pp. 164–72.

play." Colonel Stephen Fuqua, the new U.S. military attaché at Madrid, took an even grimmer view and foresaw "the consequent overthrow of the present state should [the left] bloc win a sweeping victory." Worried by the growing influence of Largo Caballero, the self-proclaimed "Spanish Lenin" who many now felt was "not a socialist of the evolutionary sort but a communist," Bowers himself admitted privately at month's end that "Spain seems bent on going into a civil war."[10]

British observers were equally concerned by the increasing appeal of the extreme left. Ambassador Chilton advised Sir Anthony Eden, the youthful knight errant of the Conservative party who had replaced Sir Samuel Hoare as foreign secretary in late December 1935, that Spanish police had in early January confiscated "2 million pesetas which had been remitted from Russian Bolshevik funds" to subsidize the Popular Front campaign. "The Socialists, Communists and Syndicalists," he added, "have been fairly quiet, to my mind ominously quiet." When left-wing disorders erupted in the Canary Islands on 20 January, frightening the British community at Las Palmas, Consul Harold Patteson blamed "the communist element" and urged Whitehall to dispatch a warship. Disheartened by the accelerating polarization at Madrid, Chilton concluded a week later that only an unexpectedly strong showing by the weak center parties could prevent Spain from being "plunged into the civil war prophesied by extremists both of the Right and the Left."[11]

By election day neither Washington nor London expected moderation to prevail at Madrid, but they disagreed over whether the Popular or the National Front was more likely to emerge victorious. Sensing that most Spaniards were both sympathetic to Azaña's brand of reformism and suspicious of the authoritarian proclivities of Gil Robles, Bowers foresaw a left-wing triumph at the polls. "A lifetime of study of political psychology and reactions," he recalled in his memoirs, "convinced me that the Leftists would win." The

---

[10]Bowers to Hull, 8 January 1936, 852.00/2130, and 15 January 1936, 852.00/2132, NA RG59; Bowers, Diary, 8, 24, and 30 January and 1 February 1936, Bowers Papers; Fuqua to G-2, 29 January 1936, 2657 S.162/8, NA RG165.

[11]Chilton to Eden, 7 January 1936, W342/62/41, and 8 January 1936, W343/62/41; Patteson to Chilton, 22 January 1936, enclosed in Chilton to Eden, 30 January 1936, W1075/627/41; Chilton to Eden, 29 January 1936, W1074/62/41, PRO FO371, vols. 20520 and 20564.

State Department had apparently resigned itself to a Popular Front victory as well, for when ITT's Frank Page suggested on election eve that the balloting would "result in the establishment of a stronger government than Spain has had in many years," the only comment by Undersecretary Phillips was a big question mark.[12] Most British observers, on the other hand, expected the right to win by a narrow margin. Sir Henry Chilton, for example, believed that conservatives such as Gil Robles would build "an insurmountable barrier to revolution." Whitehall's C. N. Stirling likewise predicted that Spain's "considerable middle class vote" would give the right "a respectable following in the next Cortes." A week before the balloting Chilton reported that the National Front now expected to win a clear parliamentary majority and assured Eden that this forecast should "prove fairly accurate."[13]

When the reckoning came on 16 February, the elections were, as most observers had expected, relatively fair and extremely close, but in the end Bowers's prediction proved more accurate than Chilton's. Bolstered by perhaps a million anarchists who went to the polls for the first time, the Popular Front eked out a narrow victory, gaining just over 50 percent of the votes cast. The left-wing coalition received some 4.7 million ballots to its right-wing rival's 4 million, while the tattered parties of the center totaled a mere 450,000. The Left Republicans headed the Popular Front contingent with 117 seats in the new Cortes, the Socialists placed second with 90, and the 30,000 member Spanish Communist party trailed badly, returning but 15 deputies.[14] While jubilant leftists celebrated in the streets, General Francisco Franco and other military leaders urged Portela Valladares to annul the election returns. But the aging prime minister, anxious to rid himself of his caretaker responsibilities and convinced that only a rapid transition to Popular Front rule could prevent serious disorders, stepped down on 18 February so that the left-wing coalition could put together a cabinet at once. When Manuel Azaña reclaimed his old post as prime minister the

[12] Bowers, *My Mission to Spain*, p. 187; Page to Phillips, 13 February 1936, 852.00/2137, NA RG59.

[13] Chilton to Eden, 24 January 1936, W797/62/41, and 29 January 1936, and minute by Stirling, 8 February 1936, W1074/62/41; Chilton to Eden, 9 February 1936, W1355/62/41, PRO FO371, vol. 20520.

[14] Brenan, *Spanish Labyrinth*, pp. 298–300, 314–15; Jackson, *Spanish Republic and Civil War*, pp. 192–94, 360–62; Payne, *Spanish Revolution*, pp. 183–84; Cattell, *Communism and the Spanish Civil War*, p. 32.

following day, Spain's political future seemed as unpredictable as ever.[15]

If the Foreign Office and the State Department had not seen eye to eye on the probable outcome of the elections, they shared a common anxiety that a Popular Front regime in Spain would open the door to the extreme left. Robert G. Caldwell, the U.S. ambassador to Portugal, warned Washington on 18 February that the Salazar regime feared the Spanish elections would "be followed by bloody disturbances and by consequent insecurity for life and property." Bowers reported a day later that the Popular Front victory had taken Spain's business community by surprise and had sent the Madrid stock exchange into a sharp tailspin. Troubled by this "decided swing to the left," Undersecretary Phillips noted that although "for the moment at least, all is quiet in Spain," even "the [Spanish] Embassy here fears communistic tendencies." Eager to dispel the "exaggerated reports of disorder in Spain in the foreign press," Bowers wired Washington on 24 February that "apart from isolated closed incidents country tranquil and Government's authority completely established." Privately, however, he expected serious trouble from Largo Caballero and the extreme left, likened contemporary Spain to France in 1792, and prophesied that "Azaña will not have a bed of roses."[16]

British officials painted an equally bleak picture of Spain in the early days of the Popular Front. On 21 February Consul Patteson at Las Palmas reported that yet another "revolutionary strike" had created a "very dangerous" situation for Britons and their property in the Canary Islands. Similar disturbances broke out the next day at Malaga, prompting Whitehall, as it had a month earlier, to have a warship stand by at Gibraltar for a possible rescue mission. Such outbreaks merely strengthened Ambassador Chilton's conviction that while the Popular Front regime might "have a fairly easy time of it for six months or a year," there were "some turbulent elements on the Left Wing" who would eventually find its reforms "too

---

[15] Azaña, "Memorias políticas y de guerra," 19 February 1936, in *Obras completas,* 4:563–70; Jackson, *Spanish Republic and Civil War,* pp. 194–95; Robinson, *Origins of Franco's Spain,* pp. 250–52.

[16] Caldwell to Hull, 18 February 1936, 852.00/2138; Bowers to Hull, 19 February 1936, 852.00/2140, NA RG59; Phillips, Journal, 20 February 1936, Phillips Papers; Bowers to Hull, tel. 24 February 1936, 852.00/2136, NA RG59; Bowers, Diary, 1 March 1936, Bowers Papers.

moderate for their tastes" and would then make serious trouble. In short, by late February Chilton like Bowers believed that Azaña "has, in fact, bitten off more than he can chew."[17]

Businessmen were even more disturbed than policy makers by the resurgent Spanish left. Top ITT executives in Spain made no secret of their right-wing sympathies during the election campaign. Telephone company technicians, for example, sabotaged the sound system at a big Popular Front rally in Madrid on 9 February by piping in speeches by several National Front candidates. Four days later a huge banner supporting Gil Robles and the parties of the right appeared high atop the Telefónica, CTNE headquarters and the tallest building in Madrid. The firm's officials blamed right-wing pranksters, but Claude Bowers viewed this incident as further proof that "the Telephone people are all monarchists, enemies of the republic, and red-hot for the Rights." He warned Washington that ITT's meddling in the elections virtually ensured left-wing reprisals should the Popular Front triumph at the polls.[18] Although British businessmen were more discreet than their American counterparts, they too were troubled by Spain's swing to the left in early 1936. Well aware that recent layoffs at the copper mines in Huelva had "increased the number of malcontents" there, Rio Tinto officials feared that a left-wing victory on election day would touch off a fresh round of "labour troubles." A Popular Front sweep of the mining district on 16 February did in fact spark a wave of strikes and riots, and when by month's end the Azaña regime proved either unwilling or unable to restore order, the firm's officials requested the Royal Navy to stand by should it become necessary to evacuate British nationals.[19]

While businessmen and bureaucrats on both sides of the Atlantic pondered the implications of this left-wing upsurge, British and American commercial relations with Spain stagnated. By late Jan-

[17] Chilton to Eden, tel. 21 February 1936, and minute by Stirling, 22 February 1936, W1576/627/41; Chilton to Eden, tel. 22 February 1936, W1607/62/41, 21 February 1936, W1639/62/41, and 27 February 1936, W1938/62/41, PRO FO371, vols. 20520 and 20564.

[18] Bowers, Diary, 10 and 14 February 1936, Bowers Papers; Bowers to Hull, 14 February 1936, 852.75 NTC/204, NA RG59.

[19] Consul F. G. Coultas (Seville) to Chilton, 31 January 1936, enclosed in Chilton to Eden, 3 February 1936, and minute by Stirling, 7 February 1936, W1140/626/41; Chilton to Eden, 28 February 1936, W1939/626/41, and tel. 29 February 1936, and minute by Stirling, 2 March 1936, W1840/626/41, PRO FO371, vol. 20561.

uary the State Department saw little hope for swift ratification of the Spanish-American reciprocal trade pact initialed the previous autumn. Spain still refused to grant U.S. exports most-favored-nation treatment and had also tightened its exchange controls so that Americans had to wait over nine months to convert their pesetas into dollars.[20] Whitehall likewise saw signs in early February that the six-month-old Anglo-Spanish trade truce was beginning to break down. Although Britons, unlike their American competitors, retained free access to foreign exchange in Spain, two weeks before the elections Madrid proposed sweeping changes in its automobile import quotas—changes that Ambassador Chilton feared would "mean a heavy reduction in British motor car exports to Spain this year."[21]

It soon became apparent that better Spanish treatment for British and American exports hinged on Madrid's ability to obtain a substantial stabilization loan in Washington or London. Spain had arranged just such a credit with France and the Netherlands in early February, but the French and Dutch bankers backed out following the Popular Front victory. Some American officials believed that the United States should step into the breach. Indeed, as early as 30 January State Department economic adviser Herbert Feis recommended that either the Reconstruction Finance Corporation or the Export-Import Bank be authorized to extend a $40-million loan to Spain to liquidate outstanding exchange arrears. Claude Bowers confirmed two weeks later that Prime Minister Azaña had hinted that "the question of payments will be handled differently" in the future provided Spain received financial assistance abroad. Washington, however, doubted that a loan would solve the long-term exchange problem and refused to consider such an arrangement until Madrid made good on its earlier pledges to restore most-favored-nation treatment to U.S. exports. The Azaña regime turned to London in desperation at month's end, but the Bank of England, like its counterparts elsewhere, declined to advance even £2.5 million until Spain liberalized its trade policies. After a short-lived truce, by the spring of 1936 Spanish commercial relations

---

[20] Bowers to Hull, tel. 20 January 1936, and tel. 29 January 1936, *FRUS, 1936*, 2:789–90.
[21] Chilton to Eden, 24 January 1936, W800/359/41, and tel. 3 February 1936, W1026/359/41, PRO FO371, vol. 20559.

with both Great Britain and the United States had once again begun to revert to cold war.[22]

The left-wing victory in the February 1936 elections was disappointing news for British and American officials, who had labored
long to engineer political and commercial rapprochements with
Spain. Both Washington and London suspected that Azaña and his
Popular Front coalition were merely stalking horses for the Kremlin
and anticipated fresh revolutionary outbursts. Multinationals such
as ITT and Rio Tinto shared similar fears, hoped that the National
Front would emerge from the polls victorious, and expected the
worst in the wake of the triumph of the left. Not surprisingly, in
the midst of such political uncertainty Spain drifted slowly from
trade truce to tariff war, first with the United States and later with
Great Britain. During the ensuing months the Spanish Republic
was swept into an even more violent maelstrom from which
neither British nor American policy makers believed it would
emerge alive.

II

During the spring of 1936 Prime Minister Azaña moved reso-
lutely to implement the more moderate aspects of the Popular
Front program, but as the Foreign Office and the State Department
had expected all along, such measures only whetted the appetite of
the extreme left. Azaña's cabinet, composed entirely of Left Republicans, quickly pardoned all political prisoners jailed during the
Asturian uprising, required all employers to reinstate workers
blacklisted for radical activities, and promised to speed up agrarian
reform. Largo Caballero and his left-wing Socialists nevertheless
dismissed such actions as mere "bourgeois" reforms. They called
instead for wholesale nationalization of Spain's major industries
and urged landless peasants forcibly to occupy hundreds of farms
throughout the country. Despite Azaña's repeated pledges to re-

---

[22]Memorandum by Feis, 30 January 1936, 611.5231/1127-1/2; Feis to Hull, 31 January 1936, 611.5231/1128-1/2; memorandum by Assistant Economic Adviser Leroy
Stinebower, 10 February 1936, 651.5231/169-1/2; Bowers to Hull, 18 February 1936,
611.5231/1148, and 11 February 1936, 852.51/323; memorandum by Feis, 26 February
1936, 852.51/335, NA RG59; Chilton to Eden, tel. 28 February 1936, W1837/1164/41,
PRO FO371, vol. 10564.

store law and order, during March sporadic strikes paralyzed out-lying provinces, left- and right-wing gunmen staged bloody street clashes, and angry anticlerical mobs sacked and burned half a dozen churches in Madrid and Barcelona. Eager to prevent this epidemic of violence from degenerating into outright civil war, the Azaña regime outlawed the right-wing Falange and pleaded with Largo Caballero to restrain his revolutionary followers. Few ob-servers, however, Spaniard or foreigner alike, felt that more seri-ous disorders could be avoided.[23]

Most American officials believed by the spring of 1936 that the Spanish Republic had entered its "Kerensky period." Claude Bow-ers, to be sure, might claim after a week-long motor trip through southern Spain in early March, that the rural areas were "as peace-ful and law-abiding as those of Westchester in New York," but he also admitted that unless Azaña took "strong measures" soon, Largo Caballero, "the evil genius of the Spanish political situa-tion," and "a Marxist and a Communist at heart," would "get out of hand." Military Attaché Fuqua agreed that the "communistic" groups were becoming bolder, confirmed that the Popular Front leaders were "losing control over the masses," and warned the War Department that persistent turmoil might eventually result in "a dictatorship in the name of law and order." By late March, Bowers himself confessed privately that "there are communistic elements in Spain that are working toward another French Revolution with its Terror."[24]

British policy makers were equally troubled by growing evidence of Soviet subversion. As the violence mounted in March, Whitehall worried that the Communists would force the Azaña regime to adopt "a programme of extreme socialist legislation" and seriously doubted "whether in case of emergency the authorities would really be in a position to take a strong line with the Extreme Left Wing." Reports from the British Embassy in Madrid strengthened Foreign Office fears that the Spanish Republic was about to suc-cumb to international communism. On 26 March Ambassador

[23] Buckley, *Life and Death of the Spanish Republic*, pp. 197–206; Payne, *Spanish Revolu-tion*, pp. 186–95; Malefakis, *Agrarian Reform*, pp. 367–71; Payne, *Falange*, pp. 98–101.
[24] Bowers, *My Mission to Spain*, pp. 201–9; Hallett Johnson to Hull, 11 March 1936, 852.00/2145; Bowers to Hull, tel. 14 March 1936, 852.00/2143, 17 March 1936, 852.00/2146, and 18 March 1936, 852.00/2147, NA RG59; Fuqua to G-2, 18 March 1936, 2657 S.126/115, NA RG165; Bowers, Diary, 20 March 1936, Bowers Papers.

Chilton forwarded a study prepared by his staff that likened conditions in Spain "to those in Russia prior to the Bolshevik Revolution." Chilton himself was "not at all happy about the situation" and warned "there will be hell to pay" should the extreme left remain unchecked. "The Communist leader, Largo Caballero, will kick out the President of the Republic, and set up a Soviet Republic, in which case the lives and property of no one will be safe," he told Sir Robert Vansittart. "If the military coup d'état, which it is generally believed is being planned, does not succeed, things will be pretty awful." Consul General Norman King at Barcelona shared Chilton's apocalyptic views and foresaw "considerable risk of revolutionary chaos in Spain, when efforts might even be made to set up Soviet Governments in parts of the country."[25]

Azaña's inability to control the extreme left forced Whitehall to confront the even more frightful possibility that the communist contagion might spread west from Madrid to Lisbon. Indeed, the Salazar regime warned British ambassador Charles Wingfield in early March that "Spain was moving fast towards Communism and a Communist Government in Spain would be exceedingly serious for Portugal." Worried by "sinister" connections between Azaña's Popular Front and Portuguese radicals, Dr. Armindo Monteiro, Salazar's minister of foreign affairs, hurried to London on 21 March to warn Foreign Secretary Eden personally that the Spanish left intended "to make of Spain and Portugal a Socialist-Communist political entity." Eden was concerned enough to ask Wingfield for a full report "on the nature of the Socialist and Communist movement in Portugal, of its strength, and of the ability and willingness of the army to suppress a possible rising, especially if backed by Spanish support." Wingfield confirmed in early April that there was considerable "communistic propaganda" in Lisbon and that "the remnants of the old Portuguese political parties . . . were known to be making common cause with the Reds in Spain." Moreover, they were rumored to be in touch with "Com-

---

[25] Ogilvie-Forbes to Eden, 3 March 1936, and minute by Stirling, 9 March 1936, W2014/62/41; Chilton to Eden, 13 March 1936, and minute by Shuckburgh, 23 March 1936, W2387/62/41; memorandum by O. A. Scott, 25 March 1936, enclosed in Chilton to Eden, 26 March 1936, W2888/62/41; Chilton to Vansittart, 26 March 1936, W4129/62/41; undated memorandum by King, enclosed in Chilton to Eden, 27 March 1936, W2872/62/41, PRO FO371, vols. 20520 and 20521.

munist and Russian agents" in Portugal as well, to plot the over-throw of Salazar.[26]

Foreign investors, like their diplomatic counterparts, grew increasingly uneasy as Spain swung to the left during the spring of 1936. Although publicly ITT officials saw "no cause for undue concern," privately Captain Logan Rock complained about Azaña's labor policies and apparently even discussed a possible coup d'état with friends in the Spanish army.[27] British multinationals in Spain encountered similar problems but on a much larger scale. Rio Tinto, for example, resisted a Popular Front decree reinstating over 1,200 miners laid off since 1934 and asked the Foreign Office to intervene on its behalf. Sir Horace Seymour, the new head of the Western Department, termed the decree "obviously idiotic," noted that it "would cause genuine hardship" for the British firm, and instructed Sir Henry Chilton to make "unofficial representations in an attempt to come to a reasonable arrangement with the Spanish authorities."[28] Such appeals fell on deaf ears in Madrid, however, and by late March the operations of British sherry producers at Jerez, banana planters in the Canary Islands, and iron smelters in the Asturias were hit by strikes too. If order was not restored soon, the British Embassy predicted, such firms "may be driven to cut their losses and clear out." Sir Evelyn Shuckburgh, who had recently succeeded C. N. Stirling as Whitehall's Spanish expert, agreed that these companies, like Rio Tinto, were "being victimized by local communists" and added that the situation "looked serious for British commercial interests in Spain" as well.[29]

---

[26]Wingfield to Eden, 4 March 1936, W2234/478/36, PRO FO371, vol. 20511; Eden to Wingfield, 21 March 1936, W2540/478/36, FO425, Foreign Office Confidential Prints, vol. 413, Public Record Office (hereafter cited as PRO FO425); Eden to Wingfield, 26 March 1936, W2676/478/36, PRO FO371, vol. 20511; Wingfield to Eden, 6 April 1936, W3358/478/36, PRO FO425, vol. 413.

[27]Memorandum by chief of the Division of Western European Affairs James Clement Dunn, 27 March 1936, 852.75 NTC/205, NA RG59; Rock's views are outlined in Bowers, Diary, 28 March 1936, Bowers Papers.

[28]Lord Bessborough (Rio Tinto) to Parliamentary Undersecretary of State Viscount Cranborne, 3 March 1936, W1957/626/41; Cranborne to Bessborough, 9 March 1936, and Bessborough to Cranborne, 11 March 1936, W1965/626/41; Chilton to Eden, 6 March 1936, minute by Seymour, 11 March 1936, and Seymour to Chilton, 14 March 1936, W2116/626/41, PRO FO371, vols. 20561 and 20562.

[29]Chilton to Eden, 13 March 1936, and minute by Shuckburgh, 23 March 1936, W2387/62/41; Chilton to Eden, 17 March 1936, W2489/626/41; minutes by Shuckburgh, 1 April 1936, W2812/626/41, and 3 April 1936, W2888/62/41, vols. 20520 and 20562.

British and American commercial relations with Spain had in fact deteriorated rapidly during the spring of 1936. Washington remained at loggerheads with Madrid over Spanish foreign-exchange regulations, which by March were forcing American exporters to wait an average of ten months to convert their pesetas into dollars. Although Undersecretary Phillips reminded Luis Calderón on 19 March that "a successful conclusion to our negotiations" hinged upon equitable treatment for U.S. trade, the Spanish ambassador replied that "any solution of this problem . . . was exceedingly doubtful" because his country still "did not have the pesetas with which to buy American dollars." Cordell Hull himself met with Calderón shortly before Easter to express his personal "disappointment and regret that the exchange situation in Spain was calculated to retard the treaty negotiations" and to urge Madrid to abandon its "purely bilateral method and policy of bartering and bargaining" and embrace "the doctrine of equality" instead. The Azaña regime hinted, as it had earlier, that a large stabilization credit would probably break the impasse, but with the proposed Spanish-American trade agreement "on the rocks" Phillips noted privately on 2 April that "it was highly doubtful whether there could be any loan either private or governmental."[30]

Despite Spain's recent pledges of most-favored-nation treatment for Great Britain, British exporters began in March and April to encounter the same convertibility problems that had plagued Americans for over a year. The Board of Trade conferred with Spanish negotiators twice in mid-March but made little headway, largely because Madrid would not reaffirm its commitment to the 1935 standstill agreement limiting tariffs or to the 1936 payments accord liquidating foreign-exchange arrears. Anglo-Spanish commercial relations eroded still further a month later after the Azaña regime announced that mounting trade deficits made it impossible to permit Britons any longer to convert their pesetas freely into sterling. "Prospects of a trade agreement are indefinitely delayed owing to the inability of Spain to meet the U.K. clearing requirements," Sir Evelyn Shuckburgh wrote on 16 April. "We have now reached a position where it is useless to attempt to secure an in-

---

[30]Bowers to Hull, 10 March 1936, 852.51/326, NA RG59; Phillips, Journal, 19 March 1936, Phillips Papers; memorandum by Hull, 25 March 1936, *FRUS, 1936*, 2:791–92; Phillips, Journal, 2 April 1936, Phillips Papers.

crease in U.K. imports to Spain because importers cannot get payment for their sales."[31] Recent developments at Madrid, then, left little doubt on either side of the Atlantic that British and American political and commercial troubles with the Spanish Republic were likely to get much worse before they got any better.

As the State Department and the Foreign Office had feared, the crisis at Madrid deepened later that spring. Although Prime Minister Azaña imposed strict censorship and proclaimed a state of alarm in an effort to prevent further disorders, mob violence became so commonplace and political killings occurred with such alarming frequency that when the new Cortes convened in early April, most of its members carried sidearms. In this ideologically charged atmosphere the deputies made a decision many would later regret. Eager to place one of their own in the National Palace, Popular Front leaders charged that President Niceto Alcalá-Zamora had technically exceeded his constitutional authority by proroguing the Cortes twice during one six-year term. Denounced by the left as a Hindenburg and by the right as a Kerensky, the hapless Alcalá-Zamora was ousted by a wide margin on 7 April. After a month of uncertainty while the legislature sought a successor, Manuel Azaña agreed to accept the largely honorific post in late April and was elected president of the republic by an overwhelming majority on 8 May. With the Popular Front now firmly in control of both the Cortes and the National Palace, many conservatives inside and outside Spain feared that the moment for the long-rumored bolshevik takeover was at hand.[32]

Despite persistent charges of Soviet subversion during the spring of 1936, Moscow seems to have adopted a relatively cautious approach to the crisis at Madrid. To be sure, the Comintern did urge Spanish Communists to redouble their support of the Popular Front and the Kremlin did repatriate a number of left-wing Spaniards, including Santiago Carrillo, who had sought refuge in Russia following the abortive Asturian revolt a year and a half earlier. Moreover, the Communist party nearly doubled its mem-

---

[31] Minutes of the Board of Trade meeting, 16 March 1936, W2502/46/41; minutes of the Board of Trade meeting, 17 March 1936, W2648/46/41; minutes of the Board of Trade meeting, 7 April 1936, and minute by Shuckburgh, 16 April 1936, W3138/46/41, PRO FO371, vol. 20518.
[32] Peers, *Spanish Tragedy*, pp. 194–98; Jackson, *Spanish Republic and Civil War*, pp. 200–206; Arrarás, *Historia de la segunda república*, 4:103–22.

bership that spring, and some Marxist firebrands, among them Luis Araquistáin, the mastermind behind Largo Caballero, stepped up their incendiary rhetoric and prophesied a proletarian revolution before the year was out. But Stalin, increasingly frightened by Hitler's Germany, was by early 1936 less interested in fomenting revolution in Western Europe than in containing the Nazis by seeking defensive pacts with Britain, or perhaps even Spain, modeled on the year-old Franco-Soviet mutual assistance treaty. As a result, in its annual May Day Manifesto the Comintern "endorsed the policy of the Spanish CP" for "loyally supporting the Government" and "oppos[ing] the destruction of the churches."[33]

Such evidence of Soviet moderation notwithstanding, British and American diplomats still worried that the latest round of political confusion at Madrid might encourge Moscow to fish in troubled waters. A. T. Beauregard, the U.S. naval attaché, reported in early April that the Kremlin had funneled "large sums of communist money" into Spain since the February elections, and Military Attaché Fuqua confirmed that the "Russian Komintern" had recently supplied over $200,000 to promote "the communistic movement which is taking place in Spain." Terming the ouster of Alcalá-Zamora later that month "a great mistake," Claude Bowers feared that "May Day in Madrid may prove to be a riotous affair" and warned Washington that if Prime Minister Azaña "fails to maintain the upper hand, the danger exists that civil war or communism may ensue."[34] Sir Henry Chilton, Bowers's British opposite number, agreed that the sudden dismissal of the Spanish president set "an unfortunate precedent in a land where the virtues of stability are not yet properly appreciated" and predicted that "the election of his successor may cause further upheavals." Distressed by "the steady strengthening of communist and extreme left-wing

---

[33] Thomas, *Spanish Civil War,* pp. 179–80; Payne, *Spanish Revolution,* pp. 194–98; Santiago Carrillo, with Regis Debray and Max Gallo, *Dialogue on Spain* (London, 1976), pp. 42–43; Anthony Cave Brown and Charles B. MacDonald, *On a Field of Red: The Communist International and the Coming of World War II* (New York, 1981), pp. 427–28; "Extracts from the Comintern's ECCI May Day Manifesto, April 1936," in De Gras, *Communist International, 1919–1943,* 3:387.

[34] Beauregard to Office of Naval Intelligence (ONI), 2 April 1936, C-10-J, 20792D ("Political Conditions—Spain"), Record Group 38, Chief of Naval Operations, Intelligence Division, Naval Attaché Reports 1886–1939, National Archives, Washington, D.C. (hereafter cited as NA RG38); Fuqua to G-2, 7 April 1936, 2657 S.168/1, NA RG165; Bowers to Hull, 21 April 1936, 852.00/2157, NA RG59.

confidence" and convinced that much depended upon whether Azaña could "prevent himself being turned into a Spanish Kerensky," Whitehall's Evelyn Shuckburgh, like many of his American counterparts, complained that "a perfectly conscious and determined effort is being made by the Communists to turn this man, and all his moderate supporters in the 'Frente Popular,' into communist stalking horses."[35]

The first concrete evidence of Soviet subversion at Madrid trickled into Whitehall and the White House in mid-April. Arthur Bryant, biographer and close personal friend of Prime Minister Stanley Baldwin, returned from a 500-mile tour in Spain convinced that "the foundations of civilisation are being undermined" and that the "revolution is beginning" with the Popular Front's blessing. "I . . . saw on the walls of every village I visited," he wrote Baldwin on 13 April, "the symbols of the Hammer and Sickle and in the streets the undisguised signs of bitter class hatred, fomented by unceasing agitation by Soviet agents among a poor and cruelly misled peasant and working class population."[36] A week later William Bullitt completed a lengthy analysis of Soviet foreign policy that found its way to the desk of President Franklin Roosevelt. Stressing that the Kremlin's united front campaign represented "the tactics of the Trojan horse," Bullitt believed that the Soviets were prepared "to take advantage of any opportunity which appears" and pointed to the Spanish Republic as a good example. "Twenty young Spaniards trained in Moscow in the technique of the Bolshevik revolution," he noted, "left Moscow yesterday for Spain."[37] Sir Henry Chilton confirmed on 27 April that a large number of left-wing militants "who had been obliged to leave Spain owing to the revolution of October 1934 and who ha[d] spent the last year and a half in Russia" had just returned to Madrid "preaching Communism."[38]

With the approach of summer few American or British observers at Madrid believed that the Azaña regime could prevent further

---

[35] Chilton to Eden, 8 April 1936, W3183/62/41, and 18 April 1936, and minute by Shuckburgh, 22 April 1936, W3449/62/41, PRO FO371, vol. 20521.
[36] Bryant to Baldwin, 13 April 1936, vol. 124, Stanley Baldwin Papers, Cambridge University Library, Cambridge, England.
[37] Bullitt to Hull, 20 April 1936, 861.01/2120, NA RG59. Roosevelt's copy is located in the FDR Papers, PSF, "Russia," box 67.
[38] Chilton to Eden, 27 April 1936, W3820/62/41, PRO FO371, vol. 20521.

polarization and bloodshed. Colonel Stephen Fuqua saw "little hope for a united Spain with a strong stabilized centralized government" in late April because Largo Caballero and his left-wing Socialists had undermined the Popular Front coalition and "turned definitely towards communism." Claude Bowers tried to minimize the Marxist danger, but even he admitted in early May that Largo Caballero had embraced "communist principles" including "a dictatorship of the proletariat."[39] The British vice consul at Almeria likewise reported widespread communist activities and claimed on 1 May that "the extremist Left rule[d] the roost" in his district. Sir Henry Chilton confirmed the next day that "the insidious propaganda of communism" was fostering the impression among Popular Front friends and foes alike that "the weak and vacillating Spanish Government had abandoned [its] power to the proletariat."[40]

Since British and American multinationals promised to be among the first victims of a successful left-wing Spanish revolution, businessmen kept a careful eye on the deteriorating political situation at Madrid. As late as 27 March ITT officials believed Azaña would "resist any extreme demands from the left groups" and remained "reasonably reassured as to the outlook generally in Spain."[41] But the publication early the following month of a scathing attack on foreign "colonization" of Spain's economy authored by Virgilio Sevillano Carbajal, the chief of the Press Department at the Spanish Foreign Ministry, must have given Colonel Sosthenes Behn and his associates pause. The book, provocatively entitled *La España . . . de quién?*, charged that American firms such as ITT and Armstrong Cork had repatriated millions of dollars to the United States, meddled in Spanish politics, and excluded Spaniards from all technical and managerial posts. Sevillano Carbajal's biggest target, however, was the Rio Tinto Company, which according to confidential government files had for sixty years reaped huge profits, paid minimal taxes, and operated the copper fields at Huelva as a virtual British colony. Terming the firm's 1873 mining concession "unconstitutional," he suggested that the Spanish

[39] Fuqua to G-2, 22 April 1936, 2657 S.162/16, and 28 April 1936, 2657 S.162/17, NA RG165; Bowers to Hull, 6 May 1936, 852.00/2165, and 11 May 1936, 852.00 P.R./448, NA RG59.

[40] Vice Consul Harrison (Almeria) quoted in Chilton to Eden, 1 May 1936, W3942/62/41; Chilton to Eden, 2 May 1936, W3946/62/41, PRO FO371, vol. 20521.

[41] Memorandum by Dunn, 27 March 1936, 852.75 NTC/205, NA RG59.

Popular Front treat Rio Tinto the same way the Soviets had treated the British-owned Lena gold fields—expropriation with only token compensation.[42]

Although Whitehall was quick to protest against this "scandalous" diatribe,[43] the book was really the least of Rio Tinto's problems. In mid-March unruly miners had clashed with armed guards protecting the firm's facilities at Huelva, touching off two weeks of labor violence. Angry Rio Tinto officials met with Prime Minister Azaña on 1 April, complained that "neither he nor anyone at present holding office" seemed aware that "at any moment there might be a serious conflict" in the mining district, and deemed it "absolutely necessary that adequate forces should be supplied" to prevent further trouble. Despite Azaña's pledge to station additional troops in the copper fields, Rio Tinto chairman Sir Auckland Geddes told Whitehall in mid-April that his and other British mining firms continued to be plagued by work stoppages and were "obliged to yield to strikers owing to inadequate police protection." Ambassador Chilton raised the matter with Spanish officials on 17 April and received fresh assurances that British interests were secure, but four days later Rio Tinto's Captain Ulick deB. Charles reported yet another "stay-in strike" and claimed that the Azaña regime was "rapidly making the situation completely intolerable for all employers of labour." Geddes confirmed that Rio Tinto had been "seriously damaged by extremist legislation." Earlier in the year, he told the firm's shareholders on 24 April, "work was proceeding smoothly" and the outlook in Spain was bright. "Then came the Elections, and the victory of the parties of the Left," he added wistfully. "Now we hardly know where we are."[44]

Other British firms operating in Spain were beset by similar difficulties that spring. At Las Palmas in the Canary Islands a town council composed of "several Socialists and three Communists"

[42] Virgilio Sevillano Carbajal, *La España . . . de quién?* (Madrid, 1936), pp. 71–82, 88–90, 129–30, 200; Chilton to Eden, 9 April 1936, W3262/62/41, PRO FO371, vol. 20521.

[43] Minute by Shuckburgh, 17 April 1936; minute by Seymour, 18 April 1936; Seymour to Chilton, 21 April 1936, W3262/62/41, PRO FO371, vol. 20521.

[44] Charles (RTZ) to Chilton, 2 April 1936, enclosed in Chilton to Eden, 3 April 1936, W3041/626/41; Paul Mason (private secretary to Cranborne) to Seymour, 14 April 1936, and Seymour to Chilton, tel. 14 April 1936, W3256/626/41; Charles to Chilton, 21 April 1936, enclosed in Chilton to Eden, 24 April 1936, W3722/626/41, PRO FO371, vol. 20562; Geddes, "Annual Rio Tinto Chairman's Address, 24 April 1936," RTZ Corporate Archives.

threatened to jail the English manager of the Yeoward Brothers banana plantation unless he rehired over one hundred workers fired since 1934. Several London-based Spanish rail lines, including the Great Southern and the Santander and Mediterranean, were plagued by sporadic strikes and sabotage. When the British owner of a small ceramics plant near Seville was physically assaulted on 30 April by a crowd of irate laborers demanding reinstatement, Ambassador Chilton delivered a blistering note to Foreign Minister Augusto Barcía demanding adequate police protection for all Britons and their property in Spain. Whitehall decried "this lawless state of affairs" south of the Pyrenees in early May but doubted whether the Azaña regime was capable of stemming "the endless illegal strikes" and reversing "the breakdown of law and order" that had fostered "a general feeling of anxiety" among British and American multinationals.[45]

With so many pressing political problems to handle, neither the State Department nor the Foreign Office devoted much time to trade troubles, and as a result U.S. and U.K. commercial relations with Spain deteriorated. Complaints from impatient American exporters unable to remit their funds from Madrid mounted during the spring of 1936, but Washington could offer precious little advice or assistance. Moreover, with Spain nearly six months in arrears on the repayment of its 1934 tobacco credit, Export-Import Bank president Warren Lee Pierson asked Secretary of Agriculture Henry Wallace on 3 April to commence legal action to collect on the default. Although Claude Bowers could still contend shortly thereafter that the Azaña regime continued "earnestly to desire that a solution to the present impasse might be found," the State Department saw no reason to expect the situation to improve in the near future.[46] Whitehall was likewise bewildered and outraged when later in April Spain unveiled a plan to boost its own coal output by drastically reducing imports from Great Britain. Terming this "a serious breach of the standstill agreement" concluded the previous

[45]Patteson to Chilton, 27 March 1936, enclosed in Chilton to Eden, 4 April 1936, W3053/626/41; Great Southern Railway to the Foreign Office, 8 April 1936, W3118/3118/41; Chilton to Barcía, 30 April 1936, enclosed in Chilton to Eden, 30 April 1936, and minute by W. H. Pollock, 7 May 1936, W3896/626/41, PRO FO371, vols. 20562 and 20569.

[46]File 601.2 Spain (January/June 1936), NA RG151; Pierson to Wallace, 3 April 1936, Credit File no. 11, NA RG275; Phillips, Journal, 3 April 1936, Phillips Papers; Bowers to Hull, 6 April 1936, *FRUS, 1936*, 2:792–93.

summer, London threatened to retaliate against Spanish produce exports unless Madrid scuttled the proposal. Once Sir Henry Chilton made it clear to the Azaña regime on 28 April that "the effect on Anglo-Spanish commercial relations would be disastrous," the plan was quickly "suspended," but British officials were left questioning whether Spain preferred a trade truce or a tariff war.[47]

Two months of left-wing rule at Madrid had done much to confirm the worst suspicions of policy makers on both sides of the Atlantic. With the country wracked by increasingly violent disorders and with the Popular Front coalition rent by bitter squabbles between the moderate Azaña and the militant Largo Caballero, bolshevism seemed to be making giant inroads. Spain's sharp swing to the left also created serious difficulties for multinational corporations such as ITT and Rio Tinto, which faced the unpleasant and expensive dilemma of either reinstating hundreds of workers dismissed since 1934 or enduring strikes and sabotage orchestrated by revolutionary extremists. Finally, Spanish commercial relations with Great Britain and the United States soured as the Azaña regime reverted to autarchic economic policies that thwarted trade negotiations with London and Washington and threatened to slash British and American exports to Spain. By May 1936 the volatile atmosphere at Madrid was sparking speculation at both the State Department and the Foreign Office that the Spanish Republic stood perilously close to the brink of civil war.

III

The weakness and ineptitude of the Left Republican government that attempted to muddle through the mounting chaos at Madrid in May and June did nothing to dispel the widespread anxiety that Spain would soon be plunged into bloody revolutionary strife. Azaña's promotion from prime minister to president of the republic on 8 May had, as expected, touched off a struggle over succession that nearly destroyed the Popular Front coalition. Indalecio Prieto, the most popular and experienced of the moderate Socialists, seemed at first the logical choice to head the new cabinet, but

---

[47]Chilton to Eden, tel. 23 April 1936, and minute by Shuckburgh, 24 April 1936, W3553/90/41; Chilton to Eden, 28 April 1936, W3828/90/41, PRO FO371, vol. 20557.

Largo Caballero, an extreme left-wing rival for party leadership, refused to support his candidacy. Eager to prevent an open breach in the center-left alliance, President Azaña chose instead to name a trusted friend, Santiago Casares Quiroga, as Spain's new prime minister on 13 May. A Left Republican veteran weakened by a long bout with tuberculosis, Casares Quiroga quickly proved a well-intentioned but ineffective leader. Azaña's ailing protégé did put together a vigorous program calculated to firm up sagging left-wing support for the Popular Front; he cracked down on right-wing extremists in late May and resurrected dormant republican labor and agrarian reforms the following month. Nevertheless, after a national maritime strike paralyzed Spain's seaports and armed squatters clashed with government troops to the south at Yeste in early June, few British or American observers held out any hope that Casares Quiroga could control the revolutionary left.[48]

Most U.S. officials in Spain were appalled by the new prime minister's apparent coddling of left-wing extremists. Military Attaché Fuqua, for example, warned in mid-May that Casares Quiroga's lax handling of disorders originating in the Cuatro Caminos, "Madrid's hotbed of communism," was bound to encourage similar outbursts in the future. Although Claude Bowers reported on 20 May that the present regime was "today in a strong position . . . to enforce its authority in all parts of Spain," he cautioned Washington "that we are going through a revolutionary period, that the public mind is still excited, and that there are bound to be sporadic disturbances for some time to come." Convinced that Azaña and Casares Quiroga faced an uphill fight against "Largo Caballero who is now as much a communist as anyone in Russia," Bowers a week later forwarded an analysis of bolshevik subversion authored by Lawrence Fernsworth, a well-known journalist who had covered Spanish politics for nearly five years. Quick to admit that it was easy to overestimate the Kremlin's role in the current crisis at Madrid, Fernsworth nevertheless pointed out that "Moscow has for a decade or more had Spain under its watchful vigilance, has its scouts in Spain, [and] has hopes of Sovietizing Spain at the opportune moment." Casares

---

[48] Jackson, *Spanish Republic and Civil War,* pp. 206–21; Payne, *Spanish Revolution,* pp. 195–98; Preston, *Coming of the Spanish Civil War,* pp. 194–97; Malefakis, *Agrarian Reform,* pp. 379–80.

Quiroga seemed destined to play Kerensky to Largo Caballero's Lenin.[49]

British diplomats were even more skeptical than their American counterparts of the new prime minister. As early as 14 May Sir Horace Seymour, the head of the Western Department, prophesied that Casares Quiroga would have "a very difficult time" with the extreme left. A short time later Consul William Oxley reported serious left-wing disturbances at Vigo and warned London that he could "no longer . . . expect any protection from the local civil authorities for British persons and property because . . . the Communists have definitely proved that they are complete masters of the situation." Shocked by this "truly alarming picture of 10,000 Communists in complete control of Vigo," Whitehall feared that similar outbreaks were "liable to arise anywhere in Spain at the present time." Indeed, the British Embassy in Moscow confirmed in late May that in the wake of the Popular Front victory in February the Comintern had detected "far more fruitful a soil for communist propaganda" in the Iberian Peninsula and was as a result rumored to be "sending money into Spain."[50]

William Bullitt, that ubiquitous apostle of anticommunism, soon corroborated Fernsworth's and Oxley's hair-raising accounts of bolshevik subversion for British and American officials. En route from Moscow to Washington for reassignment, Bullitt stopped off in London. On 25 May he dined at Cliveden, the rural estate of Lord and Lady Astor, with Thomas Jones, an intimate friend and personal confidant of Prime Minister Stanley Baldwin. The American diplomat, Jones noted that night in his diary, "made our flesh creep with his Bolshevik stories." Citing "widespread penetration of Communist propaganda" south of the Pyrenees, Bullitt reminded his listeners that only a short time ago the Kremlin had dispatched a well-trained contingent of revolutionaries to Madrid

[49] Fuqua to G-2, 16 May 1936, 2657 S.126/119, NA RG165; Bowers to Hull, 20 May 1936, 852.00/2166, NA RG59; Bowers to Daniels, 20 May 1936, Daniels Papers; undated article by Fernsworth, enclosed in Bowers to Hull, 27 May 1936, 852.00/2169, NA RG59.

[50] Chilton to Eden, 12 May 1936, and minute by Seymour, 14 May 1936, W4249/62/41; Oxley to Chilton, 15 May 1936, enclosed in Chilton to Eden, 19 May 1936, and minutes by Pollock, 4 June 1936, and Philip Leigh-Smith, 4 June 1936, W4743/62/41; Chargé d'Affaires MacKillop (Moscow) to Eden, 25 May 1936, and minute by P. Labouchere (Northern Department), 9 June 1936, N2985/75/38, PRO FO371, vols. 20521, 20522, and 20345.

"loaded with money, to stir up strife," and he warned Jones and the Astors that "Moscow foretells a Communist government in Spain in three months." While Jones passed this disturbing information along to Baldwin, Bullitt crossed the Atlantic and arrived on 2 June at the State Department, where he related substantially the same story. During a lengthy discussion of Soviet foreign policy he told Undersecretary Phillips that one of the Kremlin's major targets was the Spanish Republic. "Russia is still actively pursuing her international policy of Sovietizing other countries and has recently sent out a large number of Soviet agents supplied with ample funds to Spain," Phillips wrote in his journal that evening; "the Soviets think that, in the course of three months, Spain may become communistic."[51]

Frightened by the specter of bolshevik subversion, British and American multinationals were outraged but not surprised when their own fortunes in Spain took a turn for the worse with the approach of summer. ITT came under fire when Prime Minister Casares Quiroga carelessly permitted publication of a secret Ministry of Communications report calling for unilateral Spanish revision of the CTNE concession. Convinced that it would lead eventually to the resurrection of the 1932 expropriation campaign, ITT vice president Frank Page swiftly appealed for State Department assistance. Undersecretary Phillips instructed Claude Bowers to warn the Madrid authorities that the Roosevelt administration, like its predecessor, expected Spain to honor the telephone contract. Bowers dutifully relayed this warning to Foreign Minister Barcía on 30 May and added that ITT would "ignore" any unilateral changes in its concession "with the vigorous support of the [American] Embassy." After Barcía apologized for the apparent "misunderstanding" and promised that his government would respect all ITT's contractual rights, Bowers cabled Washington on 1 June that "I anticipate no trouble on this score."[52]

[51] Thomas Jones, *A Diary with Letters, 1931–1950* (New York, 1954), pp. 186, 188, 210–11; Phillips, Journal, 2 June 1936, Phillips Papers. Jones, who spoke with Baldwin on several occasions between May and July, noted that during a 27 July discussion of the Spanish civil war, "I *reminded* him [the prime minister] of Bullitt's prophecy made to me two months ago that Moscow looked forward to a Communist Government in Spain in 3 months." Jones, *Diary with Letters*, p. 231 (emphasis added).

[52] Rock to Behn, tel. 26 May 1936; Page to Phillips, 27 May 1936; Phillips to Bowers, tel. 29 May 1936, 852.75 NTC/206, NA RG59; Bowers, Diary, 30 May 1936, Bowers Papers; Bowers to Hull, tel. 1 June 1936, 852.75 NTC/208, NA RG59.

Rio Tinto officials, on the other hand, reported that their problems in Spain showed "no sign of diminishing." Suspecting that the present Popular Front regime intended to make Rio Tinto's operations "so unprofitable that the Company will be forced out of business," Sir Auckland Geddes sent Permanent Undersecretary of State Robert Vansittart a long memorandum on 29 May recalling the strategic importance of his firm's iron and copper exports during the Great War and outlining the issues currently at stake. "From the advent of the Republic," Geddes pointed out, "there has been a marked deterioration in the attitude of the Government towards the Company, and . . . an increasing display of animosity towards all foreign enterprises." Since neither Azaña nor Casares Quiroga was prepared to restrain the left-wing extremists who were now threatening to seize the mines and "establish something of the nature of a reign of terror in the neighbourhood," Geddes requested "the strong support of the British Government." Fearful that Madrid's "continued failure to remedy the disorderly situation at the Rio Tinto and Tharsis mines" might "at any time imperil the lives of their staffs and the safety of their property," Whitehall warned the Spanish government that any refusal to apply "normal standards of justice and equity" to these firms would "make a deplorable impression here."[53]

Other British multinationals faced even more serious problems. Arthur Loveday, the chairman of the British Chamber of Commerce at Madrid, complained that "the greater part of Spain was given over to the mob violence of the Reds" and that strikes of "the communist 'stay-in' type" had become universal. And, he added, because the Popular Front regime prohibited both domestic and foreign firms from simply closing their doors, an employer was forced "either to hand over his works to the strikers or go to prison."[54] Indeed, the London-based Alquife Mining Company confirmed in late May that the situation at its mines in Almeria "had become so bad" that it intended to suspend operations indefinitely rather than "waste any more British capital in trying to keep them open." When shortly thereafter Yeoward Brothers warned that they too "feared serious trouble at any moment" from

---

[53] Geddes to Vansittart, 29 May 1936; undated minute by Vansittart; Vansittart and Leigh-Smith to Ogilvie-Forbes, 6 June 1936, W4885/626/41, PRO FO371, vol. 20563.
[54] Arthur Loveday, *Spain, 1923–1948: Civil War and World War* (North Bridgewater, England, 1949), p. 46.

striking workers at their banana plantations in the Canary Islands, Whitehall instructed British officials at Madrid to lodge "a strong protest" against Popular Front labor policies. Chargé d'Affaires George Ogilvie-Forbes delivered the demarche in early June but did not expect the danger to British firms to lessen, because Casares Quiroga and his cabinet were "evidently unable to control the forces of disruption they have set in motion."[55]

If by late spring Madrid's political and economic relations with London and Washington had turned increasingly sour, Spanish commercial negotiations with Great Britain and the United States, deadlocked during Azaña's tenure, broke down altogether under Casares Quiroga. Ambassador Luis Calderón conferred with Cordel Hull on 11 May in a last-ditch effort to salvage a reciprocal trade agreement, but Spain's refusal to grant U.S. exporters equal access to foreign exchange remained the major sticking point. When Calderón hinted once again that a stabilization loan would help matters, the secretary of state countered that Madrid should consider devaluation. Confronted with what he regarded as Spanish intransigence, Hull insisted that "we could not permit the fundamentals of our trade program to be discredited or impaired by making vital exceptions to each country calling for the same" and abruptly asked Calderón to leave. Before departing, the Spaniard spoke with trade expert Henry Grady, who confirmed that "without some very concrete assurances regarding exchange allocation," there was no point in continuing the negotiations.[56] British commercial relations with Spain likewise reached a new low two weeks later, after Madrid reiterated its intention to reduce U.K. auto exports by five hundred units. Terming this decision a "pretty glaring . . . infraction of the standstill agreement," the Board of Trade suspended its talks with Spanish officials until they "take steps to restore the situation." Like Washington, however, London expected Madrid to make haste slowly.[57]

---

[55] J. M. Troutbeck (Western Department) to Chilton, 29 May 1936, W4637/62/41; Yeoward Brothers to the Foreign Office, 23 May 1936, and minute by Seymour, 27 May 1936, W4669/626/41; Seymour to Chilton, 26 May 1936, W4382/626/41; Ogilvie-Forbes to Barcía, 2 June 1936, enclosed in Ogilvie-Forbes to Eden, 4 June 1936, W5156/626/41, PRO FO371, vol. 20563.

[56] Memorandum by Hull, 11 May 1936, *FRUS, 1936*, 2:794–95; memorandum by Grady, 11 May 1936, 611.5231/1161, NA RG59.

[57] Sir Ronald Fraser (Board of Trade) to W. H. Pollock, 25 May 1936, and Leigh-Smith to Ogilvie-Forbes, 6 June 1936, W4716/359/41, PRO FO371, vol. 20559.

Unable to maintain law and order and unwilling to honor Spain's commercial commitments, Casares Quiroga inspired little confidence among Spaniards and foreigners alike. The Left Republican leader was powerless to tame the tidal wave of strikes that threatened by mid-June to swamp the country's economy. Spain's cities were plagued by bloody gun battles between syndicalist and falangist militias, while in the countryside the well-to-do were terrorized by roving bands of landless peasants. Appalled by the uncontrollable violence that gripped the nation, right-wing spokesman José María Gil Robles on 16 June acidly recounted for the Cortes the sorry record of Popular Front rule, citing 133 strikes, 170 church burnings, and 269 political murders in recent months as proof that Casares Quiroga could never succeed in restoring order.[58]

Spain's military leaders were even more distressed by the mounting chaos at Madrid. As early as February 1936, after Azaña had purged the army staff and exiled generals Francisco Franco and Manuel Goded to the Canaries and the Balearics respectively, right-wing officers in the clandestine Unión Militar Española had plotted the overthrow of the Popular Front regime—only to have key conspirators back out at the last minute. As left-wing disorders spread throughout Spain later than spring, however, General Emilio Mola persuaded the country's two most influential officers, Generals Franco and Sanjurjo, to lead the uprising and head the proposed military junta. Shortly thereafter a shocking incident occurred in Madrid that steeled the plotters and prevented Mola's plan from falling apart as its predecessors had. On the evening of 12 July a band of left-wing Socialists, determined to avenge the assassination of a comrade, called at the home of José Calvo Sotelo dressed in the uniforms of the republican police. Spain's leading monarchist was placed under arrest, taken away in a police wagon, and sometime later that night shot to death. The brutal murder of Calvo Sotelo dispelled any remaining hopes among the conspirators that the Popular Front might restore law and order, and on 17 July the military uprising began as scheduled in Morocco.[59] Within days

[58] Jackson, *Spanish Republic and Civil War*, pp. 220–21; Payne, *Spanish Revolution*, pp. 206–12; Malefakis, *Agrarian Reform*, pp. 223–28; Pierre Broué and Emile Témime, *The Revolution and the Civil War in Spain* (London, 1972), pp. 81–84.

[59] Jackson, *Spanish Republic and Civil War*, pp. 223–43; Thomas, *Spanish Civil War*, pp. 199–214; Payne, *Politics and the Military*, pp. 314–40; Peers, *Spanish Tragedy*, pp. 208–11.

Spain was plunged into the civil war that most observers on both sides of the Atlantic had long felt was inevitable.

American diplomats grimly watched the Spanish tragedy unfold during the summer of 1936. Claude Bowers privately admitted in early June that "conditions look stormy just now for the immediate future of Spain," largely because "the extreme left leaders . . . are now fighting bitterly among themselves." The assistant naval attaché at Madrid confirmed a few days later that the "Communists" hoped to "wreck the Left Front and bring about a new political alignment," while Hallett Johnson, Bowers's chief aide, reported an alarming increase in demands for an "Iberian Federation" composed of autonomous Basque, Catalan, and Galician republics. Convinced that the crisis had "entered upon an acute stage," the State Department foresaw "no improvement in the situation in Spain" in the near future. "The Embassy at Madrid reports strikes in increasing volume and waxing dissension in the ranks of the Popular Front," chief of the Division of Western European Affairs James Clement Dunn remarked in late June. "The Caballero Socialists," he continued, "seem disposed to support the Communists while their more moderate confreres are evidently anxious to avoid a definite decision. . . . Meanwhile, the masses are getting out of hand."[60]

British officials were also convinced that Casares Quiroga was gradually losing his grip on the situation. "The extreme left," Consul General Norman King reported from Barcelona, "seem to have got out of hand already." Spain was "faced with the choice between some sort of bolshevism and fascism," he added, and "if the present disturbed state of affairs leads to civil war, as is not unlikely, the extremists of the Left will gain the upper hand." Disgusted by the "chaotic internal condition of Spain," Chargé d'Affaires Ogilvie-Forbes complained on 16 June that Casares Quiroga was "at present unable or unwilling to govern" and was instead "tamely allowing the extremist elements to gain control."

[60]Bowers, Diary, 3 June 1936, Bowers Papers; Lieutenant T. E. Chandler to ONI, 8 June 1936, C-10-J, 20792D ("Political Conditions—Spain"), NA RG38; Bowers to Hull, 1 June 1936, and attached handwritten memorandum by assistant chief of the Division of Western European Affairs Robert Pell, 16 June 1936, 852.00 P.R./450; Bowers to Hull, 3 June 1936, and undated attached memorandum by Dunn, 852.00/ 2170, NA RG59.

Whitehall agreed that conditions in Spain had "steadily deteriorated" in recent months, mainly because the Popular Front had
been "either afraid or powerless to maintain order" since the February elections. "In many places," the Western Department's William Pollock noted on 23 June, "control of the local government,
the law courts etc. has fallen into the hands of the Extreme Left
minority," resulting "in a state of chronic strikes and lockouts and
in the virtual paralysis of a great deal of the country's business."
Noting that "the Communists have at the same time been arming
themselves and strengthening their organization," Pollock, like
Dunn, saw "no sign of improvement in the situation."[61]

British and American respect for Casares Quiroga diminished
still further after Madrid inaugurated what amounted to a tariff
war with London and Washington in early June. Convinced that it
had little to lose after commercial negotiations with Great Britain
and the United States had broken down, Spain raised its duties by
20 percent across the board on all items not specifically covered by
treaty commitments. After Claude Bowers confirmed on 1 June
that the Spaniards had indeed hiked tariffs on twenty-three products scheduled to receive most-favored-nation treatment under the
draft treaty initialed the previous autumn, the State Department
concluded that this "threat to our commerce" made any reciprocal
trade agreement with Spain out of the question. Whitehall too was
"gravely concerned at what appears to be a serious breach of the
standstill arrangement between Spain and the United Kingdom"
and threatened again to retaliate against Spanish produce unless
Casares Quiroga reversed this "disquieting precedent." Despite
the Popular Front's pledge "to be as accommodating as [was]
within their power," at month's end British merchants, like their
American competitors, still faced "heavy customs surcharges on
the great majority of goods imported into Spain."[62]

---

[61]King to Ogilvie-Forbes, 5 June 1936, enclosed in Ogilvie-Forbes to Eden, 9 June
1936, W5256/62/41; Ogilvie-Forbes to Eden, tel. 16 June 1936, W5333/62/41;
memorandum by Pollock, 23 June 1936, W5693/62/41, PRO FO371, vol. 20522.

[62]Bowers to Hull, tel. 29 May 1936, and memorandum by Morgan, 1 June 1936,
852.51/333; Bowers to Hull, tel. 1 June 1936, and undated memorandum by Morgan,
652.003/264, NA RG59; Chilton to Eden, tel. 1 June 1936, W4824/359/41; Board of
Trade to the Foreign Office, 4 June 1936, and Seymour to Ogilvie-Forbes, tel. 8 June
1936, W5055/359/41; Ogilvie-Forbes to Eden, tel. 9 June 1936, W5173/359/41;
memorandum by Pollock, 23 June 1936, W5693/62/41, PRO FO371, vols. 20522 and
20559.

British and American multinationals made no secret of their own contempt for the Casares Quiroga regime, which had placed them in an increasingly intolerable position. Although ITT officials remained outwardly "confident of our enterprise" at Madrid, the continuing turmoil in June tempted them to meddle once more in Spanish politics. Colonel Sosthenes Behn, who arrived in Spain on 20 June to assume personal control of the CTNE following the unexpected death of Captain Logan Rock, quickly made his own right-wing sympathies known. Behn maintained Rock's connections with the Spanish military and allegedly even provided assistance to the conspirators in early July. General Alfredo Kindelán, the chief of the rebel air force, later claimed that prior to the outbreak of the civil war "the American colonel who headed the Telephone Company" had set up clandestine communications links between the military plotters in Madrid and General Franco in the Canary Islands.[63]

Although it is unclear whether Rio Tinto likewise threw in its lot with the right-wing conspirators, such action would not have been surprising given the serious situation that confronted the British firm after yet another stay-in strike erupted at the copper fields in Huelva on 15 June. When the Popular Front regime refused to force the 1,400 strikers to the surface and hinted instead at nationalization, Rio Tinto officials and Chargé d'Affaires Ogilvie-Forbes suggested that Sir Anthony Eden raise the matter directly with Spanish foreign minister Augusto Barcía when the two met in the upcoming League of Nations council meeting in Geneva. Convinced that "in the present chaotic state and labor turmoil, the Spanish Govt. are really incapable of keeping any control" and worried that "if things go on as they are most British firms in Spain will be squeezed out of business," Whitehall agreed that the foreign secretary should broach the subject even though it was "always difficult to deal with extraneous matters at Geneva." On 23 June the Western Department accordingly prepared a briefing paper for Eden. It cited "considerable fears for the safety of British life and property owing to the workers getting out of hand" and

[63] Behn to Rock, tel. to be delivered to Bowers, n.d. [probably mid-June 1936], General Correspondence (1936 June–August), and Bowers, Diary, 20 June 1936, Bowers Papers; *New York Times*, 21 June 1936, sec. 2, p. 9:3; Kindelán's comments are from a personal interview with Gabriel Jackson, May 1960, as paraphrased in Jackson, *Spanish Republic and Civil War*, p. 248.

concluded that "so long as the Spanish Government fails to put its own house in order and to regain its authority, there is little hope of obtaining any real satisfaction."[64]

Sir Robert Vansittart persuaded Eden the next day that in light of "the serious state of affairs now prevailing in Spain," he must "speak strongly" to Barcía at Geneva. "Conditions are indeed disgraceful," Vansittart emphasized, "and, besides being a sad commentary on the weakness and timidity of the Spanish Government, are taking a turn detrimental to British interests." Eden arrived at the Swiss resort on 26 June and three days later, despite the press of more important matters including the Italo-Abyssinian War, he found time to discuss the Anglo-Spanish imbroglio. Noting that recent reports from Madrid made him "very anxious," he told Barcía that continual Popular Front harassment of Rio Tinto was "a disquieting example" of how "extremely difficult" it had become for British firms to do business in Spain. The Spaniard replied that Casares Quiroga was "steadily regaining control of the local situation" and fully intended to resolve all of Rio Tinto's "legitimate complaints" amicably "within a short time," leaving Eden hopeful that Britain's nagging problems with Spain might be nearing an end.[65]

Despite Barcía's assurances, however, Whitehall soon had good reason to doubt the Popular Front regime's ability to protect Britons or their property. In late June Rio Tinto was rocked by still more strikes and disorders. Within days the disturbances spread to two other London-based firms, the Zafra and Huelva Railway and the Alquife Mining Company, but the Spanish government remained "powerless or afraid" to intervene.[66] Matters became even grimmer on 2 July when Joseph Mitchell, the British manager of a Barcelona factory plagued by labor troubles, was shot to death by left-wing gunmen as he walked to work. Mitchell's assassination convinced many Britons that soon "no English businessman will be safe in

[64] Ogilvie-Forbes to Eden, 15 June 1936, W5521/62/41, 16 June 1936, W5523/626/41, and tel. 16 June 1936, and minutes by Pollock, 22 June 1936, and Seymour, 22 June 1936, W5533/62/41; memorandum by Pollock, 23 June 1936, W5693/62/41, PRO FO371, vols. 20522 and 20563.

[65] Minute by Vansittart, 24 June 1936, W5693/62/41; Consul Edmond (Geneva) to the Foreign Office, tel. 29 June 1936, W5894/626/41, PRO FO371, vols. 20522 and 20564. Eden relayed his messages to London through the British Consulate at Geneva during the League meetings.

[66] Ogilvie-Forbes to Eden, tel. 24 June 1936, W5707/626/41, tel. 25 June 1936, W5820/626/41, and 7 July 1936, W6240/626/41, PRO FO371, vols. 20563 and 20564.

Spain;" two weeks later the lack of progress on the case prompted Whitehall to complain that Madrid had "so far done nothing to show that his murderers are likely to be caught and allay fears regarding the future safety of British lives and property."[67] When faced with a left-wing threat to Britain's interests, Ogilvie-Forbes quipped sarcastically at Madrid in early July, Casares Quiroga had adopted the principle that "concession was the better part of valour." Even in the wake of Calvo Sotelo's assassination later that month the British chargé d'affaires doubted that Popular Front officials would "do anything more to preserve order than they have in the past."[68]

Although American blood had yet to be shed, U.S. officials were equally pessimistic regarding recent developments at Madrid. Four months of "widespread social unrest," Bowers warned Washington on 29 June, had rendered the Popular Front regime powerless and spawned rumors of a military coup. "As time goes on and social and economic conditions in Spain give little evidence of an early return to normality," he concluded gloomily, "the political situation is becoming daily more confused and uncertain." By early July Bowers admitted that the fate of the Spanish Republic "depends more and more upon the Government's success in restoring normal conditions," and the murders of Joseph Mitchell and José Calvo Sotelo made it clear that law and order remained a long way off.[69] The Casares Quiroga regime, Military Attaché Fuqua agreed on 14 July, was "very much disturbed and disoriented" and was almost certainly "incapable of giving successful solutions to the grave problems now confronting it."[70] Spain was clearly on the verge of a bloody upheaval, and most American observers, like their British counterparts, held the inept and pusillanimous leadership of the Popular Front responsible.

Indeed, in 1945 Spanish desk officer John H. Morgan would draft an official white paper that revealed the State Department's

[67] Consul G. Edgar Vaughan (Barcelona) to Eden, tel. 2 July 1936, W5989/62/41; Mr. Earle (Phillips Patent Company of Madrid) to Ogilvie-Forbes, 3 July 1936, W6093/62/41; Ogilvie-Forbes to Eden, tel. 6 July 1936, W6099/62/41; Vaughan to Eden, tel. 6 July 1936, W6256/62/41, and tel. 11 July 1936, and minute by D. D. MacClean, 16 July 1936, W6387/62/41, PRO FO371, vols. 20522 and 20523.

[68] Ogilvie-Forbes to Eden, 3 July 1936, W6141/62/41, and 14 July 1936, W6458/62/41, PRO FO371, vol. 20522.

[69] Bowers to Hull, 29 June 1936, 852.00 P.R./454, and 6 July 1936, 852.00 P.R./455, NA RG59.

[70] Fuqua to G-2, 14 July 1936, 2657 S.126/120, NA RG165.

ambivalence toward republican Spain on the eve of the civil war. In a series of despatches that "were regularly brought to the attention of the Secretary and Undersecretary as received," Morgan recalled, Bowers and other U.S. diplomats had described a Popular Front regime "earnestly striving to maintain public order but meeting with only limited success" due to "an atmosphere of general unrest and lack of respect for authority." In such uncertain circumstances, "three eventualities seemed possible" to American policy makers. The Casares Quiroga regime "might at last successfully consolidate its position," the "Right extremists might attempt a coup d'état," or "the more radical leaders of the left [might] assume power."[71] A quarter-century later President John F. Kennedy confronted a set of alternatives in the Dominican Republic not unlike those in Spain. Faced with the prospect of a democratic, a Trujillo, or a Castro regime, Kennedy argued in 1961 that "we ought to aim at the first, but we really can't renounce the second until we are sure we can avoid the third." Given the rough parallels with the dangerous conditions south of the Pyrenees, Hull, Phillips, and Morgan probably applied a similar "descending order of preference" to Spain in 1936.[72]

Long after the fighting ended, Britain's two highest-ranking policy makers made it clear that they shared American reservations about the Spanish Popular Front. Sir Robert Vansittart recalled that despite "good intentions," republican Spain "was smudged with religious persecution" and by 1936 actually "promised less freedom than under the dictatorship" of General Primo de Rivera. "The Republic was in fact a hotch-potch, though it was 'not the thing' to say so," Vansittart observed acidly. "It could not last. Had it done so Spain would have long since become a Soviet satellite."[73] In his memoirs Sir Anthony Eden likewise placed the blame for the Spanish civil war squarely on the shoulders of the unstable Popular Front regime. "It was the extreme left which had gained the most" during the spring of 1936, Eden pointed out, and Azaña and Casares Quiroga "could only bring peace if they showed firmness

---

[71] Morgan, "United States Policy during the Spanish Civil War July 1936–April 1939," Hull Papers, microfilm ed., reel 49, pp. 19–20 (hereafter cited as "Morgan Report"); Traina, *American Diplomacy*, p. 241.

[72] Kennedy quoted in Arthur M. Schlesinger, Jr., *A Thousand Days: John F. Kennedy in the White House* (Boston, 1965), p. 769.

[73] Vansittart, *Mist Procession*, pp. 416–17.

towards the unbridled elements among their supporters." But "this they failed to do, . . . rioting and arson soon broke out again, as extreme members of the Popular Front wreaked their will unchecked, . . . [and] by mid-summer anarchy threatened." Moreover Eden, like many other officials on both sides of the Atlantic, compared conditions in Madrid in 1936 to those in Moscow in 1917. "Spain and Russia, the two European countries which suffered bloody revolutions in this century," he remarked, "were the two most backward, where extremes of poverty and wealth existed, with little stabilizing force to weigh down extremism on either side."[74]

The parallels that Eden later drew between the Russian and Spanish revolutions reflect a central concern, one that shaped both British and American policies toward republican Spain on the eve of the civil war. Having watched the political pendulum at Madrid swing wildly to the left in 1931 and then back to the right in 1933, London and Washington feared that the Popular Front victory in February 1936 might catapult Spain irreversibly into bolshevism. Since neither the Foreign Office nor the State Department saw the Kremlin's united front as anything more than a "Trojan horse" designed to spread communism throughout Western Europe, most British and American observers doubted that the left-wing coalition of revolutionaries and reformers in Spain would outlive the election campaign. The bloody strikes and political murders that plagued first Azaña and later Casares Quiroga convinced both Whitehall and the White House that, despite outward signs of restraint from the Comintern and Spanish Communists, Moscow's agents were hard at work at Madrid. The tales of bolshevik subversion in Spain that William Bullitt and other Soviet experts recounted on both sides of the Atlantic removed any remaining doubts in London or Washington that the Spanish Republic had reached the end of its Kerensky interlude.

The United States and Great Britain grew even more skeptical of the Spanish Popular Front when it jettisoned the conciliatory attitude of its right-wing predecessors toward multinational corporations and rekindled the left-wing crusade of the early 1930s against foreign investors. American firms such as ITT and Armstrong Cork were castigated for exploiting Spanish workers or reaping exces-

---

[74]Sir Anthony Eden, *Facing the Dictators* (Boston, 1962), pp. 445–47.

sive profits but as a rule came off rather lightly through the summer of 1936, thanks largely to timely State Department intervention and, perhaps, to connections with the military. British multinationals, on the other hand, tended to fare much worse. Mining firms such as Rio Tinto and Tharsis Sulphur complained of constant intimidation, English sherry producers and banana planters saw their operations disrupted by labor violence, and railways like the Zafra and Huelva and the Great Southern were crippled by strikes and sabotage. By mid-1936 some foreign businessmen believed that only a right-wing uprising could salvage their interests in Spain.

Finally, British and American faith in the Spanish Republic diminished still further after Azaña and Casares Quiroga reneged on commercial agreements with London and Washington during the spring of 1936 and reverted to bilateral discriminatory trade policies. Having just concluded a pair of accords with Madrid designed to freeze tariffs and liquidate foreign-exchange arrears for British merchants, Whitehall was shocked and angered when the Popular Front regime unexpectedly hiked import duties and limited convertibility from pesetas to sterling. The State Department, which had spent the better part of two years hammering out a comprehensive commercial agreement with Spain, was even more outraged when most-favored-nation treatment for American exports was not forthcoming as promised. Indeed, scarcely anything could have infuriated Cordell Hull more than an assault on his cherished reciprocal trade program, especially one launched by the motley regime at Madrid. Faced with yet another huge balance-of-payments deficit for 1936, Spain once again found itself locked in commercial cold war with both Great Britain and the United States.

By July 1936 British and American relations with republican Spain were strained almost to the breaking point. The State Department and the Foreign Office agreed that the Spanish Popular Front was probably a stalking horse for the Kremlin and doubted that moderates like Azaña or Casares Quiroga could prevail over the extreme left. Neither the lives nor the property of U.S. and U.K. businessmen seemed secure in what many regarded as a prerevolutionary situation in Spain, while the trade pacts that London and Washington had recently worked out with Madrid quickly proved to be mere scraps of paper. The civil war that finally erupted on 17 July presented policy makers on both sides of the

Atlantic with an opportunity to settle old scores with a Popular Front regime whose political reliability and commercial integrity had become open questions. But it also created a major dilemma, for both Whitehall and the White House soon faced the hard choice of either assisting an increasingly suspect left-wing democracy or playing into the hands of right-wing insurgents in league with international fascism. The fate of Spain hung in the balance.

10

Malevolent Neutrality: Nonintervention in Historical Context

The political and economic troubles that had soured U.S. and U.K. relations with Spain during the spring of 1936 continued to exert a profound influence on British and American diplomacy during the first weeks of the Spanish civil war. Suspicions of bolshevik subversion deepened in London and Washington in late July as the hard-pressed Popular Front regime turned increasingly to its Communist, Socialist, and anarchist allies to combat the right-wing rebels. What British and American trade with Spain survived was reduced to a trickle by Madrid's continued intransigence and by wartime disruptions, while multinationals such as ITT and Rio Tinto saw their facilities commandeered and their funds confiscated by republican officials and armed workers. By early August few policy makers on either side of the Atlantic believed that the Spanish Republic could control its own left-wing supporters, let alone quell the military uprising. As a result many high-ranking British and American officials came to regard a Franco victory as more attractive than a Popular Front triumph in the civil war. Private preference became public policy later that summer, when both Great Britain and the United States pledged strict nonintervention in the Spanish conflict and prohibited arms sales to either side. This doctrine in theory appeared impartial, but in practice it amounted to a kind of "malevolent neutrality" that tipped the balance decisively against republican Spain.

Although the military uprising of July 1936 came as no surprise to Spaniard or foreigner alike, observers both inside and outside Spain were amazed that the ramshackle Popular Front regime did not collapse abruptly at the first whiff of grapeshot. General Franco and his rebels had quickly consolidated their hold on Spanish Morocco and soon gained a foothold on the mainland at Seville, but the army's bid to seize Madrid, Barcelona, and other major cities failed. Following futile efforts to arrange a truce with the insurgents, Prime Minister Casares Quiroga resigned on 19 July and was replaced by José Giral, another Left Republican protégé of President Azaña, who reluctantly distributed weapons to the popular militias. By month's end left-wing irregulars had fought the right-wing rebels to a standstill, derailing Franco's plans for a swift victory and ensuring that the civil war would be long and bloody.

Reliance on the popular militias, however, rapidly proved a mixed blessing for the Giral regime. Unwilling to cross swords with the staunchest defenders of the republic, the Madrid government gradually allowed much authority to pass into the hands of local committees of Socialists, Communists, and anarchists. Although Giral and Azaña urged the left to refrain from terrorism, armed workers and peasants meted out revolutionary justice during the first weeks of the civil war at an appalling rate. Anarchist contingents took the lead in hunting down rebel sympathizers, killing perhaps as many as 7,000 during a month-long rampage in Catalonia and Estremadura. Nearly twice that many "suspected fascists" were summarily executed by popular militias in the rest of the republican zone. The left-wing violence reached a bloody climax in mid-August, when guards at the Model Prison in Madrid murdered fourteen well-known right-wing politicians, including the aged republican conservative Melquiades Alvarez. With the approach of autumn hundreds of well-to-do Spaniards began to flee abroad, leaving few doubts in Washington or London that the much-dreaded bolshevik reign of terror had at last begun.[1]

---

[1] Payne, *Politics and the Military*, pp. 345–48; Jackson, *Spanish Republic*, pp. 283–87; Frank Jellinek, *The Civil War in Spain* (London, 1938), pp. 377–85; Thomas, *Spanish Civil War*, pp. 290–312; Burnett Bolloten, *The Spanish Revolution: The Left and the Struggle for Power during the Civil War* (Chapel Hill, N.C., 1979), pp. 51–61.

By late July most American officials held out little hope that the Giral regime would succeed in restraining the revolutionary left. Hallett Johnson cabled that conditions in San Sebastián, where Ambassador Claude Bowers and the diplomatic corps spent their summers, were abysmal. "There may be no authority capable of maintaining order," he prophesied, "should the armed proletariat get out of hand." Eric Wendelin, the chargé d'affaires in Madrid, confirmed that "Communist and Socialist youths" had committed so many "acts of depredation" that the streets of the Spanish capital were no longer safe. Consul George M. Graves reported that Malaga was "in the hands of Communists and other red groups," while Consul Lynn Franklin added that Barcelona had fallen under the sway of "irresponsible armed groups . . . composed of downright anarchists." Even in rebel territory American observers worried about the extreme left. Indeed, Consul Billy Corcoran at Vigo warned that a Popular Front triumph might result in "wholesale killings" because "everybody Spaniard and foreigner of bourgeois class will be marked."[2]

In Washington Secretary of State Hull read these cables with growing apprehension. Although he assured reporters on 22 July that the evacuation of American nationals from Spain was proceeding smoothly, Hull met with Admiral William H. Standley, the chief of naval operations, the next day to discuss accelerating the rescue mission. That afternoon Hull cabled President Roosevelt, who was cruising off the coast of New England, that "the situation is if anything becoming much worse," that "a completely chaotic condition may arise in Spain which may continue for some time," and that it might soon be necessary to dispatch additional warships to Spanish waters. "One of the most serious factors in this situation," Hull emphasized, "lies in the fact that the Spanish Government has distributed large quantities of arms and ammunition into the hands of irresponsible members of Left Wing political organizations." Troubled by this frightening assessment of conditions in Spain, Roosevelt authorized Hull on 24 July to send reinforcements, but with the help of the Royal Navy, the two U.S. vessels

[2]Johnson to Hull, tel. 21 July 1936, 852.00/2528; Wendelin quoted in Ambassador Jesse Straus (Paris) to Hull, tel. 22 July 1936, 852.00/2196; Graves to Hull, tel. 22 July 1936, 852.00/2202; Franklin to Hull, tel. 23 July 1936, 852.00/2209; and Corcoran to Hull, tel. 23 July 1936, 852.00/2222, NA RG59.

already on the scene were able to accommodate all the American evacuees.[3]

If the evacuation of U.S. citizens posed no major problems for the State Department, the disturbing situation in republican Spain did much to rekindle Washington's earlier fears of communist subversion at Madrid. With Ambassador Bowers stranded at the isolated resort town of Fuenterrabía near the French border, the bulk of the first-hand information that Hull and his aides received about the civil war came from foreign service officers scattered throughout the Iberian Peninsula who drew few distinctions between anarchist terror and bolshevik conspiracy.[4] Hallett Johnson feared "personal violence from Communist or other Left extremists," Consul Herbert Williams at Gibraltar claimed that "Reds" controlled the entire Mediterranean coast, and Military Attaché Stephen Fuqua at Madrid cabled that "Extremists [are] gradually controlling Government."[5] Even Luis Calderón, the Spanish ambassador to the United States, admitted during a 27 July conversation with Hull that although the Giral regime was trying "every possible way" to restrain the left-wing militias, "some time would be required to restore orderly and quiet conditions" in the republican zone. "Careful not to intimate the slightest bias" to the Spaniard, Hull privately warned Roosevelt shortly thereafter that many observers now feared that "in the event military authority should fail, mob rule and anarchy would follow."[6]

By the end of the month Hull and his aides saw little reason to question such observations. Consul Franklin at Barcelona confirmed on 29 July that the local authorities were powerless to prevent "extreme radical elements" from staging "daily assassinations of priests, nuns, monarchists and fascists." That same day Arthur Bliss Lane, the American minister to Latvia, reported

[3] Hull, "Memorandum of Press Conference July 22 1936," 852.00/2317; and Hull to Roosevelt, tel. 23 July 1936, 852.00/2265k, NA RG59; Hull, *Memoirs*, 1:475; Roosevelt to Hull, tel. 24 July 1936, FDR Papers, OF 422-C; Hull to Roosevelt, tel. 24 July 1936, 852.00/2235, NA RG59.

[4] Bowers, *My Mission to Spain*, pp. 241–54; Straus to Hull, tel. 26 July 1936, *FRUS, 1936*, 2:645–46. For a fuller discussion of Bowers's predicament, see Little, "Claude Bowers," pp. 140–41.

[5] Johnson to Hull, 24 July 1936, 852.00/2407; Williams to Hull, tel. 27 July 1936, 852.00/2292; Fuqua to G-2, tel. 29 July 1936, appended to Wendelin to Hull, tel. 29 July 1936, 852.00/2316, NA RG59.

[6] Memorandum by Hull, 27 July 1936, 852.00/2300, NA RG59; Hull to Roosevelt, tel. 27 July 1936, Roosevelt Papers, OF 422-C.

rumors of "Soviet complicity in furnishing arms and funds to communists in Spain."[7] Indeed, a fortnight after Franco's *pronunciamiento* Hallett Johnson reminded James Clement Dunn, the chief of the Division of Western European Affairs, that "today there are two revolutions in Spain: one, part of the army against the government, and two, the Syndicalists against the government." Although the popular militias were "now nominally working with the government as it suits their ends to defeat the military rebellion," Johnson warned that "should the government win it will find that the Syndicalists and other left extremists have taken the power into their [own] hands or will themselves be in revolt."[8]

British policy makers also suspected that in the event of a republican triumph in the Spanish civil war, the weak Giral regime would quickly be overthrown by the extreme left. Consul William Oxley wired Whitehall from Vigo on 20 July that his district was "virtually in the hands of the proletariat," a few hours later Consul G. Edgar Vaughan foresaw "ugly possibilities" in Barcelona because Catalan officials were "quite unable to provide any special protection for British subjects," and the next day the governor of Gibraltar warned that a victory for the "practically Communistic" forces of the Popular Front would endanger hundreds of Britons along the Mediterranean coast. "Everyone anxiously awaits the result of General Franco's coup d'etat," Consul Harold Patteson reported from Tenerife in the Canaries on 21 July. "Should he fail I believe dangerous disorders [are] bound to occur in these islands." Acting on the advice of numerous consular and diplomatic officials, the Baldwin government, like the Roosevelt administration, stationed several British warships in Spanish waters on 22 July as a precautionary measure.[9]

Whitehall's worst fears regarding the reliability of the Giral regime were confirmed on 24 July by Julio López Oliván, republican Spain's own ambassador to Great Britain. "There were three possible outcomes of the present situation," the Spaniard explained in a

[7]Franklin to Hull, tel. 29 July 1936, 852.00/2326; Lane to Hull, tel. 29 July 1936, 852.00/2316, NA RG59.

[8]Johnson to Dunn, n.d. (probably early August 1936), in Johnson, *Diplomatic Memoirs*, pp. 110–11.

[9]Oxley to Eden, tel. 20 July 1936, W6531/62/41; Vaughan to Eden, tel. 20 July 1936, W6620/62/41; Patteson to Eden, tel. 21 July 1936, W6610/62/41; governor of Gibraltar to Eden, tel. 21 July 1936, W6753/62/41, PRO FO371, vols. 20522 and 20523; Eden, *Facing the Dictators*, pp. 448–49.

long talk with his "old friend" Foreign Secretary Anthony Eden: a rebel triumph, a "communist" takeover, or continued Popular Front rule. "From the way he spoke," Eden noted, "I thought that [López] Oliván regarded a communist government as the most likely outcome of the civil war, in which event, he said, not only he, but several other members of the Spanish Embassy staff, would resign." The Spaniard reiterated his dire prophecy three days later during an interview with Thomas Jones, a personal adviser to Prime Minister Stanley Baldwin. "If the Government wins in Spain," López Oliván told Jones, "they will be superseded by the Communists to whom they have issued arms."[10]

Such reports helped harden British attitudes toward the Spanish Republic during late July from skepticism into tacit opposition. Consul Oxley at Vigo, for example, made no secret of his own pro-rebel sympathies, cabling Whitehall on 25 July that "victory for communist Government means finish of Spain." In fact, according to Henry Buckley, a journalist stationed in Spain during the civil war, most British diplomats were "very complaisantly disposed towards the Spanish Right . . . as a guarantee against Bolshevism."[11] High-ranking Conservative politicians in London were equally suspicious of the Spanish Popular Front. "The army of the Right elements, revolted by the appalling Left government, have tried a coup de main to seize power," Sir Henry Channon, an influential Tory M.P., noted on 27 July. "For a few days, we had hoped that they would win, though tonight it seems as if the Red Government, alas, will triumph." David Margesson, the chief Conservative whip, agreed shortly thereafter that "a victory for the Rebels in Spain . . . would be splendid." Prime Minister Baldwin himself confessed that he too was deeply troubled by signs of bolshevik subversion in Spain. "I told Eden yesterday," Baldwin remarked over lunch with Thomas Jones on 27 July, "that on no account, French or other, must he bring us in to fight on the side of the Russians." Jones, who later admitted that he personally favored an insurgent triumph, was quick to remind Baldwin that "Bullitt's prophecy made to me two months ago that Moscow

---

[10]Eden to Chilton, 24 July 1936, W6893/3694/41, PRO FO371, vol. 20569; Eden, *Facing the Dictators*, p. 449; Jones, diary entry for 28 July 1936, in Jones, *Diary with Letters*, p. 232.

[11]Oxley to Eden, tel. 25 July 1936, W6955/62/41, PRO FO371, vol. 20525; Buckley, *Life and Death of the Spanish Republic*, pp. 174–76.

looked forward to a Communist Government in Spain in 3 months" seemed about to be fulfilled.[12]

Ironically, however, neither Spanish Communists nor their Comintern mentors favored a proletarian takeover during the first weeks of the civil war. Such Communist leaders as Dolores Ibarruri, soon to be famous as "La Pasionaria," urged the entire left, Marxist and non-Marxist alike, to rally around Spain's embattled Popular Front. The Soviet press adopted a similar line, exhorting Spanish workers to direct their fire not at liberals like Giral but rather at the real enemy, Franco and the reactionary right. The actions of Kremlin officials and their comrades at Madrid spoke even louder than their words. In Moscow party and labor leaders raised hundreds of thousands of rubles to assist, not to overthrow, the financially strapped Giral regime. And three thousand miles to the southwest, on the plains of Castile, the charismatic Enrique Lister organized the Communist Fifth Regiment; though much smaller than the anarchist brigades, it was instrumental in thwarting the early rebel assault on republican Madrid.[13]

Despite such indications that a bolshevik upheaval was not imminent, British and American officials expressed renewed concern about Soviet subversion once the extreme left unleashed a nationalization campaign against private industry during the last week of July. After armed workers occupied factories, seized public utilities, and commandeered transport facilities, Prime Minister Giral issued a decree placing the nationalization program under governmental jurisdiction. In those regions where the central administration functioned well or where moderates held sway, as in Madrid and the Basque provinces, private property remained relatively secure, but elsewhere the drive for collectivization continued unabated. As much as one-third of the arable land in Andalusia was seized by landless peasants, while nearly half of all industry in Valencia, including the shipyards, was taken over by left-wing ex-

---

[12] Sir Henry Channon, *Chips: The Diaries of Sir Henry Channon*, ed. Robert Rhodes James (London, 1967), entry for 27 July 1936, p. 73; Margesson to Neville Chamberlain, 1 August 1936, NC 7/11/29/40, Neville Chamberlain Papers, Birmingham University Library, Birmingham, England; Jones, diary entries for 27 July and 3 September 1936, in Jones, *Diary with Letters*, pp. 231, 240.

[13] Julius Braunthal, *History of the International*, trans. John Clark, 2 vols. (New York, 1967), 2:456–57; Ronald Fraser, *The Blood of Spain: An Oral History of the Spanish Civil War* (New York, 1979), p. 145; Jackson, *Spanish Republic*, p. 257; Thomas, *Spanish Civil War*, pp. 339–41, 360–61.

tremists. The nationalization campaign reached its peak, however, in Catalonia, the stronghold of the anarchist CNT. By early August armed workers had collectivized all the textile mills, iron foundries, and utility firms in Barcelona and controlled 70 percent of other business establishments in the province as well. Although the Madrid authorities urged the CNT not to interfere with the hundred-odd British and American companies operating in Spain, the anarchists seldom distinguished between foreign and domestic enterprises. When the Giral regime proved either unwilling or unable to protect multinationals from the left-wing onslaught, both the State Department and the Foreign Office intervened.[14]

Most American holdings in Spain were located in the republican zone, placing Washington on a collision course with Madrid. As early as 22 July left-wing militiamen had seized ITT's radio-telephone transmitter in the Spanish capital, creating "a very dangerous situation" for the firm's officials, whose "greatest worry at the present time is what the mob may do the moment the fighting ceases whichever side wins."[15] A week later came the news that armed workers had seized control of the Ford and General Motors assembly plants in Barcelona. These developments were greeted with alarm on Wall Street, where stock prices for those corporations with major interests in Spain plummeted as much as 25 percent in the last three days of July. The State Department tersely acknowledged the seizures on 1 August but declined to speculate in public about what action might be taken. According to the *Washington Post,* however, American policy makers expressed grave concern over what they privately termed "the first large scale requisitioning of American property abroad since the Russian revolution of 1917." Losses in Spain, State Department officials predicted confidentially, might easily total half-a-million dollars.[16]

[14]Bolloten, *Spanish Revolution,* pp. 59–66; Payne, *Spanish Revolution,* pp. 236–53; Jackson, *Spanish Republic,* pp. 276–83; Broué and Témime, *Revolution and Civil War in Spain,* pp. 151–54.

[15]Memorandum for Hull from Paul Culbertson, 22 July 1936, 852.00/2311, NA RG59; Assistant Secretary of State Wilbur Carr to Hull, 24 July 1936, Wilbur Carr Papers, Box 13 (Memoranda), Library of Congress; Carr, Diary, 24 July 1936, Carr Papers, Box 5.

[16]Franklin to Hull, tel. 28 July 1936, 852.00/2304, NA RG59; "Memorandum of Press Conference #146, July 29, 1936," Hull Papers, microfilm ed., reel 88; *New York Times,* 30 July 1936, sec. 1, p. 1:6, and 2 August 1936, sec. 1, p. 29:1; "Revolution in Spain: Protection of Americans and Other Foreigners," 1 August 1936, *State Department Press Releases,* no. 357 (1 August 1936), p. 118; *Washington Post,* 2 August 1936, sec. 1, p. 1:5; Elston, "Multinationals & American Foreign Policy," p. 261.

After learning later that same day that the Madrid authorities had just ruled the takeovers permanent and irrevocable, Secretary of State Hull drafted a vigorous note of protest on behalf of all American multinationals in Spain. "This Government," he pointed out indignantly, "cannot admit that private property, whether in the hands of American nationals or abandoned by them temporarily because of conditions beyond their control, may be interfered with with impunity or denied the protection to which it is entitled under international law." In any case, Hull demanded "prompt and full compensation" for all American property confiscated in Spain. The Giral regime received Hull's message on 5 August and promised two weeks later to compensate U.S. citizens for all their losses, but such indemnification failed to materialize. In fact, the collectivization campaign actually accelerated. National City Bank later claimed that Catalan officials had pilfered the accounts of its Spanish subsidiary, Ford executives estimated damages to their Barcelona plant at over $1 million, and General Motors placed its losses at $3.3 million in the first three months of the civil war alone.[17]

Since many British multinationals also lay in the republican zone, the Foreign Office was eventually forced to take a strong stand against the left-wing expropriation campaign as well. As early as 27 July Consul Oxley had warned from Vigo that "if the Government and Communist hordes should win, British lives and property would be [in] serious danger." The next morning armed workers seized control of the London-based Barcelona Power Light and Traction Company. Fearful that the "proletariat" would do "willfull and serious damage to the power plants and stations involving very heavy expenditure and loss of revenue," the firm asked Whitehall "to render such assistance as is possible." Two days later Consul General Norman King confirmed "wholesale intervention [in] businesses and factories," including the BPLTC and two British banks, and warned all English entrepreneurs in

[17] Wendelin to Hull, tel. 1 August 1936, 852.00/2349, NA RG59; Hull to Wendelin, tel. 3 August 1936; Wendelin to Hull, tel. 5 August 1936, and 18 August 1936; Hull to Wendelin, tel. 12 September 1936; Acting Secretary of State R. Walton Moore to Wendelin, tel. 15 September 1936; Wendelin to Moore, tel. 22 September 1936, *FRUS, 1936*, 3:657–58, 661–62, 674, 712–13, 717–18, 725; Franklin to Hull, tel. 15 August 1936, 352.115/27; memorandum for Hull, "General Motors Losses in Spain," 2 October 1936, 352.115 GMEC/46, NA RG59; Elston, "Multinationals & American Foreign Policy," pp. 174–77, 191–93; Traina, *American Diplomacy*, pp. 62–64; Wilkins and Hill, *American Business Abroad*, p. 262.

Catalonia "that they stay at their own risk." Convinced that the extreme left intended to "take the opportunity presented to try and carry out a rebellion on the Russian plan, which might easily involve wholesale massacre and destruction of property," King complained to Catalan officials on 31 July about the confiscation of British enterprises. Although he received assurances that "all foreign property . . . is to be respected," King cautioned Whitehall that the "armed Proletariat" appeared "to be becoming daily more bloodthirsty" and "would probably not respect orders from any authority."[18]

The Foreign Office was nevertheless reluctant to lodge a formal protest "until some ordered Govt. is restored in Spain." As the assault on foreign property widened in early August, however, Whitehall was peppered with complaints from British investors calling attention to Washington's recent demarche and urging London to make similar representations. To make matters worse, the Foreign Office learned on 13 August that left-wing miners in Huelva province had seized the Rio Tinto copper fields and were holding thirty-eight British supervisors hostage in an effort to forestall the advance of rebel troops. Persuaded at last that "a warning to the Madrid Government regarding British property" would "strengthen our position vis à vis public opinion," Whitehall dispatched a "strong note" to the Giral regime on 14 August requesting its assistance in evacuating the Britons held hostage at the Rio Tinto mines. Within hours Popular Front officials were able to arrange the release of the three dozen captives, who were flown to safety by the republican air force. Once this "little scare" was "liquidated," the Foreign Office instructed Consul General King to file "a general protest . . . against the taking over of British properties," especially in Catalonia.[19] But by mid-August few diplomats or busi-

---

[18] Oxley to Eden, tel. 27 July 1936, W7009/62/41; Malcolm Hubbard (BPLTC) to Vansittart, 29 July 1936, and King to Eden, tel. 30 July 1936, W7244/62/41; King to Eden, tel. 31 July 1936, W7276/62/41, PRO FO371, vols. 20524 and 20525; Katherine, Duchess of Atholl, *Searchlight on Spain* (Harmondsworth, England, 1938), pp. 152–57.

[19] Minute by Seymour, 1 August 1936, W7244/62/41; undated statement by Lawton Fraser (BPLTC), enclosed in King to Eden, 5 August 1936, W8210/62/41; Charles Williams to Pollock, 7 August 1936, and minute by Pollock, 14 August 1936, W8152/62/41; Seymour to Milanes, tel. 14 August 1936, W8594/62/41; Milanes to Eden, tel. 15 August 1936, and minute by Pollock, 18 August 1936, W8755/62/41; minutes by Seymour, 17 August 1936, and by Mounsey, 18 August 1936, and Seymour to King, 19 August 1936, W8658/62/41, PRO FO371, vols. 20525, 20528, 20529, and 20531; Avery, *Not on Queen Victoria's Birthday*, pp. 357–64.

nessmen believed that the Giral regime could stem the wave of left-wing nationalizations.

British and American exports, like foreign investments, were severely disrupted in the first month of the civil war. When the fighting erupted in mid-summer, commercial negotiations between Washington and Madrid were already deadlocked over the issue of more equitable treatment for U.S. products. Once it became clear that the Giral regime was no more willing than its predecessors to restore most-favored-nation status to American exports, Cordell Hull concluded on 22 July that "it does not appear likely that the trade agreement will be consummated for several months or possibly longer." Any chance for real progress on commercial matters was dashed three weeks later, when Spanish officials at Tarragona proclaimed a state of emergency and confiscated $800,000 worth of U.S. raw cotton without payment.[20] British exporters fared no better. The Anglo-Spanish payments agreement, negotiated the previous winter to guarantee the convertibility of pesetas into sterling, had begun to show signs of strain as early as June 1936, and after civil war erupted the following month the arrangement ceased to function altogether. Citing a serious shortage of foreign exchange, the Giral regime suspended the accord indefinitely in early August, a move that sparked a rash of complaints from British merchants who could no longer obtain payment for their sales to Spain.[21]

The outbreak of civil war, then, exacerbated all the ideological, multinational, and commercial problems that had bedeviled British and American relations with the Spanish Republic under Popular Front rule. The rumors of bolshevik subversion in Spain, so common on both sides of the Atlantic during the spring of 1936, seemed to have become reality by late July, when armed workers and peasants imposed a revolutionary reign of terror in the republican zone. British and American firms such as the BPLTC and General Motors, long vulnerable to left-wing Spanish nationalists, saw their operations taken over by anarchists, Socialists, and Communists in early August. And U.S. and U.K. trade with Spain, already eroded by autarchic Popular Front commercial policies,

[20] Hull to Senator Warren Barbour (D-New Jersey), 22 July 1936, 611.5231/1173, NA RG59; Traina, *American Diplomacy*, p. 62.
[21] Eden to Chamberlain, 2 November 1936, W14719/46/41, PRO FO371, vol. 20518; *Board of Trade Journal*, 13 August 1936, p. 233, and 24 December 1936, p. 901; Edwards, *British Government and the Spanish Civil War*, pp. 76–81.

evaporated almost entirely with the approach of autumn as the Giral regime struggled to marshal its limited international financial resources to thwart the insurgents. Ironically, Madrid's ability to defeat Franco's rebels hinged more and more on whether it could obtain the necessary weapons from London or Washington.

II

Before the summer was out, the international overtones of the civil war in Spain were obvious to both Whitehall and the White House. The Spanish right had received encouragement and assistance from abroad for some time. As early as March 1934 a group of monarchists had paid a visit to Rome, where Mussolini pledged to support a right-wing uprising in Spain. When the civil war erupted two years later, Italy rushed weapons and aircraft to Spanish Morocco and was soon supplying military advisers as well. Equally sympathetic to Franco's rebellion, Hitler provided transport planes to ferry the insurgents from North Africa to the mainland in the early days of the fighting. Ever distrustful of Popular Front rule in Madrid, the Salazar regime allowed Spanish rebels to use sanctuaries in Portugal and later permitted the transshipment of military supplies from Lisbon across the Portuguese frontier to Franco's forces. Unable to stem the influx of men and matériel that fueled the right-wing uprising, republican Spain sought aid from the Western democracies.[22]

The embattled Giral regime turned first to Paris, where a newly elected left-wing Popular Front government might be expected to assist its counterpart at Madrid. Without hesitation, Socialist premier Léon Blum authorized the sale of French war matériel, including combat aircraft, to the Spanish Republic on 21 July. Upon his arrival in London two days later for a long-scheduled conference on European collective security, however, Blum learned that British officials opposed this decision. According to Charles Corbin, the French ambassador to Great Britain, there was "strong pro-Rebel feeling in the British cabinet," not only because "conservative cir-

---

[22]John Coverdale, *Italian Intervention in the Spanish Civil War* (Princeton, N.J., 1975), pp. 43–54; Puzzo, *Spain and the Great Powers*, pp. 60–65, 69–73; Thomas, *Spanish Civil War*, pp. 352–62.

cles" in England were "intimately allied, financially and socially, with the Spanish conservatives" but also because "British financial circles feared that the Spanish Republic would nationalize the mines and heavy industry."[23]

Blum discussed the Spanish situation informally with British officials over lunch on 23 July. Baldwin and his advisers expressed "great apprehension" regarding the French plan to aid republican Spain and urged Paris to reconsider its decision. Blum might be "honest well meaning and humane," Chancellor of the Exchequer Neville Chamberlain complained afterward, "but I doubt very much whether he understands the consequences of what he is doing." Although it is uncertain whether British policy makers resorted to any explicit threats to coerce the French, Foreign Secretary Eden privately emphasized the dangers implicit in the Spanish crisis. "It's your business," he told Blum on the evening of the twenty-third, "but I ask only one thing of you, I beg of you, please be cautious." Chastened by these words of warning, the French premier returned home the next day and discovered that several members of his own government shared British reservations. After a pair of grueling cabinet meetings Blum reversed himself on 27 July, prohibited the sale of French weapons to the Spanish Republic, and appealed for an end to all foreign intervention in the civil war.[24]

Its lifeline to France severed, the Giral regime turned next to the United States for military assistance. As early as 27 July the State Department learned that republican Spain would probably seek to purchase large quantities of American war matériel, but high-ranking U.S. policy makers did not begin to consider the question in earnest until 3 August. That morning, after dispatching a note of protest to Madrid regarding the recent confiscation of American property, Secretary of State Hull discussed the Spanish crisis with

[23] Pierre Cot, *Triumph of Treason* (New York, 1944), pp. 338–39; Joel Colton, *Léon Blum: Humanist in Politics* (New York, 1966), pp. 236–37; John Dreifort, *Yvon Delbos at the Quai d'Orsay* (Lawrence, Kans., 1973), p. 35.

[24] Testimony of Blum, 23 July 1947, in France, Assemblée Nationale, *Les événements survenus en France de 1933 à 1945*, 9 vols. (Paris, 1948), 1:216; Colton, *Blum*, pp. 242–43; Dreifort, *Delbos*, pp. 36–40; M. D. Gallagher, "Léon Blum and the Spanish Civil War," *Journal of Contemporary History* 6 (January 1971), 58; Neville Chamberlain to Hilda, 25 July 1936, NC 18/1/971, Neville Chamberlain Papers. For a different interpretation of Blum's visit, see David Carlton, *Anthony Eden* (London, 1981), pp. 86–89.

Undersecretary Phillips. Well aware that despite recent French appeals to cease meddling in Spain, Italy was still sending military assistance to what Phillips termed "the so-called rebels," both men were "naturally alarmed about possible repercussions of the Spanish situation." Even more disturbing, however, was the "great enthusiasm in Moscow" for a Popular Front regime at Madrid "which has in its folds Socialists, Communists, and even Radicalists." Late that night Phillips pondered the American alternatives. "Shall we," he wondered, "permit arms and ammunition to go to either side or both sides?"[25]

If Hull and Phillips acknowledged that the Spanish strife might in the long run spark "a European conflagration," both seemed more concerned by 4 August with the short-run danger of bolshevik subversion in the republican zone. Indeed, the two men had "several long conferences" that day about how best to handle the Giral regime's request for military assistance. "If they cannot get such supplies in Europe, they will undoubtedly turn to us and we shall be in an embarrassing situation since we have no legislation authorizing us to refuse the export of such materials even though they are destined for what amounts to a communistic government," Phillips noted. "The critical part of the situation is that if the [Spanish] Government wins, as now seems likely, communism throughout Europe will be immensely stimulated."[26] Later that evening Loy Henderson, the U.S. chargé d'affaires in Moscow, confirmed that the Kremlin had begun to provide the Giral regime with "pecuniary assistance." The news that Moscow intended to aid "the Radical or Communist Government" at Madrid convinced Phillips that the Soviets would "not hesitate to assume leadership of the Communist move [*sic*]."[27]

Hull and Phillips discussed the dangerous state of affairs in republican Spain with several other top-level State Department officials on 5 August. Although no minutes of this meeting exist, the secretary of state apparently expressed "keen interest" in the recent French proposal to prohibit arms sales to both sides in the

---

[25]Memorandum by Hull, 27 July 1936, 852.00/2300, NA RG59; Straus to Hull, tel. 2 August 1936, *FRUS, 1936*, 2:457–58; Phillips, Journal, 3 August 1936, Phillips Papers.

[26]Phillips, Journal, 4 August 1936, Phillips Papers.

[27]Henderson to Hull, tel. 4 August 1936, 852.00/2395, NA RG59; Phillips, Journal, 4 August 1936, Phillips Papers.

Spanish conflict and personally took the lead in pushing for a policy of strict nonintervention. Since current American neutrality legislation did not apply to civil wars and since Congress had already adjourned for the summer, the group decided not to issue a formal statement. Instead, Hull confidentially informed the press later that afternoon that the United States would pursue a course of total noninvolvement with regard to Spain. When Spanish ambassador Luis Calderón inquired the next day whether the republic might still purchase American weapons, Undersecretary Phillips tersely confirmed that the United States had no intention of aiding either the Giral regime or Franco's rebels but rather would maintain an attitude of impartial neutrality.[28]

Meanwhile, the State Department continued to receive graphic accounts of bolshevik intrigue and terror under Popular Front rule in Spain. Merle Cochran, a Treasury Department official stranded in the war zone for nearly three weeks, cabled Washington on 7 August that widespread "communist atrocities" had sparked "bitter resentment against direction of Spanish affairs from Moscow" among "respectable citizens [who] considered situation unbearable and were willing to risk everything in effort to overthrow Communist Government." Only "the strictest military force," Cochran concluded, could hold the "definitely communist" laborers in check. That same day, a despatch arrived from Lieutenant B. L. Hutt, an Army language student in northern Spain, which reiterated that "Russia is financing and organizing these laborers in a very determined manner." Since the armed workers had "tasted blood" and were "not going to quietly go back to hard menial labor after riding around in Packards, Cadillacs, and Hispano Suizas," Hutt prophesied that "if the present government (Frente Popular) wins out Spain will be on the verge of another situation such as Russia went through in 1917." A victory for the "so-called rebels" was the only way to ensure "a firm form of government."[29]

---

[28] Hull, *Memoirs*, 1:477; Traina, *American Diplomacy*, pp. 51–52; "Morgan Report," pp. 32–33, Hull Papers, microfilm ed., reel 49; "Revolution in Spain: Protection of Americans and Other Foreigners," 6 August 1936, *State Department Press Releases*, no. 358 (8 August 1936), pp. 131–32; Phillips, Journal, 6 August 1936, Phillips Papers; memorandum by Phillips, 6 August 1936, 852.00/2550, NA RG59.

[29] Wendelin to Hull, tel. 7 August 1936, 852.00/2464; Cochran to Hull, tel. 7 August 1936, 852.00/2463; Report no. 102–200 by Hutt, 28 July 1936 (received by the State Department 7 August 1936), 852.00/2541, NA RG59.

These harrowing reports confirmed the State Department's worst fears regarding communist subversion in Spain and strengthened its resolve to maintain a policy of strict nonintervention. Indeed, on the afternoon of 7 August Hull and Phillips drafted a circular telegram to all American officials in the Iberian Peninsula emphasizing that although the neutrality law had "no application in the present situation," the United States would "scrupulously refrain from any interference whatsoever in the unfortunate Spanish situation." Exhausted by the ongoing crisis, Hull departed for Hot Springs, Virginia, and a badly needed rest two days later, leaving Undersecretary Phillips in charge of the department. Perhaps the most bitterly anticommunist of Hull's advisers, Phillips was now in a position to make the implications of the American nonintervention policy explicit.[30]

Before the week was out, pressure was mounting on the undersecretary from both at home and abroad to clarify U.S. policy toward Spain. Recently tapped to become the new American ambassador to Italy, Phillips paid particular attention to reports from Rome indicating that Mussolini was preoccupied by "the development of Soviet propaganda and the manifest growth of communism in Europe." When the Glenn L. Martin Company called on 10 August to ask whether the State Department would object to the sale of eight aircraft to the Spanish Republic, Phillips saw an opportunity "to take a position today so that our record will be clear if any foreign government makes the above inquiry." He first contacted the White House, then telephoned the secretary of state at Hot Springs. Together, Hull and Phillips prepared a reply to the firm's query, suggesting that "the sale of aeroplanes . . . would not follow the spirit of the [U.S.] Government's policy." Since American neutrality legislation did not apply to civil wars, the pair elected to impose a moral embargo on arms shipments to Spain.[31]

Phillips encountered "strongly divided opinion in the Depart-

---

[30] Phillips, Journal, 7 August 1936, Phillips Papers; Hull, *Memoirs*, 1:477–78; Phillips to all consulates in Spain, circular tel. 7 August 1936, *FRUS, 1936*, 2:471; Harold Ickes, *The Secret Diary of Harold Ickes*, vol. 1: *The First Thousand Days, 1933–1936* (New York, 1952), p. 657, entry for 8 August 1936.

[31] Phillips, Journal, 10 August 1936, Phillips Papers; Hull, *Memoirs*, 1:478; "Morgan Report," p. 35, Hull Papers, microfilm ed., reel 49; Joseph Green (Office of Arms and Munitions Control), "Outline of Office Business June 27–Aug 14, 1936," Miscellaneous Official Correspondence and Memoranda 1935–1940, Joseph Green Papers, Seeley Mudd Manuscript Library, Princeton University, box 12.

ment on this matter." Joseph C. Green, chief of the Office of Arms and Munitions Control, felt that the nonintervention policy was probably "a wise one" but worried that the moral embargo might leave the State Department in an embarrassing predicament the next time a Latin American government appealed to the United States for military assistance in putting down a rebellion. Assistant Secretary R. Walton Moore frankly "doubted the wisdom" of the moral embargo, fearing ill-defined domestic political repercussions should the letter to the aircraft firm become public. Years later Sumner Welles would recall that other unnamed American officials had questioned the advisability of such a strategy as well.[32]

China expert Stanley Hornbeck, however, proved to be the most articulate critic of the moral embargo. He began by emphasizing that the Roosevelt administration lacked legal authority to prohibit arms sales to the warring parties in Spain. If the State Department blocked the export of weapons to Spanish republicans and rebels alike, Hornbeck warned, American officials "should be prepared to feel that the same attitude should be taken in case of civil conflict in countries other than Spain." He added that the moral embargo not only contradicted current American policy "with regard to civil conflict in certain other countries, conspicuously China," but also contained "elements of great potential unfairness." Hornbeck contended that, unless the president was willing to seek specific congressional authorization, the State Department "cannot act at all" to block arms sales to Spain.[33]

Despite these objections, Phillips pressed for the swift dispatch of the letter to the Martin Company. After conferring with Hull once again, the undersecretary sent the final draft to Roosevelt, who read it in the White House swimming pool on the afternoon of the 10th. Favorably inclined to the moral embargo earlier in the day, the president now expressed "considerable doubts" and asked to hold the letter overnight for further study. Phillips, however, stressed "the importance of getting it off this evening" and won

---

[32]Phillips, Journal, 10 August 1936, Phillips Papers; Green to Moffat, 12 September 1936, Correspondence 1936 (A-H), Moffat Papers; Moore to Hull, 5 May 1938, Moore Papers, box 19; Sumner Welles, *The Time for Decision* (New York, 1944), pp. 59–60.

[33]Memorandum by Hornbeck, 11 August 1936, 852.00/2552, NA RG59; Hornbeck to Hull, 11 August 1936, and memorandum by Hornbeck, 13 August 1936, Stanley K. Hornbeck Papers, box 455, Hoover Institution on War, Peace, and Revolution, Stanford University, Stanford, California.

Roosevelt's reluctant approval shortly before midnight. The president soon "let the cat out of the bag," leaking the contents of the letter at a press conference the following afternoon. Not wishing to embarrass the aircraft firm by disclosing the text of the letter, Phillips suggested the release of the 7 August circular telegram laying out the American strategy of nonintervention instead. "The President entirely approved," and late on the evening of 11 August the moral embargo became public policy.[34]

Some historians have argued that congressional isolationism or the fear of American involvement in a wider European conflagration was responsible for the Roosevelt administration's decision to block arms sales to Spain. Congress, however, was not even in session during the dog days of 1936. In fact, the first public display of legislative sentiment did not come until 14 August, four full days after the imposition of the moral embargo, when the White House received a telegram from Senator Gerald Nye, Representative Louis Ludlow, and eight other congressmen concurring in the president's decision. Likewise, the importance of the "war scare" during the summer of 1936 should not be overestimated. The possibility that the strife in Spain might embroil the United States in a broader conflict doubtless weighed on American policy makers, but the danger did not become paramount until rebel aircraft strafed a U.S. warship in Spanish waters on 30 August.[35] During the early weeks of the civil war, then, the State Department was less concerned with isolationist pressures at home or international complications abroad than with the unreliable and ineffective Giral regime at Madrid. The overpowering fear that bolshevik subversion in Spain would endanger American interests and contaminate Western Europe was the crucial ingredient in the making of the moral embargo of 11 August 1936.

Four days later, for remarkably similar reasons, Whitehall announced that Great Britain had accepted a French proposal calling

---

[34] Phillips, Journal, 10 and 11 August 1936, Phillips Papers; Phillips to the Glenn L. Martin Company, 10 August 1936, *FRUS, 1936*, 2:475–76; Green, "Outline of Office Business June 27–Aug 14, 1936," Miscellaneous Correspondence and Memoranda 1935–1940, Green Papers.

[35] Senators Elmer Benson, Gerald Nye, et al. to Roosevelt, tel. 14 August 1936; statement by Roosevelt at Rapid City, South Dakota, 30 August 1936, *FDR & Foreign Affairs*, 3:376, 404.

for strict nonintervention in the Spanish civil war. Worried that friction generated by the crisis in Spain might produce international repercussions, British officials had, like their American counterparts, watched with growing apprehension as conditions in the republican zone deteriorated, jeopardizing foreign lives and property. Appalled by the "wholesale butchery of priests, nuns, and decent people" in Barcelona, Consul General King advised Whitehall in late July that Spain's Popular Front leaders "have sown the wind and are now reaping the whirlwind" in Catalonia and elsewhere. "If the Government are successful in suppressing the military rebellion," King warned, "Spain will be plunged into the chaos of some form of bolshevism and acts of savage brutality can be expected." The Royal Navy reported in early August that the Biscayan and Mediterranean coasts still bristled with "armed Communists" rumored to be planning "indiscriminate looting of foreign property and probably a massacre." Even more disturbing, Spanish foreign minister Augusto Barcía informed British ambassador Henry Chilton on 3 August that the Giral regime "could not be responsible for the lives and property of foreign nationals."[36]

Not surprisingly, a consensus began to form among high-ranking British policy makers during the first week in August that London must do nothing to aid the increasingly weak and unpredictable Popular Front government at Madrid. Whitehall first learned that republican Spain might seek British assistance on 27 July, when Ambassador López Oliván called on Sir Anthony Eden, this time to discuss the possible sale of military equipment to the hard-pressed Giral regime. Eden hedged, explaining that the exportation of any British war matériel required careful consideration by the cabinet, but he made it quite clear that he was reluctant to assist the beleaguered Spanish Republic. The French ban on arms sales to Spain, which went into effect that same afternoon, proved a mixed blessing for Whitehall: while removing the danger of a left-wing Franco-Spanish alliance, it virtually ensured that Madrid would approach London directly about large-scale arms purchases.

---

[36] King to Eden, 29 July 1936, W7485/62/41; minute by Mounsey, 1 August 1936, W7648/62/41; rear admiral commanding first cruiser squadron to Admiralty, tel. 2 August 1936, W7529/62/41; Chilton to Eden, tel. 3 August 1936, W7588/62/41, PRO FO371, vols. 20525 and 20526.

"I hope," Eden sighed on 31 July as he prepared to depart for a two-week vacation in Yorkshire, "that we shall be able to avoid supplying, by some means or other."[37]

The French government offered Whitehall a way out of its dilemma two days later. Convinced by recent reports describing highly unusual Italian military operations that Franco's forces were "now receiving war matériel from abroad," the Blum regime suggested that Paris and London approach Rome about making the principle of nonintervention "a common rule" in Spain. Counselor George Mounsey brought the French proposal to the attention of Lord Halifax, who as minister without portfolio ran the Foreign Office during Eden's absence, and the two men agreed on 2 August that "we must be very careful about our answer." Blum "would no doubt like to draw us into some commitment to support, even if only morally, the present Spanish Government," Mounsey noted, "and then deter other foreign governments from sending arms to the rebels in face of Anglo-French opposition." Since Britain must strive to be "completely impartial," he and Halifax did "not think that we should *tie our hands* to any agreement which is not practically universal." As a result the reply that the two men drafted on 4 August expressed cautious interest in the nonintervention plan but withheld British approval pending prior acceptance by Italy, Germany, and Portugal.[38]

The Admiralty also wished to avoid aiding the left-wing Spanish Republic, but like Whitehall, it was reluctant to embrace Blum's proposal. On 5 August a French delegation headed by Admiral Jean Darlan arrived in London hoping to convince Admiral Ernle Chatfield, Britain's first sea lord, that it was "in the urgent interest of Great Britain to oppose, as we were attempting to do ourselves, the establishment of a Francist regime in Spain allied with Italy and Germany." Chatfield, however, dismissed French fears that Rome and Berlin planned to seize the Balearic and Canary Islands as mere "conjecture" and maintained that General Franco was "a

---

[37] Eden to Chilton, 28 July 1936, W7174/62/41; Eden quoted in minute by Seymour, 31 July 1936, W7492/62/41, PRO FO371, vols. 20524 and 20525; Eden, *Facing the Dictators*, p. 450.

[38] Chargé d'Affaires Roger Cambon to Eden, 2 August 1936 (my translation); Mounsey to Halifax, 2 August 1936 (emphasis in the original), and 3 August 1936; Eden to Cambon, 4 August 1936, W7504/62/41, PRO FO371, vol. 20526; Eden, *Facing the Dictators*, p. 452.

good Spanish patriot" who "would know how to defend himself against the influences of Mussolini or Hitler." Sir Samuel Hoare, the first lord of the Admiralty, agreed that Darlan's information was just hearsay, questioned in any case whether Italy or Germany contemplated "action of this kind at a moment when both have agreed to take part in the new Locarno conversations," and told Chatfield that "we should maintain our existing policy of neutrality" in Spain. "When I speak of 'neutrality' I mean strict neutrality, that is to say, a situation in which the Russians neither officially [n]or unofficially give any help to the Communists," Hoare emphasized. "On no account must we do anything to bolster up Communism in Spain, particularly when it is remembered that Communism in Portugal, to which it would probably spread, . . . would be a grave danger to the British Empire."[39]

The news from Spain over the following week reinforced London's unwillingness to lend even moral support to the Popular Front government at Madrid. Units of the Royal Navy stationed in Spanish waters reported on the evening of 5 August that the Giral regime was "becoming more and more communistic in character," and the next morning Whitehall received a despatch from Sir Henry Chilton confirming that much of republican Spain "is in fact in the hands of Communists." Should Giral and his Popular Front emerge from the civil war victorious, Chilton prophesied, "the next problem which will confront them will be a struggle with the Communists for supreme command." Consul William Oxley in rebel-held Vigo echoed these views on 7 August, terming the struggle in Spain "a fight between the army loyal to its national tradition allied to the middle and upper classes versus a government sold for long time past to proletariat calling itself popular front consisting of anarchists and communists." Any "success for the Madrid Government," he concluded, "would therefore mean a Soviet dictatorship."[40] Chilton reiterated the following day that the Spanish civil war had become in reality a case of "Rebel versus Rabble," with

[39] Testimony of Blum, 23 July 1947, *Les événements survenus*, 1:218; Cot, *Triumph of Treason*, p. 342; Chatfield to Hoare, 5 August 1936, and memorandum by Hoare, 5 August 1936, W7781/62/41, PRO FO371, vol. 20527.

[40] Captain D-2 to Admiralty, tel. 4 August 1936, W7696/62/41; rear admiral commanding first cruiser squadron to Admiralty, tel. 5 August 1936, W7706/62/41; Chilton to Eden, 30 July 1936 (received 6 August 1936), W7812/62/41; Oxley to Eden, tel. 7 August 1936, W7913/62/41, PRO FO371, vols. 20526 and 20527.

"the Communists, Anarchists etc" almost certain to "play absolute hell" in the wake of a republican victory. Consul Stanley Gudgeon at Oporto, Portugal, was even blunter, calling the carnage across the border a battle "between nationalism on the one hand and Bolshevism naked and unadorned on the other."[41]

If British reports on republican Spain were uniformly grim during the first week of August, the news from Paris was little better. As early as 2 August Sir George Clerk, Britain's ambassador to France, reported that the Blum regime's policy toward Spain seemed "to be shifting away from official neutrality indicated in its public announcements." Four days later the Quai d'Orsay confirmed that although it still intended "to refrain from supplying arms or munitions to Spain," clandestine Italian aid for Franco's rebels obliged France to sell the Spanish Republic five commercial aircraft easily modified for combat use. Well aware that the Blum regime was under "increasing pressure" from French Communists to abandon its "self-proclaimed attitude of neutrality as regards events in Spain," Ambassador Clerk, acting apparently on his own initiative, urged Foreign Minister Yvon Delbos on 7 August to reconsider the French decision to aid the Spanish Popular Front. When Delbos explained that Italian intervention in Spain made it impossible any longer to justify a strict French arms embargo, Clerk asked pointedly how Paris could be certain that "the Government in Madrid was the real Government and not the screen behind which the most extreme elements in Spain were directing events." In any case, Clerk warned his listener, French involvement in the Spanish civil war might "make more difficult the cooperation between our two countries" with regard to Germany.[42]

The British ambassador, who made no secret that his own "sympathies in the Spanish affair were with the rebels," probably tipped the balance against French aid for republican Spain. Already acutely sensitive to the threat of a resurgent Germany, the Quai d'Orsay doubtless hoped to avoid an open break with Whitehall. After three marathon meetings on 8 August the French cabinet

---

[41] Chilton to Mounsey, 8 August 1936, W7648/62/41; Chilton to Eden, tel. 8 August 1936, W8121/62/41; Gudgeon to Ambassador Charles Dodd (Lisbon), 7 August 1936, enclosed in Dodd to Seymour, 8 August 1936, W8538/62/41, PRO FO371, vol. 20530.
[42] Clerk to Eden, tel. 2 August 1936, W7566/62/41, tel. 7 August 1936, W7962/62/41, and tel. 7 August 1936, W7964/62/41, PRO FO371, vols. 20526 and 20528.

reaffirmed its commitment to the principle of nonintervention by the narrowest of margins, ten votes to nine. Delbos and Blum both reluctantly sided with the majority.[43] The retention of the French arms embargo, however, was extremely unpopular within Blum's left-wing coalition. Hoping to drum up support for the Spanish Republic, French Radicals and Communists organized a huge rally in Paris on 9 August, which featured impassioned speeches by Azaña, Giral, and Largo Cabellero. "One cannot help doubting whether an *effective* non-intervention arrangement is possible," Horace Seymour, the new head of the Western Department, complained three days later, "in the face of this kind of thing." Yet what troubled Seymour and his Whitehall colleagues even more was the possibility that mounting left-wing opposition to Blum's nonintervention policy might encourage the spread of bolshevism from Spain to France.[44]

Indeed, many British officials now believed that the Kremlin was using links between the Spanish and the French popular fronts to maximize Soviet influence in Western Europe. As early as 20 July Sir Maurice Hankey, the influential secretary to the cabinet, had outlined Britain's dilemma graphically. "In the present state of Europe, with France and Spain menaced by Bolshevism," he observed, "it is not inconceivable that before long it may pay us to throw in our lot with Germany and Italy."[45] As we have seen already, both Stanley Baldwin and Samuel Hoare expressed similar fears of Soviet subversion during the next three weeks, and on 8 August Sir Harold Nicolson, an astute student of British diplomacy familiar with these and other Conservative leaders, predicted that

---

[43]Chargé d'Affaires Hugh Lloyd Thomas (Paris) to Cadogan, 11 August 1936, W8676/62/41, PRO FO371, vol. 20531; "Note de la sous-direction d'Europe," 8 August 1936, France, Ministère des Affaires Etrangères, *Documents diplomatiques français, 1932–1939*, 2d ser. (1936–1939), 9 vols. (Paris, 1964–1977), 3:158–59 (hereafter cited as *DDF*, 2d ser.); Dreifort, *Delbos*, pp. 46–49; Colton, *Blum*, pp. 249–51. David Carlton has argued that since Clerk was "not speaking on behalf of his Government," his conversation with Delbos "can hardly have been of decisive significance." It is nonetheless doubtful whether the unofficial nature of Clerk's remarks on 7 August lessened their impact on French policy makers, especially in light of what occurred the next day. See Carlton, "Eden, Blum, and the Origins of Non-Intervention," *Journal of Contemporary History* 6 (January 1971), 49.

[44]Clerk to Eden, tel. 9 August 1936, and minute by Seymour, 12 August 1936, W8108/62/41; Clerk to Eden, tel. 13 August 1936, W8557/62/41, PRO FO371, vols. 20528 and 20530.

[45]Hankey, "The Future of the League of Nations," 20 July 1936, W11340/79/98, PRO FO371, vol. 20475.

"the pro-German and anti-Russian tendencies of the Tories will be fortified and increased" by the crisis in Spain.[46]

Whitehall's suspicions notwithstanding, the bolshevization of Western Europe actually seems to have been of only minor importance in Moscow, where Soviet officials in mid-1936 remained, as they had been for nearly a year, more concerned with containing international fascism than with fomenting global revolution. To be sure, Stalin continued to supply food and medicine to the Giral regime, and Marcel Rosenberg, who in August 1936 became the first Soviet ambassador ever accredited to Spain, was soon recognized as one of the three most important men in Madrid, but Russian war matériel was still noticeably absent from the republican arsenal that summer. Moreover, the Kremlin, far from attempting to spread bolshevism north of the Pyrenees, urged French Communists to step up their support for Blum's Popular Front and to make national unity, not class conflict, the watchword in the "red belt" that ringed Paris. Stalin, judged from his actions in Spain and France, apparently sought to demonstrate that the Soviet Union was no longer an implacable foe but rather a desirable ally for the Western democracies in the coming struggle with Hitler and Mussolini.[47]

British officials insisted nonetheless that Moscow was still fishing in troubled Spanish waters and concluded as a result that nonintervention in the civil war was the best antidote against the bolshevik contagion at Madrid and Paris. Sir Orme Sargent, a high-ranking Foreign Office specialist on Western European affairs, argued on 12 August that the time had come for Britain to prevent France "by hook or by crook from 'going bolshevik' under the influence of the Spanish Civil War." The Baldwin government must help the Blum regime "free itself from Communist domination, both domestic and Muscovite," because "the prospect of a France weakened or paralyzed by Communistic infection" was "bringing Germany and Italy to cooperate" with each other. Rather than "just

---

[46] Harold Nicolson, *Diaries and Letters, 1930–1939* (New York, 1966), p. 270, entry for 8 August 1936.

[47] Jackson, *Spanish Republic*, pp. 258–59; Thomas, *Spanish Civil War*, pp. 392–94; Adam Ulam, *Expansion and Coexistence: A History of Soviet Foreign Policy, 1917–1967* (New York, 1968), pp. 234–45; Franz Borkenau, *World Communism: A History of the Communist International* (Ann Arbor, Mich., 1962), pp. 405–8; Sir George Clerk (Paris) to Eden, 20 July 1936, C5278/1/17, PRO FO371, vol. 19858.

waiting for this dangerous cleavage to happen," Sargent believed Whitehall ought now to assist the Quai d'Orsay in arranging a broader system of nonintervention in Spain designed to put as much distance as possible between Paris and Madrid. Deputy Permanent Undersecretary of State Alexander Cadogan, the number-three man at the Foreign Office, agreed the next day that Britain must do all it could to ensure continued French neutrality in the Spanish civil war, but he wondered whether Blum's nonintervention policy was in the long run a wise one. "It may prevent Bolshevism in Spain and avert the immediate danger of international complications," Cadogan admitted, "but isn't there a risk that it may involve his own overthrow by Bolshevism in France?"[48]

Nevertheless, nonintervention seemed at this late date the only way to prevent Blum's France from moving closer to a left-wing alliance with republican Spain. Foreign Secretary Eden telephoned Whitehall from his retreat in Yorkshire on 14 August for an update on the situation in Western Europe. He apparently spoke with Lord Halifax, who outlined the plan to endorse the French nonintervention scheme in the near future. Halifax was convinced that the "fundamental difference between the 4 powers principally concerned" might be overcome with relative ease, because the "dangers to all of indefinite continuance of Spain" were obvious. "We certainly—nor we presume the French—do *not* want to see a Communist Govt established in Spain. And," Halifax added, "*that* we appreciate—and we understand their position—is the principal anxiety of Italy & Germany." Some kind of four-power agreement on Spain, he concluded, might "bring the war to an end" and lead to "a non-Communist Govt."[49] With Blum beginning to waver in

---

[48]Memorandum by Sargent, 12 August 1936, and minute by Cadogan, 13 August 1936, W9331/62/41, PRO FO371, vol. 20534.

[49]Eden, *Facing the Dictators,* pp. 452–53; Halifax, "Notes for Conversation with French-German-Italian," n.d. (probably mid-August 1936), SP/37/16/A, Papers of Lord Avon (Sir Anthony Eden), FO954, vol. 27A, Public Record Office (hereafter cited as Avon Papers). Although there is no date on Halifax's memorandum, it was for three reasons almost certainly written prior to September 1936. First, there is no mention of the Non-Intervention Committee, which was created on 8 September 1936 to provide a great-power forum on the Spanish civil war. Second, there is no mention of the Soviet Union, and by September 1936 Halifax and others had reason to believe that it was a power "principally concerned" with the crisis in Spain. Finally, Halifax was in charge of the Foreign Office during the first two weeks of August 1936 while Eden was on holiday in Yorkshire. And we know from a minute by Mounsey (W9151/62/41, PRO FO371, vol. 20533) that on 17 August 1936 Halifax

his commitment to neutrality in the Spanish civil war, Eden agreed that Britain must cease dragging its feet and embrace the French nonintervention scheme first proposed a fortnight earlier. Ambassador Clerk and Foreign Minister Delbos accordingly exchanged formal notes in Paris on 15 August pledging that their governments would "rigorously abstain from all interference, direct or indirect, in the internal affairs of Spain."[50]

Within two weeks nearly two dozen other nations—Italy, Germany, and the Soviet Union most prominent among them—announced their adherence to the principle of nonintervention in the Spanish civil war and agreed to establish an international committee at London to enforce an embargo on all arms sales. Despite the broad international appeal of Blum's policy, however, Whitehall soon learned that French Communists were subjecting him "to ever-increasing pressure . . . to intervene in favour of the Madrid Government." With "France growing more 'red,' " Eden returned to London in late August fearful that "this Spanish horror is going to have repercussions so wide as perhaps profoundly to modify the present alignment of European powers." For too long Britons had comforted themselves that the French "could never be communist," yet with living standards across the Channel being steadily eroded Eden worried that France might soon resemble contemporary Spain. "We may once again take comfort that this process cannot be rapid, yet it is precisely in this respect that the Spanish peril plays its part," he concluded. "If events in that country & the failure of non-intervention force the less extreme elements in the French Govt to resign, what must the consequence be?"[51]

With the approach of autumn, then, British officials were firmly

---

contacted Sir George Clerk in Paris about approaching "France and the other chiefly interested Powers in the sense of proposing to make a united appeal to the Spanish Govt.—or factions—on purely humanitarian grounds." This suggestion differed, of course, from appealing to the various Spanish factions on the basis of anticommunism, but given the left-wing complexion of both the Giral regime and the Blum government, an explicit reference to bolshevism might have been regarded in Madrid and Paris as red-baiting.

[50] Minute by Eden, 18 August 1936, W9331/62/41, PRO FO371, vol. 20534; Delbos to Clerk, 15 August 1936, and Clerk to Delbos, 15 August 1936, *DDF*, 2d ser., 3:222–23; Norman Padelford, *International Law and Diplomacy in the Spanish Civil Strife* (New York, 1939), pp. 57–69.

[51] Clerk to Eden, 17 August 1936; minute by Cadogan, 20 August 1936; and minute by Eden, 20 August 1936, C5939/1/17, PRO FO371, vol. 19858.

wedded to a policy of nonintervention, in large measure because they wished to avoid aiding a left-wing regime at Madrid that threatened to infect not only Spain but also the rest of Western Europe with bolshevism. To be sure, policy makers on both sides of the Atlantic were concerned that the Spanish conflict might eventually shatter the fragile international balance of power, but the more immediate danger was that Spain would fall prey to Soviet subversion. The real power in the republican zone, British and American observers warned repeatedly, lay not with Giral and his Popular Front but rather with the "communists" and the revolutionary left. The subsequent left-wing takeovers of multinationals such as the BPLTC and General Motors reinforced the impression in London and Washington that Spain in 1936, like Russia in 1917, was on the verge of bolshevik upheaval. Unable to bar arms sales to Spain legally, the State Department first attempted informally to discourage Americans from aiding the Spanish Republic and then announced a moral embargo on 11 August. Equally reluctant to aid the left-wing Giral regime, Whitehall pressured Paris to cut off the flow of French war matériel to Madrid in late July and then on 15 August endorsed the Quai d'Orsay's nonintervention plan. The same fears that had initially predisposed British and American policy makers to adopt what one critic labeled "malevolent neutrality" toward the Spanish Republic persisted during the months that followed, making the repeal of nonintervention unlikely.

III

Although the Giral regime was unable to obtain military assistance in London or Washington, the rag-tag republican army fought Franco's rebels to a virtual standoff in late August. Indeed, had an arms embargo been enforced impartially against both sides, the Madrid government would probably have prevailed in a war of attrition. But while both Britain and the United States made good on their pledges to halt the flow of war matériel to republican Spain, Germany and Italy actually stepped up their aid to the Spanish insurgents, supplying Franco with dozens of tanks, nearly 200 warplanes, and 10,000 rifles and machine guns during the first six weeks that the nonintervention plan was ostensibly in effect. The culmination of Mussolini's involvement in the Spanish civil war came on 3 September, when the first contingent of what by year's end would become a force of 20,000 Italian "volunteers" arrived in the rebel zone.[52]

With the insurgents' arsenal growing daily more potent thanks to Berlin and Rome and with republican war matériel dwindling rapidly thanks to London and Washington, Madrid was forced increasingly to rely on Moscow, first for food and clothing and later for military aid. The Soviets seem to have complied with the nonintervention agreement well into the autumn, shipping only noncontraband items to the beleaguered Spanish Republic. On 7 October, however, the Kremlin announced that continued German and Italian aid for Franco made it impossible for the Soviet Union in good conscience to withhold arms and ammunition from republican Spain any longer, and by the end of the month Moscow had provided Madrid with fifty warplanes, 100 tanks, and 400 Russian "advisers." Not surprisingly, such Soviet aid enhanced the reputation of the Spanish Communist party, which expanded its membership sevenfold during the last half of 1936 to an estimated 200,000. Uneasy over growing republican dependence on the Kremlin, Prime Minister Giral resigned in early September. His successor, left-wing Socialist Francisco Largo Caballero, acknowledged the Madrid regime's debts to Moscow by inviting two Communists to join his new Popular Front cabinet, one as minister of agriculture and the other as minister of education. Ironically, the British and American arms embargoes had ensured the very thing they were designed to prevent: the expansion of Soviet influence in Spain.[53]

Despite the self-fulfilling aspects of the nonintervention policy, most American observers interpreted Moscow's mounting involvement at Madrid as proof that a republican victory in the civil war would mean a bolshevik Spain. Acting chief of the Division of Western European Affairs John D. Hickerson and Undersecretary Phillips were appalled in mid-August by the "wholesale slaughter

[52]Coverdale, *Italian Intervention*, pp. 102–7; Gerhard L. Weinberg, *The Foreign Policy of Hitler's Germany: Diplomatic Revolution in Europe, 1933–1936* (Chicago, 1970), pp. 290–92.

[53]Cattell, *Communism and the Spanish Civil War*, pp. 69–75; Robert G. Colodny, *The Struggle for Madrid* (New York, 1958), p. 161; Bowers to Hull, 23 September 1936, Hull Papers, microfilm ed., reel 13; Jackson, *Spanish Republic*, pp. 310–11, 360–62; Broué and Témime, *Revolution and Civil War in Spain*, pp. 229–36; Puzzo, *Spain and the Great Powers*, pp. 82–83.

of upper classes in towns and villages" at the hands of left-wing militiamen. Moreover, a wave of "secret arbitrary executions" in Madrid, Barcelona, and other major cities later that month made it "doubtful whether protection of life and property [of] American citizens can be depended upon."[54] By early September Military Attaché Stephen Fuqua confirmed that the Spanish Republic was trapped "in the coils of the communistic serpent" and that momentum was gradually shifting to the rebels. Faced with the threat of Soviet subversion in the republican zone, U.S. officials such as Consul William Chapman found the prospect of a Franco victory increasingly appealing. "Both sides are bad to great extremes—far beyond the dimmest reaches of humanitarian conception or sentiment, but," he told Hull on 28 September, "my choice lies with the insurgents who I hope in the interest of humanity will win and beat out of Spain completely the deadly spirit of anarchy now so powerful an enemy of humanity on the side of the so-called Government" and "their Russian comrades."[55]

Only Ambassador Claude Bowers held out any hope that the Madrid government could rein in the extreme left. The Popular Front regime, he reiterated throughout August, was not committed to "communistic" policies but rather to "enlightened and constructive" reforms. Although Largo Caballero's decision to bring two Communists into his cabinet in early September did have "a sinister sound," Bowers believed the result would be a broader governing coalition "in a stronger position to put down the lawlessness of the syndicalists and anarchists." Bowers, unlike most other U.S. officials, saw the Spanish strife as a struggle between autocracy and democracy, not nationalism and communism. "This is no ordinary civil war," he noted on 10 September. "It is a battle between the 16th century and the 20th, between the most reactionary nobility and aristocracy and church in the world and the people, and the people know the significance of the fight."[56]

[54]Memorandum by Hickerson, 13 August 1936, 352.1115/1127, NA RG59; Phillips, Journal, 22/23 August 1936, Phillips Papers; Consul Thomas Davis (Valencia) to Hull, tel. 21 August 1936; Franklin to Hull, tel. 23 August 1936, *FRUS, 1936*, 2:678, 681; Wendelin to Hull, tel. 25 August 1936, 852.00/2817, NA RG59.

[55]Fuqua to Bowers, 2 September 1936, Bowers Papers, General Correspondence (September/October 1936); Chapman to Hull, tel. 28 September 1936, 352.115/1806, NA RG59.

[56]Bowers to Hull, 11 August 1936, Hull Papers, microfilm ed., reel 13; Bowers to Roosevelt, 26 August 1936, and Bowers to Hull, 7 September 1936, *FDR & Foreign*

Yet despite his sympathy for the Popular Front regime, Bowers did not oppose the Roosevelt administration's policy of nonintervention. In fact, he agreed in August that "we must not become involved in any kind of meddling with the domestic quarrel of Spain" and encouraged Washington in September to continue its moral embargo "without deviation." These views, however, reflected not a loss of faith in the Madrid government but rather the conviction that "with the Spanish people left to settle their affair, the republic would have crushed the rebellion in a week." Unfortunately, "brazen" German and Italian aid for the insurgents had prevented such an outcome and now threatened to tip the scales in favor of "the political Al Capones of Europe." Bowers nevertheless remained convinced as late as Christmas 1936 that the interests of both Spanish and global democracy could best be served if the United States set an example for the other great powers and maintained its "position of absolute neutrality and noninterference in this wretched war."[57]

Even had Bowers opposed the nonintervention policy from its very inception, however, he probably could not have persuaded Washington to rescind the moral embargo. Confined first to his "floating embassy" aboard the U.S.S. *Cayuga* off the Biscayan coast and later to his "embassy-in-exile" across the French border, "Admiral Bowers" was "out of personal touch" with the situation in Spain and became a constant source of irritation for U.S. policy makers. "Bowers has been a great trial to us," the State Department's John Hickerson complained on 14 October 1936. "One can't tell a political Ambassador that he is out of things and doesn't really count but that has been about the size of it since the first days of August." Years later Economic Adviser Herbert Feis confirmed that because Bowers had promptly taken sides in the civil war, both "Roosevelt and Hull favored his absence from Madrid since it made it easier for them to sustain their policy of detachment." With the leading American supporter of the republican cause discredited, even the most blatant German and Italian meddling in

---

Affairs, 3:395–400, 416–20; Bowers to Ambassador William Dodd (Berlin), 10 September 1936, William Dodd Papers, General Correspondence (1936 A–G), box 15, Library of Congress.

[57] Bowers to Roosevelt, 26 August 1936, *FDR & Foreign Affairs*, 3:395–400; Bowers to Dodd, 1 October 1936, Dodd Papers, General Correspondence (1936 A–G), box 15; Bowers to Hull, 10 December 1936, *FRUS, 1936*, 2:600–605.

Spain was unlikely to shake the State Department's faith in nonintervention.[58]

Although criticism of the nonintervention agreement was more widespread and more formidable in Great Britain than in the United States, the Foreign Office did not swerve from its course of malevolent neutrality during the autumn of 1936. Interpreting Whitehall's handling of the Spanish crisis as a thinly veiled Conservative attempt to settle old scores with the left-wing regime at Madrid, British trade unionists held noisy demonstrations in support of the republican cause. Moreover, a Labour party delegation called on Foreign Secretary Eden on 19 August, pointed out that "the effect of the so-called neutrality policy was to favour the 'rebels' against the government," and urged him to rescind the embargo on arms sales to the Spanish Republic. Later that same day British officials in Paris reported that Léon Blum and his Popular Front cabinet were under similar pressure from "leaders of the extreme left who accused them of being dupes of Hitler and Mussolini," that "it seemed doubtful whether the more reasonable members of the Government would be able to resist the clamours of the extremists much longer," and that as a result the Quai d'Orsay was reassessing French policy toward Spain.[59]

Despite mounting opposition to nonintervention on both sides of the Channel, Whitehall remained convinced that to assist republican Spain was in reality to facilitate bolshevik subversion in Western Europe. A strict interpretation of international law would have required London to sell arms to Madrid, Sir George Mounsey admitted on 19 August, but because "the existing Spanish Government is powerless to exercise any degree of control over the anarchist and extreme communist elements in the country, . . . our support would therefore go . . . to a regime of anarchy which could

---

[58] Bowers, *My Mission to Spain,* pp. 257–71; Hickerson to Moffat, 25 August and 14 October 1936, Moffat Papers, vol. 10, Correspondence 1936 (A–H); Hull, Draft Memoirs, 31 July 1946, Hull Papers, microfilm ed., reel 40; Herbert Feis, "Some Notes on Historical Record-Keeping, the Role of Historians, and the Influence of Historical Memories during the Era of the Second World War," in Francis L. Loewenheim, ed., *The Historian and the Diplomat: The Role of History and Historians in American Foreign Policy* (New York, 1967), p. 105.

[59] Greenwood to Eden, 18 August 1936, W9331/62/41, PRO FO371, vol. 20534; memorandum by Eden, 19 August 1936, SP/36/9, and Eden to Baldwin, 20 August 1936, SP/36/11, Avon Papers, vol. 27A; Lloyd Thomas to Cadogan, 19 August 1936, minute by Mounsey, 20 August 1936, and minute by Cadogan, 20 August 1936, W9339/62/41, PRO FO371, vol. 20534.

only plunge Spain into conditions of chaos." Alexander Cadogan likewise conceded that "if the 'existing Govt.' exercised real control and had any chance of swimming," Whitehall would have "most scrupulously observe[d] our regular and normal policy of allowing or licensing shipments to the established Govt. and not to the rebels." In the absence of a stable and moderate regime at Madrid, however, "our ordinary rule cannot be blindly followed."[60] Sir Anthony Eden echoed these views, for as he told Prime Minister Stanley Baldwin later that same day, even Labour party leaders like Arthur Greenwood "thought it possible that the outcome of this dispute would be a communist dictatorship in Spain."[61]

By the end of the month British observers in the republican zone had confirmed the worst fears of Eden and his aides. On 21 August Consul General King at Barcelona deplored the "deliberate and systematic elimination of all persons considered to have sympathy with political parties other than those of the Extreme Left." He warned the Foreign Office that those responsible for such "class warfare" intended "to carry it into other countries, including of course, Great Britain, who has hitherto considered herself immune from such calamities." Two days later Chargé d'Affaires George Ogilvie-Forbes compared conditions in Madrid to "the reign of terror in France 1789–90," a situation that on 25 August he attributed to the "growing impatience of the Government and the arrogance of the militia who are tasting blood."[62] Such reports strengthened Whitehall's conviction that a republican triumph would open the door to what Cadogan termed "constant communist disorders" in Spain, the consequences of which were quite obvious. "A Communist Spain would mean the loss of the whole of the British invested capital in Spain," Western Department chief Horace Seymour observed on 1 September, "and might also favour the spreading of communism into France." In sum, Seymour believed, the prospect of "an extreme left victory" must be disturbing

[60]Minute by Mounsey, 19 August 1936, and minute by Cadogan, 20 August 1936, W9717/9549/41, PRO FO371, vol. 20573.
[61]Eden to Baldwin, 19 August 1936, Premier 1, Records of the Prime Minister's Office (Correspondence and Papers), vol. 360, Public Record Office (hereafter cited as PRO PREM 1); minute by Eden, 21 August 1936, W9717/9549/41, PRO FO371, vol. 20573.
[62]King to Eden, 21 August 1936, W9733/62/41; Ogilvie-Forbes to Eden, 23 August 1936, W10137/62/41, and tel. 25 August 1936, W9686/62/41, PRO FO371, vols. 20535 and 20536.

"to any country which desires the maintenance of ordinary democratic government in those countries in which it still survives."[63]

Republican Spain's new foreign minister, the left-wing Socialist Julio Alvarez del Vayo, complicated matters enormously on 7 September by calling publicly for the repeal of Britain's policy of nonintervention, which he alleged was "hitting the Spanish Government only." Whitehall could not simply ignore this appeal, Spanish expert Evelyn Shuckburgh pointed out three days later, because the Madrid regime was "on strong ground" when it charged that " 'non-intervention' means in fact denying to the legitimate Govt the means of combatting a rebellion." High-ranking British officials, however, disagreed. "While it is true that from the legal point of view the Spanish Govt. has a strong case, it is undeniable that in fact, even tho not in theory, they were, long before this outbreak occurred, a Government which was failing to govern," Sir George Mounsey retorted on 12 September; "they were merely giving way, in one direction after another, to the extreme demands of labour let loose, and . . . when the outbreak occurred . . . the Spanish Govt. at once proceeded to arm all the workers and rabble, including irresponsible young boys, with the consequences we are now viewing of savage brutalities." Sir Robert Vansittart, who had just returned from "A Busman's Holiday" in Paris, agreed that "Mounsey's minute is quite correct" and warned that France too would "probably go further left, and further still in the event of a Communist victory in Spain, with all its violent consequences."[64]

Mounting left-wing influence at Madrid during the autumn of 1936 hardened London's attachment to nonintervention. By late September Arthur Pack, the British commercial attaché in Spain, warned Whitehall that "the remains of the old Frente Popular Government are too decayed to expect any kind of responsible central Government to be built upon them" in the event of a republican

---

[63] Cadogan quoted in Chargé d'Affaires Otto von Bismarck (London) to Foreign Minister Constantine von Neurath, tel. 25 August 1936, United States, Department of State, *Documents on German Foreign Policy, 1918–1945*, ser. D (1937–1945), 3: *Germany and the Spanish Civil War, 1936–1939* (Washington, D.C., 1950), pp. 57–58; Seymour to Eden, 1 September 1936, W10422/62/41, PRO FO371, vol. 20537.

[64] Ogilvie-Forbes to Eden, tel. 7 September 1936; minute by Shuckburgh, 10 September 1936; minute by Mounsey, 12 September 1936; and minute by Vansittart, 12 September 1936, W10779/9549/41, PRO FO371, vol. 20575; Vansittart, "A Busman's Holiday," 10 September 1936, 1/17, Papers of Lord Vansittart, Churchill College Library, Cambridge, England.

victory. "I cannot imagine a stable Government emerging from Largo Caballero's entourage, so that if the military coup fails we can only expect the next year or two to be given over to Bolshevism," he added. "This will be the end of our financial stake in Spain and the ruin of our commerce for years."[65] Pack's prophecy was borne out six weeks later, when Consul General King reported that the left-wing regime in Barcelona had just issued a decree "which abolishes private property and establishes a system of collectivization in Catalonia." King, who lodged "a general protest" against the ensuing violation of British property rights, termed the decree "a specimen of what may be expected if the 'Government' win the civil war." Shortly thereafter British officials in Madrid confirmed there was "little hope of compensation for dispossessed foreign interests" under republican auspices. "This memorandum shows quite clearly that the alternative to Franco is communism tempered with anarchy," the Western Department's Gladwyn Jebb concluded without hesitation on 25 November. "If this last regime is triumphant in Spain it will spread to other countries, notably France."[66]

The Kremlin's repudiation of the nonintervention agreement and the arrival of Russian war matériel at Madrid in November removed most remaining doubts among British policy makers that republican Spain had become a Soviet stalking horse. Well aware that Moscow's decision had been prompted by blatant German and Italian violations of the arms embargo, Vansittart nevertheless concluded that Soviet involvement in Spain proved that "the urge to world revolution must be much stronger in Russia than anybody has believed in the last two or three years." Pablo Azcarate, Madrid's new ambassador in London, admitted during a 9 November interview with Lord Cranborne, parliamentary undersecretary of state, that "the Spanish Government had moved a long way to the left," yet he maintained that if "they were to come out [on] top in this struggle . . . democracy would still be preserved in Spain." When Cranborne explained that many Britons still believed that a

---

[65] Memorandum by Pack, 25 September 1936, enclosed in Chilton to Eden, 25 September 1936, W12454/62/41, PRO FO371, vol. 20540.

[66] King to Eden, 4 November 1936, W15417/1164/41; Assistant Commercial Secretary K. Unwin (Madrid) to Eden, 10 November 1936, and minute by Jebb, 25 November 1936, W15925/4719/41, PRO FO371, vols. 20566 and 20570.

republican victory would mean "a dictatorship of the Left" under the influence of Russia, the Spaniard retorted that such notions were "not correct" and promised to gather evidence to refute them. "It is of no use for Senor Azcarate to get together information to refute the charges of Comintern activity in Spain before the revolt," Vansittart observed acidly on 11 November. "It was there in plenty and working hard."[67]

The lone Foreign Office critic of Britain's policy of malevolent neutrality was Sir Laurence Collier, the head of the Northern Department and Whitehall's Soviet expert. Distressed by the tendency of high-ranking British officials, including Foreign Secretary Eden himself, to ignore early German and Italian violations of nonintervention but to decry later Russian actions, Collier minimized Comintern influence in Spain in November and reminded his colleagues that the regime "against which General Franco revolted was not a Communist Government." Germany and Italy, however, were "now using anti-Communism as a cloak for their aggressive designs," which "were much more dangerous to British interests than Communism could ever be." Those who saw themselves as "Conservatives first and Englishmen afterwards," Collier warned, would live to regret their sympathy for "Mussolini's now avowed policy of spreading Fascism throughout the world as an antidote to communism." Clearly, he concluded, the nonintervention agreement had not lived up to British expectations.[68]

This warning, however, fell on deaf ears. "Mr. Collier takes the Non-Intervention Committee more seriously than I supposed anyone did," sneered Italian specialist and Southern Department chief Owen St. Clair O'Malley. "I had thought that it was generally admitted to be largely a piece of humbug, but an extremely useful piece of humbug." Although he refrained "from arguing the question of whether the dictators or the communists are the more dangerous to ourselves," O'Malley did deny that Mussolini had "started the trouble" in Spain. "My impression," he explained, "is

---

[67] Lloyd Thomas to Vansittart, 26 October 1936, and minute by Vansittart, 27 October 1936, W14793/9549/41, PRO FO371, vol. 20583; Vansittart to Eden, 26 October 1936, FO800, Foreign Office Private Collections, vol. 394 (Miscellaneous Correspondence—1936); memorandum by Lord Cranborne, 9 November 1936, and minute by Vansittart, 11 November 1936, W15511/62/41, PRO FO371, vol. 20547.
[68] Minute by Collier, 24 November 1936, W16391/9549/41, PRO FO371, vol. 20586.

that the Soviet Government or the Third International, whichever we choose to call it, had not only been asking for trouble, both in a great many countries including Spain and for many years back, but had initiated a special movement in Spain at least as early as the beginning of 1936."[69]

Others shared O'Malley's views. Sir George Mounsey agreed that "Soviet influence in Spain has been notorious for a long time before these troubles exploded, and this fact has been very much overlooked in the more recent development of German and Italian activities." Furthermore, Clifford Norton, Eden's private secretary, claimed that he had seen "evidence of Comintern intervention of no negligible nature in Spain early in 1934." Vansittart likewise termed O'Malley's summary "a very fair account of what has been the course of events," challenged Collier to identify the fascist sympathizers within the Foreign Office, and reiterated shortly thereafter that "the Soviet Government, which seems bereft of statesmanship or even card sense, must bear its share of responsibility for making Spain the cause and scene of that very ideological struggle which we are trying to prevent."[70] By late 1936, then, most British policy makers had joined the majority of their American counterparts in embracing nonintervention, as much because it promised to prevent bolshevik subversion in Western Europe as because it promised to ease international tensions.

As the Foreign Office and the State Department had expected, nonintervention tipped the balance against the left-wing Spanish Republic during the autumn of 1936. Franco's forces consolidated their staging areas along the Portuguese frontier in August, rolled back the republicans in the north to a narrow strip along the Biscayan coast in September, and laid seige to Madrid in October. The insurgents swiftly imposed martial law in the areas under their jurisdiction and sanctioned the wholesale slaughter of their left-wing opponents. A union card in the pocket or a rifle bruise on the shoulder became virtual death warrants for thousands of republican sympathizers unlucky enough to fall into the hands of the rebels. Such brutal efforts to restore law and order, however, were

---

[69] Minute by O'Malley, 30 November 1936, ibid.

[70] Minutes by Mounsey, 1 December 1936; Vansittart, 1 December 1936; and Norton, n.d., ibid.; Vansittart, "The World Situation and British Rearmament," 31 December 1936, *DBFP,* ser. 2, 17:779–80.

welcomed by frightened Spanish landowners and businessmen, many of whom greeted Franco's troops as liberators and offered them financial and administrative assistance. Privately, rebel leaders predicted victory by Christmas.[71]

Bolstered by German equipment and Italian troops, General Franco unleashed his "final offensive" against Madrid on 8 November. The insurgents registered impressive gains in the early going, but in a series of ferocious battles on the outskirts of the capital anarchist and Communist militias, assisted by the newly formed International Brigades composed mainly of left-wing volunteers from abroad, fought off the right-wing invaders. Few observers, however, expected the republic to survive the winter. In fact, as the insurgents tightened the noose around Madrid, Largo Caballero and his cabinet fled to relative safety at Valencia while Berlin and Rome recognized the Franco regime as the legitimate government of Spain. For policy makers on both sides of the Atlantic, an insurgent victory seemed by late November 1936 to be only a matter of time.[72]

The prospect of a rebel triumph in the Spanish civil war was increasingly attractive in Washington. According to assistant chief of the Division of Western European Affairs Harold Tittman, "from the outset of hostilities . . . high echelon officials were strongly pro-Franco." Most U.S. observers in Spain were convinced that the insurgents were motivated more by nationalism than by fascism. Consul Charles Bay at Seville, for example, emphasized in mid-August that the military junta recently established there was "not (repeat not) a Fascist Government." Military Attaché Fuqua likewise confirmed that "the restoration of the Monarchy [was] not among the aims of the rebels," whose "primary object" was to prevent "the soviet revolutionary movement" from converting Spain into "a socialist or communist state."[73] Even Claude Bowers

---

[71] Jackson, *Spanish Republic,* pp. 248, 297, 533–36; Payne, *Politics and the Military,* pp. 409–20, Jellinek, *Civil War in Spain,* pp. 290–97; Thomas, *Spanish Civil War,* pp. 258–68.

[72] Jackson, *Spanish Republic,* pp. 310–32; George Hills, *Franco: The Man and His Nation* (New York, 1967), pp. 262–74; Robert Rosenstone, *Crusade of the Left: The Lincoln Battalion in the Spanish Civil War* (New York, 1969), pp. 21–29.

[73] Tittman quoted in Robert A. Friedlander, "Great Power Politics and Spain's Civil War: The First Phase," *Historian* 28 (November 1965), 80; Bay to Hull, tel. 9 August 1936, 852.00/2500; Fuqua to G-2, 10 August 1936, enclosed in Wendelin to Hull, 12 August 1936, 852.00/2980, NA RG59.

admitted shortly thereafter that although General Franco was "clearly hostile to democracy," he was "not a Fascist." Franco, Bowers advised Hull on 6 October, had none of "the bluster, brag, and bulldozing manners of Hitler or Mussolini." Moreover, given the rebel leader's "nice sense of justice based on reason," Bowers believed that "our investments in Spain, the Telephone Company, the International Banking Corporation, the General Electric, the General Motors, and the Ford Plants . . . should have no trouble with the new regime." The only threat to American interests, he concluded, was that the insurgents might make "pledges to Germany, Italy, and Portugal . . . in return for military support in the rebellion."[74]

During the next six weeks, however, the State Department received information minimizing the danger that the Spanish insurgents would throw in their lot with international fascism. Ambassador George Messersmith assured Washington from his listening post at Vienna on 8 October that "the Franco Government had made no definite commitments to Italy and Germany and that the victory of the so-called National Army may not contribute to further disturbances in Europe." Three weeks later William Phillips, who had only recently moved from the number-two spot at the State Department to the U.S. Embassy in Rome, reported that Mussolini "was in no way interested in acquiring any Spanish territory" and affirmed that Italy's major goal was to prevent "an intensely Communistic sore spot" in Spain from infecting "other parts of Europe." Even after the Nazis recognized the Spanish insurgents in mid-November, Ambassador William Dodd in Berlin remained convinced that "Hitler's principal preoccupation is Central Europe" and that the German Foreign Office actually "wanted to limit its support of Franco."[75] Some Americans believed, moreover, that the most effective way to reduce Hitler and Mussolini's influence on Franco was to embrace the latter's cause wholeheartedly. ITT's Colonel Sosthenes Behn, who had just learned that his firm's Spanish subsidiary had been targeted for takeover by a German competitor, remained "very partisan to the rebels." He told Claude Bowers on 1 December that should the

[74] Bowers to Hull, 6 October 1936, Hull Papers, microfilm ed., reel 13.
[75] Messersmith to Hull, 8 October 1936, ibid.; Phillips to Hull, tel. 29 October 1936, and Dodd to Hull, tel. 19 November 1936, *FRUS, 1936*, 2:544–45, 560–61.

rebels conquer Madrid, his firm would "recognize the Franco Government without waiting on the American Government."[76]

Many Britons were equally sympathetic to General Franco, whom they regarded as an apostle of law and order. As early as 4 August British officials in rebel territory confirmed that life there was "being carried on normally." Six weeks later O. E. Scott, Ambassador Chilton's chief aide at his embassy-in-exile across the French border at St. Jean de Luz, predicted that General Franco would soon establish "a liberal military dictatorship . . . capable of giving the country what it has needed for years: firm leadership, progressive ideals, education (not purely on clerical lines), and perhaps even equal justice."[77] Relieved that the insurgents did "not intend to try and put the clock back to 1931," Whitehall by late October found "the comparative order and maintenance of agricultural and business activity in the rebel-controlled territory" a pleasant contrast to the "uncertainty, terror, and absolute stagnation which prevails in government-owned [*sic*] provinces." Although Franco did commandeer Rio Tinto pyrite shipments from Huelva on grounds of national security that autumn, most businessmen in the insurgent zone detected with the approach of winter "a general wish to see English people returning and the old trade relations resumed." As a result they expected British economic interests to fare well under military rule.[78]

Britain's growing sympathy for Franco, like that of the United

[76] Bowers, Diary, 1 December 1936, Bowers Papers. Behn's pro-Franco outlook was not all that unusual among U.S. businessmen in republican Spain. As early as 13 October Martin Glidewell, the Barcelona agent for American Steamship Lines, had told consular officials he hoped that "the insurgent forces would win and . . . put an end once and for all to communism and the other isms so prevalent in Cataluna," while George Jenkins, the managing director of Ford Ibérica, reiterated on 12 November that Franco's forces "are justified in defending themselves against the invasion of Russia to implant communism [and] atheism and [against] the criminal atrocities committed by . . . the reds in Spain." Glidewell quoted in Consul Mahlon Perkins to Hull, 13 October 1936, 852.00/3600, NA RG59, and Jenkins quoted in Elston, "Multinationals and American Foreign Policy," pp. 177–78.

[77] Undated report from Pack, enclosed in Chilton to Eden, 29 July 1936 (received 4 August 1936), W7601/62/41; memorandum by Scott, 25 September 1936, enclosed in Chilton to Eden, 25 September 1936, W12454/62/41, PRO FO371, vols. 20526 and 20540.

[78] Oxley to Eden, 5 October 1936, and minute by R. M. Makins, 7 October 1936, W12903/62/41; Coultas to Eden, tel. 20 October 1936, and minute by Mounsey, 25 October 1936, W14062/62/41; Chilton to Roberts, tel. 5 November 1936, and minute by Roberts, 13 November 1936, W15178/62/41, PRO FO371, vol. 20546; Harvey, "Politics and Pyrites," pp. 95–97.

States, was nevertheless tempered by the realization that an insurgent victory might tilt the delicate balance of power in the Mediterranean irreversibly toward Italy and Germany. Indeed, on 24 August the influential Committee for Imperial Defence (CID) expressed considerable concern that, in exchange for expanded Italian assistance to the Spanish rebels, Franco might permit Mussolini to establish permanent military bases in the Balearics or even in the Canaries. Vansittart at Whitehall likewise worried that Rome and Berlin's deepening involvement in Spain might ultimately produce "a working combination of dictators, major, minor and minimus."[79] As early as 20 August, however, the Western Department's Horace Seymour noted that if Franco dealt away the Balearics or the Canaries, "he would at once be overthrown by his own supporters, who, being of the Right, were . . . determined not to surrender Spanish territory." Mussolini, moreover, assured British officials repeatedly in late August and early September that Italy would not use the Spanish crisis as an excuse to alter the status quo in the Western Mediterranean. On 14 September Juan de la Cierva, the informal rebel representative in London, confirmed for Sir Anthony Eden that General Franco had "never made any offer of any kind to Italy and Germany" regarding military bases in return for their help.[80]

By mid-October Whitehall was determined to ensure that Franco made no such offer in the future. Well aware that Germany and Italy were on the verge of recognizing the insurgents as the legitimate rulers of Spain, Vansittart feared that unless Britain followed suit, the new regime would drift inevitably toward a fascist alliance. The best way of "countering Italian influence in the Mediterranean," he suggested on 12 October, was to "recognize Franco on the fall of Madrid, as a belligerent, & follow up by a commercial mission." Somewhat reluctantly, Eden agreed that Brit-

[79] CID, "Western Mediterranean: Situation Arising from the Spanish Civil War," 24 August 1936, CP234 (36), Cabinet 24, Cabinet Papers and Memoranda, vol. 264, Public Record Office; Vansittart, "Crying in the Wilderness: Jottings from the 1930s," *Even Now,* p. 87.

[80] Seymour to Chilton, 20 August 1936, W9248/62/41; Chargé d'Affaires Ingram (Rome) to Eden, 13 August 1936, and minute by Shuckburgh, 21 August 1936, W8997/62/41; Ingram to Eden, tel. 18 August 1936, W8980/62/41; Eden to Chilton, 14 September 1936, and minutes by Hankey, 1 September 1936, and by Seymour, 1 September 1936, W10439/62/41, PRO FO371, vols. 20532, 20534, and 20537; Edwards, *British Government and the Spanish Civil War,* pp. 23–25.

ain would shortly have to establish closer ties with the rebels. Whitehall began to move in that direction in late October and even considered dispatching an informal British representative to Burgos, the rebel capital.[81]

Paris attempted to undermine this rapprochement between London and Burgos early the next month by announcing plans to withdraw its diplomatic mission from Madrid if the city fell to the insurgents, but the Foreign Office remained convinced that Britain must make the most out of a Franco victory. "I hope we shall tell the French Govt. plainly what we think of this excursion into the moonbeams from the Larger Lunacy," Vansittart grumbled on 2 November. "If we do not watch our step more sensibly with General Franco, we shall find him in the pocket of the stronger dictators, & the Mediterranean will be bottled up the next time we are in trouble."[82] Others shared Vansittart's fears. More and more convinced that "the July rising was not merely an attempt at a coup d'etat by the military class, but rather a movement led by the army of all political parties, from moderate republicans to bigoted Catholics and Carlists," Consul General Norman King reminded Whitehall on 25 November that "the importance of not leaving until too late the establishment of friendly relations with Gen. Franco's party should not be neglected." Hopeful that London would soon dispatch a representative to Burgos, King concluded that "it would be unfortunate for British interests . . . in Spain if Gt. Britain were the last of the Great Powers to recognize General Franco."[83]

For King and Vansittart, as for many other British and American officials, nonintervention remained the most sensible course in Spain precisely because it simultaneously isolated an unsavory left-wing government at Madrid and encouraged the emergence of a right-wing regime at Burgos relatively free of Italian and German domination. This diagnosis helps to explain why, even after it be-

---

[81]Captain Hillgarth (Royal Navy) to the Foreign Office, tel. 29 September 1936, and minutes by Vansittart, 12 October 1936, and by Eden, 19 October 1936, W12501/62/41, PRO FO371, vol. 20540; Edwards, *British Government and the Spanish Civil War*, pp. 181–85.

[82]Memorandum of conversation between Cambon and Mounsey, 1 November 1936, and minute by Vansittart, 2 November 1936, W15510/62/41, PRO FO371, vol. 20547.

[83]King to Eden, 25 November 1936, W17016/62/41, PRO FO371, vol. 20551.

came obvious on both sides of the Atlantic that an arms embargo worked only to cripple the Spanish Republic, neither Washington nor London was prepared to reverse itself. Both the State Department and the Foreign Office later explained that "diplomatic inertia" had prevented them from reconsidering their policies; potential complications abroad and political or bureaucratic impediments at home made it virtually impossible to renounce nonintervention. Not surprisingly, Americans and Britons alike steadfastly asserted in public that the political proclivities of the contesting parties in Spain played absolutely no role in shaping policy.

A State Department study commissioned in 1945 employed this framework to analyze American diplomacy during the Spanish civil war. Pointing out that the 1936 moral embargo "was perhaps even more important" than had been realized at the time, the report noted that "once having adopted a policy of embargoing arms to Spain, any future deviation would have had many unpredictable ramifications" both in Europe and in the United States. Since the strategy of nonintervention seemed "so right and so routine," it was only "natural, wise and inevitable" that Congress should pass legislation on 8 January 1937 providing the Roosevelt administration with the means to enforce such a policy. "The question of whether our policy would aid one or the other factions [in Spain] was seldom raised," the study contended, "and was apparently not a determining factor in formulating opinion at that time."[84]

British officials offered a similar account of their decision making. Anthony Eden, who denied that the nonintervention policy was designed to undermine the Spanish Republic, later attributed the persistence of Britain's embargo to a lack of "feasible or acceptable" alternatives. British "neutrality" at least had had "a curbing effect upon the scale of foreign intervention" by giving "Blum and his friends sufficient cause not to take a hand in Spain." Indeed, he concluded lamely, "Any other policy . . . could only have played into Hitler's hands." Lord Halifax, Eden's successor as foreign secretary, echoed these views. The continuation of the arms embargo, he emphasized, had been necessary in order to "prevent Spain

---

[84] "Morgan Report," Hull Papers, microfilm ed., reel 49. Years later Cordell Hull confirmed this analysis. Arguing that American nonintervention "had nothing to do with our views of right or wrong in the Spanish Civil War," he concluded that had the Roosevelt administration reversed its policy, the United States "might have been responsible for a widespread conflagration." Hull, *Memoirs*, 1:192.

from becoming the opening campaign of a general European war." Despite "the unreality, make-believe, and discredit" associated with the nonintervention agreement, Halifax felt that "this device for lowering the temperature caused by the Spanish fever justified itself."[85]

Although the Foreign Office and the State Department repeatedly denied that the possible outcome of the civil war in Spain had any effect on their respective policies, one should not underestimate the role that their lingering animosity toward the Spanish Republic played in prolonging the tragic farce of nonintervention. American suspicions about the Popular Front government persisted long after 1936. James Clement Dunn, the chief of the Division of Western European Affairs and one of Hull's closest advisers, allegedly told a reporter in March 1937 that the State Department looked upon the republican regime "as a lot of hoodlums."[86] The following August a Bureau of Foreign and Domestic Commerce report warned that a left-wing victory in Spain might mean that "capitalism will be banned (as it has been in Barcelona) and in this case the value of foreign investments and credits will be extremely doubtful."[87] Seven years later Sumner Welles recalled that the presence of "communists or anarchists" in the Popular Front ranks had "created suspicion and hostility" in Washington.[88] Only "the extreme left fringe in the United States," Hull himself remarked candidly in 1946, had advocated American participation in the Spanish civil war "in favor of the so-called liberals."[89]

British officials continued to express similar doubts regarding the Spanish Republic, doubts that were probably best dramatized during a cabinet meeting on 8 January 1937. Citing fresh evidence of massive German and Italian aid to the Spanish insurgents, Foreign Secretary Eden confessed that he now had some second thoughts

[85] Eden, *Facing the Dictators,* p. 463; Earl of Halifax, *Fulness of Days* (London, 1957), p. 192.
[86] Bowers to Moore, 29 March 1936, Moore Papers, box 3. William Carney, a correspondent for the *New York Times,* told Bowers that he had spoken with Dunn and Hull in mid-March about the Spanish situation. The State Department at first denied that the meeting had taken place but later admitted that Carney had obtained an interview "of the most casual character." Needless to say, Dunn and Hull vehemently denied holding any such views. Moore to Bowers, 17 March 1937, and 10 April 1937, Moore Papers, box 3.
[87] "Outcome of Civil War," 8 August 1937, File 890 (Spain), NA RG151.
[88] Welles, *Time for Decision,* p. 59.
[89] Hull, Draft Memoirs, 31 July and 19 August 1946, Hull Papers, microfilm ed., reel 40.

about the nonintervention policy. Unless Great Britain arranged an international naval blockade to prevent further foreign assistance to the rebels, Eden prophesied, "the Germans would undertake other adventures; for example in Czechoslovakia perhaps." Nevertheless, First Lord of the Admiralty Hoare doubted whether such a blockade could be effective. Moreover, he complained, "we appeared to be getting near a situation where, as a nation, we were trying to stop General Franco from winning." Many Britons, "including perhaps some members of this Cabinet," Hoare pointed out, "were very anxious that the Soviet should not win in Spain."

The cabinet quickly deadlocked over the issue of a blockade. When Lord Halifax observed that Germany and Italy had promised to cease aiding the insurgents just as soon as the Soviet Union suspended its assistance to the republican government, Eden warned that if Rome and Berlin succeeded in engineering a rebel triumph, "there would be a great deal of complaint" in Britain. "Many people in this country," Sir Kingsley Wood, the minister of health, retorted, "would be equally troubled if the Bolshevists achieved a victory." After listening to this debate, Prime Minister Baldwin remarked that although both Germany and Italy were obviously intervening in Spain, the obstacles to a formal blockade were "insuperable." Therefore, he concluded, Great Britain must make a renewed effort to ensure that the existing nonintervention accord worked as well as possible. Even Eden confessed that at present this seemed to be the only realistic course of action.[90]

Hoare and Wood's anticommunist zeal was shared by other influential Britons on the right. Conservatives in general "were more afraid of Communism than they were of Fascism" in Spain, Lord Astor explained to Henry Stimson over lunch shortly before Christmas 1936, because "the establishment of a Communistic Spain would produce a similar development in France."[91] Early in the new year First Sea Lord Chatfield echoed Astor's support for the rebels. "I do not see how Franco can help winning," he told a friend on 16 February 1937, "because one feels that he has a much nobler cause than the Reds."[92] Five months later Sir Harold Nicol-

[90] Minutes of Cabinet Meeting, 8 January 1937, PRO PREM 1, vol. 360.
[91] Stimson, Diary, 1 December 1936, Stimson Papers microfilm ed., reel 5.
[92] Chatfield quoted in Lawrence R. Pratt, *East of Malta, West of Suez: Britain's Mediterranean Crisis, 1936–1939* (New York, 1975), pp. 43–44.

son came away from a Conservative party Foreign Affairs Committee meeting on Spain convinced that "the enormous majority are passionately anti-Govermment and pro-Franco."[93] By the autumn of 1937 officials such as Charles Howard Smith, who had recently become the new head of Whitehall's Western Department, were forced to admit that Mussolini's growing influence over Franco might "mean the establishment of a totalitarian regime in Spain which will be dependent upon Italy," a turn of events "inimical to our interests" in the Western Mediterranean. But, he was quick to point out, "we do not seem to bother about the other totalitarian form of government, viz. Bolchevism [*sic*], though a Red Government in Spain might really be dangerous to us as it would accept the doctrine of Pan-Iberianism and endeavour to absorb Portugal . . . and the Portuguese [Azore] Islands."[94]

Clearly, the specter of bolshevik subversion, which had haunted high-ranking officials on both sides of the Atlantic since 1931, continued to influence British and American policies during the civil war. Diplomatic inertia, the conviction that any change in course would spark international or domestic controversy, may help explain the transformation of the moral embargo into legal doctrine by act of Congress on 8 January 1937 or Baldwin's resolve to table plans for a naval blockade that same day, but it only obscures the origins of nonintervention. London and Washington's decisions to suspend arms sales in August 1936 had less to do with a vague fear of a general European war than with a deeper dread of left-wing revolution in Spain. For more than five years political and economic conflicts had, like a cancer, rotted Spanish relations with the United States and Great Britain. Anarchists and Communists edged ever closer to power in Madrid, multinational companies encountered increasingly serious difficulties, and U.S. and U.K. exports to Spain all but dried up. Convinced that the cancer was highly contagious and would in all probability prove fatal to Spanish democracy, the diplomatic practitioners in Washington and London elected to let the patient expire before the infection had a chance to spread. The Spanish Republic died an agonizing death three years later not succored by impartial nonintervention but rather starved by malevolent neutrality.

[93] Nicolson, *Diary and Letters, 1930–1939*, p. 307, entry for 15 July 1937.
[94] Memorandum by Howard Smith, 2 October 1937, W18656/7/41, PRO FO371, vol. 21345.

Bibliography

1. *Private Manuscript Collections*

Birmingham University Library. Birmingham, England.
  Austen Chamberlain Papers
  Neville Chamberlain Papers

Cambridge University Library. Cambridge, England.
  Stanley Baldwin Papers
  Lord Templewood (Sir Samuel Hoare) Papers

Churchill College Library. Cambridge, England.
  Lord Halifax (Edward Wood) Papers
  Lord Maurice Hankey Papers
  Thomas Inskip Papers
  Eric Phipps Papers
  Lord Robert Vansittart Papers

Herbert Hoover Institution on War, Peace, and Revolution. Stanford, California.
  Stanley K. Hornbeck Papers

Herbert Hoover Presidential Library. West Branch, Iowa.
  William B. Castle Papers
  Herbert Hoover Papers
  Irwin B. Laughlin Papers

Houghton Library, Harvard University. Cambridge, Massachusetts.
  Jay Pierrepont Moffat Papers
  William Phillips Papers

Library of Congress. Washington, D.C.
  Wilbur J. Carr Papers
  Raymond Clapper Papers
  Josephus Daniels Papers
  William Dodd Papers

Herbert Feis Papers
Cordell Hull Papers (microfilm ed.)
Harold L. Ickes Papers
George Fort Milton Papers
Key Pittman Papers
Francis B. Sayre Papers

Lilly Library, Indiana University. Bloomington, Indiana.
Claude G. Bowers Papers

Minnesota Historical Society. St. Paul, Minnesota.
Frank B. Kellogg Papers (microfilm ed.)

Seeley G. Mudd Manuscript Library, Princeton University. Princeton,
New Jersey.
Louis Fischer Papers
Joseph C. Green Papers
Arthur Krock Papers

National Archives. Washington, D.C.
John D. Hickerson Papers, Record Group 59, Department of State,
Records of the Office of European Affairs, 1934–1947

Public Record Office. Kew, Surrey, England.
Lord Avon (Sir Anthony Eden) Papers. FO 954
Lord Cranborne (Sir Robert Cecil) Papers. FO 800, Foreign Office
Private Collections
Maurice Hankey Papers. CAB 63

Franklin D. Roosevelt Presidential Library. Hyde Park, New York.
R. Walton Moore Papers
Henry Morgenthau, Jr., Papers
Franklin D. Roosevelt Papers
John C. Wiley Papers

RTZ Corporate Archives. London, England.
Rio Tinto Company Annual Reports
Rio Tinto Company Chairman's Annual Addresses

Sterling Library, Yale University. New Haven, Connecticut.
Arthur Bliss Lane Papers
Henry L. Stimson Papers (microfilm ed.)

2. *Government Archival Material*

The National Archives. Washington, D.C.
Record Group 38. Chief of Naval Operations, Intelligence Division.
Naval Attaché Reports, 1886–1939
Record Group 40. General Records of the Department of Commerce,
Office of the Secretary. General Correspondence

Record Group 56. General Records of the Department of the Treasury. General Correspondence of the Secretary

Record Group 59. General Records of the Department of State. Decimal File, 1910–1939

Record Group 84. Records of Foreign Service Posts. Part I, Records of Diplomatic Posts, 1788–1945

Record Group 151. Records of the Bureau of Foreign and Domestic Commerce

Record Group 165. Records of the War Department. General Staff, Military Intelligence Division, 1917–1941

Record Group 275. Records of the Export-Import Bank

Public Record Office. Kew, Surrey, England.

BT 11. Records of the Board of Trade, Commercial Relations and Treaties Department

CAB 23. Cabinet Conclusions

CAB 24. Cabinet Papers and Memoranda

FO 371. General Political Correspondence of the Foreign Office, 1914–1945

FO 425. Foreign Office Confidential Prints

FO 800. Foreign Office Private Collections. Miscellaneous Correspondence

FO 849. Records of the Non-Intervention Committee

PREM 1. Records of the Prime Minister's Office. Correspondence and Papers

3. Published Government Documents

France. Assemblée Nationale. Première legislature, Session de 1947. *Les événements en France de 1933 à 1945: Témoignages et documents recueillis par la Commission d'Enquête Parlementaire.* Paris: Presses universitaires de France, n.d. [1948].

——. Ministère des Affaires Etrangères. Commission de publication des documents relatifs aux origènes de la guerre 1939–1945. *Documents diplomatiques français, 1932–1939,* 2d ser. (1936–1939). 9 vols. Paris: Imprimerie nationale, 1964–1977.

Great Britain. Board of Trade. *Final Report of the Committee on Industry and Trade.* London: His Majesty's Stationery Office, 1929.

——. Board of Trade. *Statistical Abstract for the United Kingdom for Each of the Fifteen Years 1913 and 1920 to 1933.* London: His Majesty's Stationery Office, 1935.

——. Department of Overseas Trade. *Economic Conditions in Spain, 1933,* by Alexander Adams. London: His Majesty's Stationery Office, 1934.

——. Department of Overseas Trade. *Economic Conditions in Spain, 1935,* by Alexander Adams. London: His Majesty's Stationery Office, 1934.

——. Department of Overseas Trade. *Report on the Industries and Commerce of Spain, 1924,* by Captain Ulick deB. Charles. London: His Majesty's Stationery Office, 1924.

——. Foreign Office. *Documents on British Foreign Policy, 1919–1939,* ser. Ia.

7 vols. London: Her Majesty's Stationery Office, 1966–1977.
——. Foreign Office. *Documents on British Foreign Policy, 1919–1939*, ser. II. 19 vols. London: His and Her Majesty's Stationery Office, 1946–1982.
——. Foreign Office. *The Foreign Office List.* London: His Majesty's Stationery Office, various years.
——. Parliament. *Parliamentary Debates* (Commons), 5th ser. London: His Majesty's Stationery Office, various years.
——. Parliament. *Parliamentary Papers* (Commons). London: His Majesty's Stationery Office, various years.
League of Nations. Economic Intelligence Service. *International Trade Statistics.* Geneva: League of Nations, various years.
——. Economic Intelligence Service. *World Economic Survey.* Geneva: League of Nations, various years.
Spain. Dirección General del Instituto Geográfico, Catastral y de Estadística. *Anuario estadístico de España.* Madrid: Sucesores de Riva de Neyra, various years.
United States. Congress. *Congressional Record.* Washington: Government Printing Office, various years.
——. Department of Commerce. Bureau of Foreign and Domestic Commerce. *Foreign Commerce and Navigation of the United States.* Washington: Government Printing Office, various years.
——. Department of Commerce. Bureau of Foreign and Domestic Commerce. *Spain: Resources, Industries, Trade & Public Finances*, by Charles A. Livengood, Trade Information Bulletin Series Report no. 739. Washington: Government Printing Office, 1930.
——. Department of State. *Documents on German Foreign Policy*, ser. D (1937–1945). Vol. 3: *Germany and the Spanish Civil War.* Washington: Government Printing Office, 1950.
——. Department of State. *Foreign Relations of the United States. Diplomatic Papers: The Soviet Union, 1933–1939.* Washington: Government Printing Office, 1952.
——. Department of State. *Papers Relating to the Foreign Relations of the United States.* Washington: Government Printing Office, various years.
——. Department of State. *Press Releases.* Washington: Government Printing Office, various years.
——. Department of State. *Register of the Department of State.* Washington: Government Printing Office, various years.

4. *Published Reports and Speeches*

Annual Report of the Export-Import Bank. Washington, D.C.: Export-Import Bank, various years.
Klein, Julius. *American Influence and Interest in Spain . . . a Radio Talk Given by Dr. Julius Klein, March 23, 1930.* No. 13 in the series "A Week of the World's Business." Washington, D.C.: Columbia Broadcasting System, 1930.
Report of the Directors of the International Telephone and Telegraph Corporation. New York: International Telephone and Telegraph Corporation, various years.

5. *Published Memoirs, Letters, and Diaries*

Alcalá-Zamora, Niceto. *Memorias (Segundo texto de mis memorias)*. Barcelona: Planeta, 1977.

Alvarez del Vayo, Julio. *Freedom's Battle*. Trans. Eileen E. Brooke. New York: Knopf, 1940.

——. *The Last Optimist*. Trans. Charles Duff. New York: Viking, 1950.

Amery, Leopold S. *My Political Life*. Vol. 3: *The Unforgiving Years*. London: Hutchinson, 1955.

Azaña, Manuel. *Obras completas*. Ed. Juan Marichal. 4 vols. Mexico City: Oasis, 1966–1968.

Bowers, Claude G. *My Life: The Memoirs of Claude Bowers*. New York: Simon & Schuster, 1962.

——. *My Mission to Spain: Watching the Rehearsal for World War II*. New York: Simon & Schuster, 1954.

Carrillo, Santiago, with Regis Debray and Max Gallo. *Dialogue on Spain*. London: Lawrence & Wishart, 1976.

Channon, Sir Henry. *Chips: The Diaries of Sir Henry Channon*. Ed. Robert Rhodes James. London: Weidenfeld & Nicolson, 1967.

Churchill, Winston. *The Gathering Storm*. Boston: Houghton Mifflin, 1948.

——. *Great Contemporaries*. 2d ed. Chicago: University of Chicago Press, 1973.

——. *Step by Step: 1936–1939*. New York: Putnam, 1939.

Cot, Pierre. *Triumph of Treason*. Trans. Sybille and Milton Crane. New York: Ziff-Davis, 1944.

Daniels, Josephus. *Shirt-Sleeve Diplomat*. Chapel Hill: University of North Carolina Press, 1947.

Eden, Sir Anthony. *Facing the Dictators*. Boston: Houghton Mifflin, 1962.

Gladwyn, Lord (Sir Gladwyn Jebb). *The Memoirs of Lord Gladwyn*. New York: Weybright & Talley, 1972.

Halifax, Earl of. *Fulness of Days*. London: Collins, 1957.

Hoover, Herbert C. *The Memoirs of Herbert Hoover*. Vol. 2: *The Cabinet and the Presidency*. New York: Macmillan, 1952.

Howard, Sir Esme. *Theatre of Life*. Vol. 2: *Life Seen from the Stalls, 1903–1936*. Boston: Little, Brown, 1936.

Hull, Cordell. *Memoirs*. 2 vols. New York: Macmillan, 1948.

Ickes, Harold. *The Secret Diary of Harold Ickes*. Vol. 1: *The First Thousand Days, 1933–1936*. New York: Simon & Schuster, 1952.

Johnson, Hallett. *Diplomatic Memoirs, Serious and Frivolous*. New York: Vantage, 1963.

Jones, Thomas. *A Diary with Letters, 1931–1950*. New York: Oxford University Press, 1954.

Lerroux, Alejandro. *La pequeña historia*. Madrid: Afrodisio Aguado, 1963.

Maisky, Ivan. *Spanish Notebooks*. Trans. Ruth Kisch. London: Hutchinson, 1966.

Nicolson, Harold. *Diaries and Letters, 1930–1939*. Ed. Nigel Nicolson. New York: Atheneum, 1966.

Peterson, Maurice. *Both Sides of the Curtain*. London: Constable, 1950.

Phillips, William. *Ventures in Diplomacy*. Boston: Beacon, 1952.

Roosevelt, Franklin D. *Franklin D. Roosevelt and Foreign Affairs*. Ed. Edgar B.

Nixon. 3 vols. Cambridge: Harvard University Press, 1969.
——. *F.D.R.: His Personal Letters, 1928–1945*. Ed. Elliott Roosevelt. 2 vols. New York: Duell, Sloan & Pearce, 1950.
Stimson, Henry L., and McGeorge Bundy. *On Active Service in Peace and War*. New York: Harper, 1948.
Templewood, Viscount (Sir Samuel Hoare). *Complacent Dictator*. New York: Knopf, 1947.
——. *Nine Troubled Years*. London: Collins, 1954.
Thompson, Sir Geoffrey. *Front Line Diplomat*. London: Hutchinson, 1959.
Vansittart, Sir Robert. *Even Now*. New York: Hutchinson, n.d.
——. *The Mist Procession: The Autobiography of Lord Vansittart*. London: Hutchinson, 1958.
Welles, Sumner. *The Time for Decision*. New York: Harper, 1944.
Wilson, Hugh. *Diplomat between Wars*. New York: Longmans, 1941.
Yost, Charles W. *History and Memory*. New York: Norton, 1980.

6. Books

Adams, Frederick C. *Economic Diplomacy: The Export-Import Bank and American Foreign Policy, 1934–1939*. Columbia: University of Missouri Press, 1976.
Adler, Selig. *The Uncertain Giant: 1921–1941. American Foreign Policy between the Wars*. New York: Macmillan, 1965.
Aguilar, Luis E. *Cuba, 1933: Prologue to Revolution*. Ithaca: Cornell University Press, 1972.
Aldcroft, Derek H. *The Inter-War Economy: Britain, 1919–1939*. London: Batsford, 1970.
Arrarás, Joaquín. *Historia de la segunda república española*. 4 vols. Madrid: Nacional, 1956–1967.
Atholl, Katherine, Duchess of. *Searchlight on Spain*. Harmondsworth, England: Penguin, 1938.
Avery, David. *Not on Queen Victoria's Birthday: The Story of the Rio Tinto Mines*. London: Collins, 1974.
Ben-Ami, Shlomo. *The Origins of the Second Republic in Spain*. New York: Oxford University Press, 1978.
Benavides, Leandro. *Política económica en la II república española*. Madrid: Guadiana de publicaciones, 1972.
Bendiner, Robert. *The Riddle of the State Department*. New York: Farrar & Rinehart, 1942.
Blum, John Morton. *From the Morgenthau Diaries*. Vol. 1: *Years of Crisis, 1928–1938*. Boston: Houghton Mifflin, 1959.
Bolín, Luis. *Spain: The Vital Years*. London: Cassell, 1967.
Bolloten, Burnett. *The Spanish Revolution: The Left and the Struggle for Power during the Civil War*. Chapel Hill: University of North Carolina Press, 1979.
Borkenau, Franz. *The Spanish Cockpit: An Eye-Witness Account of the Political and Social Conflicts of the Spanish Civil War*. 1937; rpt. Ann Arbor: University of Michigan Press, 1963.

——. *World Communism: A History of the Communist International.* Ann Arbor: University of Michigan Press, 1962.

Brandes, Joseph. *Herbert Hoover and Economic Diplomacy.* Pittsburgh: University of Pittsburgh Press, 1962.

Braunthal, Julius. *History of the International.* Trans. John Clark. 2 vols. New York: Praeger, 1967.

Brenan, Gerald. *The Spanish Labyrinth: An Account of the Social and Political Background of the Civil War.* New York: Macmillan, 1943.

Broué, Pierre, and Emile Témime. *The Revolution and the Civil War in Spain.* Trans. Tony White. London: Faber & Faber, 1972.

Browder, Robert P. *The Origins of Soviet-American Diplomacy.* Princeton: Princeton University Press, 1953.

Buckley, Henry. *Life and Death of the Spanish Republic.* London: Hamish Hamilton, 1940.

Carlton, David. *Anthony Eden: A Biography.* London: Allen Lane, 1981.

Carr, E. H. *Twilight of the Comintern, 1930–1935.* New York: Pantheon, 1982.

Carr, Raymond. *Spain, 1808–1939.* London: Oxford University Press, 1966.

——, ed. *The Republic and the Civil War in Spain.* London: Macmillan, 1971.

Cattell, David T. *Communism and the Spanish Civil War.* Berkeley: University of California Press, 1955.

——. *Soviet Diplomacy and the Spanish Civil War.* Berkeley: University of California Press, 1957.

Cave Brown, Anthony, and Charles B. MacDonald. *On a Field of Red: The Communist International and the Coming of World War II.* New York: Putnam, 1981.

Checkland, S. G. *The Mines of Tharsis: Roman, French, and British Enterprise in Spain.* London: Allen & Unwin, 1967.

Chomsky, Noam. *American Power and the New Mandarins.* New York: Pantheon, 1969.

Colodny, Robert G. *The Struggle for Madrid.* New York: Paine-Whitman, 1958.

Colton, Joel. *Léon Blum: Humanist in Politics.* New York: Knopf, 1966.

Colvin, Ian. *Vansittart in Office.* London: Gollancz, 1965.

Connell, John (pseud.). *The "Office": A Study of British Foreign Policy and Its Makers, 1919–1951.* London: Allan Wingate, 1958.

Cortada, James W., ed. *Spain in the Twentieth-Century World: Essays on Spanish Diplomacy, 1898–1978.* Westport, Conn.: Greenwood, 1980.

——. *Two Nations over Time: Spain and the United States, 1776–1977.* Westport, Conn.: Greenwood, 1978.

Coverdale, John F. *Italian Intervention in the Spanish Civil War.* Princeton: Princeton University Press, 1975.

Cowling, Maurice. *The Impact of Hitler: British Politics and British Policy, 1933–1940.* London: Cambridge University Press, 1975.

Craig, Gordon A., and Felix Gilbert, eds. *The Diplomats, 1919–1939.* 2 vols. New York: Atheneum, 1968.

Cronon, E. David. *Josephus Daniels in Mexico.* Madison: University of Wisconsin Press, 1960.

Crozier, Brian. *Franco: A Biographical History.* London: Eyre & Spottiswoode, 1967.

Current, Richard N. *Secretary Stimson: A Study in Statecraft.* 1954; rpt. Hamden, Conn.: Archon, 1970.

Dallek, Robert. *Democrat and Diplomat: The Life of William E. Dodd.* New York: Oxford University Press, 1968.

———. *Franklin D. Roosevelt and American Foreign Policy, 1932–1945.* New York: Oxford University Press, 1979.

De Gras, Jane, ed. *The Communist International, 1919–1943: Documents.* 3 vols. New York: Oxford University Press, 1957–1965.

De la Cierva, Ricardo, ed. *Los documentos de la primavera trágica.* Madrid: Ministerio de información y turismo, 1967.

DeSantis, Hugh. *The Diplomacy of Silence: The American Foreign Service, the Soviet Union, and the Cold War, 1933–1947.* Chicago: University of Chicago Press, 1980.

Diggins, John P. *Mussolini and Fascism: The View from America.* Princeton: Princeton University Press, 1972.

Divine, Robert A. *The Illusion of Neutrality.* Chicago: University of Chicago Press, 1962.

Dreifort, John E. *Yvon Delbos at the Quai d'Orsay: French Foreign Policy during the Popular Front, 1936–1938.* Lawrence: University Press of Kansas, 1973.

Edwards, Jill. *The British Government and the Spanish Civil War, 1936–1939.* London: Macmillan, 1979.

Falcoff, Mark, and Frederick B. Pike, eds. *The Spanish Civil War, 1936–1939: American Hemispheric Perspectives.* Lincoln: University of Nebraska Press, 1982.

Farnsworth, Beatrice. *William C. Bullitt and the Soviet Union.* Bloomington: Indiana University Press, 1967.

Feis, Herbert. *1933: Characters in Crisis.* Boston: Little, Brown, 1966.

———. *Seen from E.A.: Three International Episodes.* New York: Knopf, 1947.

———. *The Spanish Story: Franco and the Nations at War.* New York: Knopf, 1948.

Fernsworth, Lawrence. *Spain's Struggle for Freedom.* Boston: Beacon, 1957.

Ferrell, Robert H. *American Diplomacy in the Great Depression: Hoover-Stimson Foreign Policy, 1929–1933.* New Haven: Yale University Press, 1957.

Foltz, Charles, Jr. *The Masquerade in Spain.* Boston: Houghton Mifflin, 1948.

Fraser, Ronald. *The Blood of Spain: An Oral History of the Spanish Civil War.* New York: Pantheon, 1979.

Gardner, Lloyd C. *The Economic Aspects of New Deal Diplomacy.* 1964; rpt. Boston: Beacon, 1971.

George, Margaret. *The Warped Vision: British Foreign Policy, 1933–1939.* Pittsburgh: University of Pittsburgh Press, 1965.

Gibb, George S., and Evelyn H. Knowlton. *History of the Standard Oil Company (New Jersey): The Resurgent Years, 1911–1927.* New York: Harper, 1956.

Gilbert, Martin. *The Roots of Appeasement.* London: Weidenfeld & Nicolson, 1966.

———. *Sir Horace Rumbold: Portrait of a Diplomat, 1869–1941.* London: Heinemann, 1973.

———, and Richard Gott. *The Appeasers.* London: Weidenfeld & Nicholson, 1963.

Grayson, George. *The Politics of Mexican Oil.* Pittsburgh: University of Pittsburgh Press, 1980.

Green, David. *The Containment of Latin America: The Myths and Realities of the Good Neighbor Policy.* Chicago: Quadrangle, 1971.

Guttmann, Allen. *The Wound in the Heart: America and the Spanish Civil War.* New York: Free, 1962.

Haithcox, John Patrick. *Communism and Nationalism in India: M. N. Roy and Comintern Policy, 1920–1939.* Princeton: Princeton University Press, 1971.

Harper, Glenn T. *German Economic Policy in Spain during the Spanish Civil War, 1936–1939.* The Hague: Mouton, 1967.

Harvey, Charles E. *The Rio Tinto Company: An Economic History of a Leading International Mining Concern, 1873–1954.* Penzance, England: Hodge, 1981.

Hayes, Carlton J. H. *The United States and Spain: An Interpretation.* New York: Sheed & Ward, 1951.

Hendrick, Burton J. *The Life and Letters of Walter Hines Page.* 3 vols. New York: Doubleday, Page, 1922–1925.

Hills, George. *Franco: The Man and His Nation.* New York: Macmillan, 1967.

Hogan, Michael. *Informal Entente: The Private Structure of Cooperation in Anglo-American Economic Diplomacy, 1918–1928.* Columbia: University of Missouri Press, 1977.

Iatrides, John I., ed. *Ambassador MacVeagh Reports: Greece, 1933–1947.* Princeton: Princeton University Press, 1980.

International Bank for Reconstruction and Development. *The Economic Development of Spain.* Baltimore: Johns Hopkins Press, 1963.

Jackson, Gabriel. *Historian's Quest.* New York: Knopf, 1969.

———. *The Spanish Republic and the Civil War, 1931–1939.* Princeton: Princeton University Press, 1965.

James, Robert Rhodes. *Churchill: A Study in Failure, 1900–1939.* Harmondsworth, England: Penguin, 1973.

Jellinek, Frank. *The Civil War in Spain.* London: Gollancz, 1938.

Jerrold, Douglas. *Georgian Adventure.* New York: Scribner, 1938.

Jonas, Manfred. *Isolationism in America, 1935–1941.* Ithaca: Cornell University Press, 1966.

Jones, Joseph M., Jr. *Tariff Retaliation: Repercussions of the Hawley-Smoot Bill.* Philadelphia: University of Pennsylvania Press, 1934.

Kahn, Alfred E. *Great Britain in the World Economy.* New York: Columbia University Press, 1946.

Katz, Friedrich. *The Secret War in Mexico: Europe, the United States, and the Mexican Revolution.* Chicago: University of Chicago Press, 1981.

Kindleberger, Charles P. *The World in Depression.* Berkeley: University of California Press, 1973.

Klein, Julius. *Frontiers of Trade.* New York: Century, 1929.

Kleine-Ahlbrandt, William Laird. *The Policy of Simmering: A Study of British Policy during the Spanish Civil War, 1936–1939.* Ambilly-Annemasse: Les presses de Savoie, 1961.

Knightly, Phillip. *The First Casualty: From the Crimea to Vietnam: The War Correspondent as Hero, Propagandist, and Myth Maker.* New York: Harcourt Brace Jovanovich, 1975.

274

Knoblaugh, H. Edward. *Correspondent in Spain.* New York: Sheed & Ward, 1937.

Kottman, Richard N. *Reciprocity and the North Atlantic Triangle, 1932–1938.* Ithaca: Cornell University Press, 1968.

Lammers, Donald N. *Explaining Munich: The Search for Motive in British Policy.* Hoover Institution Studies, no. 16. Stanford: Hoover Institution on War, Revolution, and Peace, 1966.

Larson, Henrietta; Evelyn H. Knowlton; and Charles S. Popple. *History of the Standard Oil Company (New Jersey): New Horizons, 1927–1950.* New York: Harper & Row, 1971.

Leffler, Melvyn P. *The Elusive Quest: America's Pursuit of European Stability and French Security, 1919–1933.* Chapel Hill: University of North Carolina Press, 1979.

Levin, N. Gordon, Jr. *Woodrow Wilson and World Politics: America's Response to War and Revolution.* New York: Oxford University Press, 1968.

Lewis, Cleona. *America's Stake in International Investments.* Washington, D.C.: Brookings, 1938.

Little, Richard. *Intervention: External Involvement in Civil Wars.* Totowa, N.J.: Rowman & Littlefield, 1975.

Loveday, Arthur F. *Spain, 1923–1948: Civil War and World War.* North Bridgewater, England: Boswell [1949].

McKenzie, Kermit E. *The Comintern and World Revolution, 1928–1943: The Shaping of Doctrine.* New York: Columbia University Press, 1964.

Madariaga, Salvador de. *Spain: A Modern History.* 1940; rpt. New York: Praeger, 1958.

Maddux, Thomas R. *Years of Estrangement: American Relations with the Soviet Union, 1933–1941.* Tallahassee: University Presses of Florida, 1980.

Malefakis, Edward E. *Agrarian Reform and Peasant Revolution in Spain: Origins of the Civil War.* New Haven: Yale University Press, 1970.

Martin, James J. *American Liberalism and World Politics: Liberalism's Press and Spokesmen on the Road back to War between Mukden and Pearl Harbor.* 2 vols. New York: Devin-Adair, 1964.

Matthews, Herbert L. *The Yoke and the Arrows: A Report on Spain.* New York: Braziller, 1957.

Mayer, Arno J. *Politics and Diplomacy of Peacemaking: Containment and Counterrevolution at Versailles, 1918–1919.* New York: Vintage, 1969.

Meaker, Gerald W. *The Revolutionary Left in Spain, 1914–1923.* Stanford: Stanford University Press, 1974.

Medlicott, W. N. *British Foreign Policy since Versailles, 1919–1963.* London: Methuen, 1968.

Meyer, Lorenzo. *Mexico and the United States in the Oil Controversy, 1917–1942.* Austin: University of Texas Press, 1977.

Middlemas, Keith. *The Strategy of Appeasement: The British Government and Germany, 1937–1939.* Chicago: Quadrangle, 1972.

——, and John Barnes. *Baldwin: A Biography.* London: Macmillan, 1970.

Monroe, Elizabeth. *The Mediterranean in Politics.* New York: Oxford University Press, 1938.

Naylor, John F. *Labour's International Policy: The Labour Party in the 1930s.* London: Weidenfeld & Nicholson, 1969.

Northedge, F. S. *The Troubled Giant: Britain among the Great Powers, 1916–1939*. New York: Praeger, 1966.

Offner, Arnold A. *American Appeasement: United States Foreign Policy and Germany, 1933–1938*. Cambridge: Harvard University Press, 1969.

——. *The Origins of the Second World War: American Foreign Policy and World Politics, 1917–1941*. New York: Praeger, 1975.

Orwell, George. *Homage to Catalonia*. 1938; rpt. New York: Harcourt Brace, 1952.

Padelford, Norman J. *International Law and Diplomacy in the Spanish Civil Strife*. New York: Macmillan, 1939.

Parrini, Carl P. *Heir to Empire: United States Diplomacy, 1916–1923*. Pittsburgh: University of Pittsburgh Press, 1969.

Payne, Stanley G. *Falange: A History of Spanish Fascism*. Stanford: Stanford University Press, 1961.

——. *Politics and the Military in Modern Spain*. Stanford: Stanford University Press, 1967.

——. *The Spanish Revolution*. New York: Norton, 1970.

——, ed. *Politics and Society in Twentieth-Century Spain*. New York: New Viewpoints, 1976.

Peers, E. Allison. *The Spanish Tragedy, 1930–1936: Dictatorship, Republic, Chaos*. New York: Oxford University Press, 1936.

Petrie, Sir Charles. *King Alfonso XIII and His Age*. London: Chapman & Hall, 1963.

——, ed. *The Life and Letters of the Right Hon. Sir Austen Chamberlain*. 2 vols. Toronto: Cassell, 1940.

Phillips, C. E. Lucas. *The Spanish Pimpernel*. London: Heinemann, 1960.

Pratt, Julius W. *Cordell Hull*. 2 vols. New York: Cooper Square, 1964.

Pratt, Lawrence R. *East of Malta, West of Suez: Britain's Mediterranean Crisis, 1936–1939*. New York: Cambridge University Press, 1975.

Preston, Paul. *The Coming of the Spanish Civil War: Reform, Reaction and Revolution in the Second Republic, 1931–1936*. New York: Harper, 1978.

Puzzo, Dante A. *Spain and the Great Powers, 1936–1941*. New York: Columbia University Press, 1962.

Ramos Oliveira, Antonio. *Politics, Economics and Men of Modern Spain, 1808–1946*. Trans. Teener Hall. London: Gollancz, 1946.

Ratcliff, Dillwyn F. *Prelude to Franco: Political Aspects of the Dictatorship of General Miguel Primo de Rivera*. New York: Las Americas, 1957.

Reynolds, P. A. *British Foreign Policy in the Inter-War Years*. New York: Longmans, Green, 1954.

Robinson, Richard A. H. *The Origins of Franco's Spain: The Right, the Republic and Revolution, 1931–1936*. Newton Abbott, England: David & Charles, 1970.

Rock, William R. *British Appeasement in the 1930s*. New York: Norton, 1977.

Rose, Norman. *Vansittart: Study of a Diplomat*. London: Heinemann, 1978.

Rosenstone, Robert. *Crusade of the Left: The Lincoln Battalion in the Spanish Civil War*. New York: Pegasus, 1969.

Rotvand, Georges. *Franco Means Business*. Trans. Reginald Dingle. New York: Devin-Adair, n.d.

Rowse, A. L. *Appeasement: A Study in Political Decline, 1933–1939*. New York: Norton, 1961.

Royal Institute of International Affairs. *Political and Strategic Interests of the United Kingdom*. New York: Oxford University Press, 1939.

——. *Survey of British Commonwealth Affairs*. Vol. 2, pt. 1: *Problems of Economic Policy, 1918–1939*, by W. K. Hancock. London: Oxford University Press, 1940.

——. *Survey of International Affairs, 1937*. Vol. 2: *The International Repercussions of the War in Spain (1936–7)*, by Arnold Toynbee. London: Oxford University Press, 1938.

Russell, Ronald S. *Imperial Preference: Its Developments and Effects*. London: Falcon, 1949.

Sampson, Anthony. *The Arms Bazaar: From Lockheed to Lebanon*. New York: Viking, 1977.

——. *The Seven Sisters: The Great Oil Companies and the World They Shaped*. New York: Bantam, 1976.

——. *The Sovereign State of ITT*. New York: Stein & Day, 1973.

Sanchez, José M. *Reform and Reaction: The Politico-Religious Background of the Spanish Civil War*. Chapel Hill: University of North Carolina Press, 1962.

Sayre, Francis B. *America Must Act: What We Do to Assure Jobs—Wages—Markets—Peace*. World Affairs Pamphlets no. 13. New York: World Peace Foundation, 1936.

Schlesinger, Arthur M., Jr. *A Thousand Days: John F. Kennedy in the White House*. Boston: Houghton Mifflin, 1965.

Schmitt, Karl. *Mexico and the United States, 1821–1973: Conflict and Coexistence*. New York: Wiley, 1974.

Schulzinger, Robert D. *The Making of the Diplomatic Mind: The Training, Outlook, and Style of United States Foreign Service Officers, 1908–1931*. Middletown: Wesleyan University Press, 1975.

Sedwick, Frank. *The Tragedy of Manuel Azaña and the Fate of the Spanish Republic*. Columbus: Ohio State University Press, 1963.

Sevillano Carbajal, Virgilio. *La España . . . de quién? Ingleses, franceses y alemanes en este país*. Madrid: Gráficas Sánchez, 1936.

Skidelsky, Robert. *Politicians and the Slump: The Labour Government of 1929–1931*. London: Macmillan, 1967.

Smith, Rhea Marsh. *The Day of the Liberals in Spain*. Philadelphia: University of Pennsylvania Press, 1938.

Smith, Robert Freeman. *The United States and Revolutionary Nationalism in Mexico, 1916–1932*. Chicago: University of Chicago Press, 1972.

Southard, Frank A. *American Industry in Europe*. Boston: Houghton Mifflin, 1931.

Stimson, Henry L. *Democracy and Nationalism in Europe*. Princeton: Princeton University Press, 1934.

Sundiata, I. K. *Black Scandal: America and the Liberian Labor Crisis, 1929–1936*. Philadelphia: Institute for the Study of Human Issues, 1980.

Tasca, Henry J. *World Trading Systems: A Study of American and British Commercial Policies*. Paris: International Institute of Intellectual Cooperation, League of Nations, 1939.

Taylor, A. J. P. *The Origins of the Second World War*. 2d ed. Greenwich, Conn.: Fawcett, 1966.

Taylor, F. Jay. *The United States and the Spanish Civil War*. New York: Bookman Associates, 1956.

Thomas, Hugh. *The Spanish Civil War.* 3d ed. New York: Harper, 1977.

Thompson, Neville. *The Anti-Appeasers: Conservative Opposition to Appeasement in the 1930s.* New York: Oxford University Press, 1971.

Traina, Richard P. *American Diplomacy and the Spanish Civil War.* Bloomington: Indiana University Press, 1968.

Trotsky, Leon. *The Spanish Revolution (1931–1939).* Ed. Naomi Allen and George Breitman. New York: Pathfinder, 1973.

Ulam, Adam. *Expansion and Coexistence: A History of Soviet Foreign Policy, 1917–1967.* New York: Praeger, 1968.

Ullman, Richard. *Anglo-Soviet Relations, 1917–1921.* 3 vols. Princeton: Princeton University Press, 1961–1973.

"Unknown Diplomat." *Britain in Spain: A Study of the National Government's Spanish Policy.* London: Hamish Hamilton, 1939.

Van der Esch, Patricia. *Prelude to War: The International Repercussions of the Spanish Civil War, 1936–1939.* The Hague: Nijhoff, 1951.

Vicens Vives, Jaime. *An Economic History of Spain.* Trans. Frances M. López-Morillas. Princeton: Princeton University Press, 1969.

Waterfield, Gordon. *Professional Diplomat: Sir Percy Loraine of Kirkharle Bt., 1880–1961.* London: Murray, 1973.

Watkins, K. W. *Britain Divided: The Effect of the Spanish Civil War on British Political Opinion.* New York: Nelson, 1963.

Weil, Martin. *A Pretty Good Club: The Founding Fathers of the U.S. Foreign Service.* New York: Norton, 1978.

Weinberg, Gerhard L. *The Foreign Policy of Hitler's Germany: Diplomatic Revolution in Europe, 1933–1936.* Chicago: University of Chicago Press, 1970.

White, Stephen. *Britain and the Bolshevik Revolution: A Study in the Politics of Diplomacy, 1920–1924.* New York: Holmes & Meier, 1979.

Wilbur, Donald N. *Riza Shah Pahlavi, 1878–1944: The Resurrection and Reconstruction of Iran.* Hicksville, N.Y.: Exposition, 1975.

Wilkins, Mira. *The Maturing of Multinational Enterprise: American Business Abroad from 1914 to 1970.* Cambridge: Harvard University Press, 1974.

——, ed. *British Overseas Investments, 1907–1948.* New York: Arno, 1977.

——, and Frank Ernest Hill. *American Business Abroad: Ford on Six Continents.* Detroit: Wayne State University Press, 1964.

Williams, William Appleman. *American Russian Relations, 1781–1947.* New York: Rinehart, 1952.

——. *The Contours of American History.* New York: World, 1961.

——. *The Tragedy of American Diplomacy.* 2d ed. New York: Delta, 1972.

Wilson, Joan Hoff. *American Business and Foreign Policy, 1920–1933.* Lexington: University Press of Kentucky, 1971.

——. *Ideology and Economics: U.S. Relations with the Soviet Union, 1918–1933.* Columbia: University of Missouri Press, 1974.

Wood, Bryce. *The Making of the Good Neighbor Policy.* New York: Columbia University Press, 1961.

Yergin, Daniel. *Shattered Peace: The Origins of the Cold War and the National Security State.* Boston: Houghton Mifflin, 1977.

7. *Articles*

"The Ambassadors of the United States of America." *Fortune* 4 (July 1931), 46–51, 94–105.
Araquistáin, Luis. "The October Revolution in Spain." *Foreign Affairs* 13 (January 1935), 247–61.
——. "The Struggle in Spain." *Foreign Affairs* 12 (April 1934), 458–71.
Beck, Peter J. "The Anglo-Persian Oil Dispute, 1932–33." *Journal of Contemporary History* 9 (October 1974), 123–51.
Bell, J. Bowyer. "French Reaction to the Spanish Civil War, July–September 1936." In *Power, Public Opinion, and Diplomacy: Essays in Honor of Eber Malcolm Carroll by His Former Students*, pp. 267–96. Ed. Lillian P. Wallace and William C. Askew. Durham: Duke University Press, 1959.
Ben-Ami, Shlomo. "The Dictatorship of Primo de Rivera: A Political Reassessment." *Journal of Contemporary History* 12 (January 1977), pp. 65–84.
Blumel, André. "La non-intervention en Espagne." In *Histoire du front populaire*, 2d ed., annex no. 17, pp. 494–500. Ed. Georges LeFranc. Paris: Payot, 1974.
Bowers, Robert E. "Hull, Russian Subversion in Cuba, and the Recognition of the U.S.S.R." *Journal of American History* 53 (December 1966), 542–54.
Carlton, David. "Eden, Blum, and the Origins of Non-Intervention." *Journal of Contemporary History* 6 (January 1971), 40–55.
Chandler, Alfred D. "The Growth of the Transnational Industrial Firm in the United States and the United Kingdom: A Comparative Analysis." *Economic History Review*, 2d ser., 33 (August 1980), 396–410.
Colodny, Robert G. "Notes on the Origin of the Frente Popular of Spain." *Science & Society* 31 (Summer 1967), 257–74.
Desmond, Raymond T. "The Aftermath of the Spanish Dictatorship." *Foreign Affairs* 9 (January 1931), 297–310.
——. "Dictatorship in Spain." *Foreign Affairs* 5 (January 1927), 276–92.
Diffie, Bailie W. "Spain under the Republic." *Foreign Policy Reports* 9 (20 December 1933), 234–44.
Feis, Herbert. "Some Notes on Historical Record-Keeping, the Role of Historians, and the Influence of Historical Memories during the Era of the Second World War." In *The Historian and the Diplomat: The Role of History and Historians in American Foreign Policy*, pp. 91–121. Ed. Francis L. Loewenheim. New York: Harper & Row, 1967.
Fernsworth, Lawrence. "Back of the Spanish Rebellion." *Foreign Affairs* 15 (October 1936), 87–101.
——. "Mass Movements in Spain." *Foreign Affairs* 14 (July 1936), 662–74.
——. "Whither Spain?" *Foreign Affairs* 12 (October 1933), 110–23.
Fleming, Shannon E., and Ann K. Fleming. "Primo de Rivera and Spain's Moroccan Problem, 1923–1927." *Journal of Contemporary History* 12 (January 1977), 85–99.
Flinn, M. W. "British Steel and Spanish Ore." *Economic History Review*, 2d ser., 8 (August 1955), 84–90.

Friedlander, Robert A. "Great Power Politics and Spain's Civil War: The First Phase." *Historian* 28 (November 1965), 72–95.

Gallagher, M. D. "Léon Blum and the Spanish Civil War." *Journal of Contemporary History* 6 (January 1971), 56–64.

Greene, Thomas R. "The English Catholic Press and the Second Spanish Republic, 1931–1936." *Church History* 45 (March 1976), 70–84.

Harvey, Charles E. "Business History and the Problem of Entrepreneurship: The Case of the Rio Tinto Company, 1873–1939." *Business History* 21 (January 1979), pp. 3–22.

——. "Politics and Pyrites during the Spanish Civil War." *Economic History Review*, 2d ser., 31 (February 1978), 89–104.

Hubbard, John R. "How Franco Financed His War." *Journal of Modern History* 25 (December 1953), 390–406.

"I.T.&T. Ends a Brilliant Decade." *Fortune* 2 (December 1930), 34–45, 118–24.

Jackson, Gabriel. "The Azaña Regime in Perspective." *American Historical Review* 64 (January 1959), 282–300.

Jessup, Phillip C. "The Spanish Rebellion and International Law." *Foreign Affairs* 15 (January 1937), 260–79.

Jones, Geoffrey. "The Expansion of British Multinational Manufacturing, 1890–1939." In *Proceedings of the Fuji Conference*. No. 9: *Overseas Business Activities*, pp. 125–53. International Conference on Business History. Tokyo: University of Tokyo Press, 1984.

Klein, Julius. "Commercial Forces in Contemporary Spain." *International Communications Review* 6 (July 1930), 45–54.

Lammers, Donald. "Fascism, Communism, and the Foreign Office, 1937–1939." *Journal of Contemporary History* 6 (January 1971), 66–86.

Lingelbach, William. "Conservative Rule in Spain." *Current History* 42 (September 1935), pp. 655–57.

Linz, Juan J. "The Party System in Spain: Past and Future." In *Party Systems and Voter Alignments: Cross-National Perspectives*, pp. 197–282. Ed. Seymour M. Lipset and Stein Rokkan. New York: Free, 1967.

Little, Douglas J. "Antibolshevism and American Foreign Policy, 1919–1939: The Diplomacy of Self-Delusion." *American Quarterly* 35 (Autumn 1983), 376–90.

——. "Claude Bowers and His Mission to Spain: The Diplomacy of a Jeffersonian Democrat." In *U.S. Diplomats in Europe, 1919–1941*, pp. 129–46. Ed. K. Paul Jones. Santa Barbara, Calif.: ABC-Clio, 1981.

——. "Twenty Years of Turmoil: ITT, the State Department, and Spain, 1924–1944." *Business History Review* 53 (Winter 1979), 449–72.

Nicholas, S. J. "British Multinational Investment before 1939." *Journal of European Economic History* 11 (Winter 1982), 605–30.

O'Connell, James R. "The Spanish Republic: Further Reflections on Its Anticlerical Policies." *Catholic Historical Review* 57 (July 1971), 275–89.

Preston, Paul. "Spain's October Revolution and the Rightist Grasp for Power." *Journal of Contemporary History* 10 (October 1975), 555–78.

Shubert, Adrian. "Oil Companies and Governments: International Reaction to the Nationalization of the Petroleum Industry in Spain, 1927–1930." *Journal of Contemporary History* 15 (October 1980), 701–20.

Smith, Robert Freeman. "Republican Policy and the *Pax Americana*, 1921–

1932." In *From Colony to Empire: Essays in the History of American Foreign Relations*, pp. 253–92. Ed. William Appleman Williams. New York: Wiley, 1972.

Stopford, John M. "The Origins of British-Based Multinational Enterprises." *Business History Review* 48 (Winter 1974), 303–35.

Taussig, F. W. "Necessary Changes in Our Commercial Policy." *Foreign Affairs* 11 (April 1933), 397–405.

Valaik, J. David. "American Catholic Dissenters and the Spanish Civil War." *Catholic Historical Review* 53 (January 1968), 537–55.

———. "Catholics, Neutrality, and the Spanish Embargo, 1937–1939." *Journal of American History* 54 (June 1967), 73–85.

Vincent-Smith, J. D. "The Portuguese Republic and Britain, 1910–1914." *Journal of Contemporary History* 10 (October 1975), 707–27.

Warner, Geoffrey. "France and Non-Intervention in Spain, July–August 1936." *International Affairs* 38 (April 1962), 203–20.

Watt, Donald C. "The Historiography of Appeasement." In *Crisis and Controversy: Essays in Honour of A. J. P. Taylor*, pp. 110–29. Ed. Alan Sked and Chris Cook. London: Macmillan, 1976.

Whealey, Robert. "How Franco Financed His War—Reconsidered." *Journal of Contemporary History* 12 (January 1977), 133–52.

Wilkins, Mira. "Modern European Economic History and the Multinationals." *Journal of European Economic History* 6 (Winter 1977), pp. 575–95.

Wilkinson, Ellen. "Terror in Spain." *Nation* 140 (6 March 1935), 272–74.

8. Unpublished Theses

Adams, Frederick C. "The Export-Import Bank and American Foreign Policy, 1934–1939." Ph.D. diss., Cornell University, 1968.

Elston, James Mitchel. "Multinational Corporations and American Foreign Policy in the Late 1930s." Ph.D. diss., University of Michigan, 1976.

Heider, Hans Karl. "International Operations and Growth of the Firm: A Study of the Experience of General Motors, Ford, and Chrysler." Ph.D. diss., Cornell University, 1975.

Little, Douglas James. "Malevolent Neutrality: The United States, Great Britain, and the Revolution in Spain, 1931–1936." Ph.D. diss., Cornell University, 1978.

Index

Index

Library of Congress Cataloging in Publication Data

Little, Douglas, 1950–
  Malevolent neutrality.

  Bibliography: p.
  Includes index.
  1. Spain—History—Civil War, 1936–1939—Causes.   2. Spain—Foreign
relations—1931–1939.   3. Spain—Foreign relations—Great Britain.   4. Great
Britain—Foreign relations—Spain.   5. Spain—Foreign relations—United
States.   6. United States—Foreign relations—Spain.   7. Neutrality.   I. Title.
DP257.L53   1985   946.081   84-19930
ISBN 0-8014-1769-4 (alk. paper)